Edward Augustus Freeman

English Towns and Districts

A series of addresses and sketches

Edward Augustus Freeman

English Towns and Districts
A series of addresses and sketches

ISBN/EAN: 9783337012120

Printed in Europe, USA, Canada, Australia, Japan

Cover: Foto ©ninafisch / pixelio.de

More available books at **www.hansebooks.com**

ENGLISH TOWNS AND DISTRICTS

ENGLISH TOWNS AND DISTRICTS

A SERIES OF ADDRESSES AND

SKETCHES

BY

EDWARD A. FREEMAN, M.A., Hon.D.C.L. & LL.D.

HONORARY FELLOW OF TRINITY COLLEGE, OXFORD

'Illa quidem longe celebri splendore beata
Glebis, lacte, favis, supereminet insula cunctis.
Testes Londoniae ratibus, Wintonia Baccho,
Hereforda grege, Wirecestria fruge redundans,
Batha lacu, Salesbira feris, Cantuaria pisce,
Eboracum silvis, Excestria clara metallis,
Norvicium Dacis, Hibernis Cestria, Gallis
Cicestrum, Norwageniis Dunelma propinquans.
Testis Lincoliae gens infinita decore,
Testis Ely formosa situ, Rovecestria visu.'
HEN. HUNT.

WITH ILLUSTRATIONS AND MAP

London

MACMILLAN AND CO.

1883

All rights reserved

LONDON: PRINTED BY
SPOTTISWOODE AND CO., NEW-STREET SQUARE
AND PARLIAMENT STREET

PREFACE.

I HAVE here brought together papers of two kinds. The shorter ones, reprinted from the Saturday Review, are of exactly the same character as those which I have collected in my two small volumes, 'Historical and Architectural Sketches, chiefly Italian,' and 'Sketches from the Subject and Neighbour Lands of Venice.' Their subjects are English, instead of Italian, Greek, or Illyrian; that is all. The longer ones come nearer to the nature of the papers on cities and countries in the third series of 'Historical Essays,' such as 'The Normans at Palermo,' and 'The Illyrian Emperors and their Land.' There is only the difference which is implied in the fact that those papers were written merely to be read, while those now reprinted were written to be heard by considerable bodies of hearers. They were addresses to various societies, several of them being presidential addresses delivered at the opening of the Historical Section at various meetings of the Archæological Institute. They have mostly appeared in the Archæological Journal or Macmillan's Magazine, or both; that on Carlisle appeared in the Contemporary Review. In both kinds of papers I have, in revising them for the reprint, made any changes that seemed to be called for, whether by adding, leaving out, or any other form of improvement. Of some places I found that I had both a longer and a shorter account, both a shorter sketch in the Saturday Review and a longer address read before one of the societies. In such cases I have reprinted the longer discourse, working into it any matter in the shorter sketch which was not in the longer and which seemed worth preserving.

One piece is of a different character from any of the others. I had not at first thought of giving a place in the volume to the paper headed, 'The Case of the Collegiate Church of Arundel.' For it is more of the nature of a legal argument than either of an address or of a sketch. But, in going through the other papers, I found so many references to the class of churches divided between a parish and a body of monks or clergy that I thought that a paper dealing more generally and directly with that subject would not be out of place. And, considering that this paper, written for use at the time of the trial between the Duke of Norfolk and the Vicar of Arundel, had a kind of history of its own, I have reprinted it just as it was originally written, and I have kept most of the notes and references. The whole subject of these divided churches is a very curious one, and it would be quite worth the while of any one to make it the subject of a thorough-going monograph, with ground-plans of each. To one such church I wish to call special attention, one to which, had I thought of it earlier, I should have liked to give a paper in this volume. This is the very singular priory church of Waybourne in Norfolk, which is referred to in a few words in the paper on Arundel. Here the division was made in a way quite unlike any other. The monastic tower, of Primitive Romanesque style, has the monastic choir to the east of it. The parish choir is built against the tower to the south, with the parish nave to the west, so that the monastic and parochial churches are not in a line with one another. I had a paper on this church many years ago in the Gentleman's Magazine, but I could not have reprinted it without unduly enlarging the volume. I have therefore done all that I could by giving a view of the building.

The illustrations, some from my own drawings, some from photographs, have been made by the same process and by the same artists as those in the 'Subject and Neighbour Lands of Venice.' I have specially had in view the study of the towers of the Primitive style, the ancient style common to England with the rest of Western Europe. This is a subject on the general bearings of which I have said what I have to say in the fifth volume of the Norman Conquest. In choosing other subjects for illustration I have taken buildings which are comparatively little known, rather than the great cathedral and abbatial churches which everybody has seen either in the original or in a picture. In the case of Glastonbury, where everything turns on the relations between the eastern and western churches, a ground-plan seemed what was wanted, and I have given one, modified for my own purposes from that given by Professor Willis. The paper headed 'The Shire and the Gá,' I have illustrated by a map chiefly founded on one of Dr. Guest's, showing the successive waves of West-Saxon conquest which led to the formation of the land of the *Sumorsætan*. About the conquests of Ceawlin and Cenwealh there seems no reasonable doubt; but in the extreme west of Somerset it is not easy to say how much was won by Centwine and how much by Ine, and the question is further complicated by the difficulty of fixing by what road and at what date the West-Saxons entered Damnonia.

The main object of such a collection as this is, not to go into the topographical and antiquarian details of each place with the minuteness of a local antiquary, but to point out the chief historical and architectural features of each place, as a contribution to the general history of England. Many of us, in these days of foreign travel, have very little notion of the treasures of art and history which still live in the towns and villages of our own country. And many of us have not fully grasped the truth how largely in every land national history is made up of local history. It is a wise saying of Polybios (iii. 1) that the historian must study the parts through the whole and the whole through the parts. No man understands the history of a city like Lincoln or Exeter, unless he puts the city in its fitting place, as part of the history of the kingdom. And no man can really understand the history of England unless he knows something of the characteristic history of the several English cities, unless he grasps the different ways in which the several English kingdoms were formed, and the different relations in which modern divisions stand to ancient ones within the boundaries of the several kingdoms.

One of these points at least was grasped, as it was grasped by no other man, by the brilliant painter of history whom we have just lost. Mr. Green was good enough, in the dedication of one of his volumes, to speak of me as one of his 'masters in the study of English history.' In this matter at least he was my master. I may be allowed here to copy what I said twelve years ago in the preface to the first edition of the fourth volume of the Norman Conquest. 'I may truly say that it was from him that I first learned to look on a town as a whole with a kind of personal history, instead of simply the place where such and such a church or castle was to be found.' From Mr. Green I learned that, be it at Chester or be it at Rome, the city itself and its history are something greater than any particular object in the city. To him is due the happy phrase of the 'Making of England' to describe the process in which many of the towns and districts here spoken of played no small part. And I trust that I am not to blame in having brought in, as I believe I have once or twice done, that happy phrase in the revision of papers which were written long before he had thought of it.

SOMERLEAZE, WELLS: *March* 12, 1883.

CONTENTS.

	PAGE
SOUTH WALES:	
CARDIFF AND GLAMORGAN	3
LLANTHONY	20
ANGLIA TRANSWALLIANA	33
SOUTH PEMBROKESHIRE CASTLES	40
WESSEX:	
THE PLACE OF EXETER IN ENGLISH HISTORY	49
GLASTONBURY BRITISH AND ENGLISH	76
THE SHIRE AND THE GÁ	103
BRADFORD-ON-AVON	134
DEVIZES	142
WAREHAM AND CORFE CASTLE	149
SILCHESTER	157
CHRISTCHURCH, TWINHAM	165
CARISBROOKE	172
MERTON PRIORY	181
MERCIA:	
LINDUM COLONIA	191
YORK AND LINCOLN MINSTERS	222
CHESTER	230

MERCIA (*continued*):

    Præ-academic Cambridge 238
    Præ-academic Oxford 249
    Saint Albans Abbey 257

NORTHUMBERLAND:

    Points in Early Northumbrian History . . . 265
    Kirkstall . . . 294
    Selby 302
    Notes in the North Riding 309
    The Percy Castles 316
    Bamburgh and Dunstanburgh 324

SUSSEX:

    The Case of the Collegiate Church of Arundel . . 333
    Appendix. *Worksop and Blyth* 363
    Cowdray 367
    Chichester 374

COLONIA CAMULODUNUM:

    Colonia Camulodunum . . 383

CARLISLE:

    The Place of Carlisle in English History . . . 421

LIST

OF

ILLUSTRATIONS.

LLANTHONY PRIORY, LOOKING NORTH-EAST	To face p.	24
LLANTHONY CHURCH, NORTH-WEST VIEW	,,	25
KIDWELLY CHURCH AND CASTLE	,,	30
GROUND PLAN OF GLASTONBURY CHURCH	,,	98
CHURCH OF SAINT LAURENCE, AND BRIDGE, BRADFORD-ON-AVON	,,	136
TOWERS OF SAINT MARY-LE-WIGFORD, AND ST. PETER-AT-GOWTS, LINCOLN	,,	211
HOUSE OF SAINT MARY'S GUILD, LINCOLN. With Architectural Details.	,,	212
TOWER OF SAINT MICHAEL'S, OXFORD.—TOWER AND BELFRY ARCH, SAINT BENET'S, CAMBRIDGE	,,	244
SAINT GREGORY'S MINSTER, LASTINGHAM, AND CRYPT	,,	314
TOWERS OF BYWELL CHURCH AND OF TRINITY CHURCH, COLCHESTER	,,	323
WAYBOURNE PRIORY, NORFOLK	,,	343

MAP.

SOMERSET AND THE NEIGHBOURING LANDS	,,	118

SOUTH WALES

CARDIFF AND GLAMORGAN.

1871.

[This paper was read as the Presidential Address to the Historical Section of the Archæological Institute at its Cardiff Meeting. As the first address of the kind that I was called on to make to that body, it may serve as a kind of introduction to those that follow. It will be remembered that Dr. Guest was then still living.]

I AM well pleased that my first appearance in any official character before a body with which I have had so long had to do as the Archæological Institute takes place in a district of which I have already some degree of knowledge, and one than which no part of the kingdom offers a wider field to the historical student. In the seven and twenty years which have passed since our Society first came into being, we have visited famous cities and trod on ground hallowed by the deeds of famous men. We had our birth in the land which witnessed the birth of the English realm and the English Church; we started on our path from that illustrious corner of our island which was the first prize alike of Cæsar, of Hengest, and of Augustine; we drew our first corporate breath in the old metropolis of Canterbury, beneath the walls of the mother church of England. Since then, year after year, we have gone from city to city, spying out the minsters and castles and fields of battle where the history of England has been wrought. From the Old Minster and the royal hall of Winchester, the home alike of Ælfred and of William, we have looked up to the hills hallowed to English hearts as the scene of the martyrdom of

Waltheof. From the awful ruins of Glastonbury, the common sanctuary of contending races, the one tie which binds the Church of the conqueror to the Church of the conquered, we have looked up from beside the rifled graves of Arthur and the Eadmunds to the prouder Tor of the Archangel, hallowed wherever truth and right are held in honour as the scene of the martyrdom of Whiting. As at Winchester and at Glastonbury, so also at Waltham and Crowland and Evesham, we have mused over the spots where the dust of the noblest heroes of England has been scattered to the winds at bidding of the destroyer. We have stood on the hill of the elder Salisbury, within the mighty ditches which have formed the bulwarks of so many successive races, and we have looked on the plain where Cynric overthrew the Briton, where William mustered his host after the overthrow of England, and where now the most graceful of West-Saxon minsters covers the ground which was once the chosen meeting-place alike of armies and of councils. At Silchester, at Wroxeter, at either Dorchester, we have traced the works alike of the Briton and the Roman, and we have seen the relics which bear witness to the wasting havoc wrought by Englishmen in the days of their first conquests. At Warwick we have looked on the mound of Æthelflæd; at London and Rochester and Newcastle and Norwich we have looked on the mighty towers reared by the Conqueror, his companions, and his successors. At Oxford and Cambridge we have seen how our ancient Universities seem but creations of yesterday within the walls of boroughs which had played their part in English history before a single scholar had come to learn Christian theology at the feet of Robert Puleyn, or to hear Vacarius expound the mighty volume of the Imperial Law. Time would fail to tell of all that we have seen; but we cannot forget how, within the ramparts of old Eboracum, the minster of Paullinus and Thomas of Bayeux seemed young in the home of Severus and of Constantine; nor can we forget how, where the Ouse flows between the two castles of the Conqueror, we thought how often Scandinavian fleets had sailed up those waters to ravage or to deliver England. And we may deem perhaps that York itself taught us less than the sight of the ancient City of the Legions, where the monks of Bangor fell beneath the sword of Æthelfrith, where the forsaken walls stood for three hundred years to record the havoc of his victory, and where the Lady of the Mercians bade the city rise once more to life, to stand forth in English history as the last of English cities to own the Norman as her lord. And York and Chester themselves may yield to the charm of the long history of the height crowned by the Colony of Lindum, the home of Briton, Roman, Englishman, Dane, and Norman; its walls, its houses, its castle, and its minster, bearing the living impress of its successive conquerors; where on the height we call up the memory of those ancient Lawmen, those proud patricians who once bade fair to place Lincoln alongside of Bern and Venice, and where, in the plain below, a higher interest is kindled by the stern yet graceful towers which tell us how Englishmen, in the days of England's bondage, could still go on, with the Norman minster and castle rising above their heads, building according to the ruder models of the days of England's freedom. Such are the spots which we have seen and mused on in the twenty-seven years of our corporate life, spots whose history makes up the history of England and the older history of the land before it bore the English name. And in spots where there has been so much to learn we have seldom lacked worthy interpreters. We have had minsters expounded by the unerring acuteness of a Willis, and castles called up to their first life by the massive vigour of a Clark. And below the ditches of Salisbury, beside the boundary streams of Avon and of Severn, we have heard the great master—I would rather say the great discoverer—of early English history, bring together the combined witness of records and monuments and nomenclature to call forth the true tale of Saxon and Anglian conquest out of what, in other hands, had seemed but a chaos of myth and legend. One spot still remains: we have not yet gone over all the cities of England. Some strange freak of destiny, some mysterious cause too deep for common intellects to fathom, has during all these years kept us out of the great city of the West. Damnonia is still untrodden ground to us; we have caught a kind of Pisgah view out of neighbouring shires, but Exeter, the city which beat back Swegen and all but beat back William, is still a place which we know by the hearing of the ear, but on which our eyes have not yet rested. Some day surely the ban will be removed; some day surely we may hear from the lips of Dr. Guest how the process of conquest, which he has traced to the Axe and the Parret, went on further to the Tamar and the Land's End; some day surely we may be allowed to listen while our other guides set forth all that is to be said of the city where walls which at least represent the walls of Æthelstan still fence in the Red Mount of Baldwin of Moeles and the twin minster towers of William of Warelwast.

But while we are thus shut out from that part of our island which was anciently known as West-Wales, I must congratulate our body on the choice of a place for its meeting, now that the Archæological Institute of Great Britain and Ireland has for the first time assembled beyond the bounds of England. I hear a murmur, but I speak advisedly. That the Institute has visited the extreme north of England I fully admit; that it has met beyond its northern border I deny. I can listen to no geography which tells me that the earldom of Lothian and the Borough of Eadwine are other than English ground. Edinburgh then I claim as English; Dublin, like Exeter, is a place which we have heard of but never seen; but now we have at last crossed the border. Whether we place that border at the Wye, the Usk, or the Rumney, there is no doubt that here, on the banks of the Taff, we are standing on genuine British ground. I say genuine British, I do not venture to say purely British; for one of the advantages of this district for historical study is that it is not purely British nor purely anything; there is no part of the island where all the successive races which have occupied it or overrun it have left more speaking signs of their presence. We are here emphatically in a border district, and a border district is always specially rich in materials for history. A glance at the map, a glance at any list of local names, shows how many races and tongues have had their share or their turn in the occupation or the superiority of the district. In the greater part of England well nigh every name is English or Danish, according to the district; if here or there a river or a great city keeps its British name, that is all. Even in districts like Somerset and Devonshire, which keep somewhat of a border character, districts where the Briton was subdued and assimilated, but not utterly wiped out, though British names are found in comparative abundance, they are still, after all, but a small minority. There are large districts of Wales, on the other hand, where every local name is British; where if a stray English name is found by any chance, it is at once felt to be a modern intruder. In districts like these we see that the Briton is still in full possession; it is a mere political change, not any real disturbance of the population, which cuts him off from the days of Howel the Good and Roderick the Great. The land in which we are now met, the land of Gwent and Morganwg, presents phænomena different from any of these. Cast your eye at random over the map of this county of Glamorgan, and it may haply light on the name of a place called Welsh Saint Donats. Such a name is enough to set one a-thinking. In what state of things is it needful to mark out a place as Welsh, to distinguish Welsh Saint Donats from another Saint Donats which is not Welsh? If you are in Cardiganshire, you have no need to distinguish a place as Welsh Llanfihangel; if you are in Kent, you have no need to distinguish a place as English Dartford or English Sevenoaks. Such a name as Welsh Saint Donats implies that you are in a district partly, chiefly, but not wholly, Welsh. Look on more carefully through the list of names; it is easy to see that the mass of them are purely Welsh, Llandaff, Llantrissaint, and a crowd of others. But some, like Cowbridge and Newton, are purely English; others are English translations of Welsh names, as where English Michaelston has supplanted Welsh Llanfihangel. But here and there we stumble on a name like Beaupre, which is neither Welsh nor English, but good French. And here and there we find a name like Flemingston, which not only points by inference to the presence of other races, but tells us on the face of it what those races were. A district which has such a local nomenclature as this, where so many nations and languages have left their abiding traces, is shown, without further proof, to be a district specially rich in materials for historical study. We see a district in which the old British race is still the prevailing element, but into which intruders of more than one nation have made their way. And they have made their way, not simply as visitors or plunderers or momentary conquerors, but as men who have settled down in the land, who have given their own names to its fields and houses, and who have made themselves essential elements in the population of the district alongside of its earlier possessors.

We have here then, on the face of it, a district of paramount interest to the historical inquirer. We see in the nomenclature of the district signs of the presence of several successive races; but those signs alone could not tell us at what time or by what means those successive races made their way into the land. The general course of history will tell us that the Welsh names are older than the English; but, without taking in other special means of information, we could hardly get beyond that. Let us try and find out, in a vague and general way, what more special research is likely to tell us, what points for further inquiry it is likely to suggest to us, as to the history of a district whose phænomena show themselves, at the first blush, as so remarkable.

We may begin with the old question of all, Who were the first inhabitants of the country? As far as recorded history goes, as far as spoken language goes, there is nothing to suggest the presence of any inhabitants earlier than those who still form the bulk of the population, the Britons, Cymry, or Welsh. But on points of this kind it is often needful to go beyond the teaching either of recorded history or of spoken language. Two views, each of which has been maintained with no small ingenuity, suggest the presence of races older than the oldest now existing in the country. Were the Britons the earliest wave of Aryan migration in these lands, or were they preceded by an earlier Aryan and Celtic race, that namely which consists of the Scots both of Britain and Ireland, and which, on the lips of the Cymry as on their own, still bears, in various forms, the name of *Gael* or *Gwyddyl?* That is to say, is the wide distinction between the two branches of the Celtic race in these islands, between the Scots or Gael and the Welsh or Britons, a distinction which arose after they settled in these islands, or do they represent two successive waves of Aryan migration? In this last case, there can be no doubt as to putting the Gael as the earlier settlers of the two. The evidence, as far as there can be any direct evidence on a præhistoric matter, consists mainly of certain spots in various parts of Wales which still bear the name of the *Gwyddyl*. Many of them are wild headlands; a few are inland spots equally wild, such as Nant-y-Gwyddyl in the heart of the Black Mountains, in the upper part of the deep dale where stands the elder priory of Llanthony. Are these simply spots occupied by rovers from Ireland who undoubtedly harried these coasts in later times, or are they spots where the older Gaelic population made their last desperate stand against the British invader? Is *Nant-y-Gwyddyl* in Gwent a name analogous to *Wallcombe* in Somerset, a name which records the former presence of the Gael in the land of the Briton, as its possible fellow certainly records the former presence of the Briton in the land of the West-Saxon? And again, can either branch of the Celtic race, Gael or Briton, claim to be the first inhabitants of the land? The Celt, in some shape, was undoubtedly the first Aryan inhabitant, but was he the first human inhabitant of any kind? No one doubts that a large part of Western Europe was overspread by non-Aryan races, relics of which, in the extreme North and again in one stubborn corner of Gaul and Spain, still retain their primæval languages. Was the same the case in Britain, and was our island also once inhabited by non-Aryan races, kinsfolk, it may be, of the Fins and Laps of the North, or of the Basques of the Pyrenees? Have we existing monuments of their workmanship among us? We are here in a land not poor in primæval antiquities; this county contains one of the largest cromlechs in Britain, and it is as well to remember that one theory at least attributes these gigantic graves—I suppose there is no one here so behind the world as to dream about Druid altars—not to Celts, British or Gaelic, not to Aryans of any race, but to the strangers who held the land in the old times before them. And this question has been still more strongly pressed upon our minds by a very modern controversy. It has been held, not only that Britain was occupied by a non-Aryan race before either Gael or Briton made their way into it, but that this same non-Aryan race still survives, that it still forms a main element in the population of some parts of the island, especially of that part in which we are now come together. It has been held by two writers, both of great name, but with a long interval of ages between them—by Tacitus and by Professor Huxley—that the Silurians of South Wales and the neighbouring districts were really a people closely akin to the Iberians of Spain, and therefore not Celtic, not Aryan at all. I do not know how this doctrine sounds in the ears of men of British blood. Speaking myself as a Saxon, I can only say that it fairly took my breath away. I know not whether Britons will be ready to give up Caradoc as a British brother; I should certainly be unwilling to give him up as an Aryan cousin. Still here is a doctrine which is supported by great names, and which at least deserves to be thoroughly gone into from all points of view. One thing is plain, that if the people of South Wales are really of a non-Aryan stock, the process of Aryan assimilation has been very thoroughly carried out. The British tongue, I need not say, is still a living thing in these parts; but if Basque, or any other non-Aryan speech, is now spoken in any part of Morganwg, we must, I think, look for it, not among the native inhabitants of either the vale or the mountains, but among the strangers whom commerce has brought from all corners of the earth to the busy haven of Cardiff.

Here then are questions as to the præhistoric state of the district well worthy of being tested in every way. We will pass on to the more certain facts of history. Whether the people of this district are genuine Britons or Iberians who have somehow changed into Britons, it is certain that, as far as either recorded history or local nomenclature can carry us back, the land has been a British land, and its prevailing tongue has been the British tongue. But the people and the language are to a great extent their own monument. It is a point of marked contrast between the archæology of Wales and that of Ireland, that, while in Ireland the land is full of buildings of very early date, I never saw in Wales any building—I mean buildings strictly so called, works of masonry—which I felt any inclination to assign to a date earlier than the Norman invasion. The land was full of churches, and specially full of saints, for the churches of Wales commonly bear the name, not of the canonized heroes of the Church at large, but of the local worthies who were their own founders. They have left behind them their names, their memory, and their foundations; but their actual works have, as far as I know, everywhere given way to later buildings. Still less is it needful to show that all the great military structures of the country, the castles, great and small, which form such a characteristic feature in its landscape and in its history, are all of later date than the coming of the Norman. If then the primæval sepulchres belong to an earlier race, and the ecclesiastical and military structures to a later, for British antiquities, in the strictest sense, we must look to the lesser remains of the country. For British remains of heathen times we must look among ruder defensive works, camps and earthworks like those of Caerau, and in Christian times we must seek them among a most interesting class of minor ecclesiastical antiquities, the sculptural crosses and inscribed stones, which have attracted deserved attention at the hands of several inquirers, and several of which will be found within our present district. I commend this question to the consideration of Celtic antiquaries: Why it is that Ireland has a marked national style of ecclesiastical buildings, beginning long before and continued long after the English Conquest, while in the Celtic parts of Scotland we have only a few analogous structures, like the round towers of Brechin and Abernethy, and while in Wales nothing of this class finds any counterpart? The ecclesiastical buildings of South Wales have much of deep interest; they have much of local character: but there is absolutely nothing which reminds us of Glendalough, of Clonmacnois, and of Monasterboice; their connexion with the days of early British Christianity is, even at places like Saint David's and Llandaff, like Llantwit and Llancarfan, a connexion wholly of history and association; it in no case extends to the actual stones.

I have been carried on too far at the expense of chronological order, for the first conqueror of the Briton has not failed to leave important traces behind him. Two famous seats of Roman occupation stand forth among the chief antiquarian attractions, if not of Morganwg, at least of Gwent. On the banks of the Usk the Roman fixed an Isca, a City of the Legions, which once was a rival both to the other City of the Legions by the Dee and to the other Isca by the Damnonian Exe. Not far off too are the remains of the Silurian Venta, which once needed to be so distinguished from that other Venta which became the royal city of the West-Saxons, and from the third Venta in the east, which has fallen the most utterly of the three, but which is in some sort represented by a greater city than any of those of which I have spoken. The Silurian and the Belgian Venta still remain as habitations of man; but the Icenian Venta lives only in the rime which tells how

Caistor was a city when Norwich was none,
But Norwich was built of Caistor stone.

The Briton then remains in his speech and in his own presence; the Roman and his speech have vanished utterly, but his works remain. The relations of the Briton to his next invader supply a more instructive subject of study. The results of the English conquest were widely different in various parts of Britain. In the greater part of the land the fate of the Celtic inhabitants was utter extirpation; in a considerable, but far smaller, district it was assimilation. Men of British blood submitted to the English conquerors, and they gradually adopted the language and feelings of Englishmen. How slow the process sometimes was we see in the long endurance of the British tongue in Cornwall. Now I need not show that neither of these processes has taken place to any great extent in this district. English does advance; but, except in great centres of population, like that where we are now met, it advances very slowly. English has taken far longer to advance from the Wye to the Usk than it took to advance from the German Ocean to the Wye. Except in the great towns, the land is essentially British, so far British that anything else is exceptional. But it is not purely British, like large parts of central and northern Wales, which were conquered under Edward the First, but which never received any large amount of English settlers. In this district we see something more than the mere political conquest of Cardigan or Merioneth, something less than the extermination of Kent or the assimilation of Devonshire. Strangers have conquered and settled in the land, but, except in small districts here and there, they have neither driven out nor assimilated the earlier inhabitants. The cause of this difference was doubtless the time when the conquest of this country took place. The old wars of extermination, when the heathen English swept away everything Roman, British, or Christian before them, had ceased before Gwent and Morganwg had any dealings with the English in peace or in war. The West-Saxon Kings, from Ecgberht onwards, were satisfied with an external supremacy, which was nominal or real, according to the degree of power which the overlord had to enforce it. It was not till the time of Eadward the Confessor that anything like real conquest was even attempted. Then we find a Bishop of Llandaff receiving his see from the King and Witan of England. In the last years of Eadward's reign, after the overthrow of Gruffydd ap Llywelyn, I have no doubt that, along with certain districts in northern and central Wales, the land of Gwent, between the Wye and the Usk, was formally annexed to England. The hunting-seat which Harold raised for the king at Portskewet, and which was presently swept away by Caradoc ap Gruffydd ap Rhydderch, was no doubt meant to be a solemn taking of seizin, a speaking sign that, within these limits at least, the King of the English was to be no mere overlord, but an immediate ruler. The events which immediately followed hindered any plans of

English settlement from being carried out; they even hindered the deed of Caradoc from meeting with any punishment. Nor did William himself ever do more than pass through the district on his way to the shrine of Saint David, receiving the submission of the land in a general way, and providing for the liberation of English or Norman captives. I ask those who know the local history better than myself, how far we can trust the entry in the Welsh Chronicles which places the beginnings of the castle of Cardiff in the days of the Conqueror. He may have taken some such precaution to secure the fidelity of his new vassals, but further than this I see no signs of anything strictly to be called a conquest in his time. The real conquest came in the next reign, and it is to its peculiar nature that the characteristic phænomena of the district are owing. Gwent and Morganwg were not conquered by heathen invaders, spreading mere slaughter and havoc before them; neither were they conquered, as a political conquest, by a Duke of Normandy or a King of England, at the head of a national Norman or English army. The conquest was more like the conquest of Ireland a generation or two later than it was like either the English conquest of Britain or the Norman conquest of England. The scramble for lands and dwellings, which some people seem to fancy took place under the strict civil police, the stern military discipline, of William the Great, really did take place when a crowd of Norman knights and their followers swept down on the devoted districts, each man seeking to carve out a lordship for himself. The land was won by the sword, but it was by the sword of private adventurers, not by the armies of a regular government. The land was conquered, the land was divided, to a large extent it was settled, but its former inhabitants were neither destroyed, expelled, nor assimilated. Each chief came with a motley following. Normans and Frenchmen pressed on from the conquest of England to complete the conquest of the rest of Britain. Englishmen, conquered in their own land, could, alike in Maine and in Morganwg, appear as conquerors out of it; and Normans and English forgot their mutual hatred when carrying on a common aggression under a common banner. And along with Normans and English came the near kinsman of the Englishman, the keen-witted and hardy Fleming, equally ready and skilful in the pursuit of gain, whether war, commerce, or manufacture, offered itself as the means of its pursuit. To this peculiar character of the invasion we owe the peculiar character of the antiquities of the district. Castles arose far thicker on the ground than in England itself, for every leader among the invaders needed a stronghold for the safety of himself and his followers. A Norman knight, who in England would have been satisfied with a manor, made perhaps in some slight degree defensible, here needed a fortress, smaller and less splendid, but as strictly a military work as the Towers of London or Rochester. The Norman too was essentially devout; wherever he dwelled, wherever he conquered, he founded monasteries and parish churches; but in such a land as this a monastery could not fail to be a fortress; a church was driven to be on occasion a house of warfare. Of the fortified monastery no better example can be seen than the priory of Ewenny; as to the smaller churches, the real necessities of one age became the mere tradition of a later, and something of a military character was impressed on the church towers of South Wales down to the very end of mediæval architecture. And, besides castles and churches, the new settlers soon began to seek at once strength and enrichment by the foundations of chartered towns, whose privileged burgesses would consist of a motley assemblage of French, English, Flemings, anything in short but Britons. Every castle, every town, was thus a foreign settlement, a settlement of men with arms in their hands, who had to keep what they had won against the enmity of those who had lost it. Wherever it was convenient and possible, the natives would be utterly driven out, and the result would be such a purely English-speaking district as that of Llantwit and Saint Donats. The land remained a scene of predatory warfare, of a truly national strife, long after men of all races and all tongues within England itself had sat down side by side in common obedience to a common law.

A district with such a history as this is rich above most districts alike in antiquarian interest and in picturesque incident. The student of language, of ecclesiastical or military architecture, of ecclesiastical or municipal foundations, will each find a rich store of the objects of their several studies, a store all the richer because it contains many objects of all classes which are at once small in scale and eccentric in character. And I believe that a field equally wide is opened to the lover of genealogy and family history, pursuits which, in a district of this kind, certainly connect themselves more closely with real history than elsewhere. I will myself touch on only one point of detail. I mentioned the Flemings among the settlers in South Wales. Now about the Flemish settlement in Pembrokeshire there is no kind of doubt. It is a matter of history, recorded by contemporary writers. But the alleged Flemish settlements in Glamorgan, in Gower and about Llantwit, do not rest on any such certain evidence as this. They seem to rest only on inference and tradition, tradition balanced by other statements which make the Teutonic inhabitants of Gower, not Flemings, like those of Pembrokeshire, but West-Saxons from the opposite coast of Somerset. Here then is a special point to be thoroughly worked out by some one who has the opportunity. The language of the alleged Flemish districts of Glamorgan should be carefully compared with the language of the known Flemish districts of Pembrokeshire, with the spoken language of Flanders, and with the dialect of Somerset. But such an inquiry must be made in a thoroughly scientific way. Local inquirers into local dialects constantly mark as local every word which has gone out of use in high-polite English. A word is thus set down as characteristic of Kent which is equally characteristic of Northumberland or Cornwall. Points of likeness between Gower and Somerset, between Gower and any other district, prove nothing, unless it can be shown that they are also points of unlikeness to other districts.

I give this as an example of the kind of questions, suggested by local phænomena, but having an interest far more than local, which are brought before us by the varied antiquities of the land in which we are met. It is a land in which men of all the races which have occupied this island may alike feel at home, for each and all may trace out the memorials of their own forefathers. Briton, Englishman, Norman, Fleming, have all contributed to the population, to the speech, to the existing antiquities, of the district. Our Danish friends in the North and East have perhaps less part and lot in the matter, but it may comfort them to remember that wiking fleets were often seen in the Bristol Channel, and that down to the eleventh century the Black Heathen were ready to destroy all that men of the other races were ready to rear up. On spots where our fathers met in arms, we, living men of those various races, can meet in friendship to trace out their deeds. The castles which were once badges of bondage of which men loathed the sight and the name, are now the witnesses of a time which has happily passed away, witnesses whose silent teaching we can listen to with curiosity and even with reverence. And, if the castles remind us of the old separation, the old hostility, of contending races, another class of buildings reminds us of their union. The ecclesiastical history of Wales is certainly no pleasant page in the history of England. One reads with a feeling of shame of the revenues of ancient Welsh churches swept away, in the twelfth century and in the sixteenth, to enrich English foundations at Gloucester, Tewkesbury, and Bristol. Yet, in the days of war and tumults, it was something that men of contending races could at least worship together, that they could agree to look with reverence on spots like the holy places of Saint Teilo and Saint Iltyd. And it is something on the other side that, in one point at least, the nineteenth century may hold up its head alongside of any of its forerunners. No church of its rank in South Britain had ever fallen so low, few have now risen so high, as the cathedral church of the diocese in which we are met. If there were nothing else to draw us hither, it would be goal enough for our pilgrimage to see the ancient minster of Llandaff, not so many years back a ruin and worse than a ruin, stand forth, as it now does, among the model churches of our land.

LLANTHONY.

1853-1876.

EVERY ONE knows that the Cistercian monks, whether of set purpose or through a happy accident, always placed themselves in the most picturesque parts of our island. Monks needed wood and water; Cistercian monks needed special retirement from the common abodes of men. We should hardly have looked for any other order in a solitary vale fenced in by lofty hills which in southern Britain rank as mountains. Yet at two times far away from each other, in the twelfth century and the nineteenth, this very obvious rule of monastic propriety seems to have passed out of sight. The vale of Llanthony has been chosen in the later period as the dwelling-place of self-styled Benedictine monks, as in the earlier period it was chosen as the dwelling-place of real Austin canons. But the original founder of Llanthony might at least plead that he could not well have planted Cistercians there, as his foundation was made before the beginning of that great Cistercian movement in Britain which created Tintern and Neath as well as the abbeys of Yorkshire. But the Benedictines themselves would hardly have been more out of place than the Austin canons, whom, about 1108, Hugh of Lacy planted in the heart of the Black Mountains. The Austin canons, an order which may be called intermediate between the seculars and the stricter regulars, were often placed in towns, witness Bristol and Carlisle, and seldom in such utter solitudes as that of Llanthony. The Austin canons themselves seem to have been of the same mind. Less than thirty years after their beginning, in 1136, they found that the life in the mountain valley did not suit them. They procured a transfer of the house to a site outside the walls of Gloucester, which better suited their notions of civilized life. There arose the monastery of Llanthony the Second, while Llanthony the First still remained among the hills.

There is something very singular in this transfer of the monastery to so great a distance. The special reason assigned is one of historical importance. Llanthony the First was founded in the days of the Lion of Justice, and, while he ruled, even the wild Britons were kept in some kind of order. He was hardly in his grave before their incursions began again, and the canons of Llanthony were among the first to suffer. But, besides this, it is plain that they did not like the place itself. How should they? The first set of canons were brought to Llanthony from the priory of Saint Botolf outside the walls of Colchester. The change must have been frightful. We must remember that they would have no feeling of the picturesque, no admiration for the scenery of the mountain valley. Perhaps even now a man who was obliged always to live at Llanthony might admire the scenery less than one who visits it only now and then. Landor himself, with all his poetry and all his zeal to improve his neighbours, did not stay there all his days. But in the earlier days a transfer from Colchester to Llanthony must have been a banishment which would make any Austin canon of them shudder. When the brotherhood had moved to Gloucester, the historian of the house draws an elaborate contrast between the position of Llanthony the First and that of Llanthony the Second. The comfortable Gloucester site was much more to his mind. Yet the valley is not barren; it has rich pastures enough; but we may believe that the very presence of the hills, which to us is the chief charm of the spot, was to them a matter of horror. Anyhow, Llanthony the Second became more popular than Llanthony the First. It also became much richer. But of Llanthony the Second but little is left, and of the church nothing at all. At Llanthony the First enough remains both of the church and the other buildings to form a most instructive study of architectural style and monastic arrangement.

There is also another singular point in the transfer, namely the removal of the name to a place where it was utterly without meaning. There are indeed many other instances of the transfer of monasteries, and indeed of the transfer of names. But it would perhaps be hard to find another case of the transfer of a name to a spot where it was so grotesquely out of place. Llanthony is not, as many people seem to think, the church of Saint Anthony. It is a contraction of Llanddewi-nant-Honddû—that is to say, the church of David in the vale of the Honddû. The vale of the Honddû is a deep mountain valley, in which the older Llanthony stands, with the stream of the Honddû rushing along it to find its way into the Usk, the 'Welsh Axe' of our forefathers. So far the name was indeed descriptive. Yet, after all, it was, even in its beginning, a delusion. Llanddewi-nant-Honddû was not in truth a Llanddewi at all. It is said to have taken its name from an earlier chapel of Saint David which the canons found standing there; it is certain that their own church was dedicated to Saint John Baptist. The transfer to Gloucester made the rest of the name meaningless. At Gloucester, by the banks of the Severn, there was no Honddû and no vale—none, at least, in the same sense as the narrow glen through which the mountain torrent makes its way. Either the name must have conveyed but little meaning to those who inhabited the place called by it, or else they must have had a deeper affection for the name than would have seemed from their eagerness to quit the place. Anyhow, a new Llanthony, a new church of David in the vale of Honddû, arose far away from the vale of Honddû, and this time bearing the dedication neither of Saint David nor of Saint John, but of Our Lady.

The history of the two monasteries after the removal to Gloucester in 1136 is very obscure. The Gloucester Llanthony was designed to be merely a cell; but, as we have seen, it grew into a distinct house. But Llanthony the First, though much poorer than Llanthony the Second, still went on. It does not seem, as some have thought, to have become in turn a cell to its own child. There is a document of Edward the Fourth's reign uniting the two Llanthonies, but it would seem not to have taken effect, as they were distinct houses with distinct properties at the Dissolution. Anyhow, it is the elder Llanthony which now survives in its old place among the mountains. The church takes its place in the series of the great churches of South Wales, being clearly intermediate between the nave of Saint David's and the nave of Llandaff. It supplies one of the best examples of the Transition. The pointed form shows itself in all the main constructive arches, but it is only in the west front that it becomes predominant in the smaller decorative arches as well. The work is just what suits a great church in such a position. Every detail is good and well finished; but there is a stern simplicity, a casting aside of all needless ornament, which seems thoroughly in place in the church and the dwelling of men who had of their own free will chosen the wilderness as their home. Saint David's is plain without, because, where it stands, external adornment would have been carved only to crumble away. But then, as becomes the head church of a great diocese, Saint David's makes up for its plainness without by lavish gorgeousness within. Llanthony, on the other hand, though its design is clearly to some extent modelled on that of St. David's, does not reproduce any of the rich ornament of the mother church, and affects altogether different proportions. The nave arches of Saint David's are round, and of remarkable width; those of Llanthony

are pointed, and much narrower, having an arcade of
eight in a length a little shorter than that which at Saint
David's is filled by six. The plainness of the pillars, most
of them without capitals, is striking, but the effect is
good throughout. The short eastern limb, much shorter
than that of Saint David's even in its first estate, has
never, like Saint David's, grown out into eastern chapels,
so that the whole length of Llanthony is very much
smaller than that of the mother-church. And again,
while Saint David's has gone through changes at every
date and in every style, few minsters could have been so
little changed as Llanthony between the foundation and
the Dissolution. No innovation seems to have happened
beyond the insertion of a large east window, and a recasting of the side chapels, exactly answering to that of
Saint David's.

We said that Llanthony filled a place intermediate
between Saint David's and Llandaff; but it is much less
easy to compare it with Llandaff than with Saint David's.
A comparison can be one only of architectural detail, for
the peculiar outline of Llandaff, its lack of transepts and
central tower, puts it out of all comparison as regards
general effect. As far as this last goes, the outline of
Llanthony, with its three towers, was far more ambitious
than that of either of the two episcopal churches. But as
regards architectural style, as Llanthony, with all its
severity, is an advance on Saint David's, so Llandaff is a
further advance on Llanthony. Each marks a stage in
the great change by which the pointed arch and its appropriate ornaments supplanted the round arch and its
appropriate ornaments. At Saint David's—we speak of
the nave—the round arch is dominant, though the pointed
arch is coming in. At Llandaff the pointed arch is
dominant, though the round arch is not quite forgotten.
At Llanthony we see the two in a moment of equal
struggle. Yet, with all this, there is a likeness of work
and feeling which binds the three churches together, as

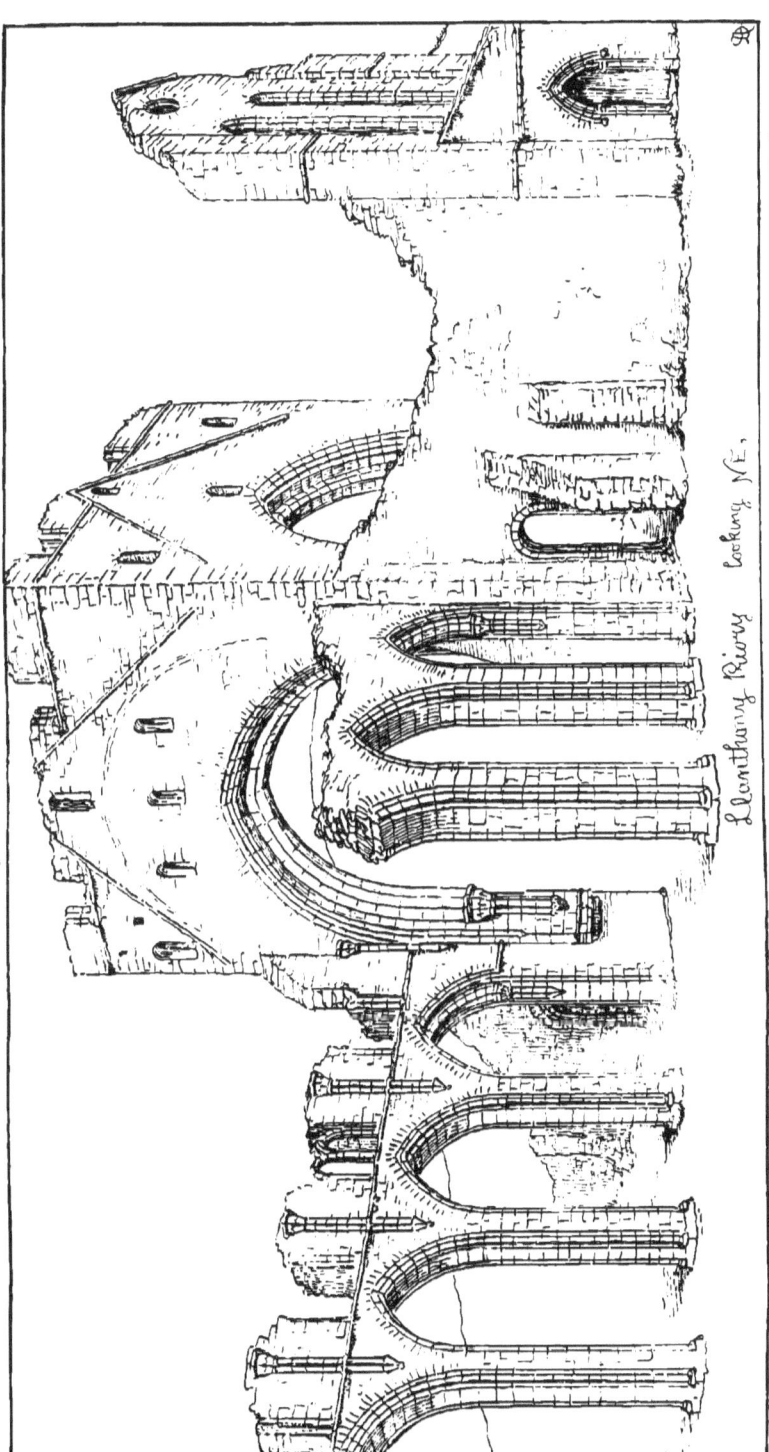

Llanthony Priory, looking N.E.

To face p. 24.

Llanthony. NW view.

To face p. 25.

if they were the work of a single architect, or of a single school of architects gradually feeling their way towards successive stages of developement. A more instructive study in the history of art can hardly be found than that which is supplied by the gradual changes of style to be traced in the three best preserved among the great churches of South Wales.

Of the church of Llanthony the remains are very extensive. In fact, though it is less perfect than some other monastic ruins, there is enough to make out every essential feature. But much more was standing, even within living memory. Old prints show much more both of the west front and of the central tower than is now standing, and the southern arches of the nave fell only about forty years ago. The remains of the monastic buildings are considerable. The chapter-house is still there, though broken down, and there are signs left of the substructure of the refectory. The building which immediately joins the south-western tower, and indeed the south-western tower itself, are made partly into a farm-house, partly into a small inn, where the traveller who does not need very splendid quarters may pass a day or two while examining the priory and its neighbourhood. And among the monastic buildings stands the small parish church, seemingly of the same date as the priory. Its existence appears to have puzzled some of the earlier visitors to Llanthony, and indeed some of its earlier historians. They seem not to have understood how a parish church could be needed in such a place. But the very existence of the monastery implied the presence of a certain lay population, and the only choice was either the creation of a distinct parish church or the division of the minster itself between the parishioners and the canons. The latter was the rule among Austin canons; but the position of Llanthony was an exception to all rule. Most houses of Austin canons stood in towns, where the people had something to say to the matter. In such a place as

Llanthony, the canons must always have had everything their own way, and they may have been best pleased to keep their church all to themselves.

In short, what with the old Austin canons, what with Landor, what with the modern Benedictines, Llanthony seems to have had a way of coming before the world by fits and starts. One fit or start in the last days of the twelfth century gave us one of the most instructive pieces of ecclesiastical architecture in our island, and placed perhaps in a more remarkable site than any other.

KIDWELLY.

1849-1870.

In speaking of Kidwelly, castle, church, and town, let us, first of all, give a warning as to the name. The traveller who draws near to Kidwelly by the most likely road, that is, by the road which will take him either from London or from Bristol, will, before he reaches Kidwelly, pass by Llanelly. This name may suggest to him that he has reached a fit place for practising that sound so mysterious to modern Englishmen, but which their forefathers uttered with perfect ease whenever they had to speak of either a loaf, a lord, or a lady. In the name Llanelly the sound which has vanished from the modern forms of *hláf*, *hláford*, and *hlǽfdige* has certainly to be uttered twice. The Llanelly of the south is as great a problem as the Llangollen of the north. But let no one who has succeeded in giving the due sound to Llanelly be sc puffed up with his success as to go on further and pronounce Kidwelly after the same pattern. The *ll* in Kidwelly is a mere English barbarism; the first syllable is spelled a dozen ways in the Welsh Chronicles, but the latter part of the word is always *weli*, or something to that effect. In short, the English visitor to Kidwelly need give himself no trouble about the name of the place. He will come nearest to the true British sound if he sounds the name as he would sound it if he came upon it in Kent or Norfolk.

The visitor who thus reaches Kidwelly by the Great Western Railway will find a small town—if he is very metropolitan in his ways of thinking, he may be inclined to call it a village—of which the most prominent feature in the immediate neighbourhood is a tall spire, a most unusual feature in that neighbourhood. Further off, beyond the little river Gwendraeth, he will see, rising above church and town, a castle which is very far from being the largest of the South-Welsh castles, but which, as a real artistic design, may hold its own against any military building in South-Wales or anywhere else. The castle, the church, and the collection of houses dignified with the name of a borough, are commonly the elements which go to make up one of these small Welsh towns. In some cases however the church is absent. That is to say, the town was an absolutely new creation of the Norman or English conquerors, whichever we are to call them. In such cases the town does not form an ecclesiastical parish; it simply stands within some elder parish, the church of which may be near or far off, as may happen. Thus at Newport on the Usk the castle and town were founded by the river-side at the foot of the hill. The old parish church of Saint Woollos stands at the top of the hill, and it is only the modern growth of Newport which has carried the town up to the church. But in other cases, and at Kidwelly among them, the town was not a new creation of the conquerors; it was simply a place taken possession of by them and applied to their own uses. The town in such cases existed already; what the conquerors did was to give it new inhabitants, to build a castle to protect or threaten it, and sooner or later to give it an English municipal constitution. And very commonly the church grew into a religious foundation of some kind or other. In all these ways Kidwelly is typical; the castle, the priory, and the borough, are all there. The municipal history of these Welsh towns is a subject which it would be specially worth the pains of some one versed in municipal matters to work out thoroughly. Each of them was a foreign colony in a conquered land,

and in each of them men of all nations except the conquered were welcome. Ages after the Christian æra Alexandria was still, in its own belief, peopled by men of Macedonia—that is to say, men of anywhere except native Egyptians. So the burghers of Kidwelly, in the twelfth century and doubtless long after, were distinguished among themselves as French, English, and Flemish. The Briton had no place at all. If he was allowed to dwell within the municipal circuit, he was at least not admitted to municipal rights. At Kidwelly, as in so many other places, there is an old town and a new. The old town stood on the same side of the river as the castle, while the new town, with the priory, was on the other side. That is, most likely, the castle supplanted an older native settlement on the high ground, while the new town of the French, English, and Flemish burgesses arose, where there was more room for it, on the other side of the stream. Thus far the history of Kidwelly is a miniature copy of the history of Lincoln and Cambridge. The town, with its ancient bridge, and the ancient houses which here, as elsewhere, are fast giving way to modern love of destruction, has that peculiar air which belongs to towns of the smallest and least busy class, towns which have an air of far less life than the mere open village. The municipal archives of Kidwelly are said to be rich, and the borough, like London, New Romney, and some others, still remains unreformed.

But while the municipal element in Kidwelly, though still there, has in some sort to be looked for, the ecclesiastical and still more the military element force themselves at once on the eye. The South-Welsh coast is, as a whole, rather rich in churches—that is, if the traveller will accept a kind of wealth which does not consist in size or splendour, but in a class of buildings which almost always have a good picturesque outline, which suit the scenery, and which bear on them the impress of the history of the country. The military towers of the churches along this whole coast, from Monmouthshire to Pembrokeshire, are well worth study; but Caermarthenshire, as a whole, has less to show in the ecclesiastical way than its neighbours on either side. But Kidwelly, as becomes a monastic church, is one of the exceptional class of larger and finer buildings which ever and anon diversify the small and plain, but picturesque, churches which are characteristic of the country. Not that Kidwelly priory would pass as a fine church in Somerset or Norfolk, not that it has in the least the character of a minster; still it is large and striking and stately after its own fashion. A long, broad, aisleless nave, cruelly cut short at the west end, would, if it were only vaulted, not be out of place in Anjou or Aquitaine. The tower and spire on the north side look as if a local architect, used to the military towers of the district, had made a journey into Northamptonshire, and had brought back some rude notions of a broach spire. The church is cruciform, though without a central tower, and the choir, with some eccentricities, such as a strangely flat chancel arch, is not a bad specimen of work of the fourteenth century. The priory was a cell to the abbey of Sherborne; the date of its foundation is doubtful, but it existed in 1291. But the connexion of the place with Sherborne is much older. The famous Bishop Roger, the founder of Sherborne as a distinct monastery, gave to that house lands at Kidwelly, at which time the burghers of the three nations also granted certain tithes. And it is to be noticed that, among the witnesses to Roger's grant, we find two men with purely English names holding the two most important local posts: 'Edmundus qui tunc castellum de Cadweli custodiebat, et Alwinus presbyter villæ.'

The castle then was in being, and in English hands, in the time of Henry the First. It had already been ravaged by English invaders as early as 993, and, exactly a hundred years later, came the invasion, Norman or English, as we may call it, with which the history of the place really

Kidwelly, NW.

Kidwelly Castle.

To face p. 30.

begins. Somewhat after Bishop Roger's time, it belonged to a certain Maurice of London, of the house of London or *Londres*, a house which plays a leading part in the history and legend of the conquest of Glamorgan. He, with his son William, made grants to the church of Kidwelly and to the monks of Sherborne. According to the received pedigree, this Maurice, whose date was about 1150, is made fourth in descent from William, the alleged conqueror of 1093. It may be so; but the generations of the house of London would seem to have been wonderfully short, and in singular contrast to the length of those of the family which is said to have succeeded them. We are told of a certain Patrick of Chaworth or Cahors, who was living in 1194, but whose father came in with the Conqueror. Here we are landed in the chronology of Ivanhoe, and we turn from the pedigree-makers to the fact recorded in the Welsh Chronicles, that in 1190 the Welsh prince Rhys built the castle of Kidwelly. At that time then the house of London could not have been in actual possession. And in truth there is no doubt that Kidwelly had been, on the conquest of Shrewsbury, granted again by Henry the First to the Welsh prince Howel. All this is important, rather as showing the kind of materials out of which the history of Wales will have to be put together when any real scholar shall take it in hand, than as throwing any light on the buildings which are now actually standing at Kidwelly. Whatever either Maurice or Rhys may have built, it is not there now. The present castle clearly belongs to the latter part of the thirteenth century, when it was certainly in possession of the house of Cahors or Chaworth. From them it passed by marriage to the earls and dukes of Lancaster, and so became part of the Lancaster duchy, from which in later times it has again passed into private hands. Save the later gate-house, the whole building is of a piece —a court surrounded by four round towers. Two other large round towers flank the gateway, and another stands at its outer side. Few castles have an outline at once so compact and so picturesque; but the distinguishing feature of the dwelling is to be looked for at the eastern side, where the art of the military and that of the ecclesiastical architect have worked together with a skill which is beyond praise. At Kidwelly the chapel was to be a main feature of the building. It was not to be a mere room stowed away in one corner, where the inquirer finds it with difficulty. But in a castle by no means on the greatest scale, it was not to be a separate building, as at Bamburgh and once at Alnwick; still less was it to be a miniature minster as at Warkworth, or a miniature Saint Sepulchre as at Ludlow. A polygonal projection—the chapel tower—was thrown out from the east face of the castle, and an apsidal end was thus provided for the chapel in its upper story. A projection again from this tower provides in its upper stage the quarters of the chaplain; the castle, in short, has an ecclesiastical quarter, and that one which stands forth from the main line of defence, as if trusting to its sacred character. Nothing was ever more skilfully devised as a matter of arrangement; nothing was ever more skilfully carried out in the matter of execution. The castle chapel at Kidwelly is the very model of its own class; no form, no details, could have been better devised for a building which forms part of a military structure, but which is not itself military. The work, well finished but not richly ornamented, exactly suits its position. Its range of trefoil lancets proclaims the chapel as a part of the building which has a character of its own, while they do not stand out in any violent contrast to the plainer and more strictly military parts of the buildings. The actual founder of the castle can only be guessed at; the name of his architect has utterly perished; but, like so many other builders of churches and castles whose names we cannot hope to recover, he must have been a man of no mean order of genius in his own art, and his employer, one would think, must have been one who was able to appreciate his skill.

ANGLIA TRANSWALLIANA.

1851-1876.

THE last Teutonic settlement in Britain often passes without notice. The Englishry of Pembrokeshire, 'Little England beyond Wales,' can hardly be said to be an unknown land while it contains the well-known watering-place of Tenby. But we may guess that a good many visitors to Tenby come away with very faint notions of the remarkable ethnological phænomena of the land which they have been visiting. To many it is doubtless enough that they are in Wales; one part of Wales is the same as another. And certainly the authorities of Tenby have done their best to lead their visitors astray. On the castle-hill of Tenby is a statue of Prince Albert, with a legend in English and Welsh, in which the Prince has borrowed the epithet of the great British law-giver, and appears as 'Albert Dda.' Moreover there is a display of heraldry, and a legend—in the British tongue only—about the Red Dragon of the Cymry. Now there is exactly as much reason for setting up a Welsh inscription at Tenby as there is for setting one up at York or Canterbury. The Welsh tongue was doubtless once spoken in all three places, and all three places are called by modifications of Welsh names. For Tenby must not be mistaken for a Danish *by*; the name is British, the same as the Denbigh of North Wales. It is possible that the *bych* may have been changed into the likeness of Danish *by* by the same kind of process by which Jerusalem becomes *Hierosolyma*; but that is the full amount of the connexion,

D

if there be any. In this purely English town in a purely English district, one looks up at the strange beast and the strange tongue with a feeling that the Lion of Justice has in some measure laboured in vain. King Henry took some pains to plant good seed in his field; whence then these tares of Red Dragons, and of legends in a tongue not understood of the people of Tenby and of all South Pembrokeshire? Laying parables aside, we are, at Tenby and the coasts thereof, in a district of the highest historic interest. We are within the bounds of the last Teutonic settlement in Britain, as in Kent, on the opposite side of the island, we are within the bounds of the first. Henry wrought the last act of the drama which was begun by Hengest. We are here in the Englishry, in Little England beyond Wales. We are in a district where language universally, where local nomenclature generally, is as Teutonic as it is in Norfolk. To its inhabitants 'Albert the Good' may give an idea; but 'Albert Dda' is quite thrown away upon them. The Red Dragon of the Cymry was to their forefathers only as the Snark or the Jabberwock, a noisome beast to be hunted down without mercy. The strange fancy of Englishmen for turning their backs on themselves, for wiping out their own history to make room for the legends of somebody else, surely never took a stranger shape than in an outbreak of Welsh nationality at Tenby.

There is no doubt, as was hinted in an earlier paper, from the direct witness of William of Malmesbury and other contemporary writers, that Henry the First, among his measures to keep the Welsh in order, planted a colony of Flemings in Dyfed, the modern Pembrokeshire. In the district allotted to them, the southern part of the county, they must have done their work thoroughly. The Briton has left but few traces. The one speech of the district is English, and most of the places have received English names. Most of them are called after individual settlers—Johnston, Williamston, Haroldston,

Herbrandston, names which exactly answer to the Danish names in Lincolnshire, save that they end in English *ton* instead of Danish *by*. Here and there a place keeps a Welsh name, specially the towns of Pembroke and Tenby, just like London, Gloucester, and Winchester, in other parts of the island. Whatever we say of the alleged Flemish settlements elsewhere, the settlement in Pembrokeshire is an undoubted fact. King Henry's colony is always expressly described as a colony of Flemings. It is recorded both by the English and by the Welsh writers; but the fact that the colony, which was originally Flemish, now speaks English has given rise to a good deal of puzzledom, and to the talking of no small amount of nonsense. Any one who knows the district will have heard the question raised over and over again. In local books too we constantly see mention of 'Flemish houses,' 'Flemish architecture,' 'Flemish chimneys,' and even a 'Flemish court of justice,' as if the Flemings had brought over some special style of art with them from their own country. We have even seen an elaborate comparison, which was meant to prove something, between the 'Flemish houses' in Pembrokeshire and a house in some other part of England—in Cumberland, if we rightly remember—belonging to a family named Fleming. It would have been easy to improve upon this last notion; for, in some versions of the story, the Flemings whom Henry settled in Pembrokeshire are said to have been before that settled in the North of England. But the so-called Flemish houses are in no way distinctively Flemish, and they were built ages after the settlement of the Flemings. They are simply good, solid, stone-built houses, with pointed doorways and round chimneys. They show that the district must have been fairly prosperous at a time when so many stone houses could be built; but they also show in slight military touches that the days of warfare, or at all events the traditions of the days of warfare, had not wholly passed away. On the other hand, it is only in an old-fashioned district where there has been comparatively little change, that so many of them could have lived on to our own day. But there is nothing special or mysterious about them, nothing on which to found any ethnological theory. To call them Flemish houses, attaching any distinct meaning to the word Flemish, is as much to the purpose as it would be to talk of a West-Saxon style in the stone houses of Somerset, or of a Middle-Anglian style in the stone houses of Northamptonshire.

We have brought in this last analogy of set purpose; for of course the great puzzle always is, how a Flemish settlement came to speak English. People constantly ask how the Flemings came to change their language. The difficulty is by no means a new one; it is as old as Randolf Higden, who looked on Flemings as barbarians, and says that in his day they had left off their barbarous tongue, and spoke good Saxon ('dimissa jam barbarie Saxonice satis proloquuntur'). And of the two Welsh chronicles known as the Brut, the later, fuller, and less trustworthy, tells us how Henry planted Englishmen—in Welsh, of course, 'Saxons,'—among the Flemings to teach them English, and how into the writer's day they were English. It is a standing local puzzle how Flemings could have come to speak English. What they were expected to speak, what the natural language of Flemings left to themselves was supposed to be, does not appear. Perhaps they were expected, as coming from the modern kingdom of Belgium, which uses French on its coins, to speak French rather than English. That native Britons should have come to speak English was clearly thought a much slighter difficulty than that Flemings should have done so. It seemed like a paradox to many to be told that the settlers in Pembrokeshire had never changed their language at all, to be told that there was no need to ask how the Flemings came to speak English although they are Flemings, while the simple fact was that they spoke English because they were Flemings. To one who really takes in the history and the relations of the Teutonic dialects of Britain there is no difficulty at all in the matter. The Flemish tongue is one dialect of Low-Dutch; the English is another. Even now the nearness between modern Flemish and modern English must strike every one who thinks at all upon such matters, and the nearness in the twelfth century, before English had gone through those changes which have parted it off from its fellows, must have been far closer than it is now. The true way of looking at the matter is, as we have already said, to look on the Flemish occupation of Pembrokeshire as simply the last stage of Teutonic settlement in Britain. The Flemings may fairly pass as another English tribe, like Angles, Saxons, or Jutes, only coming so many ages later. Between them comes a Teutonic settlement of another kind, that of the Danes. The Flemish settlement has far more in common with the earliest settlements of all than the intermediate Danish settlement has. For the Danes settled at the expense of earlier Teutonic inhabitants, while the Flemings settled almost wholly at the expense of the Celts, just as the Angles and Saxons did ages before. There have been later settlements in Britain, settlements from the same part of the world which sent forth the Flemish settlement in Pembrokeshire. Intercourse with the Netherlands, and the reception of refugees from the Netherlands, has given a certain tinge to East-Anglia in more ways than one. But here was a settlement altogether of the old kind, a settlement where the colonists drove out the old inhabitants, where they divided the land among themselves, and gave places new names from their new owners. The causes and circumstances of the Flemish settlement in Pembrokeshire were altogether different from those of the earliest English settlements in Britain. But the process of settlement must have been very much the same; the only difference was that the Flemings were not, like the first Angles and Saxons, heathen destroyers. But to the second stage of Anglian and Saxon conquest, the stage represented by Cenwealh and Ine and other Christian conquerors, the settlement of the Flemings must have presented an exact parallel.

In short, the processes which created the standard English tongue, or rather the processes which brought it to the front amid a crowd of local dialects, have affected the Teutonic speech of Pembrokeshire, as well as the Teutonic speech of other parts of the island. The Fleming of Pembrokeshire speaks English for the same cause that the Dane of Lincolnshire speaks English. That is to say, one form of standard English is common to all. How far all parts actually speak it is another matter. It is for some local philologer to find out whether there are any local peculiarities in the Nether-Dutch of Pembrokeshire, and whether they at all approach to any peculiarities in the Nether-Dutch of Flanders. After such complete separation for so many ages, we should not expect to find much special likeness between the two dialects. Still the point is quite worth looking into; and, though the colony was certainly mainly Flemish, we need not suppose that every single man in it came from Flanders. There may be truth in the Welsh chronicler's statement that King Henry planted Englishmen among the Flemings, though it is not likely that he did it for the purpose of teaching the Flemings English. We may be sure that there were both French-speaking and more strictly English-speaking settlers among them. Normans, English, Flemings, when they got into Wales, largely forgot their differences, and formed one whole as against the Britons. Pembroke Castle was a strictly Norman foundation, the work of Arnulf of Montgomery before the Flemish settlement began. And the foundation of the castle would naturally lead, at Pembroke as everywhere else, to the settlement of both French-speaking and English-speaking burgesses around it. And there is every probability that the Flemish settlement was a revival, or a continuation, or a strengthening, of an earlier Teutonic settlement from quite another quarter. Though the name of Tenby is not Scandinavian, yet other names in the district are. Such names as Hasgard and Freystrop seem to point, not only to Scandinavian occupation, but to Scandinavian occupation in heathen times. Whatever we make of Hasgard, it seems hardly possible that any place could have got the name of Freystrop—that is doubtless Freysthorp—if it had not been founded by people who still believed in Frey. If any Scandinavian settlements stayed on till the time of Henry the First, they would merge with the Flemings and the English into one Teutonic community, just as the Saxons of Bayeux were lost among the Normans, but helped to keep Bayeux Teutonic later than other parts of Normandy. In all these points of view, ethnological and linguistic, this little out-of-the-way corner of the Teutonic world is of very high interest, and its local history and peculiarities have never been thoroughly worked out from a scientific point of view. It has points in common with another isolated Teutonic land at the other end of Britain. The Scandinavian islands, Orkney and Shetland, speak English. Indeed we have seen documents in those islands drawn up in the Scottish form of English before they were mortgaged by Denmark. Both cases teach the same lesson, how easily a standard form of any language assimilates all the kindred dialects of a country, but how little effect it has on dialects which are not kindred. English has not assimilated, though it has largely displaced, the Welsh and Gaelic tongues, with which it has no connexion beyond the remotest Aryan kindred. But the tongues of the Dane and the Fleming, as well as those of the Angle and the Saxon, have all been drawn together by the attraction of a single type of standard English. The actual local speech of different parts still remains very different. But all understand the same standard tongue, and all read the same English Bible in which that standard tongue appears in its best form.

SOUTH PEMBROKESHIRE CASTLES.

1851-1876.

THE Flemish district of Pembrokeshire—in what sense Flemish we have already explained—is as rich in castles as Northumberland itself, and for exactly the same reason. The inhabitants were settlers in a conquered land, with dangerous neighbours on their borders; they held a small isolated territory which lay open to attack from the whole of a large district. Each town therefore needed its fortress to guard it; each dwelling of a considerable lord became itself a fortress. Yet perhaps castles are not so thick on the ground here as they are in some other districts. They are hardly so thick on the ground as they are in Glamorgan. Perhaps the difference is in some measure owing to the different nature of the settlement. The settlement of Glamorgan was essentially a settlement of lords with their followers. The Flemish colony can hardly fail to have been of a more popular character. Every parish church seems to have had its tower designed as a stronghold in time of need, and, as we have said, a military touch may be seen in the ordinary houses. And the churches as well as the houses are well worth studying. That they have less of ornamental detail than the ancient churches of almost any other part of the island is in no way surprising, nor is it in any way blameworthy. And what they lack in ornamental detail they make up in picturesqueness and complexity of outline. They add too the almost universal presence, though certainly in the simplest of forms, of the stone vault, so rare in all other parts of Britain, except in churches of a far greater size. In South Pembrokeshire, contrary to the rule of the rest of the world, a wooden roof in a church is a sign of finer work. It is a sign that the building is not a specimen of the local style of the district, but that it has been built after the pattern of churches of a richer type elsewhere. Where we see, as we now and then do, elaborate windows and other work of the fourteenth century, the plain local barrel vault would be felt to be out of place. So it is at Carew, so it is at Hodgeston, where a modern architect has ruthlessly mutilated the most graceful feature of the building; so it is lastly in the most characteristic of the greater churches of the district, the priory of Monkton close to Pembroke.

From the churchyard of Monkton the view is one which is eminently characteristic of the district. Nowhere do we more thoroughly feel where we are than in Little England beyond Wales. The great physical feature of the district is brought strongly home to the mind of the traveller who passes from the town of Pembroke to its suburb Monkton. South Pembrokeshire is, before all things, a land of inland seas, of peninsulas, and of islands. It is not a land of mountains, but it is pre-eminently a land of hills. The English district is largely made up of two peninsulas, the northern of which is separated from Dewisland, the immediate patrimony of Saint David, by the noble bay of Saint Bride, curving round like the bay of Penzance, or even of Naples, and with the islands off either horn suggesting memories of Ischia and Capri. This northern peninsula, itself made up to a considerable extent of smaller peninsulas, is cut off from its southern fellow by the haven of Milford. Here again we seem to see a Scandinavian trace. The *ford* here is surely neither an English *ford* nor a Welsh *ffordd*, but a Scandinavian *fiord*, like Waterford and Wexford. And a *fiord* of very truth it is; a fiord with endless creeks running far up the country, so that points far inland stand on the salt water. We are here on a fiord of the Ocean, subject to the law of tides, so that the look of one of these inland creeks varies greatly from one hour to another. But, at a favourable moment, the great fiord of Pembrokeshire may suggest the noblest gulf of the Hadriatic; on the bosom of the haven of Milford, we are tempted to say that we only lack the mountains to feel ourselves on the *mouths* of Cattaro. The creeks which run thus far inland wash the bases of three of the chief castles of the districts. At Haverfordwest, the most northern point of the haven— the spot where the traveller leaves the iron road of modern times to betake himself how he can to the ancient city of Saint David's—at this border stronghold of the Englishry, castle and town rise proudly over the low ground at their feet, low ground where, at the favourable moment, the inland sea shows itself. But the castle, noble in its position and outline, is degraded and disfigured by its modern use as a gaol. At Haverfordwest the objects of greatest attraction are ecclesiastical. There is the church of Saint Mary, of an uncouth outline enough outside, but which shelters pillars and arches of the thirteenth century which might stand part of the richest minster. And there is the ruined priory by the water, with the shell of its aisleless cruciform church, once seemingly, with its long lancets, the fellow of the little cathedral at Killaloe. From Haverfordwest the railway will lead us to its most distant point at Neyland or New Milford, with Pater or Pembroke Dock opposite to it. Here we are in the thick of the works of modern times. But we have only to cross the hill between the main haven and one of its creeks, and we come in sight of the opposite heights crowned by the castle of Pembroke and the priory of Monkton. The narrow inlet of the ocean, dwindled to the size of a small stream, ebbs and flows between the two hills, and the proud fortress which grew out of the wooden structure of Arnulf of Montgomery rises straight from the rocks which form one of its coasts. A cave, the

Wogan—the British name survives for a natural object —not quite of the size of Wookey Hole in Mendip— perhaps its namesake—or of the Devil's Hole in the Peakland, but big enough to be striking and solemn, burrows, as it were, under the hall of the castle, and is itself taken into the line of the defences. The walls with their towers, the huge round tower—not quite the rival of Coucy, but the nearest surviving approach to it in Britain—the stately hall itself with its late thirteenth-century windows, the gateway, the whole circuit of the castle, all join to form a group worthy to be the head of the Flemish land, worthy to be the home of the great earls of whom the one gained his fame by sheltering the youth of Henry of Winchester, and the other by withstanding his misrule.

The castle stands nobly, whether as seen immediately from below or from the opposite side. But the Monkton view, though it brings out the architecture of the castle itself less perfectly, is perhaps the most characteristic of all. The priory stands on its height, one of that class of double churches whose arrangements seem at best to be beginning to be understood—a church without transepts, with a graceful choir and Lady chapel of the fourteenth century, now in ruins, attached to a ruder nave of the native type. In its churchyard—so it is said on the spot— not so long ago stone seats still remained for the hearers of the out-door sermon which was preached from the churchyard cross. Below it stands, not exactly a castle, but a fortified house, a 'domus defensabilis,' thoroughly characteristic of the district. On the opposite side are the castle, the town wall, the massive tower of Saint Mary's church, contrasting with the slender one of the priory itself, but both such as could be found nowhere else. In mere extent the town of Pembroke does not rank above an English market-town; but, just as with the small towns of Germany, its position gave it importance. As the capital of the conquered land, the seat of the local chief and of the burgesses gathered under the shade of his fortress, a town of this class really ranked rather with Exeter and Lincoln than with the petty places on whose level its mere physical size would place it.

While one horn of the haven reaches to Haverfordwest and another to Pembroke, each washing a fortress which protects a considerable town, a third horn washes a third fortress, which stands all alone, the stronghold of a lord, not the shelter of a civic settlement. This is Carew, a place whose name calls for a short lecture on its pronunciation. The name is British, *caerau*, camps, a name handed on from some encampment of the race who were driven out. But the received English spelling is *Carew*, keeping in its last syllable a survival of the British plural; and its received English sound is exactly the same as *Carey*, not deviating very much from the sound of the Welsh original. From the place a family took its name, and, till within a generation or two, the name of both place and family was always sounded *Cárey*. But, as Smith becames *Smythe* and *Smijth*, so *Caroó* was thought to have a finer sound, and the barbarous pronunciation is actually making its way from the family to the castle. The castle itself is in some points a contrast to that of Pembroke. While at Pembroke we have a purely military castle, mainly of the thirteenth century, at Carew we can trace the steps by which the mere fortress gradually changed into the great house. The gates and towers are there after the old pattern, but the great hall was thoroughly recast in the days of Henry the Seventh by Sir Rhys ap Thomas, a person who plays some part in general history, and who holds a very great place indeed in local imagination. Joining on to his work, built on by a most violent contrast against one of the original towers with its vast spur buttresses, is a range of large rooms of the confirmed domestic architecture of the Elizabethan age. The whole is forsaken and roofless; but, as often happens, the latest part of the building is the most ruinous. Huge square windows, with their mullions and transoms, are not so well fitted to weather storms as the massive walls of a Norman keep.

The castle of Carew then is not only striking in its general outline and worth studying in many of its details, but it is specially instructing from its combination of military and domestic architecture. But on the road from Pembroke to Carew the traveller will do well to turn aside to take such a view as is allowed him of another forsaken and roofless building of the ecclesiastical-domestic class, the once episcopal manor of Lamphey. The building, once a favourite residence of the bishops of Saint David's, is well worth the attention of the special student of domestic architecture; but in a more general aspect it is chiefly remarkable for the question which has been raised, whether its peculiar arcaded parapet, which bears a faint likeness to the beautiful parapets of the palace of Saint David's and the castle of Swansea, is the work of the same architect, the famous Bishop Henry Gower of the fourteenth century. But, compared with the work in the other building, the Lamphey parapet looks so very poor that it must surely be a weak imitation of later times. We may with more confidence look for the hand of Gower in the neighbouring church of Carew, one of the best of those in the district which do not conform to the local type.

From Carew, castle and church, the wayfarer will naturally make his way to Tenby, but he will do well to turn aside to give a glance to the church of Gumfreston on its slope, with a singular mineral well at the bottom of the dell in which either the natural philosopher or the physician may find some interest. The church itself has no detail of any kind, but no better specimen can be found of the strange, wild, picturesque character of the local type. At Tenby itself, the huge church has nothing local but the tower; but the process by which it has swelled to its present form is worth comparing with Grantham and Great Yarmouth. The most really interesting thing at Tenby is the town wall, which remains very nearly perfect throughout the whole of one side. Of the castle only fragments are left; but the peninsular hill stands nobly, looking over the sea two ways, to the island known as Caldy on the one side, and on the other side to the Worm's Head, the western promontory of Gower, the Saxon or Flemish fellow of the Scandinavian *Orms* Head of Gwynedd. From Tenby the favourite excursion is, not without reason, to the castle of Manorbeer, the birthplace of Giraldus. Five-and-twenty years back there was not much to be made out here beyond a picturesque outline of walls and round towers. But the chief features have lately been brought clearly to light, a hall and a chapel whose changes are well worth study, and among which are parts of Giraldus' own day or earlier. The castle stands well on the south coast, looking down on a small bay, and with the wildest and strangest even of Pembrokeshire churches on the side of an opposite hill. As to the origin of the name of this place many strange guesses have been made. It may be well to preserve the strangest. At some unrecorded time the land was laid waste by a huge and savage bear. For a while no means were found of killing, trapping, or otherwise getting rid of the enemy. At last a stout knight of those parts met the terrible beast in single combat. At last he slew him, but not till after so long and hard a struggle that it was for a while doubtful to which victory would fall, 'man or bear.' Wherefore the name of the place was called Manorbeer.

WESSEX

THE PLACE OF EXETER IN ENGLISH HISTORY.

[Read at the Exeter Meeting of the Archæological Institute, July 30, 1873. Some few passages have been worked in from an earlier article on Exeter in the 'Saturday Review,' June 11, 1870.]

THE thought sometimes comes into the mind of the English traveller in other lands that the cities of his own land must seem but of small account in the eyes of a traveller from the lands which he visits. I speak of course as an antiquary; I speak not of modern prosperity and modern splendour; I speak of the historical associations of past times and of the visible monuments which past times have left behind them. Our best ecclesiastical and our best military buildings, the minsters of Durham and Ely, the castles of Rochester and Caernarvon, are indeed unsurpassed by buildings of the same class in any other land. But buildings of this kind are few and far between; the English town, great or small, does not, as a rule, make the same impression, as an artistic and antiquarian object, as a town of the same class in Italy, Germany, Burgundy, France, or Aquitaine. The ordinary English market-town has commonly little to show beyond its parish church. Its history, if it has any history, is simply that it has been, so to speak, the accidental site of some of the events of general English history, that it has been the scene of some battle or the birth-place of some great man. In many parts of the Continent such a town would have its walls, its gates, its long lines of ancient houses; it would have too a history of its own, a history

of our island. None has in all ages more steadily kept
the character of a local capital, the undisputed head and
centre of a great district. And none has come so near to
being something more than a local capital. None has
had so fair a chance as Exeter once had of becoming an
independent commonwealth, the head of a confederation
of smaller boroughs, perhaps the mistress of dependent
towns and subject districts, ruling over her περίοικοι or
Unterthanen as Florence ruled over Pisa, as Bern ruled
over Lausanne.

I think then that it is not with mere words of course
that I may congratulate the members of this Institute on
finding themselves at last within the walls—here it is no
figure of speech to say within the walls—of the great city
of Western England. For years we have been, like Swegen
or William himself, knocking at the gates. At least we
have stood outside, and we would have knocked at the
gates, if any gates had been left for us to knock at. We
have, wherefore no man knoweth, dealt with the Damnonian Isca as the last among the great cities of England,
but it has assuredly not been because it is the least.
We have seen York and Lincoln and Chester; and, if
Exeter must yield to York and Lincoln and Chester in
wealth of actually surviving monuments, it assuredly does
not yield to any of them in the historic interest of its long
annals. It has in truth a peculiar interest of its own, in
which it stands alone among the cities of England. It
is one of the few ties which directly bind the Englishman
to the Roman and the Briton. It is the greatest trophy
of that stage of English conquest, when our forefathers,
weaned from the fierce creed of Woden and Thunder,
deemed it enough to conquer, and no longer sought to
destroy.

The first glimpse of the city shows the traveller that
it is one of a class which is common on the Continent but
rare in England, and which among West-Saxon cities is
absolutely unique. From Winchester onwards—we may

say from Dorchester, for the forsaken sites must not be
forgotten in the reckoning—the seats of the West-Saxon
bishoprics, as a rule, lie low. Take the most familiar
test; besides Exeter, Sherborne is the only one to which
the traveller on the railway looks up, and to Sherborne
he looks up far less than he looks up to Exeter. From
Sherborne indeed the Lotharingian Hermann took a high
flight to the waterless hill of the elder Salisbury; but
Richard Poore redressed the balance by bringing church
and city down into the plain of Merefield. Dorchester
looks up at the camp on Sinodun; Winchester looks up
at the place of martyrdom on Saint Giles's hill. Wells
crouches at the foot of Mendip; Glastonbury, on her
sacred island, crouches at the foot of the Archangel's Tor.
Bath has in modern times climbed to a height like that
of Lincoln or Durham, but the site of her abbey shows
how the true Bath, the Aquæ Solis that Ceawlin conquered, the Old Borough where Eadgar wore his crown, was
built, as the Jew says in Richard of the Devizes, 'ad por-
tas inferi.' But Exeter tells us another tale at the first
glance. The city indeed looks up at heights loftier than
itself, but the city itself sits on a height rising far above
railway or river. Exeter, Isca, Caer Wisc, is in short a
city of the same class as Bourges and Chartres, as com-
munal Le Mans and kingly Laon, as Lausanne and
Geneva by their lakes, as Chur and Sitten in their Alpine
valleys. We see here, what we see so commonly in Gaul,
so rarely in Britain, the Celtic hill-fort, which has grown
into the Roman city, which has lived on through the
Teutonic conquest, and which still, after all changes,
keeps its place as the undoubted head of its own district.
In Wessex such a history is unique; in all southern
England London is the only parallel, and that but an imperfect one. The name carries on the same lesson which
is taught us by the site. *Caer Wisc* has never lost its
name. It has been Latinized into *Isca*; it has been Teu-
tonized into *Exanceaster* and cut short into modern *Exeter*;

Anderida, Calleva, Uriconium, remain desolate to this day. All this is the natural result of the history of the country. The tie which binds the history of the Roman to the history of the conquered provincial on the one hand and of the Teutonic conqueror on the other is weaker in Britain than in other lands. Nowhere else did the Roman find so little of native groundwork on which to build; nowhere else was his own work so utterly swept away. The grass which once grew over the temples and houses of Deva and Aquæ Solis, the grass which still grows over the temples and houses of Calleva and Anderida, is the best witness to the difference between the English Conquest of Britain and the Gothic, Burgundian, and Frankish conquests of other lands.

Yet the very fact that the cities of England must yield in antiquity, in artistic wealth, in historical associations, to the cities of other European lands, does not fail to give them a special interest of their own. The domestic history of an English town, which was always content to be a municipality, which never aspired to become an independent commonwealth, seems tame beside the long and stirring annals of the free cities of Italy and Germany. Yet, for that very reason, it has a special value of its own. Because the city has not striven after an independent being, it has done its work as a part of a greater whole. Because it has not aspired to be a sovereign commonwealth, it has played its part in building up a nation. And the comparison between the lowly English municipality and the proud Italian or German commonwealth has also an interest of another kind. The difference between the two is simply the difference implied in the absence of political independence in the one case and its presence in the other. This difference is purely external. The internal constitution, the internal history, sometimes the internal revolutions, often present the most striking analogies. In both we may often see the change from democracy to oligarchy and from oligarchy to democracy.

In both we may see men who in old Greece would have taken their place as demagogues, perhaps as tyrants. Here, as in other lands, the city has often had to strive for its rights against the neighbouring nobles. Exeter has something to tell of earls and countesses of Devon : Bristol has something to tell of its own half citizens, half tyrants, the lords of Berkeley. We may see germs of a federal system among the Five Danish Boroughs of Mercia, among the Cinque Ports of Kent and Sussex, and in the Hansa of the Burghs of Scotland. We may see germs too of the dominion of the city, ruling, like Sparta or Bern, over surrounding subject districts, so long as the county of Middlesex neither chooses her Sheriffs herself nor receives them from the central Government, but has to accept such Sheriffs as may be given her by the great neighbouring City. To that city her inhabitants stand thus far in the relation which a Spartan knew as that of πɛρίοικοι, and a Berner as that of *Unterthanen*.

In the free cities of the Continent in short we see what English cities might have grown into, if the royal power in England had been no stronger than that of the Emperors, and if England had therefore split up into separate states, like Germany, Italy, and Gaul. A city or borough, with its organized municipal constitution, could, if the central power were either gradually or suddenly removed, at once act as an independent commonwealth. It is plain that a county could not do so with anything like the same ease. It has been the constant tendency to unity in England, the tendency to subordinate every local power to the common King and the common Parliament, which has made the difference between a municipality like Exeter and a commonwealth like Florence. And here, in this city of Exeter, thoughts of this kind have a special fitness. No city of England has a history which comes so near to the history of the great continental cities. No city in England can boast of a longer unbroken existence; none is so direct a link between the earliest and the latest days of the history

perhaps hardly known beyond its own borders, but still a
history; some tale of its lords or of its burghers, of lords
ruling over a miniature dominion, of burghers defending
a miniature commonwealth, but still lords and burghers
who have a history, no less than kingdoms and commonwealths on a greater scale. In towns of a higher class,
the peers of our shire-towns and cathedral cities, the
palace of the prince, the council-house of the commonwealth, perhaps a long range of the dwellings of old
patrician houses, speak of the greatness of a city which
once held its rank among European capitals, as the
dwelling-place of a prince or as a free city of the Empire.
I speak not of world-famous cities which have been
the seats of mighty kingdoms, of commonwealths which
could bear themselves as the peers of kingdoms, or of
the Lords of the World themselves. I speak not of
Venice or Florence, of Trier or of Ravenna. I speak
of cities of a class one degree lower. I speak of the
last home of Carolingian kingship on the rock of Laon;
I speak of the walls of successive ages, spreading each
round another, like the circles of Ecbatana—the works
of Gaul and Roman and Frank, of counts and bishops
and citizens—gathering around the minster and the castles of Le Mans. I speak of the Bern of Theodoric by
the Adige and of the Bern of Berchthold by the Aar.
I speak of the council-houses of Lübeck and Ghent, of
Padua and Piacenza, of the episcopal palace at Liége
and the ducal palace at Dijon, of the castled steep which
looks down on the church of Saint Elizabeth at Marburg,
of the hill, with its many-towered church, its walls, its gateways, its rugged streets, which rises above the island home
of Frederick at Gelnhausen. We have few such spots as
these, spots so rich at once in history and in art. And
yet we need not grieve that we are in this matter poorer
than other nations. Whatever is taken away from the
greatness of particular cities and districts is added to the
general greatness of the whole kingdom. Why is the

history of Nürnberg greater than the history of Exeter? Simply because the history of England is greater than the history of Germany. Why have not our cities such mighty senate-houses, such gorgeous palaces, as the seats of republican freedom or of princely rule among the Italian and the Teutonic cities? It is because England was one, while Italy and Germany and Gaul were still divided. Our cities lack the stately buildings, they lack the historic memories. But they lack them because England became an united nation too soon to allow of her nobles and prelates growing into sovereign princes, too soon to allow of the local freedom of her cities and boroughs growing into the absolute independence of sovereign commonwealths.

And if the cities of England are less rich in historic memories, less thickly set with historic buildings, than the cities of the Continent, they must no less yield to them in mere antiquity. We have no cities like Massalia and Gades, which can trace up an unbroken being and an unbroken prosperity to the days of Greek and even of Phœnician colonization. It is only here and there that we can find a site which can even pretend to have lived on, like the ancient towns of Italy and Gaul and Spain, as a dwelling-place of man from the earliest recorded times, the home in turn of the Briton, the Roman, and the Englishman. Perusia, Tolosa, Remi, a crowd of others in the south-western lands, are cities which have lived on, keeping their own names or the names of their tribes. They are cities reared by the Etruscan, the Iberian, and the Celt, or become possessions of Roman, Gothic, and Frankish masters. In our land Dr. Guest has shown that London itself has but doubtful claims to an unbroken being from the days of the Briton. Even of the cities raised in Britain by the Roman, though many are still inhabited, though some have been constantly inhabited, yet many others, like Bath and Chester, rose up again after a season of desolation, while other sites, but the city by the Exe has, through all conquests, through all changes of language, proclaimed itself by its name as the city by the Exe. For the Exe is of no small moment in the history of Exeter. The city is not only a fortress on a height; it is a fortress on a height overhanging a river. Every one must feel the difference between a position of this kind and one, like that of Bristol or Châlons, where the town was built close on, or rather in, the river. At Châlons this kind of site was chosen, because in the Catalaunian Fields no hill-tops were to be had, and next to a hill-top an island in a river was the safest site. At Bristol, a comparatively modern town, of purely English name and origin, the same kind of site was chosen for another reason. Bristol was a commercial town from the very beginning; the merchant borough of course needed defences, but the post was not in itself a military one. At Exeter, a British hill-fort, strength of position was the first object; commerce was something which came after. The walls ran round the crest of the hill; it was only at one point that they came down to the river, where the Quay Gate opened to receive a commerce which, in the early middle age, was one of the richest in England.

The name and the site go together. The name has had a more perfectly continuous being than the names of most of the cities of northern Gaul. At Rheims, Paris, Bourges, a crowd of others, the name of the tribe has supplanted the true name of the city; but Isca, like the cities of the south, like Burdigala and Massalia, has never exchanged its own name for the name of the Damnonian people. Name and site together at once distinguish Exeter from any of the ordinary classes of English towns. They distinguish it from Teutonic marks which have grown into modern towns, and which, like Reading and Basingstoke, still keep the clan names of the Rædingas and Basingas. They distinguish it no less from Roman towns like Bath and Chester, which rose again after a season of desolation—from towns like Wells and Peterborough, which grew up under the shadow of some great minster—from fortresses or havens like Taunton or Kingston-on-Hull, which sprang into life at the personal bidding of some far-sighted king—from towns like Durham and New Salisbury, where church and city arose together when some wise bishop sought, on the peninsular hill or on the open meadow, a home more safe either from foreign invaders or from unkindly neighbours. Exeter is none of these; like Lincoln it stands on a site which Briton, Roman, and Englishman have alike made their own; like Lincoln it is a city set on an hill, it has a temple built on high; on the whole, Lincoln is its nearest parallel among the cities of England; in some points the histories of the two present a striking likeness; in others they present differences not less instructive than their likenesses.

Exeter then, as a hill-fort city, has, more than almost any other city of England, a close analogy with the ancient cities of Gaul. But there is another point in which the history of Exeter altogether differs from theirs. The Gaulish city has almost always been the seat of a bishopric from the days of the first establishment of Christianity. The cathedral church and the episcopal palace stand, and always have stood, side by side, on the highest point of the hill on which the city stands. The city is indeed older than the bishopric, because it is older than Christianity itself. But the bishopric is something which was firmly established during the days of Roman dominion, something which, as far as the Teutonic conquerors were concerned, might be looked on as an inherent and immemorial part of the city. There had been a time when Bourges and Chartres and Paris had not been seats of bishoprics; but it was only as seats of bishoprics that their Frankish conquerors knew them. The Roman bishopric, like so many other things that were Roman, lived on through the Teutonic conquest, and, except in the case of very modern unions and suppressions, it has lived on till at a place whose name, though written in different ways, we should certainly understand to be Exeter if there were no reason to the contrary. It is certainly hard to bring the West-Saxon conquerors even to the Devonshire borders at any time earlier than the days of Ine, when the powerful King Gerent reigned over Damnonia, and when Taunton was a border fortress of the Englishman against the Briton. Yet it may be that the difficulty arises only from taking for granted that the West-Saxon entrance into Devonshire must have been made by this line of conquest, the line, in modern geography, of the Great Western Railway. It is possible that the West-Saxons may have come in by the South-Western line, by way of Dorset and not of Somerset, and Exeter may have been an English possession when Taunton was still a border fortress against Britons dwelling north of Exeter. And this view is strengthened by the fact which has been very ingeniously put forward, that the dedications of the churches of the city fall into two classes, English and Welsh, and that the Welsh dedications are found in its northern part. One thing is certain, that under Æthelwulf Devonshire was English, and that the men of Devonshire, as West-Saxon subjects, fought valiantly and successfully against the Danish invader. This is the first distinct mention in our Chronicles which marks the district as an English possession, while their first mention of the city, as I have already said, comes later in the same century, in the wars of Ælfred. But though it was English by allegiance, it was not till two generations later that the city became wholly English in blood and speech. In Æthelstan's day the city was still partly Welsh, partly English. We can, if we please, according to many analogies elsewhere, conceive the two rival nations dwelling side by side within the same enclosure, but separated again by enclosures of their own. Britons and Englishmen would thus each form a city within a city, the British city lying north of the English. To this state of things the Lord of all Britain, the conqueror of Scot and Northman, the lawgiver of England, deemed it time to put a stop, and to place the supremacy of the conquering nation in the chief city of the western peninsula beyond all doubt. Exeter was a post which needed to be strongly fortified, and its fortification was to be put in no hands but such as were thoroughly trustworthy. The British inhabitants were driven out; the city became purely English; and, to the confusion of those who tell us that Englishmen could not put stones and mortar together till a hundred and forty years later, it was encircled by a wall of square stones, and strengthened by towers, marking a fourth stage in the history of English fortification. Ida first defended Bamburgh with a hedge or palisade; a later Northumbrian ruler strengthened it with a wall or dyke of earth. Eadward the Elder surrounded Towcester with a wall of stone; Æthelstan surrounded Exeter with a wall of squared stones. This is is not theory, but history. If any one asks me where the wall of Æthelstan is now, I can only say that a later visitor to Exeter took care that there should not be much of it left for us to see. Yet there are some small fragments, huge stones put together in clear imitation of the Roman fashion of building, which may well enough be remains of the wall of Æthelstan. His defences doubtless followed the line of the Roman wall which doubtless helped at least to supply them with materials, and the plan of the city has not been seriously interfered with in later repairs. It still keeps the plan of the Roman *chester*, modified somewhat by the ground. The four limbs are there, though the course of one of them has been changed in later times. The gates, as we have seen, are gone, though in some cases they have left their memorial in the shape of hinges.

Now the distinguishing point in this stage of the history of Exeter is this, that it, alone of the great cities of Britain, did not fall into the hands of the English invaders till after the horrors of conquest had been softened by the influence of Christianity. Whatever was the exact

the bishoprics within the Empire, the bishops of those
cities grew to a height of temporal power to which no
prelate, not the Palatine of Durham himself, ever reached
in England, and which the bishops of Exeter were among
those who were furthest from reaching. At Chur the
church and palace of the bishop, with its surrounding
quarter, grew into a fortified akropolis, where the bishop
still reigned as prince, even when the lower city had
become independent of his rule. At Sitten church and
castle stand perched on the twin peaks of Valeria and
Tourbillon. But the castle was the fortress, not of king
or duke, but of the prelate himself. In some English
bishoprics too the bishop was, if not prince, at least
temporal lord. At Wells, for instance, the city simply
arose outside the close, and its municipal franchises were
the grant of its episcopal lords. At Exeter, where the
bishop came as something new into a city which had
stood for ages, it was as much as he could do if he could
maintain the exemption of his own immediate precinct,
at all events when the civic sword was wielded by a mayor
of the ready wit and the stubborn vigour of John
Shillingford.

It is not however my business to dwell at any detail on
either the ecclesiastical or municipal history of the city.
My business is with the city in its more general aspect.
I have pointed out two of the characteristic features of its
history, how it is rather continental than English in its position, as a hill-fort city living on from Roman and British
times, while it is specially English in the modern date
of the foundation of its bishopric. The first question
which now suggests itself is one which I cannot answer.
When did the city first become a West-Saxon possession?
When did the British *Caer-Wisc*, the Roman *Isca*, pass
into the English *Exanceaster?* Of that event I can find
no date, no trustworthy mention. In the days of Ælfred,
as every reader of the Chronicles knows, Exeter figures
as an English fortress, and a fortress of great importance,

more than once taken and retaken by the great king and his Danish enemies. But I am as little able to fix the date of the English conquest of Isca as I am to fix the date of its original foundation by the Briton. John Shillingford tells us that Exeter was a walled city before the Incarnation of Christ, and, though it is not likely to have been a walled city in any sense that would satisfy either modern or Roman engineers, it is likely enough to have been already a fortified post before Cæsar landed in Britain. Nor can I presume to determine whether Isca ever bore the name of *Penholtkeyre*, which sounds rather like a British name read backwards with an English word thrown in by the way. Nor can I say what was the exact nature of Vespasian's dealings with the city at the time when we hear of a mysterious sale of thirty Jews—some say, only their heads—for the price of one penny. In a later age, another civic worthy, the famous John Hooker, tells us that Vespasian, when Duke under the Emperor Claudius, besieged the city by order of his master, but was driven away, like some later besiegers, by the valour of the citizens, and betook himself to Jerusalem as an easier conquest. These questions are beyond me; but the identity of the British Caer-wisc, the Roman Isca, the English Exanceaster, is witnessed by a crowd of authorities. Still I know of no evidence to fix the point at which Isca became Exanceaster, any more than to fix the point when Isca came into being. As the story of Saint Boniface runs, we are told that he was born at Crediton, and brought up at Exeter. This would of course imply that, before the end of the seventh century, Isca was already an English town, and a town where some place of education had already come into being. Now for the birth of Boniface at Crediton there is no authority earlier than the fourteenth century, though the unbroken and uncontroverted tradition may be allowed to count for something. His education at Exeter rests on the reading of a passage in his biographer Willibald; he is said to have been brought up

our own day. In England, on the other hand, besides the
union of some bishoprics and the division of others, there
has been a wandering to and fro of the immediate seats
of episcopal rule to which there has been no parallel in
Gaul. In Gaul but few bishoprics have been moved—as
distinguished from being united or divided—from their
original seats; in England it is rather the rule than the
exception that a bishopric should have changed its place
once or twice since its foundation. The causes of these
differences go very deep into the history of the two
countries: it is enough to say here that the character
of the English Conquest, as a heathen conquest, hindered any place within the oldest England from being
the unbroken seat of any Roman and Christian institution.
Add too that in Britain neither Celts nor Teutons, unused
as both of them were to the fully-developed city-life of the
South, ever strictly followed the rule which was universal
in Italy, Spain, and Gaul, that of placing the seat of the
bishop in the chief town of his diocese. Hence, while on
the Continent, the city and its bishopric are both, from a
Teutonic point of view, immemorial,—that is to say, both
existed before and lived through the Teutonic conquest—
in not a few English cities the bishopric is a comparatively
modern institution. The bishop has not been there from
the beginning; he has been placed there by the Confessor
or by the Conqueror, by Henry the First or by Henry the
Eighth, or by virtue of acts of Parliament which we can
ourselves remember. So it is conspicuously at Exeter.
The hill-fort has grown into the city; the city has lived
through all later conquests; but the bishopric is something which, in the long history of such a city, may
almost seem a creation of yesterday. Bishops of Exeter
have played an important part both in local and in general
history; but the city of Exeter had begun to play an important part in the history of Britain ages before bishops
of Exeter were heard of. This fact is stamped on the
outward look of the city. As we now look at the city,

the episcopal church seems to stand out only less conspicuously than Bourges or Geneva, as the roof and crown of all; but for ages its predominance in the landscape must have been more than disputed by the castle on the Red Mount; and Isca had lived and flourished for a thousand years before its height was crowned with a stone of either minster or castle. In truth, if the cathedral church is the prominent object, it is so mainly because of the lack or destruction of other objects. The castle is practically gone, mutilated and disfigured as it is by modern buildings; its gateway alone and the vast ditch below represent it, and these do not show in the general view. There was no abbey without the walls, no Saint Ouens or Saint Augustines, to rival the church of the bishop. And, as in some other cities, Canterbury and Winchester among them, the episcopal church draws some part of its importance from the remarkable poverty of the parish churches. Prominent as Exeter cathedral is in the first view, we find, when we come to study the city more minutely, that it is not the real centre, like those head churches of the old Gaulish cities which often supplant some older temple of paganism. It is in truth a new comer stowed away in its own corner.

It may here be well to compare Exeter for a moment with two continental cities in which the points both of likeness and of unlikeness seem to reach their highest degree. As Exeter stands upon its hill, but is still surrounded by loftier hills that look down upon it, so the loftier heights of Chur and Sitten are looked down upon by the snowy peaks of the Pennine and Rætian Alps. Vast as is the difference of scale, there is a real likeness of position, as compared with the isolated hill of Chartres, rising in the midst of its vast corn-land. Like the Damnonian Isca, Sedunum and Curia Rætorum are cities which have lived on from Roman to modern times. But in them, not only the city, but the bishopric also has lived on through all changes. And, following the common law of

date of the conquest of Devonshire, it was certainly after
Birinus had preached the faith to that most heathen nation
of the Gewissas, after Cynegils and Cwichelm had been
plunged beneath the waters of baptism, and had built the
minster of Dorchester and the Old Minster of Winchester.
When Caer-Wisc became an English possession, there was
no fear that any West-Saxon prince should deal with it as
Æthelfrith had dealt by Deva, as Ceawlin had dealt by
Uriconium and Aquæ Solis, as Ælle and Cissa had dealt
by Anderida. The Norman came to Exeter as he came to
Pevensey, but he did not find the walls of Isca, like the
walls of Anderida, standing with no dwelling-place of
man within them. Neither did they stand, like the walls
of Deva, again to become a city and a fortress after a desolation of three hundred years. When Isca was taken,
the West-Saxons had ceased to be destroyers and deemed
it enough to be conquerors. Thus it was that Exeter
stands alone, as the one great English city which has
lived an unbroken life from præ-English and even from
præ-Roman days. Whatever was the exact date at which
the city first became an English possession, it was not
till the driving out of the Welsh inhabitants under
Æthelstan that it became a purely English city. As
such it fills, during the whole of the tenth and eleventh
centuries, a prominent place among the cities of England,
and a place altogether without a rival among the cities of
its own part of England. Its complete adoption into the
English fold was accompanied by a meeting of the Witan
of the whole realm within the newly-raised walls, and at
that meeting one of the collections of laws which bear the
name of Æthelstan was put forth. Later in the century
the fortress by the Exe begins to play its part as the chief
bulwark of Western England during the renewed Danish
invasions of the reign of Æthelred. That it could play
such a part, that such a site as Exeter was for ages
deemed a position of great strength, is a good commentary
on the difference between ancient and modern warfare.

A siege of Exeter would be a very easy business to an army possessed of modern cannon; but as against the offensive arms of the tenth and eleventh centuries, few positions could be stronger. The hill is peninsular, cut off by ravines, which on each side lead nearly to the river and form a kind of natural moat. The only approach on level ground is the narrow isthmus to the north-east leading to the great eastern gate, and by that path those conquerors of Exeter whose path can be traced seem always to have entered it.

These early sieges of Exeter form a spirit-stirring tale. In our national Chronicles the second millennium of the Christian æra is ushered in by the record which tells us how the heathen host sailed up the Exe and strove to break down the wall which guarded the city—how the wall of Æthelstan defended by the valiant burghers bore up against every onslaught, how fastly the invaders were fighting, and how fastly and hardly the citizens withstood them. It was no fault of those valiant citizens that, as ever in that wretched reign, the valiant resistance of one town or district only led to the further desolation of another. Exeter was saved, but the Unready King had no help, no reward, for the men who saved it; the local force of Devonshire and Somerset had to strive how they could against the full might of the invader; and the overthrow of Pinhoe and the wasting of the land around followed at once upon the successful defence of the city. The very next year Exeter became part of the morning-gift of the Norman Lady, and for the first time—a foretaste of what was to come before the century was out—a man of foreign blood, Hugh the French churl, as our chroniclers call him, was set by his foreign mistress to command in an English city. With no traitor, with no stranger, within their walls, the men of Exeter had beaten off all the attacks of the barbarians; but now we read how, through the cowardice or treason of its foreign chief, Swegen was able to break down and spoil the city, and

F

how the wall of Æthelstan was battered down from the east gate to the west. I do not pretend to rule whether this means the utter destruction of the wall or only the destruction of two sides of it; but it is certain that sixty years later, when Exeter had to strive, not against Norman traitors within but against Norman enemies without, the city was again strongly fortified according to the best military art of the times. It may be noticed that, in the description of Swegen's taking of Exeter, though we read of plundering and of breaking down the walls, we do not, as we commonly do when a town is taken, hear of burning. As a rule, houses in those days were of wood; and it is sometimes amazing how, when a town has been burned, we find it spring up again a year or two later, sometimes only to be burned again. Whether in a city which was so early fortified with towers and walls of squared stones, other buildings too may not have been built of stone earlier than was usual in other places, I leave to local inquirers to settle.

After the capture by Swegen, we hear nothing more of the city itself during the rest of the Danish wars. Doubtless it submitted, along with the rest of western England, when Æthelmær the Ealdorman of Devonshire and all the thegns of the west acknowledged Swegen as King at Bath. In the war of Cnut and Eadmund the men of Devonshire fought on the side of England at Sherstone, but we hear nothing specially of the city. Our only knowledge of Exeter between the Danish and the Norman invasions consists of the fact of the foundation of the bishopric, and of the further fact that the city which had been part of the morning-gift of Emma became also part of the morning-gift of her successor Eadgyth. The two facts are connected. The special relation of the Lady to the city accounts for the peculiar ceremony which, though the charter in which it is recorded is marked by Mr. Kemble as doubtful, can hardly be mere matter of invention. In that charter we are told that Leofric, the first bishop of the new see, was led to his episcopal throne by the King and the Lady, the King on his right side and the Lady on his left. Here, as everywhere else in these times, in every expression and in every ceremony, the strong *Regale*, the undoubted ecclesiastical supremacy of the King and his Witan, or to speak more truly, the identity of the nation and the national Church, comes out plainly. The Bishop is not only placed in his bishopric by the King, but the Lady, as the immediate superior of the city, has her part in the ceremony. The foundation of the bishopric was accompanied by several circumstances which mark it as an event belonging to an age of transition. It was among the last instances of one set of tendencies, among the earliest instances of another. The reign of Eadward the Confessor is the last time in English history, unless we are to except the reign of Edward the Sixth, when two English bishoprics were joined together, without a new one being founded to keep up the number. Such an union had happened more than once in earlier times: it happened twice under Eadward, when the bishoprics of Devonshire and Cornwall were united under Leofric, and when the bishoprics of Dorset and Wiltshire were united under Hermann. But this translation is also the first instance of a movement which, like so many other movements, began under the Normannizing Eadward and went on under his Norman successors. This was the change which brought England under the continental rule that the bishopric should be placed in the greatest city of the diocese. The translation of the see of Saint Cuthberht to Durham was not a case in point; Ealdhun sought a place of safety, and he chose one so wisely that a city presently grew up around his church. But the translation of the West-Welsh bishopric from Bodmin and Crediton to Exeter was the beginning of a system which was further carried out when the great Mid-English bishopric was moved from Dorchester to Lincoln, and when the East-Anglian bishopric was moved from Elmham, first to Thetford and then to Norwich. Again, the first bishop himself represents in his own person more than one of the tendencies of the age. He represents the dominion of the Englishman over the Briton; he represents the close connexion of the Englishman of that generation with his Teutonic kinsmen beyond the sea. Leofric, a native of his own diocese, is described as a Briton, that is, I conceive, a native of Cornwall. But, like the great mass of the landowners of Cornwall in his day, he bears a purely English name. Either he was the descendant of English settlers in the British land, or else he was the descendant of Britons who had so far gone over to English ways as to take to English proper names, just as the English a generation or two later took to Norman proper names. In either way he represents the process through which the list which Domesday gives us of the landowners of his diocese in the days of King Eadward reads only one degree less English than the list of the landowners of Kent and Sussex. But Leofric, whether English or British by blood, was neither English nor British by education. His bringing up was Lotharingian, and he was the first prelate of his age to bring the Lotharingian discipline into England. He thus represents the high position which was held at the time, as seminaries of ecclesiastical learning and discipline, by the secular churches of Germany, by those especially of that corner of the Teutonic kingdom which might be looked on as the border-land of many, Gaul, and Britain, and which drew scholars from all those lands. Leofric represents further that close connexion, especially in ecclesiastical matters, between England and the Teutonic mainland which began under Æthelstan and Eadgar, which went on under Cnut, and which reached its height when Godwine and Harold found it an useful counterpoise to the Norman and French tendencies of King Eadward. Leofric again, in the constitution which he brought into his church, the stricter discipline of Chrodegang, marks the beginning of a tendency which was afterwards carried on by Gisa at Wells, and for a moment by Thomas at York, but which presently gave way to the system which Remigius brought from Rouen to Lincoln, and which, in theory at least, still remains the constitution of the old-foundation churches of England. Leofric survived the Norman invasion; he survived the great siege of Exeter, in which his name is not mentioned. Insular by birth, but continental in feeling, he was succeeded by one of the Norman settlers in England who became an Englishman at heart. Osbern, a son of the famous Gilbert of Brionne, a brother of the fierce Earl of Hereford, came to England, like so many of his countrymen, to seek his fortune at the court of King Eadward. Of him alone among the foreign prelates of that day we read that in his manner of life he followed the customs of England, and had no love for the pomp of Normandy. Of his English tastes we have still a negative witness among us. Throughout his episcopate, down to the fourth year of Henry the First, the church in which Englishmen had been content to worship still stood. The oldest parts of the present church of Exeter date from the time of his successor, William of Warelwast, the former enemy of Anselm, and it is his work that gives the church its distinctive character. Every one knows its strange and unique outline. No western towers, no central lantern but those two side towers which have been irreverently likened to paddle-boxes, and which the smaller church of Ottery Saint Mary has, perhaps dutifully, but somewhat servilely, reproduced. And the outside has affected the inside in a way which, whether we approve or not, is at least unique. The absence of a central tower, or of a lantern of any kind, has made room for what is likely to be the longest unbroken vaulted roof in the world.

The great ecclesiastical change of the eleventh century has carried us on, in point of date, beyond the great time which stands out above all others in the history of Exeter, the time when we may say that for eighteen days

Exeter was England. The tale of the resistance of
the western lands and their capital to the full power of
the Conqueror is one which ought never to pass away from
the memories of Englishmen. The city, with its walls
and towers again made ready for defence—the mother and
the sons of Harold within its walls—the march of the
conqueror to the Eastern gate—the faint-heartedness of
the leaders—the strong heart of the commons, who en-
dured to see their hostage blinded before their eyes—
the resistance as stubborn against William as it had been
against Swegen—the breach of the walls by arts which to
the simpler generalship of Swegen were unknown—the
escape of Gytha and her companions by the water-gate—
the bloodless entry of the Conqueror—the foundation of
the castle to curb the stout-hearted city—the raising of
its tribute to lessen the wealth which had enabled it to
resist—all form a tale than which, even in that stirring
time, none, save the tale of the great battle itself, speaks
more home to the hearts of all who love to bear in mind how
long and how hard a work it was to make England yield
to her foreign master. Our hearts beat with those of the
defenders of Exeter; we mourn as the mother of the last
English king flees from the last English city which
maintained the cause of the house of Godwine. But we
see none the less that it was for the good of England that
Exeter should fall. A question was there decided, greater
than the question whether England should be ruled by
Harold, Eadgar, or William, the question whether England
should be one. When Exeter stood forth for one moment
to claim the rank of a free Imperial city, the chief of a
confederation of the lesser towns of the West—when she,
or at least her rulers, professed themselves willing to
receive William as an external lord, to pay him the tribute
which had been paid to the old kings, but refused to
admit him within her walls as her immediate sovereign—
we see that the tendency was at work in England by which
the kingdoms of the Empire were split up into loose col-

lections of independent cities and principalities. We see that the path was opening by which Exeter might have come to be another Lübeck, the head of a Damnonian Hansa; another Bern, the mistress of the subject lands of the western peninsula. Such a dream sounds wild in our ears, and we may be sure that no such ideas were present in any such definite shape to the minds of the defenders of Exeter. But any such conscious designs were as little likely to be present to the minds of those who, in any German or Italian city, took the first steps in the course by which, from a municipality or less than a municipality, the city grew into a sovereign commonwealth. In a record of what did happen that separate defence of the western lands which ended in a separate defence of Exeter is simply an instance of the way in which, after Harold was gone, England was conquered bit by bit. York never dreamed of helping Exeter, and Exeter, if it had the wish, had not the power to help York. But it is none the less true that, when a confederation of western towns with the great city of the district at their head, suddenly started into life, to check the progress of the Conqueror, it shows that a spirit had been kindled, which, had it not been checked at once, might have grown into something of which those who manned the walls of Exeter assuredly never thought. We cannot mourn that such a tendency was stopped, even by the arm of a foreign conqueror. We cannot mourn that the greatness of Exeter was not purchased at the cost of the greatness of England. But it is worth while to stop and think how near England once was to running the same course as other lands, how easily the Earls of Chester and Shrewsbury might have grown into sovereign princes, margraves of their border principalities—how easily the Palatine Bishops of Durham might have grown into spiritual princes, like their brethren of Speier and Bamberg—how easily Exeter and Lincoln might have taken their places as the heads of confederations of free cities in the *Wealh-cyn* and among the Five Danish boroughs. From such a fate as this, from the sacrifice of the general welfare of the whole to the greater brilliance of particular members of the whole, we have been saved by a variety of causes, and not the least of them, by the personal character of a series of great kings, working in the cause of national unity, from West-Saxon Ecgberht to Norman Henry. The tendency of the patriotic movements in William's reign was a tendency to division. The tendency of William's own rule was a tendency to union. The aims of the Exeter patricians could not have been long reconciled with the aims of the sons of Harold, nor could the aims of either have been reconciled for a moment with the aims of the partisans of the Ætheling Eadgar, of the sons of Ælfgar, or of the Danish Swegen. Our hearts are with the defenders of Exeter, with the defenders of York and Ely and Durham, but we feel that from the moment when England lost the one man among her own sons who was fit to guide her, her best fate in the long run was to pass as an undivided kingdom into the hands of his victorious rival.

With the submission of Exeter to William we might fairly end our tale of the place of Exeter in English history. It was now ruled for ever that the city by the Exe was to be a city of the English realm. It was to be no separate commonwealth, but a member of the undivided English kingdom, yet still a city that was to remain the undisputed head of its own district. Its history from this time, as far as I am concerned with it, is less the history of Exeter than the history of those events in English history which took place at Exeter. It still has its municipal, its ecclesiastical, its commercial, history; it still had to strive for its rights against earls and countesses and bishops; it could, in later days, bear its share in the great seafaring enterprises of commerce and discovery. But from the entry of William, Exeter has no longer a separate political being of its own. It is no longer an object to be striven for by men of contending nations. It is no longer something which might conceivably be cut off from the English realm, either by the success of a foreign conqueror or by the independence of its own citizens. In the other sense of the words, as pointing out those events of English history of which Exeter was the scene, the place of Exeter in English history is one which yields to that of no city in the land save London itself. It was with a true instinct that the two men who open the two great æras in local history, English Æthelstan and Norman William, both gave such special heed to the military defences of the city. No city in England has stood more sieges. It stood one, perhaps two more, before William's own reign was ended, indeed before William had brought the Conquest of the whole land to an end by the taking of Chester. The men of Exeter had withstood William as long as he came before them as a foreign invader; when his power was once fully established, when the Castle on the Red Mount, reared by the stranger on the earthworks of earlier days, held down the city in fetters, they seem to have had no mood to join in hopeless insurrections against him. When, a year and a half after the great siege, the castle was again besieged by the West-Saxon insurgents, the citizens seem to have joined the Norman garrison in resisting their attacks. According to one account, they had already done the like to the sons of Harold and their Irish allies. The wars of Stephen's reign did not pass without a siege of Exeter, in which King and citizens joined to besiege the rebellious lord of Rougemont, and at last to starve him out within the towers which legend was already beginning to speak of as the work of the Cæsars. I pass on to later times; the days of the Tudors saw two sieges of the city, one at the hands of a pretender to the crown, another at the hands of the religious insurgents of the further West. Twice again in the wars of the next century do we find Exeter passing from one side to the other by dint of siege, and at last we see her receiving an invader at whose coming no siege was needed. The entry of William the Deliverer through the Western Gate forms the balance, the contrast, and yet in some sort the counterpart, to the entry of William the Conqueror through the Eastern Gate. The city had resisted to the utmost, when a foreign invader, under the guise of an English king, came to demand her obedience. But no eighteen days' siege, no blinded hostage, no undermined ramparts, were needed when a kinsman and a deliverer came under the guise of a foreign invader. In the army of William of Normandy Englishmen were pressed to complete the Conquest of England; in the army of William of Orange strangers came to call her sons to the work of her deliverance. In the person of the earlier William the crown of England passed away for the first time to a king wholly alien in speech and feeling; in the later William it in truth came back to one who, even in mere descent, and yet more fully in his native land and native speech, was nearer than all that came between them to the old stock of Hengest and Cerdic. The one was the first king who reigned over England purely by the edge of the sword; the other was the last king who reigned over England purely by the choice of the nation. The coming of each of the men who entered Exeter in such opposite characters marks an æra in our history. And yet the work of the two was not wholly alien to each other. The later William came to undo the work of the earlier, so far as it was evil, to confirm it so far as it was good. With the one began the period of foreign domination which seemed to sweep away our ancient tongue and our ancient law. With the other began that period of internal progress, every step of which has been in truth a return to the old laws of England before the Norman set foot upon her shores. And yet, after all, William the Conqueror did but preserve what William the Deliverer came to restore. His conquest ruled for ever that England should remain an undivided kingdom, and, in so ruling, it ruled that the old laws and freedom, trampled on indeed but never trampled out, should live to spring up again in newer forms. When the one William renewed the laws of Eadward, it was but a link in the same chain as when the other William gave his assent to the Bill of Rights. In the one case the invader came to conquer, in the other he came to deliver; but in both cases alike the effect of his coming was to preserve and not to destroy; the Conqueror and the Deliverer alike has had his share in working out the continuous being of English law and of English national life. The unwilling greeting which Exeter gave to the one William, the willing greeting which she gave to the other, marked the wide difference in the external aspect of the two revolutions. And yet both revolutions have worked for the same end; the great actors in both were, however unwittingly, fellow-workers in the same cause. And it is no small place in English history which belongs to the city whose name stands out in so marked a way in the tale alike of the revolution of the eleventh century and of the revolution of the seventeenth. It is no small matter, as we draw near by the western bridge or by the eastern isthmus, as we pass where once stood the Eastern and the Western Gate, as we tread the line of the ancient streets, to think that we are following the march of the Conqueror or of the Deliverer. It is no small matter, as we enter the minster of Leofric and Warelwast and Grandison, to think that on that spot Te Deum was sung alike for the overthrow of English freedom and for its recovery. It is no mean lesson if we learn to connect with the remembrance of this ancient city, among so many associations of British, Roman, and English days, two thoughts which rise above all the rest—the thought that there is no city in the land whose name marks a greater stage in the history of its conquest and in the history of its deliverance.

GLASTONBURY BRITISH AND ENGLISH.

[Read as the President's Opening Address at the Meeting of the Somerset Archæological and Natural History Society at Glastonbury, August 17, 1880. I have cut short some minute discussions, and worked in some passages from another address.]

THE history of Glastonbury follows in some sort naturally upon the history of Exeter. The two spots have a common characteristic; and that characteristic is the one which gives its historic position to both. What Exeter is among the cities of Britain, that Glastonbury is among the churches of Britain. Let us ask then more minutely, What is the history of Glastonbury? Every one can at once answer that it is the history of a great monastery. The history of Glastonbury is the history of its abbey. Without its abbey, Glastonbury were nothing. The history of Glastonbury is not as the history of York or Chester or Lincoln; it is not as the history of Bristol or Oxford or Norwich or Coventry. It is not the stirring history of a great city or of a great military post. The military, the municipal, and the commercial history of Glastonbury might be written in a small compass, and it would very largely belong to very modern times. The history of Glastonbury is a purely ecclesiastical history, a history like that of Wells and Lichfield, of Peterborough and Crowland. Again, unlike the history of Wells and Lichfield, but like the history of Peterborough and Crowland, it is a purely monastic history. No one who has read the signatures to the Great Charter can fail to know that there have been bishops of Glastonbury; but Glastonbury looked on its bishops only as momentary intruders, and was glad to pay a great price to get rid of them. But even the short reign of the bishops did not affect the purely monastic character of Glastonbury; no one ever tried at Glastonbury, as was tried at Winchester, at Coventry, and at Malmesbury, to displace the monks in favour of secular priests. But again, among monastic histories, the history of Glastonbury has a character of its own which is wholly unique. I will not insult its venerable age by so much as contrasting it with the foundations of yesterday which arose under the influence of the Cistercian movement, which have covered some parts of England with the loveliest of ruins in the loveliest of sites, but which play but a small part indeed in the history of this church and realm. Glastonbury is something more than Netley and Tintern, than Rievaux and Fountains. But it is something more again than the Benedictine houses which arose at the bidding of the Norman Conqueror, of his house or of his companions. It is something more than Selby and Battle, than Shrewsbury and Reading. It is, in its own special aspect, something more even than that royal minster of Saint Peter, the crowning-place of Harold and of William, which came to supplant Glastonbury as the burial-place of kings. Nay, it stands out distinct, as having a special character of its own, even among the great and venerable foundations of English birth which were already great and venerable when the Conqueror came. There is something at Glastonbury which there is not at Peterborough and Crowland and Evesham, in the two minsters of Canterbury and in the two minsters of Winchester. Those are the works of our own people; they go back to the days of our ancient kingship; they go back, some of them, to the days of our earliest Christianity; but they go back no further. We know their beginnings; we know their founders; their history, their very legends, do not dare to trace up their foundations beyond the time of our own coming into this island. Winchester indeed has a tale

which carries up the sanctity of the spot to Lucius the
King and Eleutherius the Pope; but legend itself does
not attempt to bridge over the whole space; it does not
venture to deny that, whatever Lucius and Eleutherius
may have done, Cenwealh and Birinus had to do over
again, as though it had never been done. The mighty
house of Saint Alban, in its site, in its name, in the very
materials of its gigantic minster, carries us back beyond
the days of our own being in this land. But it is only in
its site, in its name, in its materials, that it does so. If
the church of Roman Alban was built of Roman bricks
on the site of Alban's martyrdom, it was built by English
and Norman hands; it was built because an English
king had of his own choice thought good to honour the
saint of another people who had died ages before his
time. But there is no historic or even legendary continuity between the days of Alban the saint and the days
of Offa the founder. It is at Glastonbury, alone among
the great churches of Britain—we instinctively feel that
on this spot the name of *England* is out of place—that
we walk with easy steps, with no thought of any impassable barrier, from the realm of Arthur into the realm of
Ine. Here alone does legend take upon itself to go up,
not only to the beginnings of English Christianity, but to
the beginnings of Christianity itself. Here alone do the
early memories of the other nations and other Churches
of the British islands gather round a holy place which
long possession at least made English. Here alone,
alongside of the memory and the tombs of West-Saxon
princes who broke the power of the Northman, there still
abides the memory, for ages there was shown the tomb,
of the British prince who, if he did not break, at least
checked for a generation, the advancing power of the
West-Saxon. The church which was the resting-place of
Eadgar, of his father and of his grandson, claimed to be
also the resting-place of Arthur. But at Glastonbury this
is a small matter. The legends of the spot go back to

the days of the Apostles. We are met at the very beginning by the names of Saint Philip and Saint James, of the twelve disciples, with Joseph of Arimathæa at their head. Had Wells or even Bath laid claim to such an illustrious antiquity, their claims might have been laughed to scorn by the most ignorant; at Glastonbury such claims, if not easy to prove, were at least not easy to disprove. If the Belgian Venta claims ten parts in her own Lucius, the isle of Avalon claims some smaller share in him. We read the tale of Fagan and Deruvian; we read of Indractus and Gildas and Patrick and David and Columb and Bridget, all dwellers in or visitors to the first spot where the Gospel had shone in Britain. No fiction, no dream, could have dared to set down the names of so many worthies of the earlier races of the British islands in the *Liber Vitæ* of Durham or of Peterborough. Now I do not ask you to believe these legends; I do ask you to believe that there was some special cause why legends of this kind should grow, at all events why they should grow in such a shape and in such abundance, round Glastonbury alone of all the great monastic churches of Britain. And I ask you to come on to something more like history. Elsewhere even forged charters do not venture to go beyond the days of Æthelberht. But Glastonbury professed to have a charter, dating, as far as chronology goes, only from the days of Æthelberht, but which claimed, truly or falsely, to belong to a state of things which in Kent would carry us back before the days of Hengest. In one page of his history William of Malmesbury records a charter of the year 601 granted by a king of Damnonia whose name he could not make out, to an abbot whose name—will our Welsh friends, if any are here to-day, forgive him?—at once proclaimed his British barbarism. Then follows a charter of 670 of our own West-Saxon Cenwealh. Then follows one of 678 of Centwine the King, then one of Baldred the King, then the smaller and greater charters of Ine the glorious King.

Except the difficulty of making out his name, there is nothing to hint that any greater gap parted the unknown Damnonian from Cenwealh than that which parted Cenwealh from Centwine, Baldred, and Ine. One to be sure is King of Damnonia, another is King of the West-Saxons. But that might be a mere change of title, as when the King of the West-Saxons grew into the King of the English. The feeling with which we read that page of William of Malmesbury's History of Glastonbury is the same as the feeling with which we read those lists of Emperors in which Charles the Great succeeds Constantine the Sixth, with no sign of break or change. It is the feeling with which we read those endless entries in Domesday from which we might be led to believe that William the Conqueror was the peaceful successor of Eadward the Confessor. In this, as in ten thousand other cases, the language of formal documents would by itself never lead us to understand the great facts and revolutions which lurk beneath their formal language.

But we must stop to see what legends and documents prove as well as what they do not prove. We need not believe that the Glastonbury legends are records of facts; but the existence of those legends is a very great fact. I will not as yet search into the genuineness of either the Damnonian or the West-Saxon document. They are equally good for my purpose, even if both of them can be shown to be forgeries. The point is this. Compare Glastonbury and Canterbury. We have no legends tracing up the foundation of Christ Church or Saint Augustine's to the days of the Apostles, or to the days of any Roman emperor or British king. Instead of such legends we have a bit, perhaps of genuine history, at all events of highly probable tradition, which seems to show that, in setting up new churches for men of English race, some regard was paid to the still remembered sites and ruins which had once been the churches of men of Roman or British race. In most places we do not find even this much of remembrance of the state of things which had passed away; at Canterbury we do find this much. But this is widely different from the absolute continuity of the Glastonbury legends, in which Joseph of Arimathæa and Dunstan appear as actors in different scenes of the same drama. So again, no monk of Christ Church or Saint Augustine's, not the boldest forger that ever took pen in hand, would have dared to put forward a charter of Vortigern in favour of his house, immediately followed by a charter of Hengest. In Kent at least the temporal conquest of the Briton by the Jute, the spiritual conquest of the Jute by the Roman, were too clearly stamped on the memories of men, they were too clearly written in the pages of Bæda, to allow of any confusion about such matters. There at least men knew that, if the reign of Woden had given way to the reign of Christ and Gregory, the reign of Christ and Cæsar had once given way to the reign of Woden. There at least the great gulf of Teutonic conquest still yawned too wide for either legends or documents to bridge it over. But here, in the isle of Avalon, legends and documents go on as if no such gulf had ever yawned at all. The truth is that this unbroken continuity of legends — it matters not whether true or false — of documents — it matters not whether genuine or spurious — is the surest witness of the fact that in the isle of Avalon Teutonic conquest meant something widely different from what it meant in the isle of Thanet. In our Glastonbury story Teutonic conquest simply goes for nothing. My argument is that it could not have gone for nothing, even in the mind of an inventor of legends or a forger of documents, unless it had been, to say the least, something much less frightful on the banks of the Brue than it was on the banks of the Stour. I argue that the coming of our forefathers was not here, as it was there, something which made an utter break between the days before it and the days after it. It was a mighty change indeed, but still a change through

G

which men and their institutions might contrive to live. They were not driven simply to perish or to flee away, leaving behind them only feeble memories or shattered ruins.

The simple truth then is this: among all the greater churches of England, Glastonbury is the only one where we may be content to lay aside the name of England and to fall back on the older name of Britain. As Exeter is the one great city of Britain that lived on an unbroken life through the storm of English Conquest, the one city which lived on as equally great in the old state of things and in the new, so Glastonbury is the one great religious foundation of Britain which lived through the storm of English conquest, and in which Briton and Englishman have an equal share. At no other place do we so fully stand face to face with the special history of the land which lies south-westward from the Axe. Nowhere else can we so plainly see the living on of a certain Celtic element under Teutonic rule; nowhere else can we so plainly see the process by which the Britons of certain parts of the island were neither wholly slaughtered nor wholly driven out, but were to a great extent, step by step, assimilated with Englishmen. Nowhere else, in short, do we so clearly see the state of things which is pictured to us as still fresh in the laws of Ine, but which had come to an end before the putting forth of the laws of Ælfred. The church of Glastonbury, founded by the Briton, honoured and enriched by the Englishman, is the material memorial of the days when Briton and Englishman, conquered and conqueror, lived under the same law, though not an equal law, under the same protection, though not an equal protection, on the part of the West-Saxon king. Nowhere is there the same unbroken continuity, at all events of religious life. At Canterbury Christ was worshipped by the Englishman on the same spot on which he had been worshipped by the Briton. But there was a time between, a time in which, on the same spot or on some spot not far from it, Englishmen had bowed to Woden. But, as there never was a moment when men of any race bowed to Woden on the hill of Exeter, so there never was a moment when men bowed to Woden in the isle of Avalon. Men on either spot had doubtless bowed, in days which in Cenwealh's days were ancient, to the gods of the Briton and the Roman; but no altars ever smoked to our Teutonic gods within the shores of the holy island or on the peak of the holy mount which soars above it. The cause of the difference is a simple one. Whatever was the date of the English conquest of Exeter, it was assuredly later than the English conquest of Avalon. And we read in the Chronicle thirteen years before that fight at the Pens which made Avalon English— 'Her Cenwealh wæs gefullod.' Here then the Teutonic conqueror was one who had been himself washed, enlightened, made whole; in other words baptized into the faith of Christ. Those whom he conquered were his brethren. He therefore came not, as Hengest and Ælle, simply to destroy. In other parts of the West-Saxon realm the coming of Cerdic and Ceawlin had been as fearful as the coming of Hengest and Ælle. But Avalon and the coasts thereof, the land of the Sumorsætan from the Axe westward, was the prize of a conqueror who was Hengest and Æthelberht in one. Under him the bounds of English conquest were still enlarged; but English conquest no longer meant death or slavery to the conquered; it no longer meant the plunder and overthrow of the temples of the Christian faith. The victor of Bradford and the Pens had, before he marched forth to victory, done over again what men fondly deemed to be the work of Lucius; he had timbered the old church at Winchester. He was therefore ready to spare, to protect, to enrich, to cherish as the choicest trophy of his conquest, the church which he found already timbered to his hand in Ynysvitrin.

And now what will be said if, after all this, I go on to tell you that I am strongly inclined to the belief that the monastery of Glastonbury, with all its long legendary history, is not a foundation of any astounding antiquity? I believe that, in mere point of years, it may, as Dr. Guest hinted long ago, very likely be younger than Christ Church at Canterbury. If ever anything bore on the face of it the stamp of utter fiction, it is what professes to be the early history of Glastonbury. It is going too far when the tale brings in such an amazing gathering of saints from all times and places to shed their lustre on a single spot. Setting aside the Apostles and Joseph of Arimathæa and King Lucius, the object is too apparent by which Patrick and David and Columb and Bridget and a crowd of others are all carried into the isle of Avalon. It is too much in the style of the process which invented a translation of Dunstan's body from Canterbury to Glastonbury. It is too much in the style of that amazing Joseph-worship which sprang up in the fifteenth century, while in the earlier legend Saint Joseph holds a very modest place among the other worthies of the spot. This legendary history will be found in two works of the same writer, in the first book of William of Malmesbury's History of the Kings and in his special treatise on the Antiquity of the Church of Glastonbury. The main story is much the same in the two, but there is a good deal of difference in the way of telling it, and also in many of the details. The History of the Kings was written apart from any special Glastonbury influences, and it gives the legend in a comparatively moderate shape. The tale contains plenty that is purely fictitious; but fiction is as it were kept in some degree of order by being embedded in a work of which the main substance is historical. But the treatise on the Antiquity of the Church of Glastonbury is a work of another kind. The object of its writer was to put in a clear and attractive shape such stories as the Glastonbury monks of his day told him. Wonderful things, to be sure, they did tell him; still they did not tell him the same things which Glastonbury monks would have told him a very few years later. The object of the stories which they told him was to exalt the glory and the antiquity of Glastonbury; it was not to exalt the glory of Arthur, or in any way to connect Glastonbury and Arthur together. A few years after William of Malmesbury wrote, the wonderful tale of his younger contemporary Geoffrey of Monmouth had come into vogue. But when William of Malmesbury wrote, the tale of Geoffrey had not yet come into vogue, if it had been written or thought of at all. As we see from several passages in the History of the Kings, the fame of Arthur was great and growing; but it had not yet reached its full height. When it did reach its full height in the hands of Geoffrey, we see its effect at Glastonbury. Not long after the complete legend of Arthur had been invented, the tomb of Arthur was fittingly invented also. The tale of William of Malmesbury no longer suited those who had an interest in the new form of the story. His original work, wonderful enough in itself, was further interpolated to suit the new local creed. In the History of the Kings the name of Arthur appears in several passages which have no reference to Glastonbury, but in no passage which has a reference to Glastonbury. Least of all does William, in the History of the Kings, look on Glastonbury as the burial-place of Arthur, for he distinctly says that the burial-place of Arthur was unknown. We must then, I think, unhesitatingly cast away, as the interpolation of some Glastonbury monk, a passage in his Glastonbury History in which he is made to assert the burial of Arthur at Glastonbury. For this directly contradicts the deliberate statement of his graver work. But I shall not object if any one chooses to claim as a genuine piece of William of Malmesbury a passage in which Arthur appears simply as one prince and one benefactor among others. He is made to found certain monks in memory of the valiant Ider who overthrew the giants who infested Brent Knoll, a knoll which then was doubtless, like our other knolls great and small, an island, and which, it seems, was then known as the mount of frogs. Such a story is very silly, very mythical, it sounds very much like an interpolation; but it is just possible that William of Malmesbury may have heard it at Glastonbury and have written it down; for it at least does not contradict anything in the History of the Kings. We must carefully distinguish between two sets of legends, both of which are equally untrustworthy, but which are put together with quite different purposes. It is the more needful to distinguish them, because the second set of tales comes so very closely upon the heels of the first. William of Malmesbury and Geoffrey of Monmouth were both alive at the same time; very likely they were both writing at the same moment. But William, while he had his own stories of Arthur, knew nothing of those more famous stories of Arthur which Geoffrey presently gave to the world.

I look then on the Glastonbury History of William of Malmesbury, even as he wrote it, as essentially legendary; but I do not at all deny that these legends, like other legends, may very likely contain here and there some kernel of truth. But if we are in search, not of mere kernels of truth, but of direct statements of fact, we may safely cast aside everything earlier than the first year of the seventh century. We may see our first bit of anything savouring of real history in the grant of the Damnonian king whose name so puzzled William of Malmesbury, but which Dr. Guest, with the greatest likelihood, supplies as Gwrgan Varvtrwch. Dr. Guest holds that Glastonbury did not become the head sanctuary of the Britons till after the loss of Ambresbury. It is hard to rule such a point; but do not let any one think that, if this date of 601 should be accepted as marking the beginning of the greatness of Glastonbury, it therefore necessarily marks the beginning of the existence of Glastonbury, even as the place of a religious foundation, much less as a place of human dwelling. We may be sure that such a site as Glastonbury, a site which had so many attractions in early times, was inhabited from a very early time indeed, though ages may have passed before its name found a place in history or legend. If we fix 601 as the likely date for the beginning of a great monastery on this spot, let no one take me as fixing that year as the date of the coming of the first human being, of the coming of the first Christian man, or even of the coming of the first monk. And indeed this first entry, if we can at all trust its words, points, not to the setting up of anything absolutely new, but to the enlarging and enriching of something which was there already. The king—Gwrgan, we will say—is made to give Ynysvitrin to the old church. Now the 'old church' may simply mean old in the time of William of Malmesbury, not old in the time of Gwrgan. But the grant of Ynysvitrin, that is, of Glastonbury itself, strikes me as having a special force. Gwrgan may have found a church, he may have found a monastery, already in the island. But it is he who is represented as giving the monastery its great temporal position; it is he who first makes the island itself a monastic island. Now this kind of statement has at least a negative force. It fixes our date one way. The document may be forged; the grant may be imaginary; the position bestowed by the grant may not have begun till much later. But we may be quite sure that it did not begin earlier. I am inclined to attribute to the document a higher value than this. Let it even be a forgery: I do not believe that any man would go forging charters of Gwrgan—men might have forged charters of Arthur—unless he had seen or heard of a real charter of Gwrgan. And a forger would most likely have written the name of his king clearly enough for William of Malmesbury to read it. I am therefore disposed to attach some positive importance to the entry of 601. But in any case it has a negative importance; it gets rid of all earlier claims of the monastic house of Ynysvitrin to have held the temporal possession of the soil of Ynysvitrin.

There is another quite independent legend which

seems to me to fall in with a belief in the earlier existence of Ynysvitrin, but which sets Ynysvitrin before us in a state quite unlike that of the seat of a great monastic body. This is the story contained in the Life of Saint Gildas. The date and author of the piece are uncertain; but it must be older than the great days of the fame of Arthur; that is, it must be older than Geoffrey of Monmouth. It gives us a familiar part of the Arthurian story in a much earlier and simpler shape than that in which we are used to see it. In this story, Arthur is not conqueror of the world; he is not even King of all Britain; he is simply 'tyrant' in Cornwall and Devonshire. His overlord is Meluas, who is king in the 'æstiva regio,' that is surely in *Somerset*. We must of course take the word 'tyrant,' neither in its old Greek sense nor in its common modern sense; it must be taken in that later Latin sense in which it means a rebel prince, one who has set himself up against a lawful emperor or king. And so, directly after the place where he is called tyrant, Arthur is yet more distinctly called 'rex rebellis.' But the lawful king has done the tyrant a great private wrong by carrying off his wife Guenever. He has carried her off to Ynysvitrin, to keep her safe in the inaccessible island, where he is presently besieged by the tyrant Arthur with a countless host of the men of Cornwall and Devonshire. At this moment Gildas comes to the island, an exile, driven by the pirates of Orkney—wikings put a little out of their place—from his hermitage on the Steep Holm, where for seven years he had lived on fish and birds' eggs. He wrote, as we know, a 'Liber Querulus;' one might expect that, if it was during this time of his life that he wrote it, it would be a 'Liber Querulus.' He now sails up to Ynysvitrin; he is there received by the abbot; he reconciles the two kings by persuading Meluas to give up Guenever; they become sworn brothers, and promise for the future to obey the abbot.

Now I hold this Life to be purely legendary, if for

no other cause, yet for this, that it represents Gildas as having a great deal to do with Arthur. Gildas himself, while speaking of so many other British princes, has not, in his extant writings, one word to say about Arthur. The tyrant of Cornwall, even if he won the fight of Badbury, was clearly, in the eyes of Gildas, a much smaller person than Maelgwyn of Gwynedd, the great dragon of the isle of Dywyganwy. Giraldus indeed gives a good reason for this silence. He explains how Gildas actually wrote a book of the acts of Arthur; but, having a private quarrel with the King, he threw his book into the sea. I venture to look on this as simply an attempt to account for the silence of Gildas about Arthur, and I look on any story which brings Gildas and Arthur together as legendary on the face of it. But this legend, like many other legends, unconsciously preserves a kernel of truth. I must not hide the fact that there is another passage in the Life which speaks of Arthur as 'rex totius majoris Britanniæ.' But this only makes the other passage more precious. The two descriptions come from different sources. The writer, clearly writing in days when the fame of Arthur was growing but had not yet reached its full height, preserved, without marking the inconsistency, an older story which painted Arthur in a much lowlier guise. The tyrant Arthur, in rebellion against the king of the 'æstiva regio,' is something which neither the biographer of Gildas nor any one else would have invented; it must be a bit of genuine tradition. And that tradition represents Glastonbury as a place to which a king who carried off the wife of one of his under-kings was likely to carry her. This is not the picture of Glastonbury to which we are used. If any later king, any of our West-Saxon kings, had designed such a crime as that of Meluas, he would not have chosen Glastonbury for the scene of it. The wildest scandal-monger did not make Eadgar take Wulfthryth or Ælfthryth to the old home of Dunstan. The story indeed brings in an abbot; but the abbot is most likely brought in simply because men could not conceive Glastonbury in any age without an abbot. The value of a tale of this kind always lies in those parts which are most likely to have happened, because they are least likely to have been invented. I am very far from pledging myself to the historical truth of the statement that Meluas carried off Guenever wife of the tyrant Arthur, and hid her in the isle of Avalon. But I do say that that statement belongs to a stage of Arthurian legend much earlier than any of those to which we are used. I do believe that, whether it does or does not preserve a memory of real facts, it does preserve a memory of a real state of things. It helps us to a picture of the isle of Avalon very different either from the Glastonbury of Eadgar or from the Ynysvitrin of Gwrgan.

We get another incidental notice of early Glastonbury in a better quarter than the Life of Gildas. This is in the Life of Dunstan by a Saxon from the Old Saxony. We here find that, in the days of Dunstan's youth, Irish pilgrims, learned men from whose books Dunstan himself learned much, were in the habit of coming to Glastonbury to worship at the tomb of one of their own worthies, either the elder or the younger Patrick. It must therefore have been believed in Ireland that Glastonbury was the resting-place of an ancient Irish saint. Now such a belief as this could not have taken root, if the connexion between Glastonbury and the elder Celtic Church had been the invention of West-Saxon monks at any time between Cenwealh and Dunstan. Surely nothing but an independent Irish tradition could have led Irish pilgrims across the sea. This tradition clearly sets Glastonbury before us as being already a holy place even before Gwrgan. But it is quite consistent with the belief that it was Gwrgan who raised Ynysvitrin to be, according to the British formula, one of the three great choirs of the isle of Britain.

I am thus, on the whole, strongly inclined to believe,

on the one hand, that it was a true tradition, something indeed more than tradition, which connected Glastonbury, as an ecclesiastical foundation, with days before the English invasion, but to believe also, on the other hand, that, at the time of the English invasion, it was not a foundation of any great antiquity. I am inclined to believe, though I would not take upon myself at all positively to assert, that, perhaps not the existence, but anyhow the greatness, of Glastonbury as a religious foundation, dates from Gwrgan at the beginning of the seventh century. I am inclined to think that it was then that Ynysvitrin took its place as the great sanctuary of the Britons, to supply the loss of fallen Ambresbury. As a great monastic house it would thus have stood little more than fifty years when it passed into West-Saxon hands. It would be, as I said, actually younger in years than Christ Church at Canterbury. But what is younger in years may often belong to an older state of things. I have constantly to insist on this fact in the history of buildings. I have to try to make people understand that the fact that some buildings of the Old-English type are later in date than some buildings of the Norman type is the strongest of all proofs that there was an Old-English style earlier than the Norman style. There are few buildings more deeply interesting than the work of Prætextatus beneath the Roman Capitol, a pagan temple younger than the oldest Christian churches on the Lateran and the Vatican. And may I class with this last my own neighbour church of Wookey, with its chapel built and fitted up for the worship of the days of Philip and Mary, younger therefore than the Cornish church of Probus, built and fitted up for the worship of the days of Edward the Sixth? In the like sort, if, in a reckoning of years, we set down Glastonbury at the beginning of the seventh century as younger than Canterbury at the end of the sixth, yet in historic order, Glastonbury still remains older than Canterbury. If we should accept Gwrgan, not only as the benefactor and enlarger, but as the very beginner, of the house of Ynysvitrin, there still will be no need to unsay a single word of what I said earlier in this discourse. The sentiment of antiquity would doubtless be more fully gratified if we could give the house of Ynysvitrin a British existence of five hundred years than if we give it a British existence of only fifty. But the unique historic position of the place is the same in either case. In either case Glastonbury is the one great church of the Briton which passed unhurt into the hands of the Englishman. In either case it is, in a way that no other great church is, a tie between the state of things represented by the names of Arthur and Gildas and the state of things represented by the names of Eadgar and Dunstan. In either case we may truly say, as I have often said, that that talk about the ancient British Church, which is simply childish nonsense when it is talked at Canterbury or York or London, ceases to be childish nonsense when it is talked at Glastonbury. Nay, as tending to draw the tie still tighter, we can forgive the invention of the tomb of British Arthur to match the real tombs of our West-Saxon Eadgar and our two mighty Eadmunds. We can almost forgive the baser fraud which changed the western church, the true church of the Briton, into the freshly devised chapel of Saint Joseph, and which must have gone far to bring down that lovely building by so daringly scooping out a crypt beneath it. The fraud almost becomes pious when it helps to keep up, even in an exaggerated and distorted shape, the memory of a connexion with the elder time which here, and here alone, is history and not fable.

But there is no need to carry back the memories of the spot one moment further than sober history will let us. If we believe that Glastonbury was a British foundation, but that, as one of the great monastic houses of Britain, it dates only from the last age of British occupation, from days when the English conquest had already begun, we surely open a new source of historic interest. There is

surely something striking in the picture of the British
king and his people, driven from their elder sanctuary by
the advancing tide of English invasion, still keeping up
their hearts, still cleaving to their faith, raising or renewing
for themselves another holy place in the venerated island,
in the very teeth of triumphant heathendom entrenched
upon the hills which bounded their landscape. Let us
try and call up before us the general look of the 'æstiva
regio,' in the days when Avalon and all its fellows were
truly islands in the deep fen. The mount that crowns
the holy isle itself looked down, through long months at
least, on a waste of waters, relieved here and there by
smaller spots of land where alone man could dwell and
till and worship. In truth the dwelling-places of man,
still almost wholly confined to the ridges and the bases of
the isolated hills, must have then occupied very much
the same extent which they do still; the change lies in
the state of the flats—what we call the moors—between
them. Avalon, larger and loftier than its fellow islands,
was a shelter admirably suited either for devout monks
or for runaway queens. By Gwrgan's day it had become
one of the last shelters, at once centre and outpost, of a
race and a creed which must have seemed to be shrinking
up step by step, till both should pass away from the soil
of Britain. That race has not passed away; that faith
has won back the lands which it had lost. We are tempted
to ask whether Gwrgan, in the summer land, when he
bade Ynysvitrin take the place of Ambresbury, had heard
that one realm of the heathen invaders had become the
spiritual conquest of teachers from beyond the sea, and
that new temples were at the same moment rising for the
same faith at the bidding of British and of English rulers.
But the Christian Jute was far away; the heathen Saxon
was at his gates. The high ground to the north and
to the east, the long range of Mendip, the hills of the
Wiltshire border, stood like a mighty castle-wall fencing
in the strongholds of Woden and Thunder. At any

moment the great march of Ceawlin might be renewed towards new points; the summer land and the long peninsula beyond it might be as the land by the Severn and the two Avons; the holy place of Avalon in its island, the strong city of Isca on its hill, might be as Glevum and Aquæ Solis, as Corinium and Uriconium. It was not then as when men hear of their enemies in distant lands or on some distant frontier of their own land. It was as when the Corinthian, jealous of the growth and power of Athens, had but to climb the steep of his own citadel to see with his own eyes the mighty works which were rising on the lowlier height of the rival akropolis. And, from our side too, what was it that kept our fathers from swooping down on the prey which lay before their eyes? Why did they pause for nearly eighty years before they came down from their hill fortress to make a lasting spoil of the rich plains and islands at their feet? Could there be some dim feeling that Woden and Thunder were gods of the hills, but were not gods of the valleys? Whatever was the cause, the work was not to be done by men who bowed to Woden and Thunder. Gwrgan could build and endow his church in safety, while the gorges of Cheddar and Ebber, while Crook's Peak and Shutshelf and Rookham, were strongholds of heathen men. The Saxon was at last to pour down from his height, to smite the Briton by the Pens and to chase him to the banks of Parret. But the blow was not to come till it was lightened by coming from the hands of men who were brethren in the same faith. The Saxon was to win Avalon; he was to win Isca; but he was not to deal by them as he had dealt by Uriconium and Corinium. Through the long years of watching between the march of Ceawlin and the march of Cenwealh, the Tor of Avalon, the island mount of Saint Michael, not perhaps as yet hallowed by the archangel's name, but standing as the guardian of the holy places, new and old, which gathered at its foot, might look forth day by day towards the threatening rampart, with somewhat of the old note of

Hebrew defiance—'Why hop ye so, ye high hills? This is God's hill, in the which it pleaseth him to dwell, yea the Lord will abide in it for ever.'

The day at last came, the day when one race was to give way to another, but when the transfer of dominion from race to race no longer carried with it the transfer from creed to creed. The founder of Winchester became at once the conqueror and the protector of Ynysvitrin. With the change of race came a change of name, and British Ynysvitrin passed into English Glastonbury. I have in this discourse freely used the names Ynysvitrin and Avalon, while speaking of this place in its British stage. I have done so, because I needed some name to speak of the place by in its British stage, and so to bring out more clearly the fact that the place had a British stage. But if any one chooses to arraign those particular names of Avalon and Ynysvitrin as lacking in authority, I shall not be over careful to answer him in that matter. I believe that there is no authority for either earlier than the treatise of William of Malmesbury and the Life of Gildas. And we have seen that the treatise of William of Malmesbury is a work written to order in the interests of Glastonbury, and which has further been largely interpolated. There is something very odd in an English gentile name suddenly displacing the British name; there is something suspicious in the evident attempts to make the English and British names translate one another, in the transparent striving to see an element of *glass* in both. *Glæstingaburh*, it must be borne in mind, is as distinctly an English gentile name as any in the whole range of English nomenclature; *Glastonbury* is a mere corruption; the syllable which has taken a place to which it has no right in Hunt*ing*don and Ab*ing*don has in Glas*ton*bury been driven out of a place to which it has the most perfect right. The true origin of the name lurks, in a grotesque shape, in that legend of *Glæsting* and his sow, a manifestly English legend, which either William of Malmesbury himself or some interpolator at Glastonbury has strangely thrust into the midst of the British legends. Glæsting's lost sow leads him by a long journey to an apple-tree by the old church; pleased with the land, he takes his family, the *Glæstingas,* to dwell there. This might almost be taken as a kind of parable of the West-Saxon settlement under Cenwealh. There is no mention of earlier inhabitants; but the mention of the church implies that there were or had been such; in any case the Glæstingas settle by the old church—the main work of the middle of the seventh century, as far as Glastonbury is concerned. But there is certainly something strange in the sudden way in which we find the *Glæstingas* so comfortably settled in their own *burh* within the isle which has so lately been British Avalon. The old-world gentile name seems in a manner out of place in a conquest so recent and so illustrious. There is something unusual in such a place altogether changing its name, above all in its taking the gentile name of a certainly not famous *gens.* Other chief places which passed in the same manner from British to English rule, if they changed their names at all, did not change them after this sort. Isca, for instance, to look back again to the greatest case of all, lived on under its old name as English Exeter. Still we have the fact which we cannot get over, that Glastonbury was already spoken of as an old name in the days of Winfrith, at the end of the seventh century or the beginning of the eighth. And on the other hand, unless we throw aside the whole history of West-Saxon advance, as we have learned it from Dr. Guest and as, to me at least, it seems to be clearly written in the pages of the Chronicle, we cannot carry our *Glæstingas* to *Glæstingaburh* at any time earlier than the time of Cenwealh.

As for the British names themselves, the two names of Avalon and Ynysvitrin stand to some extent on different grounds. There certainly is a degree of suspicion about the name Ynysvitrin and its alleged meaning of *insula vitrea.* It is tempting to look upon it as simply a name made up as a kind of translation of the supposed meaning of *Glas*tonbury. But it is just as likely that it is a real British name, having no more to do with glass than Glastonbury has, but on which that meaning was put by the same kind of etymological pun of which we have many examples, and of which the turning of Jerusalem into *Hierosolyma* is a familiar case. At all events it is older than the tales of Arthur and Glastonbury in their present shape. It may be that Avalon is a name transferred hither with a purpose, after that name had become famous in the legends of Arthur. But it is just as likely that, as there undoubtedly were Avalons in other Celtic lands, so there may have been an Avalon here also. The spot on which we are met may stand to the Avalon of legend in the same relation in which the Olympos of geography stands to the Olympos of legend. As for the external authority for the names, it is much stronger in the case of Ynysvitrin than in the case of Avalon. Yet even on behalf of Avalon I think it may be possible to find a small piece of negative evidence. It comes in the legend of Glæsting and his sow. I do not greatly care whether this legend comes from William of Malmesbury or from an interpolator. Surely no interpolator writing after the invention of Arthur would have brought in the name of Avalon in so lowly a connexion. This strikes me as going a long way to show that Avalon was known as a name of Glastonbury before the legends of Arthur had taken possession of the name. But I have no wish to insist positively on a matter which is certainly difficult and doubtful. On one point I think we shall all agree: if Glastonbury really be Avalon, we must cast aside the belief that no rain falls in Avalon as a poet's dream.

On the architectural details of the buildings I shall not enter. But there is one general aspect of those buildings which directly connects their peculiar character with the peculiar history of the place. There is a special character about the church—to be perfectly accurate, I should say the churches—of Glastonbury, because there is a special character about the history of Glastonbury. There the old British sanctuary lived on under English rule, and fell only at the hands of destroyers of baser mould in days which, by comparison, seem as yesterday. The very arrangements of the ruined minster still live as a speaking witness to tell us what stood on that venerable spot in days before our fathers came. I conceive that there was a time when Ynysvitrin had, like Glendalough or Clonmacnois, a group of small churches, the Celtic fashion of building where Roman usage would have dictated the building of one large church. One of these, the oldest and most venerated, the old church, the wooden church, the church of wicker and timber, 'vetusta ecclesia,' 'lignea basilica,' lived on, and by living on stamped the buildings of Glastonbury with their special character. It lived on through English, Danish, and Norman conquests. It was enriched by the gifts of Ine. It beheld the devotions of Cnut when he made his offerings for the soul of the murdered Eadmund. To the east of that primæval church there arose in English times a church of English fashion, a church of stone, of which Ine was the first founder, and which was rebuilt in a statelier guise by Dunstan himself. The two churches, differing so greatly in scale and in material, stood side by side, witnesses of the presence of two successive nations, till both alike yielded to the grander conceptions of the architects of the twelfth century. Then the wooden church of the Briton gave way to the loveliest building that Glastonbury has to show, the gem of late Romanesque on a small scale, the western church, the western Lady chapel, corruptly known since the fifteenth century as the chapel of Saint Joseph. Meanwhile the English church, the stone church, the church of Dunstan, gave way in the course of the same century to the church of Norman Herlwin, as that before long gave way to the mighty pile which still stands in ruins. The

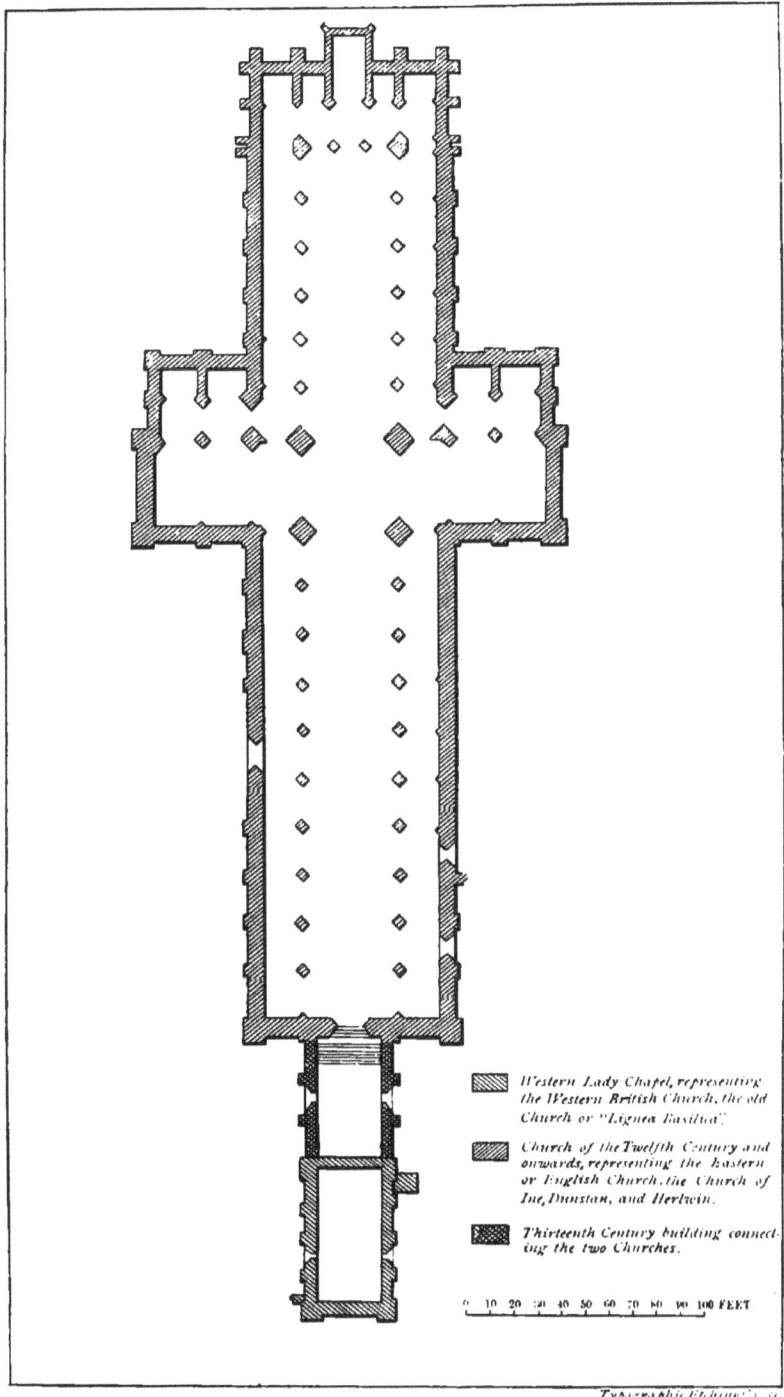

To face p. 98.

wooden basilica and the church of Dunstan have both perished; not a stick is left of one, not a stone is left of the other. But both live in a figure there still. Each has its abiding representative. The western church still stands in the site and stead of the wooden building of the Briton, the representative of the church in which Arthur may have prayed. The greater church to the east of it no less represents the church which Ine built, which Dunstan built afresh, and around whose altar were gathered the tombs of the greatest rulers of the tenth and eleventh centuries. Had the two vanished churches not stood there, in the relation in which they did stand to one another, the minster of Glastonbury could never have put on a shape so unlike that of any other minster in England. Nowhere else do we find, as we find here, two churches—two monastic churches—thrown together indeed in after times into one continuous building as seen from without, but always keeping up the character of two wholly distinct interiors. For nowhere but at Glastonbury was there the historical state of things out of which such an architectural arrangement could grow. Nowhere else did the church of the Briton live on untouched and reverenced by the side of the church of the Englishman, a witness of the Christianity of those ancient times when our fathers still pressed on in the name of Woden and Thunder to overthrow the altars and smite the ministers of Christ.

But the material fabric is not all. Within its walls the memories still live which, while the fabric was still untouched, were something more than memories. The Briton, the Norman who had listened to his lore, believed that Arthur lay before the high altar in the tomb which bore his name. The Englishman knew that those walls sheltered the shrine of Eadgar the Giver-of-peace, the tomb of Eadmund the Doer-of-great-deeds, and the tomb of his descendant and namesake, the mighty Ironside. There is no other spot in Britain which, like this, gathers round it all the noblest memories, alike of the older and of the newer dwellers in the land. Less exalted in ecclesiastical rank, less often in later times the scene of great events, less happy in having been handed over to the wanton will of the most ruthless of destroyers, the church of Glastonbury, in its ruined state, still keeps a charm which does not belong either to the mother church of Canterbury or to the royal abbey of Westminster. From one form of wrong its ruin has saved it. The pile is roofless; the Christian tombs which it once sheltered have vanished, and the dust of kings and saints and heroes has been scattered to the winds. But it has been spared the intrusion of the debased art and the depraved fashion of modern times. Its walls and pillars have been broken down; they have at least not lived on to be blistered with busts and tablets and fulsome panegyrics in prose and verse. Its aisles are open to the sky; they are at least not darkened by statues in the garb of modern debate or modern warfare—happy when they keep the garb of modern debate and modern warfare, and have not fallen back on a garb which they never wore, or on the lack of any garb at all. The altars of God, the images of his saints, have vanished. They are at least not shouldered by the graven forms of the very dæmons of heathendom. The fall of Glastonbury is great; but there is a fall still lower. Amid the ruins of Avalon we may at least be thankful that Avalon is not as Westminster.

Through the long later history of Glastonbury I am not called to go on at length. My special subject has been those early fortunes of the place which have given its church a character wholly unique among the minsters of England. I would fain say somewhat of the stern rule of Thurstan, when the monks were shot down before the altar, because they chose still to sing their psalms after the ancient use of Glastonbury and not after a new use of Fécamp. I would fain say somewhat of the lights thrown upon the state of Glastonbury and all Somerset by the Glastonbury entries in Domesday. I would fain say somewhat of the long struggle with the Bishops which makes up so great a part of the local history both of Glastonbury and of Wells. I would fain say somewhat of the last scene of all, of the heroic end which winds up the tale which, at Glastonbury as in other monastic houses, had for some centuries become undoubtedly unheroic. The martyrdom of Richard Whiting, following on the ordinary story of an English abbey after abbeys had lost their first love, reads like the fall of the last Constantine winding up the weary annals of the house of Palaiologos. But of one group of names, of one name pre-eminently among them, I must speak. We cannot meet at Glastonbury without in some shape doing our homage to the greatest ruler of the church of Glastonbury, the greatest man born and reared on Glastonbury soil. Earliest among the undoubted worthies of Somerset, surpassed by none who have come after him in his fame and in his deeds, we see, on this spot, rising above the mists of error and of slander, the great churchman, the great statesman, of the tenth century, the mighty form of Dunstan. Not a few famous men in our history have been deeply wronged by coming to be known only as the subjects of silly legends or, worse still, of perverted and calumnious history. So have Leofric and Godgifu suffered; so has Ælfred himself suffered; but Dunstan has suffered more than all. I doubt not that to many minds his name still calls up no thoughts but that of one of the silliest of silly legends; or, worse still, it calls up the picture, most unlike the original, of a grovelling and merciless fanatic. Think, I would ask you, under the guidance of true history, more worthily of the greatest son, the greatest ruler, that Glastonbury ever saw. Think more worthily of one who was indeed the strict churchman, the monastic reformer, who called up again the religious life at Glastonbury after a season of decay—but who stands charged in no authentic record as guilty of any act of cruelty or persecution, but who does stand forth in authentic records as the great minister of successive West-Saxon kings, of successive Lords of all Britain, in days when Wessex was the hearth and centre of English rule, and when Glastonbury stood first among English sanctuaries, the chosen burial-place of kings. Let us think of him as the friend of Eadmund, the counsellor of Eadred, the victim of Eadwig, the friend and guide of Eadgar the Giver-of-peace. So mightily under him grew the fame of Glastonbury that a greater name than all was drawn within its spell, and men at the other end of England deemed that it was at Glastonbury, and not at Athelney, that Ælfred himself held his last shelter, when the bounds of Wessex, the bounds of England, reached not beyond the coasts of a single island of the Sumorsætan. But, in that century of West-Saxon greatness, the local history of this spot can dispense with any single word or touch that the strictest criticism would reject. The home of Dunstan, the burial-place of Eadgar and the Eadmunds, gathers around it the greatest memories of the great age which made the English kingdom. Yet these memories are all of a kind which are shared by other famous spots within the English realm. What Glastonbury has to itself, alone and without rival, is its historical position as the tie, at once national and religious, which binds the history and memories of our own race to the history and memories of the race which we supplanted.

THE SHIRE AND THE *GÁ*.

[Read as the President's Opening Address to the Historical Section of
the Archæological Institute, at Taunton, August 7, 1879.]

THE Archæological Institute met last year in Northamptonshire; it has met this year in Somerset. In neither case has it shown itself for the first time within the borders of the district in which it came together. But in each case its earlier visit was to a border city, an ecclesiastical city; it is only at the second gathering in each district that a temporal centre has been chosen as the place of meeting. The Institute met at Peterborough before it met at Northampton; it met at Bath before it met at Taunton. It would be hard to find two English cities whose histories are more unlike than the places of those two meetings. The settlement which grew up around the great fenland monastery of Saint Peter, the holy house of Medeshampstead, grew by degrees into a borough, and, by later ecclesiastical arrangements, into a city, a city and borough to which the changes of our own day have given a growth such as it never knew before. Here is a marked history, old and new; yet, far nobler as are its existing architectural monuments, we should hardly venture to compare the history of Peterborough with the history of the Roman city, the English monastery, the Norman bishopric—the old borough Acemannesceaster, which by another name men Bath call. Yet, in the history of this Institute, a meeting at Bath and a meeting at Peterborough have thus much in common. From neither point would it be possible to make anything like an exhaustive examination of the land in which the city stands. In both cases it is the second meeting which first gives the opportunity for any study of the land itself, as a land. A Northampton meeting ought to lead to a typical, even, as far as opportunities may allow, to an exhaustive examination of the region of which Northampton is the centre, and to which Northampton gives its name. A Taunton meeting ought to lead, if not to an exhaustive, at least to a typical, examination of the region of which, I must remind you at starting, Taunton is not the centre, and to which it does not give its name. Bear in mind that distinction from the beginning. Taunton does not stand to Somerset in the same relation in which Northampton stands to Northamptonshire. Still, if we look on the land of the Sumorsætan, not as a circle but as an ellipse, those who, like myself, come from the spot which is in some sort the rival of Taunton, must freely allow that Taunton is one centre out of two.

In passing from Northamptonshire to Somerset, the Institute passes from one of the regions of England most favoured in antiquarian wealth to another region no less favoured. The comparison and contrast between the two with regard to their buildings is attractive, almost fascinating; but I will not enter on it here at any length; it belongs to another section. I will point out one feature of contrast only, one which is in some sort connected with my present subject. Northamptonshire is, among all the shires of England, one of the richest, perhaps the very richest, in buildings of Romanesque date and style. It abounds in every variety of round-arched architecture, from those arches in the basilica of Brixworth which, whatever may be their date, are surely Roman in material, Roman in style, to those arches in the minster of Peterborough whose mouldings show that nothing but conformity to an elder design kept their builders back from adopting the constructive forms of the then new-born Gothic. In the average Northamptonshire parish church we look at least for a Norman doorway, while in not a few we find other features of that style, reaching their climax in the rich capitals and arches of Saint Peter's in Northampton. And Northamptonshire has relics more precious still. Fragments of earlier days, arches, doorways, whole towers, built in that Primitive style which our earliest teachers brought from Rome, are there usual enough to cease to be wonderful. Here in Somerset, one may go miles without seeing a trace of even Norman work, and I doubt whether a midwall shaft is to be found between the Avon and Exmoor. I would ask you to bear in mind this single point of architectural difference between Northamptonshire and Somerset. The difference is incidental; it may be accidental; but, from my point of view, it is not without its teaching.

But my immediate point is that, while Northamptonshire and Somerset alike claim their place among the most historic regions of England, the historic interest of the two regions is of quite a different kind in each, and that the difference is of a kind which is not accidental, but one the cause of which goes up to the very beginnings of the English nation. The difference may be summed up in a few words. To what proportion of my hearers will my words convey a meaning, if I say that the difference is this, that Somerset is an immemorial *gá*, while Northamptonshire is a comparatively modern department, a *shire* in the literal sense? If these words do not convey a meaning as yet, I trust to make them convey a very distinct meaning before I have done. As yet I will only ask you to notice some outward points of difference between the two regions, some palpable facts, some familiar ways of speaking, by which I hope to lead you up to that perhaps still mysterious definition as the only key which will explain them. I have already asked you to remark that Taunton does not hold the same position in the land where we are now met which Northampton holds in the land where the Institute met last year. I asked you to notice the very obvious truth that Northamptonshire is called after the town of Northampton, while Somerset is not called after the town of Taunton. But, more than this, as the land of Somerset is not called after the town of Taunton, so neither is it called after any other town. There is indeed within its borders a town bearing a kindred name, the King's town of Somerton. But the land of Somerset is not called after the town of Somerton; the names of the land and of the town are simply cognate, derived from a common source, but neither of them derived from the other. But the difference is not merely a difference of names: it is also a difference of facts. There is no town, Taunton or any other, which stands to the land of Somerset in the same relation in which the town of Northampton stands to the shire of Northampton. Northampton is beyond all doubt the local capital; no other town in the shire is likely to dispute its precedence. It has every claim to that rank. First of all, it is very central. It is possible that some of the smaller towns may be geographically still more central; but, if so, the difference is so slight as to be altogether overbalanced by the fact that Northampton is, and always has been, the greatest town in the shire. If it happens that there is any Northamptonshire magistrate here present, I would ask him whether it ever came into his head to propose that the assizes or sessions of his county should be held anywhere but at Northampton. I can remember when, at a Northamptonshire election, the one polling-place was Northampton; and, if there was to be only one polling-place, it was certainly the best place for the purpose. But here in Somerset we have no one town which holds, or ever did hold, the same indisputable position as the local capital. The largest town is the Roman city of Bath; but that, lying as it does in a corner, is wholly unsuitable for such a purpose. Taunton does not lie so completely in a corner as Bath;

but we of Wells sometimes keenly feel that Taunton is not a geographical centre, and the map will show you that it is a great deal nearer to Devonshire than it is to Gloucestershire. Wells, more central than Taunton, is much smaller; Glastonbury, most central of all, is smaller still. Somerton has its kindred name and its precedence in Domesday; but it would hardly assert any more recent claims to the rank of a capital. Ilchester, rival of Bath in antiquity, has really more historic claim to be looked on as the local capital than any of the towns which I have spoken of. It was the place of the county elections down to the first Reform Bill; it kept its county gaol later still. But Ilchester lives only in the past; it has the memory of its elections and the memory of its siege; it has the presence of the beautiful mace of its chief magistrate; but it would hardly venture now to put forward a claim to be deemed the head of Somerset. As for assizes and sessions, they have been held at all manner of places, at Bridgewater and at Chard, and I doubt not at other places also, as well as at the towns which I have named. The present arrangement is to hold them alternately at Wells and at Taunton; and I do not think that it has ever been proposed at Wells that Taunton should be deprived of that privilege. In short, while there is no question as to what town is the one capital of Northhamptonshire, there is no town which has any grounds, geographical, historical, or practical, for putting itself forward as the one capital of Somerset. Now such a difference as this is not accidental; it must have some ancient historical cause. What that cause is we shall see presently; but before we come to it, I will ask you to notice one or two more points of difference between the two regions.

Look then at the names of the two districts. When I have spoken of Northamptonshire, I have always called it Northamptonshire; there is no choice in the matter; there is nothing else to call it, except the more formal style of 'county of Northampton,' which comes to the same thing. But have any of you noticed that, up to this point in my discourse, I have avoided using the word Somerset*shire*? I have spoken either of *Somerset*, or, when I meant to be a bit archaic, of the land of the *Sumorsætan*. I do not know whether anybody has noticed it as a peculiarity that I said *Somerset* rather than *Somersetshire*; but I am sure that, if any one noticed it as a peculiarity, no one had any difficulty in knowing what I meant. Now one must always say Northampton*shire*, because a distinction must be drawn between the shire and its capital. Here, where there is no capital, *Somerset* and *Somersetshire* are both justified by common usage. But *Somerset* is the form to be preferred on the ground of ancient usage, and in some phrases it is preferred in modern usage. I think we always speak of the parliamentary divisions as East-, West-, and Mid-*Somerset*. I believe that a point of view might be found from which the form *Somersetshire* may be thought to be more correct than *Somerset*; for it might be argued that in strictness a *Somerset* was a man, one of the *Sumorsætan*, and that *Somersetshire* was the proper name of the 'shire of the Sumorsætan.' And I hope very soon to show you an actual ancient instance of such an use of the word. But in actual use the word *Somerset* represents the tribe-name *Sumorsætan*, the *Sumersete* of Domesday being an intermediate stage. Now, in my own centuries, eleventh and twelfth, the ending in *shire* was familiarly added to the name of some *pagi*, only the 'pagus Sumersetensis' is one of those to which, as a rule, it is not added. In several passages the contrast is very marked between Somerset and other lands bearing tribe-names, and those lands which are commonly spoken of as *shires*. Take for instance some entries in the Chronicles. In 878 the inhabitants of three *pagi* of Wessex flock to the banner of Ælfred. They are 'Sumorsǽte ealle and Wilsǽte and Hamtúnscir se dǽl þe hire beheonan sǽ was.' In 1015

Cnut harries 'on Dorsætum and on Wiltunscíre and on Sumorsæton.' In 1051 Odda is made Earl 'ofer Defenascire, and ofer Sumorsæton, and ofer Dorseton, and ofer Wealas [West-Wales or Cornwall].' The next year Harold lands at Porlock 'neh Sumersætan gemæran and Defenescíre.' Henry of Huntingdon represents the second of these passages in his Latin by 'prædavit Dorset et Sumerset et Wiltsire.' In Domesday the forms are 'Sumersete,' 'Sumerseta,' while we have 'Devenescire,' and 'Wiltscire.' One passage alone looks the other way; but it is very clearly one of those cases where, according to the true force of the saying, the exception proves the rule. On the night of July 24, 1122, among other fearful things seen and heard, there was an earthquake 'ofer eal Sumersetescire and on Gleauccestrescire.' The 'eal' here makes all the difference. It is like Cnut's special title of King of all England, as distinguished from the title of 'King of England' unknown till long after his day. Remembering that this is the one case in which the land of the Sumorsætan has the shire-ending, we may fairly translate it, as I hinted above, 'over all the shire of the Sumorsætan and in Gloucestershire.' It would have been hard to mark in any other way the whole land of Somerset as distinguished from the seemingly partial range of the phænomenon in Gloucestershire. But throughout the period of English history with which I have had most to do, save in this single case, the ending *shire* is no more added to Somerset—or to Dorset either—than it is added to Kent or to Cornwall.

Why then is this? I answer for the present that certain *pagi* of England were called *shires* because they were shires, that certain other *pagi* were not called *shires* because they were not shires. Somerset belongs to one class, Northamptonshire belongs to the other. I ask you for the present to put up with this very unsatisfactory answer. I am yet only piling together my points of difference; I have not yet come to their explanation. We have as yet established these points of difference between the two districts which I am comparing. Somerset is not in early times called a shire; it is not called after a town; it has not, and never has had, any one town as its undoubted capital. It is essentially what in Switzerland is called *Land* as opposed to *Stadt*. It is a land of certain extent, meted out simply as a land, without reference to towns at all. It has no one natural centre and meeting-place; its meeting-places have shifted from time to time, as has been found convenient from time to time. Northamptonshire, on the other hand, is strictly the district attached to a town. It takes its name from a town; it gathers round that town as its natural centre and meeting-place. One in short is the shire of Northampton; the other is the land of the Sumorsætan.

I would again crave your indulgence while I go off into another most important point of contrast; in short, I would ask to complete my collection of phænomena before I begin the explanation of the phænomena. Let us now compare the position which the two districts hold in the general history of the larger whole, the kingdom of which they alike form parts. The contrast which is thus supplied is most striking and instructive. Both are historic regions, full of great historic associations; but their historic memories are of different kinds, and for the most part they belong to different ages. Northamptonshire is the richer of the two in contributions to the general history of England, while Somerset may claim the special interest which belongs to a land which has a history of its own. Let me put it in another way; the land of the Sumorsætan is older than England; the shire of Northhampton is younger than England. Northamptonshire is simply part of England: it has no separate historic being of its own; Somerset is one of the earlier wholes by whose union England was made up. It has, in a certain sense, a history which may be said to end when the history of England as England begins. If we look through the history of England, at least from the eleventh century onwards, we shall find that an unusually large proportion of great national events, of battles, of councils, of national settlements, took place within the borders of Northamptonshire; but there is no history of Northamptonshire itself. There is a history of the borough of Northampton; there is a history of the abbey of Peterborough; there is doubtless a history, if we could only get at it, of every smaller town and parish within the shire. But of the shire itself, as a shire, there is no history. Northamptonshire doubtless has its local annals, its lists of sheriffs and parliamentary representatives; but it has no history in the sense which I mean. Here in Somerset the case is different. The list of great events in English history which took place within its borders is not small; but we shall hardly be wise if we set up our land as in this respect a rival to Northamptonshire. We have made our contributions to the general history of the kingdom, even in later times; but we shall do well to allow that Northamptonshire surpasses Somerset both in the number and in the greatness of the national events which it has beheld. But, if we go back to times before the eleventh century, the prominence of Somerset over Northamptonshire in our national annals is yet more undoubted. That is to say, Somerset has, what Northamptonshire has not, a history of its own, a history set down in our national Chronicles, which carefully record the gradual making of Somerset as no small part of the gradual making of England. We hear of the land, its towns, its fortresses, as early as the sixth century; we hear of its folk by their own name early in the ninth. Of Northampton town we get our first mention early in the tenth century; its great historic importance begins in the second half of the eleventh. The first mention of the northern *Hamptonshire* —carefully to be distinguished from the much earlier mention of the southern—as a separate district bearing that name, comes earlier in that century, in the year 1011.

The name of Northampton borough thus first comes before us in the wars of Eadward the Unconquered; it was one of the towns which had to be won back from the Dane. The name of Northamptonshire first comes before us in the later struggle with the new Danish invaders, Swegen and Cnut. From that time onward, the shire, and above all its capital, stand forth, as I have already said, as the scene of a very large proportion of the great events of English history. Northampton might dispute with Oxford the honour of being the great national meeting-place of northern and southern England. If it was at Oxford that under Cnut Danes and English agreed to dwell together under Eadgar's law; it was at Northampton that Harold held the great Gemót which acknowledged the earl whom Northumberland had chosen, and in which northern and southern England agreed to dwell together under the law of Cnut. If Oxford saw the granting of the great Provisions, Northampton saw the Parliament which carried on the work of Harold's Gemót yet further, by acknowledging Scotland as an independent kingdom. How high a rank Northampton held among the cities and boroughs of England, how it had supplanted cities of far greater and earlier fame, we see by a witness which is none the less certain because of the strange form that it takes. On the day that King Eadward was alive and dead, the four greatest cities of England were held to be London, York, Winchester, Lincoln. In the reign of Stephen, Exeter had supplanted Lincoln. But when the body of the quartered David had to be divided among the chief towns of England according to their rank, London got the head without doubt; York and Winchester disputed over the shoulders, which should have the right; the right leg went to Bristol, the left to Northampton. That is to say, the inland borough, of comparatively recent origin, no centre of trade, no dwelling-place of ancient kings or bishops, had risen to rank fifth among the towns of England, next after the ancient and immemorial cities and after the merchant borough whose happy position and far-reaching traffic had raised it to a level with them.

But the historical associations belonging to Northampton and Northamptonshire press thick upon us. It was the earldom of Waltheof, his old earldom along with Huntingdon, before he received Northumberland from the Conqueror. After his death, his martyrdom as his countrymen deemed it, it passed with his daughter to Simon of Senlis, the founder alike of the priory of Saint Andrew and of the castle which overlooked the river. This was after the survey, after the death of the Conqueror, so that of Northampton castle there is no notice in Domesday. The entries of both shire and borough in that great record are meagre, but they are instructive in their meagreness. They show that, while Lincolnshire and Bedfordshire were among the parts of England where Englishmen most largely kept their own, Northampton and Northamptonshire were among the parts which were most thoroughly handed over to the possession of strangers. This, I need not say, speaks well for the people of a land on whom the Conqueror's hand fell thus heavy. In the following reigns the borough is again called to fill its old place as one of the great seats of national gatherings; but now that calling begins to be shared with the local capital by other points within its shire. It was within the borders of the shire, though not within the walls of its capital, in the castle and by the forest of Rockingham, that Anselm, the born saint, in the simple might of his true holiness, stood face to face with the power and the wrath of the Red King. It was in the castle of Northampton itself that his imitator, Thomas, the artificial saint, withstood in another spirit a king of another mould, when in more than a figure cross and sword met as hostile weapons, and when the appeal was made from the king of Angles to the king of angels. It was again within the borders of the shire, in the vanished monastery of Pipewell, that Richard of

I

Poitou, in the former of his two short visits to England,
held his great market for the sale of lands, honours, and
pardons. It was there that—within the same shire which
saw the acknowledgement of Morkere of Northumberland
and of David of Scotland—he sold back to the Scottish
Lion the special rights which his father had won over the
Scottish realm. And these are only a few out of a crowd
of councils and parliaments held within the shire, most of
them in its capital. If we take in the history of the
great abbey of Peterborough, we may bring it many a
stirring tale, from the raid of Hereward and the stern rule
of Turold to the days when old Scarlett buried two queens
within the minster. And, if report speak true, it was the
fact that the minster of Peterborough held the grave
of Katharine which caused it to be spared to receive the
grave of Mary. And the same land which saw Mary's
burial, saw also her beheading. Not many miles off, by
the banks of the same sluggish river, stands Fotheringhay, where the fallen choir of the church held the tombs
of the princes of the house of York, where the small fragments of the castle remind us of the day when their descendant laid her head on the block within its hall. Once
landed in the region of personal incident, we might even
mention that a Northamptonshire village was the scene of
the romantic adventure which led Edward the Fourth to
raise the widow of Sir John Gray to the throne which had
been meant for a princess of Castile or of Savoy. And,
going back again to the wider events of history, if
Northampton and Northamptonshire have been the scene
of councils, they have no less been the scene of battles.
The great year whose later months saw the victory of
freedom at Lewes had seen in its earlier months a heavy
blow dealt to freedom at Northampton. The town was
taken by the forces of Henry the Third; its defender,
the younger Simon, was made a prisoner; the burghers
were mercilessly plundered; according to one account they
were ruthlessly slaughtered, on a charge, strange indeed,

of a design to burn the city of London. In another and less noble strife two hundred years later, when Englishmen were wasting their blood in genealogical disputes, the spot which had seen the victory of one Henry saw the captivity of another; in the meadows below Northampton the king-maker won the second of his battles, and for the second time had his king at his mercy. And, last of all, when the strife of the thirteenth century was fought again in the seventeenth, it was not indeed at Northampton itself, but within the bounds of Northamptonshire, that the victors of Naseby could give their glad answer to the question—

> O wherefore come ye forth, in triumph from the North,
> With your hands and your feet and your raiment all red?
> And wherefore doth your rout send forth a joyous shout,
> And whence be the grapes of the wine-press which ye tread?'

Now I think that, after going through this long string of great events in our national history, we must allow that, for many centuries past, at least from the twelfth century onwards, more great questions have been disputed or decided, more great assemblies have been held, more great battles have been fought, on the soil of Northamptonshire than on the soil of Somerset. The reason is plain; it is a geographical reason. It is the central position of Northampton and Northamptonshire which caused so many important scenes of national history to be acted within the borders of the shire, and specially within or under the walls of the town. The central land of England, the land into which not a brook flows from any other shire, but out of which rivers flow into three seas, swelling the waters of the Wash, the Thames, and our own Severn sea, was, from its mere place in the map, likely to be the scene of great events. A national assembly must be held somewhere. In days when there is free choice in such matters, when all the business of three kingdoms is not done in a single town in a corner of one of them, that national assembly is most naturally held in some place near the centre of the kingdom. So, when armies are in the field, they will meet in battle somewhere; and, when two armies of Englishmen are engaged in civil war, they are more likely to meet for their decisive struggle in Northamptonshire than in Northumberland or in Cornwall. But mark that the exact place depends on the accidents of warfare. If one army had been a little quicker or another a little slower, the battle of Edgehill might have been fought in Northamptonshire or Oxfordshire, and the battle of Naseby might have been fought in Leicestershire. Those battles were not fought in the shires in which they were fought out of any reason specially affecting those shires; they were not struggles waged by the men of those shires for any special objects of their own. Nearly all the events which I have gone through help to bear out my proposition that, though Northamptonshire is a land which plays so great and constant a part in English history, there is no such thing as a history of Northamptonshire itself.

And I do not any the more shrink from saying this, because there is one most important point in which we may truly say, perhaps that Northamptonshire itself, certainly that a region of which Northamptonshire is a very considerable member, has in some sort given the law to England. I mean in the matter of language. The polite and literary speech of England, while it is neither the speech of Northumberland nor the speech of Wessex, is the speech, if not exclusively of Northamptonshire, at least of a region of which Northamptonshire is part. But again what is the cause? Doubtless the central position of that region. The strongly marked Saxon speech which has fallen back from Kent to Somerset was not likely to make disciples in Yorkshire. The strongly marked Anglian speech, fresh wrought under Danish influences throughout a large region, was not likely to make disciples either in Kent or in Somerset. But Yorkshire, Kent, and Somerset might all silently agree to take as their common classical standard the intermediate speech of the intermediate lands, a speech which could be understood by the men at either end, while the men at either end could hardly understand one another.

Now my position was that, while Somerset cannot pretend to have been the scene of so many of the great events of English history as Northamptonshire has been, it has the advantage of Northamptonshire in having in the strictest sense a history of its own. This feature actually comes out most strongly in the earliest parts of English history; but it comes out in the latest parts also. In the civil war of the seventeenth century Somerset can boast of no one event like the fight of Naseby; the land had its share in the struggle, but its share was mainly of a local kind. What we most think of in connexion with Somerset during the whole of the seventeenth century is the number of names which it contributes to the roll of the worthies of the age. The name of Phelips still lives at Montacute; the greater name of Pym is not forgotten at Brymore; the memory of Blake dwells at Bridgewater where he was born and at Taunton which he defended; none, I should deem, visit Wrington without giving a thought to the memory of Locke. Nor are the worthies all on one side; all cavaliers were not like Rupert and Goring; and Wells, ever prudent in the choice of its members, need not be ashamed of having been represented by Sir Ralph Hopton. But here I would again notice that the chief local events of Somerset in the seventeenth century are essentially local events; they are local in a sense in which the fight of Naseby is not a local event in Northamptonshire. When Blake defended Taunton, he was not merely defending a strong military post which military needs required should be defended; he was something like the defender of a free city; he was the defender of a town which had a character and an interest of its own; he was the leader of burghers who knew for what they were fighting and whose hearts were thoroughly in the cause. Taunton in the West was as eager to keep Goring outside its walls as Colchester in the East was eager to get rid of him when he had got inside. Only Taunton has the advantage over Colchester that its siege has not become the subject of a myth. But go on a little later, to the last fighting which this part of England has seen, to the days of Monmouth's insurrection. Perhaps I should not call Sedgemoor the last fighting, as there was a skirmish at Wincanton a few years later; but Sedgemoor was, as Macaulay says, the last fighting in England which deserves the name of battle. Now that battle was essentially a local battle; it was not merely part of a general struggle which happened to be decided in Somerset, as the fight of Naseby happened to be decided in Northamptonshire; it was a local warfare, a warfare which the men of the shire, or a large party among them, waged on their own account. It was strictly local; it was strictly popular; it was a struggle in which Taunton again plays its characteristic part; it is a struggle which is but a small matter in the general history of England, but which fills a great space in the special history of Somerset.

But it is after all in the earliest days of the history of England that we can best see the special character of the history of Somerset. Nowhere else can we so well see a land in its making. Nowhere else can we so well trace out the process by which a land became bit by bit an English possession, how this battle gave our forefathers the dominion of such an amount of British soil; how, after a lapse, sometimes only of a few years, sometimes of a whole generation, the frontier was again pushed forward as the result of another battle. Three, perhaps four, periods of conquest, three or four swoops down on the devoted land, made the whole region from the Avon to Blackdown English. The territory thus won bit by bit from the Briton became one of the constituent parts of the West-Saxon realm, the land of the Sumorsætan. The same process doubtless went on in other parts of Britain; but nowhere else are we allowed to see it before our eyes

with the same clearness. In Kent and Sussex we can trace the formation of a kingdom; but those kingdoms reached their full extent at an earlier period of their growth. It is in the history of the West-Saxon kingdom that we can best see how a kingdom went on growing; how it made a conquest; how it received a check; how it waited years before it made another conquest; how it lost on one side and gained on another, till it took the final shape in which it became one of the component parts of the greater whole of England. And no part of the growth of Wessex is so clearly written as that which sets before us the making of the land of Somerset by the conquests of Ceawlin, Cenwalh, Centwine, and Ine. The process is a part of general English history; for it is a part of the growth of England. But it is part of the growth of England only by being the growth of one of those smaller settlements by whose union England was to be made.

The land of the Sumorsætan was thus formed, in the space between the years 577 and 710, as one of the states which made up the kingdom of the West-Saxons. It was ruled, we can hardly doubt, by one of the under-kings of the royal house, of whom we know that there were at one time as many as five at once. As the unity of the kingdom grew, under-kings gave way to ealdormen, and more than one ealdorman of the Sumorsætan plays his part in the great struggle with the Danes. And I need not add that one, and the greatest, of the kings of the West-Saxons made one spot in Somerset the centre from which to win back the West-Saxon realm when for a moment it was lost. But remember that it was only for a moment that Wessex was lost, and it is the fact that it was only for a moment that it was lost which makes the main difference between the historical position of Somerset and of Northamptonshire, between the historical position of the West-Saxon and the Mercian shires generally. We have seen that we have a history of Wessex, a history of Somerset, from the earliest possible moment. We have no such history of Mercia as we have of Wessex; but that is simply because it is not recorded; the same process of gradual conquest from the Briton must have gone on in both cases. And as we have a history of Somerset, so we might, if it had chanced to be recorded, have had a history of any of the states which went to make up the Mercian whole, of the Wocensætan, the Cilternsætan, the Pecsætan, and the Elmetsætan, of the Gyrwas and the Lindesfaras, of Noxga *gá* and of Ohta *gá*. None of them could have had so long a history as the history of Somerset, because those divisions and names had perished before the tenth century, while Somerset, both division and name, has lived on till now. Neither could Northamptonshire, as Northamptonshire, have so long a history, because Northamptonshire, as Northamptonshire, is not heard of till the making of England is over. Or rather it is not heard of till a large part of England has to be made again, and till Northampton came into being as part of this second making.

I think you will see by this time that there is an essential difference between a land of which we can trace the gradual formation from the sixth century onwards and a land whose name is not heard of till the eleventh century —between a land gathered round a town, called from a town, of which that town is the natural head and centre, and a land which has no head town, no natural or historical centre, above all, which does not bear the name of a people. Here we at last come to the main difference: the one is the *shire* of Northampton, the other is the *gá* of the Sumorsætan. Let me use this old word *gá*, the High-German *gau*. We can just prove that it was in English use; for we know that there was somewhere in Mercia a Noxga *gá* and an Ohta *gá*, though Mr. Kemble himself was unable to find out exactly where those *gás* lay. This most ancient name has been fairly driven out of the language by a name younger, though still very ancient, the name *shire*. *Gá* and *scir* alike translate the Latin *pagus*, the district which we now call *shire* or *county*. But the two names look at the district from different lights; their own etymological meaning is wholly different; they seem to point to difference in the districts called by each. Now in English the name *gá* or *gau*, still familiar in Germany, everywhere died out, but the name *shire* did not everywhere come in. To many counties of England the ending *shire* is never added. Some of us may have heard the phrase of going into 'the shires,' as distinguished from those parts of England which are not shires. No one ever adds the word to Kent, Cornwall, Sussex, Essex, Middlesex, Norfolk, Suffolk, Northumberland, Cumberland, or Westmoreland. No one who knows local usage ever adds it to Rutland. And, leaving that last mysterious little district alone, the reason in the other cases is plain. None of those districts are historically *shires*. A *shire* is in strictness a division, something *sheared* off from a greater whole. Now the lands which I have mentioned are not divisions; they are not sheared off from anything greater; they are not divisions of the kingdom of England; they are ancient kingdoms and principalities whose union helped to make the kingdom of England. And the like rank I claim for the lands of Somerset and Dorset. They are not shires cut off from anything greater; they are the territories of tribes, in other words *gás*, which went to make up the kingdom of Wessex, and thereby the kingdom of England.

The root of the whole matter is that the names Somerset and Dorset are strictly tribal names. The name of the tribe and the name of their land is one. A thing is always done 'on Sumorsætan,' 'on Dorsætan,' while things done in the neighbouring lands may be done 'on Defenan,' 'on Wilsætan,' but may also be done 'on Defenascire,' 'on Wiltûnscire.' This usage of language is exactly as when a thing is done 'on West-Seaxum,' 'on East-Englum,' 'on Myrcnan;' the land has no name apart from its people. So it is with old Greek names like *Lokroi* and

Leontinoi; so it is with modern German names, like *Preussen, Hessen, Sachsen*. In our own language the plural form *Wales* is another case of the same usage: it is clearly *Wealas*, the name of the people used as the name of the land. *Somerset* then, *Sumersete, Sumerseta, Somersetania*, all the forms that the name takes in English or in Latin, is the land of the *Sumorsætan*; *Somerton* is their town. I will not pretend to decide what is the origin of the first half of the name; the derivation which makes *Somerset* the *æstiva regio* is so easy and tempting that one is half afraid that it cannot be right. But as to the second half of the name there is no doubt. *Sætan* is a word of the same origin as *sit, settle*, and other kindred words; we use the same phrase every day when we talk of *settlers* and *settlements* in Australia and elsewhere. The *sætan* in any district are those who *sit* down or *settle* in it; the form is therefore a common ending of tribe-names. In Wessex we have the Sumorsætan, the Dorsætan, the Wilsætan. In Mercia we have seen the names of some ancient tribes whose memory has perished from the map and even from history. Such are the *Pecsætan* or settlers on the Peak, the *Wocensætan*, whom Mr. Kemble takes to be rather *Wrocensætan*, the settlers by the Wrekin. So among a kindred folk we have the land of *Elsass*. Its English form would be *Ilsætan, Ilset*. Or was the river which gave its name to *Alsatia* once the *Ivel*, to bring us as strangely near to our own Ivelchester and Ivelminster, Ilchester and Ilminster, as *Strassburg, Strateburg*, brings us near to our own *Street?* So again there is *Holsatia, Holtset*, the land of the *Holtsætan*, the woodfolk, whose High-Dutch name of *Holstein* might easily put us on a wrong scent. And there are two Mercian tribe names which have not perished with the rest. The land of the *Magesætan* is now known as Herefordshire; but their name is not wholly lost; it lives possibly in *Maisemore*, more surely on *May Hill*, the high hill between Gloucestershire and Herefordshire. Had Herefordshire kept its tribe name, the modern shape of that name would be *Mayset*. But the *Scrobsætan* have done more than this; they have given their name to *Shropshire*, the only Mercian shire which keeps a tribe-name; and like our own *Sumersætan*, *Dorsætan*, and *Wilsætan*, the shire contains a town with a cognate name, the borough of the *Scrobsætan*, *Scrobbesburh* or *Shrewsbury*. Shropshire and Rutland are the only two Mercian shires which have strictly names of their own, not taken from any town.

A crowd of curious questions might be asked as to the names and the origin of the West-Saxon lands and shires. Some of them I have tried to answer elsewhere; some I might find it a little hard to answer. But I cannot enter upon them here. My object now is to contrast counties which are undoubted tribal settlements and which bear undoubted tribal names, a class of which Somerset is the best example, with counties which are mere *shires* or divisions, a class of which Northamptonshire is as good an example as any other. All the Mercian shires, save Shropshire and Rutland, are called, like Northampton, directly after a town. And, just as in the case of Northamptonshire, the town after which the shire is named is commonly one which lies conveniently central, and, except when it has been outstripped by the growth of other towns in later times, it is the greatest town in the county. I could go through the few apparent exceptions at some length, but I will mention only one, because I think it is the only one which concerns us. Buckinghamshire, a land once West-Saxon, is the only Mercian shire in which there is any room for questionings as to which town is to be deemed the local capital. But there is room for such questionings in every shire of Wessex in the later and wider sense—that is, in every shire south of the Thames— save only in Devonshire and Dorset, where the position of the Roman cities of Exeter and Dorchester forbade all rivalry.

The name of every one of these shires suggests some curious point or other. But all that concerns us now is

to point out the difference between counties like Somerset
keeping an immemorial tribe-name, and which have no
central town, and counties like Northamptonshire which
have a central town, and which bear its name. Now
what is the cause of this distinction? I believe it to be
this, that West-Saxon England was made only once,
while Mercian England had to be made twice. The
Mercian *shire* is another thing from the West-Saxon *gá*,
because Mercia, or the greater part of it, was conquered
and divided by the Danes in 877, while the Danes tried in
vain to conquer and divide Wessex in 878. In Mercia,
save, it would seem, in the land of the Scrobsætan, the old
divisions, Gyrvan, Pecsætan, and the rest, passed away,
as the ancient names of Derby and Whitby passed away,
as the elder names of a crowd of smaller places must have
passed away when they took names from Danish lords.
When Eadward the Unconquered and his sister the Lady
of the Mercians won the land back for England and for
Christendom, when they founded many towns and fortresses, they seem to have mapped out the recovered land
afresh. It may be, though I will not insist on what cannot be proved, that Ælfred himself began the work in that
part of Mercia which he held with his West-Saxon kingdom, and that we have here the kernel of truth in the
myth which describes him as dividing all England into
shires. Perhaps then partly the great king himself, in
any case his children, made new shires, shires in the
strictest sense, divisions, departments. Only, unlike
modern French departments, they called them after the
chief towns; they called a shire Northamptonshire; they
did not call it the department of Nen and Welland. And
to each of these chief towns they allotted such a territory,
such a *shire*, as lay conveniently round the town as a
central meeting-place. There are some anomalies; nothing
human is without them. But this account is true of Mercia
as a whole; it is emphatically true of Northamptonshire,
especially if we look on the *soke* of Peterborough as a

separate district. In Wessex, on the other hand, and in
the South of England generally, the Danes never settled.
They came and ravaged; for a moment they conquered;
but they never occupied the land or divided it among
themselves. At no time then was there any need for any
general recasting of the districts which made up southern
England. There was nothing to hinder an old kingdom,
an old *gá*, from living on as a modern county. And some
at least of the old kingdoms, of the old *gás*, have lived on
as modern counties. We have Kent and Sussex; we have
Somerset and Dorset. Somerset and Dorset therefore, no
less than Kent and Sussex, are no shires, no divisions, no
departments, but component elements of England, older
than England. Northamptonshire was made by the great
King or the great Lady of the tenth century. Somerset
was never made; it grew; it grew bit by bit from the
victories of Ceawlin to the victories of Ine. It has therefore a history of its own, a history of its own growth, a
history which in the nature of things comes to an end
at a time somewhat earlier than the time when the new-
made Mercian departments, which in the nature of things
have no history of their own, first begin to show themselves on the general field of the history of England.

Up to a certain point then, a point early in the eighth
century, the history of Somerset and the history of Wessex
are in some sort the same. The growth of the *gá* was the
growth of the kingdom. In Ine's day the new land was
fully formed, as one of the lands which make up the kingdom. From that time of course its local history becomes
secondary to the general history of the kingdom, first of
Wessex, then of England. But till Wessex is finally
merged in England, or rather has grown into England—
till the West-Saxon name has passed away, lost in the
name of the kingdom into which Wessex has grown—the
land of the Sumorsætan keeps its place as one of the parts
of the kingdom which is richest in its supply of historical
incident and historical instruction.

And now comes in the distinction which I drew long ago as to the nature of the strictly architectural wealth of the two regions. We all know that the architectural wealth of Somerset consists mainly of works in the later styles. Both lands are rich in ancient houses; but among houses we take a lower standard of antiquity than we do among churches, and whether in Northamptonshire, in Somerset, or in anywhere else, we set down a house older than the fourteenth century as something remarkable in itself. It is in the churches that the distinction comes out. The churches of Somerset, as I have already noticed, contain but little of Romanesque of any kind, while of the earliest form of Romanesque I think I may safely say that they contain none at all. I hardly know why this is, as the abundance of good building-stone in both districts would doubtless cause stone to be freely used in both earlier than in most parts of England. But as a matter of fact, the memorials of the earliest style may be almost said to abound in Northamptonshire; in Somerset, if they ever existed, they have vanished. Now, even if this fact be accidental, there is a kind of poetical justice in it. Northamptonshire, which, setting aside the great abbey which hardly belongs to it, is barely visible in the earliest records of English history, keeps abundance of material memorials of those days, to remind us that the land which became Northamptonshire was already there, though under some other name. Somerset, where so large a part of the earliest English history happened, which holds so prominent a place in our earliest records, could better dispense with material memorials of the days of which its very name is a witness.

For if the land—I may now say the *gá*—of the Sumorsætan is less rich than Northamptonshire in great historical associations from the time of the Norman conquest onward, yet, wherever the visitor treads in that land, he is treading in the very thick of West-Saxon history. Almost every spot has made its contribution to the history

of the West-Saxon realm; almost every spot has its
memories of kings and saints and heroes. We meet in
the castle of Taunton, in the fortress of Norman times
hard by the ancient *burh* of Ine. That later fortress at
least represents the town and stronghold which Ine reared
to guard his newly-won land against the British enemy,
the town and stronghold which Æthelburh did not shrink
from burning, when it was turned about to purposes of
home-born strife. We make our way to Dunster; there
we look down on a coast almost every inch of which has
beheld some stage of the warfare of the ninth, tenth,
and eleventh centuries. There is the Parret's mouth,
where in Ecgberht's day the invaders were smitten by
Bishop Ealhstan and Ealdorman Osric; there, on either
side, are Watchet and Porlock, where again they were
smitten in the days of Eadward the Unconquered—Porlock
where again Harold and Leofwine landed on their return
from their Irish shelter. And some have placed within
the circuit of the same bay the site of the Danish landing
which led to the camp of Athelney and the fight of
Ethandun, to the baptism at Aller and the chrisom-loosing
at Wedmore. The geographical position of the land, the
wide flat fenced in by hills, enables us to trace out the
successive waves of conquest almost as in a map. The
long line of Mendip guards the frontier stream of Ceawlin;
the wilder heights of Quantock and Exmoor proclaim
themselves as the natural strongholds where the Briton
held out till the days of Centwine and Ine. The intermediate frontier of the Parret is less strongly marked in
the general view of the landscape; but the conquest of
Cenwalh is not without its visible memorial; the tor of
Glastonbury stands as at once the sanctuary and the
central point of the land which the second wave of settlement added to Somerset, to Wessex, and to England. In
the Mendip line the greatest of its natural features, the
pass of Cheddar, forms no marked object in a distant view;
we cannot, save in their own immediate neighbourhood,

look on the rocks which saw the perilous chase and
deliverance of Eadmund the Doer-of-great-deeds; but the
memory of his repentance and gratitude may rise before
us even among the great memories of Glastonbury. We
visit the ground which once bore Æthelstan's minster of
Machelney, and thence we pass to the more famous spot
of Montacute. And at Montacute, Montacute itself must
not be forgotten. Besides the church, the priory, the
houses of the town, the mansion which preserves the
memory of one of our local worthies, the hill of Leodgaresburh, the true *Mons Acutus*, may claim some thoughts.
We may surely find our feelings as Englishmen stirred as
we look on the hill round which gather so many memories
of the days of England's struggle and overthrow and
second birth. It was on that hill that the pious sacristan
found, so the tale went, the wonder-working rood; it was
at the foot of that hill that the willing oxen of the proud
Tofig, unwilling as long as the names of the greatest
English minsters were spoken, started at once as soon as
they heard the name of Waltham as the goal of their
journey. It was in honour of the cross of Leodgaresburh
that Tofig first reared his minster, that Harold enlarged
alike its foundation and its material fabric. It was the
name of the Holy Cross, the holy cross found on that West-
Saxon hill, which gave the war-cry to the host which
gathered around England's last native king, alike on the
day of victory at Stamfordbridge and on the day of overthrow on Senlac. And surely that cry was heard again
when Leodgaresburh had newly become Montacute, when
the sharp peak, hallowed in English eyes, had become the
vulture's nest of the stranger, when the stronghold of the
devouring Count of Mortain crowned the venerable height,
foremost among those dens of oppression which made
Englishmen shudder at the name of castle. There it was,
around that height, that the last fight was fought for the
freedom of the Western lands, the fight which sets the
name of Montacute beside the names of York and Ely.

When Exeter had fallen, when the whole land seemed conquered, when London and Salisbury were constrained to send their English contingents to the foreign host, the men of Somerset and Devonshire still rose in arms to wage war against the hated fortress, to fight, but to fight in vain against overwhelming odds, to be borne down by the arms of their own countrymen, and to feel in their hour of overthrow that the plunderings of the Norman Count were after all less sharp than the subtler cruelty of the Norman Bishop. No one name lives at Montacute, as the name of Waltheof lives at York, as the name of Hereward lives at Ely; but the men who last fought for England on the spot which gave England her war-cry are as worthy of a place in the bede-roll of England's defenders as their fellow-workers in other parts of our land whose personal exploits still live in history and legend.

I change the scene to give a few words to another spot whose memories are not of warfare. If it were not a safe rule that comparisons and contrasts are but of little value, except when there is some strong groundwork of likeness between the objects contrasted, it might be curious to contrast in detail the two greatest ecclesiastical buildings in the two districts of which we are speaking. But the churches of Wells and Peterborough are so utterly unlike, both in history and in architectural character, that it is almost impossible to contrast them. The one monastic, the other secular, the one among the greatest triumphs of Romanesque, the other a building in which not a Romanesque stone is to be found, they stand too far apart for comparison. The west fronts indeed are pretty much of the same date and style, but here again comparison is forbidden. The portico of Peterborough is unique; the noblest conception of the old Greek translated into the speech of Christendom and of England has no fellow before it or after it. As for the front of Wells, I would only hint in the most delicate way that those who wish to admire really good design, and who come to the church

of Saint Andrew to look for it, had better go to the
north, to the south, or above all to the east. But when
we get beyond the walls of the two churches, Wells
certainly has the advantage. It has more to show in its
own way. Peterborough has some grand remains of its
monastic buildings, but it has hardly so much to show as
some of its monastic fellows. But we can better mark at
Wells than anywhere else the arrangements of a great
secular foundation which never, like so many others, put
on the monastic garb. At Wells a greater number of the
original ecclesiastical buildings, palace, prebendal houses,
and vicars' close, still remain than in any other foundation
of the same class. Nowhere else is so large a number of
ancient buildings still applied to the purposes for which
they were first designed. And mark too at Wells how an
English bishopric differs from a continental one. The
continental bishop was the bishop of a city; the English
bishop, in the sees which are most purely of English origin,
was the bishop of a land or a people. Bishop of Wells, still
more Bishop of Bath and Wells, is the style of a later day.
The Bishop of the Sumorsætan did not fix his *bishopsettle* in
any city, as bishops afterwards did at Exeter and Norwich.
He fixed it in his church of Wells, within his lordship of
Wells. The little city grew up at the bishop's gate, and
received its municipal rights from the bishop's grant.
Here then is another class of town, a class specially English. An abbot's borough might arise anywhere; no better
instance can be found than the borough of Saint Peter
itself, that Golden Borough which often came to be called
distinctively the Borough without further epithet. But a
bishop's borough could hardly arise out of Britain. Here
is one to speak for itself, a bishop's borough and nothing
else. By the king's town of Somerton, by the abbot's town
of Glastonbury, by the lay lord's town of Dunster, we
place, as an example of a rarer class than any of those,
and as having a special history, the bishop's town of
Wells.

But in the general history of Wessex and of England, I might say with truth, in the history of Britain and of Europe, the abbot's town counts for more than the bishop's town. Glastonbury, the common sanctuary of Briton and Englishman, sets before us, as we have clearly seen, more strongly than any other spot in the land of the Sumorsætan, one special historic characteristic of the land where, for the first time on a large scale, Englishman and Briton sat down side by side as subjects of a common king, obeying a common law, and living under its protection. The laws of Ine are a marked contrast to the laws both of earlier and of later date. The earlier laws of the Kentish kings know only one race and speech in the land; all their enactments are made for men of English race only. So again, the later West-Saxon laws, the laws of Ælfred and his successors, are the laws of a realm in which, if all men are not of the same blood, all at least are of the same speech and the same law. In the intermediate time of Ine we see another state of things. In his day the King of the West-Saxons ruled over a realm in which the barrier between two distinct races was broadly drawn. He legislates for a land in which Englishmen and Welshmen dwelled side by side, not yet indeed on terms of perfect equality, but still as subjects of the same prince, each in his place protected by that prince's law. In the realm of Ine, as there were Englishmen, so there were Welshmen, of various ranks. Among both nations there were bond and free; among the free there were men without land and men holding large estates. But in all cases the value of the Welshman, the value of his life, the value of his oath, is appraised at a lower rate than the value of an Englishman of the same rank. This clearly marks the position of the conquered, as men personally free, under the protection of the law, not forbidden the possession of landed property and its accompanying privileges, but still clearly marked as a race inferior to their conquerors. This is something widely different from

the grievous choice of death, exile, and bondage which
was all that the Briton had set before him in the days of
Ceawlin. But it is also something widely different from
the state of things a hundred and eighty or two hundred
years later, when in the laws of Ælfred the distinction of
Englishman and Welshman is found no longer. A British
population had remained in the land, but they had learned
to adopt the name, tongue, and the feelings of Englishmen. And it must have been in Somerset that this new
state of things, this dwelling of Englishman and Welshman side by side, was first seen on a great scale. It was
to Somerset and to a small part of Wiltshire that this
portion of the laws of Ine must have mainly applied.
There could have been no great need of them in the older
West-Saxon lands. If we had those laws of Offa of which
Ælfred made use no less than of those of Ine, we should
most likely find that legislation of the same kind as that
of Ine was needed on the British march of Mercia, no less
than on the British march of Wessex. But such legislation could not have been needed in the days of Ine or of
Offa either in the Northern or in the Southern Hamptonshire. There could have been few or no free Britons,
whether *eorls* or *ceorls*, dwelling on the banks of the
Itchin or of the Nen.

Thus in the days between Ine and Ælfred the British
population in the land of the Sumorsætan must have been
so thoroughly anglicized that the distinction between them
and the English was forgotten. In the central land of
England there could have been no such distinction to
forget. Northamptonshire, long before it was known by
that name, must have been wholly English. It remains
so still. If a Danish *by* here and there, the Ashby of the
Castle and the Ashby of the Canons, reminds us that other
Teutonic settlers have made their way into the land, yet
Englishman and Dane are one as opposed to either the
Briton or the Norman. Here again comes in the broad
distinction between the two lands. Northamptonshire is

simply part of England. Somerset had to take a part in making England. In one part of the work which made Britain England a large share fell to the lot of the West-Saxon settlers in the *æstiva regio*. Among them and among their neighbours the Englishman had to assimilate the conquered Briton, as he had afterwards throughout the land to assimilate the conquering Norman. It was as the chief of an united realm that the greatest of West-Saxon kings, the greatest of English kings, went forth from his shelter at Athelney to the fight at Ethandún, the storm at Chippenham, the meeting of diplomatists at Wedmore. The spot which sheltered Ælfred when all hearts but his had failed is after all the most memorable spot in this historic land. No trace is left of the abbey which the thankful heart of the great king bade to arise on the small island in the marsh which for a few weeks was the whole extent of free English soil in Britain. Yet the spot speaks perhaps more eloquently in its desolation. The patriotic magistrates of the oldest Wessex sold the lead of Ælfred's coffin to ease the burthens of Hampshire ratepayers. His foundation at Athelney, his burial-place at Hyde, keep no outward memorial of him. But his memory still lives wherever the English tongue is spoken; above all should it live, as the highest and noblest of many high and noble memories, in the land which his sojourn in his dark hour has made more truly his own than either the burying-place from which he has been cast forth or the birth-place where he is still held in honour.

BRADFORD-ON-AVON

1858–1872.

The name Bradford conveys to the world in general the idea of a huge Yorkshire manufacturing town, which has covered a site which in itself must have been not unpicturesque, and where an unusual number of stately public buildings of late erection may raise some questions as to the architectural taste of its inhabitants, but leave no doubt as to their public spirit. It suggests a place which has had a considerable share in many of the political movements of our own time; but no name seems less connected with the history of ancient times. Manchester is mentioned in the Chronicles; Leeds hands down to us the name of a British kingdom; Wakefield at once calls to mind a memorable fight of later days; but Bradford has, as far as we remember, no such place in our early history. The records of the town are purely local—its entry in Domesday, its connexion with the house of Lacy and the Castle of Pontefract, the notices of its infant mills as early as the fourteenth century. Local pride may well remember the comparison made by Leland, that Leeds, though as large as Bradford, was not so 'quick,' a description which some have hinted is not wholly untrue in our own time. Still this is no very great amount of history for eleven centuries; the real share of the northern Bradford in the history of England begins with the civil wars of the seventeenth century. But, as some people are gradually awakening to the truth that there are two Dorchesters, so it is well to put on record the further truth that there are also two Bradfords. Indeed, if we come to minute accuracy, there are more than two, as is not wonderful, seeing that wherever there is a river there is the chance of a broad ford. But besides the better known place of the name, there is one other Bradford which is of historical importance. Bradford-on-Avon, in the north-western part of Wiltshire, is far less known to the world in general than its Yorkshire namesake, but there are points of analogy between the two besides the mere likeness of name. In fact the likeness of name necessarily implies a certain likeness of site. Where there is a ford there must be a stream, and thus is established at least as much of likeness as was to be found between Macedon and Monmouth, though it may be doubted whether the stream at the northern Bradford is entitled to so dignified a name as that of river. Whether there are salmons in either we should think more than doubtful; indeed whether any fish at all could live in the neighbourhood of so many mills is a point which we may leave to the proper authorities of the two districts. This last sentence implies that there are mills at the southern as well as the northern Bradford, and in truth the southern Bradford is, and has been for ages, a seat of manufactures, though hardly on the same scale as its namesake. A consciousness of this last fact has perhaps led the Post-Office authorities to decree that the Wiltshire town should exchange its later name of Great Bradford for the more picturesque and more ancient description of Bradford-on-Avon. The Isle of Britain, we all know, is rich in Avons, and Wiltshire alone can boast of at least two. Of these the Bradford Avon is not that which runs southward by Salisbury and Christchurch, but that which makes its way into the estuary of the Severn by the greater cities of Bath and Bristol. Those cities, we may add, have free communication with Bradford, being the only parts of the world thus privileged. From other places the ancient town is somewhat hard to get at, being placed on that tangled mass of branch railways which join together, or keep asunder, Salisbury, Chippenham, Weymouth, Devizes, and Wells. When it is reached, Bradford is found to lie on both sides of its own Avon, occupying a site of unusual picturesqueness among English towns. The houses and other buildings are spread irregularly over the immediate height, and they command wider views of the hills in the further distance. But Bradford, as its name implies, is a river town; it has climbed the hill, like Bristol and Bamberg. Its ancient buildings stand mainly on the lower ground; a single small chapel alone crowns the height. The parish church, a building of various dates from the twelfth century onwards, the vast barn, the stately mansion known as the Duke's house, the ancient bridge, with its chapel suggesting that of Wakefield, but at once humbler in itself, and shorn of its projecting chancel—all stand at the bottom, or but a very little way up the hill. The building which gives Bradford its chief attraction in antiquarian eyes stands a little higher, but it hardly reveals itself at the first sight.

It is a remarkable thing that Mr. Kemble should, in the Index to the Codex Diplomaticus, have transferred to a Bradford in Dorset—Bradford Abbas we presume—several notices in the charters which clearly belong to Bradford-on-Avon. We do not know whether he would have done the same by the notice of Bradford in the Chronicles, which has been so clearly explained by Dr. Guest. Bradford was the site of a battle which marks one of the great stages in the advance of the English power in the Western peninsula. It was the scene of the first victory of the Christian West-Saxon over the Christian Briton, the first English victory after which the conquerors dealt with the vanquished, no longer as wild beasts to be slaughtered, driven out, or enslaved, but as men, looked on undoubtedly as men of a lower race, but still fellow-men and fellow-Christians, whose lives and goods and oaths had their value in the eye of the law.

St. Laurence. Bradford on Avon.

Bradford Bridge.

To face p. 136.

In 652, seven years after his own baptism, a year before the conversion of the Middle-Angles, six years before the fight that gave him Avalon, 'Cenwealh fought at Bradford by Avon.' This battle, as Dr. Guest has shown, won for Wessex that long strip of land in the modern Wiltshire which held out after the conquests of Ceawlin. The battle of Bradford gave to Wessex, not only the site of Bradford but the site of Malmesbury, and the two places are brought together in the next notice of Bradford which we come across. William of Malmesbury, in his Life of Saint Ealdhelm, traces out a crowd of monasteries and churches which were founded or enlarged by him. First and foremost was William's own Malmesbury. Ealdhelm increased the original foundation of Meildulf and built a more stately church, which William himself had seen, and which did not seem to him contemptible in point either of size or of ornament ('tota majoris ecclesiæ fabrica celebris et illibata nostro quoque perstitit ævo, vincens decore et magnitudine quicquid usquam ecclesiarum antiquitus factum visebatur in Angliâ'). The church of Ealdhelm at Malmesbury was thus the immediate predecessor of the present building, of which at least the destroyed eastern parts were doubtless built in William's own day. But, besides this chief minster, there was also standing at Malmesbury within William's memory, though seemingly not when he wrote, a smaller church, which local tradition believed to be the original building of Meildulf ('parva ibi admodum basilica paucis ante hoc tempus annis visebatur, quam Meildulfum ædificasse antiquitas incertum si fabulabatur'). This custom of building two churches, a greater and a lesser, for the use of the same foundation, a custom of which Glastonbury is so conspicuous an example, seems to have prevailed in most of the monasteries of this time. There were also two churches at Bruton, the greater of which, whose choir had been enlarged in William's own time, was also attributed to Ealdhelm ('est ibidem et alia major ecclesia in sancti

Petri nomine, quam a beato viro factam et consecratam non negligenter asseverat opinio. Hujus orientalem frontem nuper in majus porrexit recentis ædificationis ambitio'). In William's day then there might have been seen at Bruton a church with a new Norman choir, but whose nave was believed to be the work of Ealdhelm. At Frome too he founded a monastery, which in William's time had come to nought as a monastery, but one at least of its churches was supposed still to be standing ('stat ibi adhuc, et vicit diuturnitate sua tot sæcula ecclesia ab eo in honorem sancti Johannis Baptistæ constructa'). Lastly, he founded the monastery at Bradford, which, like Frome, had vanished as a monastery, but the little church of Saint Lawrence was still standing. Besides these there was also a church at Wareham which was built by Ealdhelm, but of which the ruins only remained in William's time ('ejus domus maceriæ adhuc superstites cælo patuli tecto vacant; nisi quod quiddam super altare prominet, quod a fœditate volucrum sacratum lapidem tueatur'). There is certainly nothing now standing at Wareham, Malmesbury, Bruton, or Frome, which can have the least claim to be looked on as a work of Ealdhelm or his time. But at Bradford the case is widely different. A building is there standing which there can be no reasonable doubt is the 'ecclesiola' spoken of by William of Malmesbury, and which he believed to be the work of Ealdhelm. Even those whom some strange superstition makes so eager to maintain that no Englishman before 1066 could have put two stones together do not venture to pretend that it is later than the time of William of Malmesbury. We see therefore still standing the original 'ecclesiola,' the little church of which William of Malmesbury speaks. The only question is whether William of Malmesbury was right in believing it to be the work of Ealdhelm.

The building of which we speak stands at a little distance to the north-east of the parish church, and is an *ecclesiola* indeed, consisting of a nave, chancel, and north porch, but measuring within from east to west less than forty feet. But its proportionate height is most remarkable; the walls of the nave are as high as the nave is long, while in the chancel the height again, without reckoning the roof, is considerably greater than the length. Its style is undoubtedly Primitive Romanesque. We believe that we are safe in saying that no one ever mistook it for Norman, though at a first distant glance it is easy to mistake it for *cinque-cento*. But it has some peculiarities of its own. As it has no tower, there is no opportunity for midwall shafts in belfry-windows. The single perfect window has the double splay, but it is by no means so rude as those of Benedict Biscop at Jarrow. Both nave and chancel are enriched with flat pilaster-strips, and with a flat arcade cut out of single stones, which also runs round the flat east end, there being no east window. In the gables and in the porch the arcade seems to have been exchanged for small shafts not supporting arches, as in many Italian churches. The masonry is remarkably good, being made of square stones, though now unluckily some ugly gaps are seen between them. The doorway and the chancel-arch are of distinctly Primitive Romanesque, and very narrow, the chancel arch especially wonderfully so. Over the chancel are two carved figures of angels very like some of those in early manuscripts, especially in the Benedictional of Saint Æthelwold.

Such is the 'ecclesiola' which William of Malmesbury believed to be the genuine work of Ealdhelm. Was he right in so thinking? We know of only one historical notice of the church or monastery of Bradford at any date between the days of Ealdhelm and those of William. This is in a charter of Æthelred (Cod. Dipl. iii. 319), in which the monastery of Bradford is given to the nuns of Shaftesbury as a place of refuge to which they might flee with the body of the newly martyred King Eadward in case of Danish incursions ('quatenus adversus barbarorum insidias ipsa religiosa congregatio cum beati martyris cæterorumque sanctorum reliquiis ibidem Deo serviendi impenetrabile obtineat confugium'). This description of Bradford as a place likely to be safe against invaders falls in singularly well with the fact that the district had held out against the West-Saxon arms for seventy-five years after the first conquest of Ceawlin. In the words of the charter there is nothing which directly proves anything as to the date of the building. The words would seem to imply an existing building, but it is of course possible that the nuns of Shaftesbury, on coming into possession, rebuilt such buildings as they found, and that of such rebuilding the 'ecclesiola' is the result. But this is pure surmise. All that we really know is that William of Malmesbury believed the church to have been built by Ealdhelm, and that we have no other historical statement which either confirms or contradicts his belief. Is his belief then so incredible in itself that it must be set aside on à *priori* grounds? For our own part, we see no difficulty whatever in believing as William did. We see no objection to his belief, except the vague notion that Ealdhelm, at the end of the seventh century or beginning of the eighth, could not have built anything. But this is simply the dream of people to whom all Old-English history is a blank, who fancy that all 'the Saxons' lived at one time, and who sometimes argue as if Bæda's account of the rudeness of Scottish buildings in the seventh century proved something about English buildings three or four hundred years afterwards. The masonry at Bradford is certainly smoother than most early Romanesque work in England. It has a good deal the air of the work of Stilicho by the *Porta Maggiore* at Rome. But this is the characteristic of finished Primitive work. It is built 'more Romano' in a sense in which Norman is not. But, before Ealdhelm, Wilfrith had already built at Ripon 'ex polito lapide.' The work at Bradford is better finished than the work at Jarrow; but Jarrow is a generation older, and Ealdhelm, with King Ine at his back, might be expected to build in the very best way that anybody could build in his time. In fact, as we see the matter, we have William of Malmesbury's statement on the one hand; we have a mere superstition on the other. We have very little doubt as to which of the two we should choose.

The 'ecclesiola' of Bradford was long desecrated and disfigured, almost hidden by parasitic buildings. It has now been saved, and restored, in the true but rare sense of that word. The building itself has been preserved; it has not had something else put in its place. It is in fact the one perfect surviving Old-English church in the land. The ground-plan is absolutely untouched, and there are no mediæval insertions at all. So perfect a specimen of Primitive Romanesque is certainly unique in England; we should not be surprised if it is unique of its own kind in Europe.

DEVIZES.

1874.

The name of the town of Devizes at once strikes the ear as something which does not readily fall under any of the classes into which English place-names commonly fall. It is not a Roman or British name which has lived through the English Conquest. Nor is it an English name, either describing the place itself or else preserving the memory of a tribe or of an early owner. Nor yet is it, like Beaulieu and Richmond, a name palpably French, witnessing to the days when Norman and other foreign settlers had made French the polite speech of the land. The name is Latin without being Roman. For once the Latin name is not made from the English, but the English from the Latin. The castle 'ad Divisas' has become Devizes, or rather 'the Devizes.' The article was used as late as Clarendon's time, and, we fancy, much later; the popular local name of the place is 'the Vize.' It is plainly called from a boundary or division of some kind, but what boundary or division is not at first sight very clear. It must be remembered that the name 'Divisæ' is not found till the foundation of the castle by Bishop Roger of Salisbury in the time of Henry the First, of which more anon. The town is one of the same class as Richmond, one which has arisen around a castle of comparatively late foundation. Why then did Bishop Roger give his fortress so odd a name? Dr. Guest points out that the town of Devizes overlooks the Avon valley, that it stands just on the border of that narrow slip of territory which the Britons kept up to the battle of Bradford in 652. He holds that the march district was called 'Divisæ,' and that the castle took its name from the district. He refers to the town of Mere in the same county, a good deal south-west of Devizes, where the name, an English equivalent, as he remarks, of *Divisæ*, is clearly derived from the border position of the place. It is very seldom, and always with great diffidence, that we set up our judgement against that of Dr. Guest, but this is a case in which we are strongly tempted to do so. *Mere* is an English word, and the name may be as old as the first English occupation of the district. *Divisæ* is a Latin word, and Dr. Guest does not bring any instance of the name being used before Bishop Roger's time. It would certainly be strange if a district had, for five hundred years, kept a Latin name of which no trace can be found. It certainly seems more likely that the 'divisæ' from which the castle took its name were some smaller local boundary, and we believe that local antiquaries are ready with more than one explanation of this kind. And as for the oddness of the name, it must be remembered that it is not a name which arises from any settlement or tradition, but from the fancy of one man. In such cases eccentric names have often been given in all ages.

Another question may arise, what was the nature of the place before the foundation of the famous castle. Most of the great Norman castles were reared on earlier sites; the mound and the ditch, as we have been taught by Mr. Clark, are for the most part English works—works most commonly of Eadward the Elder, or of his sister the Lady of the Merciana. But their works are placed along the line of defence against the Danes, and they are found in places which bear intelligible names, whether of English or earlier origin. One hardly sees why Eadward should fortify a post in the heart of Wessex, and, if he did, the place would bear some name, and it is not likely that that name would be *Divisæ*. But, whether the earthworks belong to their day or to some earlier time, it is certain that it was by Bishop Roger that the vast ditch, the mighty mound which the unseen railway now passes under, were first crowned by a castle in the later sense. Certainly no place brings more strongly home to us the temporal position of a bishop in those days. The episcopal castle and the episcopal palace are two very different things. The palace, in strictness of speech, is the bishop's dwelling in the episcopal city. It is only a piece of modern affectation which, since both the English metropolitans have forsaken their natural homes, speaks of the manors of Lambeth and Bishopthorpe as *palaces*. The episcopal palace, hard by the episcopal church, sometimes actually joining it, is for the most part in strictness a house. Standing most commonly within a walled town, it needed no great amount of defence; even when, as at Wells, some degree of fortification was needed, it was plainly no more than was needed for protection in case of danger. Episcopal castles in the episcopal city, castles like those of Durham and Llandaff, are quite exceptional, though they may be easily explained by the circumstances and history of the places where they are found. At Durham Bishop Walcher was placed by William as both temporal and spiritual ruler among a fierce and half-conquered people, who had slain two former earls, and who were in the end to slay the bishop himself. It is not wonderful that he was set to dwell in a fortress, even within the episcopal city. At Llandaff a bishop placed among the turbulent Welsh, and whose city was a mere unwalled village, needed a fortress no less than his more princely brother of Durham. Wolvesey, the castle of the bishops of Winchester, not actually within the city, but just outside of it, was more remarkable and unusual. But among episcopal dwellings away from the cities, the castle is, in the days with which we are dealing, the rule. The bishop of the days at once following the Norman Conquest, turned by the Norman polity into a military tenant of the Crown, dwelling commonly as a stranger among a strange and often hostile people, often raised to his see as the reward of temporal services to the Crown, as soon as he got away from the episcopal city and its more peaceful associations, as soon as he found himself on his rural estates, began to feel like any other baron on his rural estates. He raised for himself, not a house, not a palace, but a castle in the strictest sense; a fortress not merely capable of defence in case of any sudden attack, but capable of being made a centre of military operations in case the bishop should take a fancy, in times of civil strife, to make war upon some other baron or upon the King himself. And Roger of Salisbury was not likely to be behind his brethren in this matter. The poor clerk who had won the fancy of the Ætheling Henry by the speed with which he gabbled over the service in his lowly church in a suburb of Caen, and who was thereon declared to be the fittest of all chaplains for soldiers, had risen with the fortunes of his patron. As the chief minister of the Lion of Justice, he was the most powerful man in the realm. Architecture, both military and ecclesiastical, was a special taste of his, and it would seem from the description of his works given by William of Malmesbury that the later form of the Norman style, the form where a finer masonry and more elaborate kind of ornament came into use, was in some measure his creation. As Bishop of Salisbury—that is, not of the new Salisbury in the plain, but of that elder Salisbury where the city itself was the mightiest of fortresses, but where the bishop was not the lord of the city—Roger was not unnaturally stirred up to the raising of fortresses on the episcopal estates which might be wholly his own. At Malmesbury he gave great offence to the monks by building a castle within the very precincts of their monastery. At Sherborne, the town which his last predecessor but one, the Lotharingian Hermann, had forsaken for the old British hill-fort, he built another castle; but, unlike Malmesbury, it stands quite distinct,

L

and at some distance from the minster. But his great work was at the Devizes; the huge earthwork which he found there was crowned with a castle which was said not to be surpassed by any castle in Europe. Its fragments show that it must have been an example of a rich form of the style of which its founder was such a master, a form intermediate between the stern simplicity of the days of the Conqueror and the lavish gorgeousness of the days of Henry the Second. But unluckily all that is now to be seen consists of mere fragments here and there, fragments for the most part built up again as meaningless ornaments in the midst of the most fearful piece of modern gimcrack that human eyes ever beheld. But the mound and the ditch at least are there. It would need more than another Roger to get rid of them, and we can without much difficulty call up before our eyes that remarkable episode in the most troubled time of our history of which the castle of the Devizes was the scene.

The sudden imprisonment of Bishop Roger by command of Stephen seems to have been the turning point of his reign. It at once set the clergy against him, and it seems besides this to have awakened general wonder as something so unlike the general character of the King. He who was held to be, in the words of the Chroniclers, a 'mild man and soft and good, and who did no justice,' suddenly turns about, and, without any very clear reason, seizes in the most ignominious way on two of the chief men both in Church and State. People were struck both with the act in itself and with its strangeness in a man like Stephen, who, whatever were his faults, is not at any other time charged with cruelty, or even with lack of generosity, in his own person. But the moral difficulty is perhaps not very great. When a man like Stephen, mild and gentle rather from temper than from principle, is once stirred up to what he is told is an act of energy, he is very likely to overdo matters, and to be energetic at the wrong time and in the wrong way. Anyhow, here was the great Bishop Roger, the most powerful man in England, the minister of the late King, suddenly seized along with his nephew Alexander, Bishop of Lincoln, and his avowed son Roger the King's Chancellor, during the sitting of a great Council at Oxford, and threatened with all manner of threats, unless all their castles and possessions were surrendered to the King. But our concern is only with the one castle which was Roger's great work. Another nephew, Richard Bishop of Ely, managed to escape to his uncle's fortress, 'ad Divisas fortissimum oppidum,' where the chief tower ('principalis munitio') was held by the younger Roger's mother, Matilda of Ramsbury, who was likely enough the Bishop of Salisbury's unacknowledged wife. The King comes before the castle, on the site doubtless of the present approach from the town, swearing in his wrath that the younger Roger shall be hanged and the elder kept without food, unless the castle is at once surrendered. Another version indeed makes the fast a voluntary offer on the part of the Bishop of Salisbury; he promises, in the hope of making his nephew yield, that he will not eat or drink till the castle is given up. In short, according to what may be a general Aryan usage, one certainly well known in India and not unknown in Ireland, he 'sits *dharna*' at his nephew's door. In either case we have the picture of the mild Stephen suddenly turned as fierce as William Rufus, with his three prisoners, the two bishops and the Chancellor, the bishops just released, it would seem, from their wretched imprisonment, one in an ox's stall, the other in some miserable shed not otherwise defined. There is the great Bishop Roger, suddenly fallen from his pomp and power, standing faint and hungry before the walls, to do what he can, by the sad sight and by his sad words, to move his obstinate nephew the Bishop of Ely to surrender, if only to save the life of his uncle. We see the pair on the walls; the Bishop of Ely is unmoved by his uncle's pleading and ready to let him or anybody else

starve rather than give up the stronghold within which
he has found shelter. Then the King is moved to further
wrath; a gibbet is set up; the Chancellor is to be hanged
at once. But his mother holds the strongest tower; her
heart is moved for her son, if the Bishop's heart is not
moved for his uncle; she will give up anything for her
child. The great tower is at once surrendered, and after
that the resistance of the Bishop of Ely and his followers
is all in vain. We read the story; we go to the spot and
try to call up the scene. If the castle stood there untouched, it would be easy; if nothing stood there at all,
it would not be very hard; but when the castle of Bishop
Roger is turned into a grotesque modern mockery, what
is to be done?

Some comfort however may be drawn from a visit to
the two churches of the town. They have not fared worse
than churches commonly do in the space of seven hundred
years. They have at least not been deliberately and of
malice aforethought turned into shams. There are not
many towns in England which still keep two vaulted
Norman choirs, one of which is not unlikely to be the
work of Roger himself.

WAREHAM AND CORFE CASTLE.

1875—1882.

THE name of Corfe Castle is familiar to most people as the scene of one of those isolated legends which, in so many eyes, make up the whole of our earliest history; and the name of its neighbour Wareham, less familiar perhaps to the world in general, must be well known to all who have studied modern parliamentary history. Up to the first Reform Bill, Wareham and Corfe Castle each sent two members to Parliament; now a district which takes in both places sends one only. As Wareham thus belongs to the class of rural boroughs, it was spared at the last suppression, when other boroughs fell which had a larger number of real burgesses than Wareham, but whose nominal population was not swelled in the same way by the addition of the neighbouring villages. A reformer from Yorkshire or Lancashire would most likely sneer at Wareham and Corfe alike as 'miserable villages in the south of England.' But, as Wareham is still a good deal bigger than Corfe, so the parliamentary history of the two places is quite different. Wareham has sent members ever since the reign of Edward the First. Corfe sent them for the first time in the reign of Elizabeth. That is to say, Wareham is represented in Parliament because there was a time when it deserved to be represented; Corfe never deserved to be represented at all, and was enfranchised simply in order to be corrupt. Both places play an important part in English history, and that mainly in military history, as the seats of two renowned castles. But Wareham is a case of a castle founded in an existing town. Corfe is a case of a town, or rather village, growing up round a castle. We cannot conceive that Corfe was ever greater than it is now; of Wareham we have the evidence of our own eyes that it once was far greater. Wareham, in short, is one of those towns which have not only, like most of the ancient towns of England, been outstripped by younger rivals, but which have absolutely decayed. It is like Rome or Autun or the Westphalian Soest, where, starting from the centre of the town, we gradually leave the streets and find ourselves among lanes, fields, and gardens, till we at last come to the town wall. Wareham has in the same way shrunk up. It is not, as at Chester and Colchester, where there are fields and gardens within the walls, but where the space thus left void is more than made up by the growth of the town in other directions beyond the walls. Wareham has not grown at all, except in the sense of growing smaller; the walls are there, but the modern town is very far from filling up the whole space within them. But the walls of Wareham differ from the walls of Colchester in another most important point. They are indeed rectangular, or nearly so; but they are not walls in the stricter sense, walls of stone or brick, but vast ramparts of earth. Their nearest parallel is to be found in the kindred earthworks of Wallingford, a town whose history has in many points a near likeness to that of Wareham. In each case a rectangular earthwork forms three sides of a space, square or nearly so, leaving the fourth side to be defended by a river. Wallingford has but one river, but that is one of the great rivers of England, the great border stream of Thames. Wareham has two rivers, but rivers of less renown. The town stands at the head of its landlocked haven, a branch of the greater haven of Poole, on the isthmus of a peninsula formed by the confluence of the southern Frome and the Piddle. This last stream in older writers shares the name of Trent with one of the great rivers of central England; for, when Asser and Florenec speak of Wareham as lying 'inter duo flumina Fraw et Terente,' they can hardly mean that the place lies between the Frome and the more distant Tarrant. But the position of Wareham between its two streams is one of its characteristic features. The side towards the south, which is sheltered by the greater stream of the Frome and the once doubtless swampy land beyond it, was left wholly unfortified. The northern side, towards the lesser stream of the Piddle, is fortified, but less strongly than the eastern and western sides, where there is no river at all. Now the question at once arises, by whom were these earthworks thrown up; that is to say, by whom was the town of Wareham first founded? The defences are, in a certain vague sense, Roman. That is to say, their rectangular shape shows they are the work of men who had some knowledge of the rules of Roman castrametation. But they are not Roman in material; and that they are not Roman in date—that is, that they are not older than A.D. 410—is almost proved by the place bearing the purely English name of Wareham, instead of being marked as Roman by the ending *chester*. The most probable opinion is that the earthworks both of Wareham and of Wallingford were thrown up by the Welsh, who at Wallingford have left their name, as defences against the invading English. The argument which attributes these works to the Danes, on the ground that they must be the work of men who already commanded the water, does not apply. By the time that the West-Saxon arms reached Wareham, the days of invasion by sea had come to an end, and Cerdic or his descendants were pushing their way both westward and northward by land.

The military importance of Wareham arose from its commanding the approach to the peninsula which lies between it and the open sea, that island of Purbeck which is still less of an island than the greater island

of Pelops. The isle of marble is one of the ends of
the world. The nineteenth century has effected a lodge-
ment in the shape of the watering-place of Swanwich;
otherwise Purbeck, with its cliffs, its long views, along
the coast on either side, its ancient houses, its venerable
church of Studland, seem all cut off from the everyday
world by an impassable barrier. And the barrier is
physically there. A little south-east of Wareham lies
Corfe. A glance shows the essential difference between
the two places. Wareham is a fortified town; Corfe is a
simple fortress. The great line of hills which runs along
the peninsula, and which shuts off both Corfe and Wareham from the open sea, here makes a sudden gap. Such
a gap bears in all languages names which translate one
another. The endless *Pylai* of the Greeks have their
parallel in *Corfes-geat*. In the midst of the gate, like the
massive pier in the middle of the double gateways of
the Roman Wall, stands a lower conical hill, crowned
first by a West-Saxon royal house, and then by the
famous Norman castle. Not far from the little town is a
clearly marked earthwork, which must have played its
part in the days before castles were. Both Corfe and
Wareham figure in our early history, and the first time
that Corfe is spoken of, the second time that Wareham is
spoken of, the two places have both their share. Wareham first appears in history in 876, when the Danes
marched thither from Cambridge, therefore by land, and
after swearing oaths and giving hostages to Ælfred,
marched the next year to Exeter. The words of Asser
and Florence, 'castellum quod dicitur Werham'—the
Chronicles simply say 'bestæl se here into Werham West-
seaxna fyrde'—might seem to imply that they made use
of the existing fortifications as they did of the 'waste
chester' further north in 894. Our next mention of the
two places is at the death of Eadward the Martyr in 979.
Every one must have seen the picture of the young King
stabbed at the gate of the castle, a confusion doubtless

with the *Corfes Gate* itself. The Chroniclers merely record the fact of his death with the time and place, and add a bitter wail for a deed than which none worse had been done since the English came into Britain. But their very silence as to the doer of the deed strongly confirms the story which is found in its simplest form in Florence, and which gathers fresh details in every later writer, that according to which the murder was the deed of Eadward's stepmother Ælfthryth. The murdered king was buried without any kingly worship at Wareham, but was in the next year translated by Ealdorman Ælfhere, the enemy of monks, with mickle worship to King Ælfred's minster at Shaftesbury. The steps by which the tale grew into the elaborate piece of hagiology to be found in Brompton form, like everything else of the kind, a curious study of comparative mythology. The main facts there is no reason to doubt; but the common way of treating such stories is not honest, namely, to take the legend in its full-blown form, and, leaving out all that is miraculous, to treat the remainder as authentic history.

In Domesday Wareham appears as a borough, and, as if to keep up the parallel with Wallingford in every point, it appears that in King Eadward's days it formed one of the special quarters of the King's housecarls. Many houses had been destroyed, perhaps on William's march to Exeter. No castle of Wareham is mentioned in the account of Wareham itself, but there is an incidental entry which says that William obtained its site by an exchange with the abbey of Shaftesbury. Nor is any castle of Corfe, by that name, entered in the Survey, and before William's coming the dwelling of Ælfthryth had ceased to be a royal possession. Corfe appears in Domesday as the former holding of two Englishmen named Wada and Ægelric, and as the present possession of Robert son of Gerold. From this a local antiquary of high authority has argued that the Domesday entry of Wareham Castle really refers to Corfe.

The confusion of names would be much the same as when the castle of Tickhill not uncommonly bears the name of Blyth, a place several miles distant and in another county. But it is strange if a castle did not arise on the mound of Wareham, a place which had so long been a fortress, in the early days of the Conquest; and, if the Domesday entry of 'Wareham' refers to Corfe, we shall be driven to understand of Corfe not a few other entries which more naturally refer to Wareham. Wareham castle was one of the many places of imprisonment of Duke Robert and the more lasting prison of Robert of Bellême. Are we to infer that here too Corfe and not Wareham is meant? In the beginning of Stephen's reign both castles were certainly in being. Among the long string of fortresses which the Winchester annalist reckons up as built or strengthened by Earl Robert of Gloucester, Wareham and Corfe are both found. This sets aside anything that might be inferred from the language of the 'Gesta Stephani,' where Baldwin of Redvers lands at the *city* of Wareham, and occupies the strong castle of Corfe ('apud civitatem Warham applicuit, susceptusque in Corpha uno omnium Anglorum castello munitissimo'), with no mention of the castle of Wareham.

At Wareham the castle has vanished, but its site is plain enough. Like so many others, it has arisen on a mound of English work in the south-east corner of the town, overlooking the Frome. At Corfe no artificial mound was needed. There nature had thrown up a mound greater than the works of the Lady of the Mercians at Warwick or at Tamworth. On that hill the castle still stands, more utterly shattered by the great siege of the seventeenth century than perhaps any other building which has not been purposely destroyed. The square keep, the Conqueror's work, as some hold, crowns the height, and graceful fragments of later work are left beside it. Below it are the remains of a building of earlier masonry which inquirers not given to credulity on such points have deemed to be most likely the remains of the house of Eadgar's widow. Both fortresses are constantly mentioned in the twelfth and thirteenth centuries, Wareham being more prominent in the earlier and Corfe in the later period. Both were often chosen as the places of safe confinement of important prisoners. Among notable prisoners at Corfe we find the Welsh prince Gruffydd in 1198, and Henry of Montfort in 1275. But between those dates Corfe had been chosen as the scene of two of the blackest of the crimes of John. Had they but met with a sacred poet, the two-and-twenty continental supporters of the cause of Arthur who were starved to death in the still existing tower of Corfe in 1202 might have been as famous as those who, before the century had run its course, shared the same doom in Pisa's vanished Tower of Hunger. Again, twelve years later, it was at Corfe that the unlucky Peter of Pontefract, whose prophecy had been so strangely fulfilled, was drawn and hanged as the first act of authority of the new papal vassal. It would even seem that Corfe had fixed itself in men's minds as the special scene of deeds of horror, as one chronicler, the annalist of Bermondsey, transfers thither from Berkeley the fate of the second Edward. Of the importance of the post we have other and less hideous reminders, in the constant occurrence of the name Corfe in lists of the great fortresses of the kingdom.

Neither Wareham nor Corfe was ever the seat of any great ecclesiastical foundation. A monastery of nuns is mentioned as being there at the time of the Danish occupation; and, as it is not mentioned afterwards, it probably perished then. In the time of Henry the First, Robert Earl of Leicester—is this the famous Count of Meulan or his son?—founded a priory at Wareham, as a cell to the abbey of Lire in Normandy, which, at the suppression of alien houses, passed to the Carthusians of Shene. This priory seems to have been attached to the chief, if not only, surviving church of Wareham, known, by a kind of tautology, as Lady Saint Mary. It will hardly be believed that, about thirty years back, the great Norman nave of this church was destroyed at the instance of one of the Church Building Societies, whose grant for some repairs or reseating was made conditional on an act worthy of a Pope's nephew or of the grantee of a suppressed monastery. But in a side chapel, alongside of some fine thirteenth century tombs, are some fragments of Primitive Romanesque, which are said to have been built into the wall of the Norman building, and which may have seen the hasty burial of the martyred king. Instead of this hideous destruction, it would have been a better work to call to life again one of the disused and mutilated churches which show how much Wareham has fallen from its greatness either in the days of Cerdic or in the days of Stephen.

SILCHESTER.

1873.

THE Britain which our forefathers turned into England is, for the most part, to be looked for below the ground. That so it should be was one of the necessary results of the means by which that great change was made. At first sight it might seem as if the phænomena of our own country in this respect differed but little from the phænomena of other lands. Take for example the city which, of all the cities of Northern Europe, is richest in vestiges of Roman dominion. Rich as Trier still is in its remains above ground, its amphitheatre, its basilica, its palace, and the mighty pile of its *Porta Nigra*, there can be no doubt that far more extensive remains of Augusta Treverorum lurk below. The vaults, the pavements, which are hidden under the mediæval and modern houses must be endless. But this is what always happens in a town which has never ceased to be inhabited. Nothing is so lasting as a street; nothing is so little lasting as the particular houses of which the street is made up. In Exeter, for instance, there are few houses even of mediæval date, but the main lines of the Roman city are there as plain as ever. Not a fragment, to the best of our knowledge, of the Damnonian Isca is standing above ground, but we should be surprised if there is not a good deal of it to be still found underneath. In cases like these the city is destroyed by the fact of its being preserved. It perishes piecemeal, because there was no moment when it was utterly swept away. Now on the Continent, as a rule,

the Roman cities have been continuously inhabited down
to our own time; in Italy, Gaul, and Spain, the Roman
life has never wholly died out. If therefore the Roman
remains in those countries are on the whole much more
scanty than we should have looked for, it is chiefly because they have perished through the wear and tear of
ages; mediæval buildings gradually supplanted buildings
of Roman date, as modern buildings are gradually supplant-
ing buildings of mediæval date. The exceptions are to
be found in those parts of the Continent where the circumstances were nearly the same as in our own island, in
those border lands of Germany, Gaul, and Italy, where
the Teutonic conquest or reconquest trod out the remains
of Roman life almost as thoroughly as it did in Britain.
But, comparing the Continent in general with our own
island, especially comparing that land of Gaul which it is
most natural to compare with our own island, we find one
main distinction to be, that in Gaul, as a rule, the Roman
towns have been continuously inhabited, while in Britain,
as a rule, they have not. We cannot in every place
pronounce dogmatically. We know that Exeter, as not
having been conquered by the English till after their
conversion, has never ceased to be inhabited. But we
know also that Chester, Bath, and Cambridge stood
desolate for several centuries, and we know that Anderida
has stood desolate till our own time. On the other hand,
if Canterbury, York, London, and Lincoln ever stood
desolate, the time of their desolation could not have been
very long. But the point is that, in marked contrast to
the continental rule, a great number of the Roman cities
of Britain were utterly wasted, and that many of them
have never been rebuilt. Parts of some sites have been
occupied by small villages; other sites stand altogether
waste; of some Roman settlements it is even hard to find
the site at all. The cases where a Roman town still
exists as a considerable English town can hardly be the
majority. Those which can be shown to have been unin-

terruptedly inhabited are a very small minority indeed. In France and Aquitaine, on the other hand, in utter contrast to Britain, the chief Roman towns still remain the chief towns in our own day. In Aquitaine and Provence they even commonly retain their names of Roman or earlier date, not forgetting that the still surviving names of Massalia and Antipolis carry us back to a state of things to which Britain has no parallel at all.

Now this utter destruction of the Roman cities, the desolation of so many of their sites down to our own day, is the most speaking witness of the wasting and exterminating character of the English Conquest. The fact that we know so little about it, the yawning gap between Roman and English history in Britain, a gap which has no parallel in continental lands, teaches us better than anything else what was the real nature of the settlement made by our forefathers. It is a striking fact that no ornamental Roman building is to be found standing above ground in Britain. Not a single perfect Roman column remains in its place throughout the whole land. This is not the mere work of time. To say nothing of Egyptian remains, Greece, Italy, and Sicily still keep abundant remains of Hellenic antiquity; it is owing to a mere accident of modern warfare that the Parthenôn itself does not remain as perfect as when the Slayer of the Bulgarians paid his thanksgiving within its walls. It is because Britain was overrun by an enemy far more destructive than the Goth, the Frank, or the Turk himself. It is a speaking fact that of what must have been one of the greatest Roman cities of Britain we have absolutely no history whatever. Antiquaries are, we believe, now pretty well agreed that Silchester is the Roman Calleva Atrebatum—in Gaul the place might have been called Arras and its district Artois —and it is so marked in Dr. Guest's map. But this is merely a geographical and not an historical fact. Calleva is simply a name in the Itineraries; nothing that we ever heard of is recorded to have happened there. Nor do we add very much to our knowledge if we conceive Silchester to have been the Caer Segeint of the so-called Nennius; for his one fact, that the elder Constantius was buried somewhere in those parts, can hardly be true, seeing that he died at York. Of the origin of the city we have no account; nor have we, as we have in the case of Anderida, Bath, and other cities, any statement, or even any direct clue, as to the time of its destruction. That we know nothing of its origin is most likely owing to the fact that Calleva was more of a town and less of a fortress than most of the Roman settlements in Britain. Its polygonal shape, which it shares with Durolipons or Godmanchester, stands in marked contrast to the quadrangular shape of the camps which grew into York and Lincoln, Chester, Gloucester, and Exeter. And the space contained within the walls is far greater than what is contained within the walls of their *chesters*. The cause of the difference doubtless is that those were *chesters* in the very strictest sense, foundations of the early age of warfare; the city arose out of the camp, and spread itself around the walls of the camp. Here there was no camp, no *chester* in the strictest sense. The spot was settled after the Roman Peace was fully established in southern Britain; in after days, when the Roman power was threatened, the inhabited space, as it then stood, was walled in. So it was at Rome itself, in this matter the least Roman of Roman cities, alike in the days of Servius and in the days of Aurelian. As to the time of its destruction, it is plain from the discovery of coins of Honorius and Arcadius that the site was occupied as long as the Roman occupation of Britain lasted. The general indications which have been followed by Dr. Guest in tracing out his maps lead us to set it down as having been in English occupation—and English occupation just then was the same thing as destruction—before the great check which the English arms received at the hand of Arthur in 520. The destroyers therefore were Cerdic and Cynric; but we have no such notice of its overthrow as we get in Henry of Huntingdon, and even in the Chronicles, of the overthrow of Anderida at the hands of Ælle and Cissa. The whole history of the site is shrouded in darkness, but it is darkness more instructive than any amount of light.

The place is easy of access, lying from three to four miles from the Mortimer station of the branch of the Great Western Railway between Reading and Basingstoke. The French name of Mortimer, coming between the two Teutonic tribe names of the Rædingas and the Basingas, and serving as the point of starting for the old Roman city, gives us a lesson in British nomenclature. As usual, the Roman, the Englishman, and the Norman have all left their mark; the Briton alone is utterly wiped out. When we reach the spot, the first feeling is perhaps one of disappointment; the walls do not stand out in the same stately sort as the walls of Anderida, those walls which stood as they stand now when William landed beneath them. We doubt whether there is any place in the whole circuit where the outer surface has not been thoroughly picked away. In a country where stone is precious, Silchester walls and Reading abbey church have alike been found useful as quarries. The wall is there in its whole extent, save where the gates have utterly perished, whether as part of the special work of the first conquerors, or because they supplied a tempting store of good stones in aftertimes. The wall is there, but it is often sadly broken down; in some places it has to be traced. Nowhere is its Roman character forced upon the eye as it is at Anderida, and in the smaller fragments at York and Lincoln. But, when we get within the enclosure, utterly unoccupied except by a small church and a single farmhouse in one corner, our feeling is that of amazement at its great extent. The two largest diameters of the irregular polygon are, one rather more, one rather less, than half a mile. And when we come to examine the treasures below ground which have been brought to light by the zealous care of

M

Mr. Joyce, we find that Silchester is indeed one of the great spots of our island. The excavations have as yet been carried over only a small part of the enclosure, but the foundations of a great number of public and private buildings have been brought to light. In some cases it is plain that changes took place while the city was still inhabited. An ingenious conjecture has found a name and a probable use for everything that has been brought to light. We cannot enter into all of these; but two buildings of extraordinary interest must be spoken of. The excavations of the Forum, which seems to be almost perfectly made out, have brought to light the unmistakeable foundations of a gigantic basilica. The foundations of the two rows of columns are there, and here and there fragments of the columns themselves, with noble Corinthian capitals, have been brought to light. They doubtless supported entablatures; there is no reason to think that the great invention of Spálato had been forestalled at Calleva Atrebatum. The internal arrangement of the basilica must have been awkward as compared with that of the ecclesiastical basilicas at Ravenna and elsewhere. In these the semicircle of the apse continues on either side the lines formed by the two ranges of columns. At Silchester it is otherwise. Here the semicircle is greater than a semicircle would be which continued the ranges of columns, so that the ends of the columns, the two ranges of which seem to an ecclesiastical eye to stand strangely near together, must have abutted upon the chord of the semicircle, so as to throw the two ends of the apse itself into obscurity. Any one who remembers Torcello or Classis will feel how utterly the effect of the apse must have been ruined by such a ground plan. Still, though the perfection of the basilican arrangement was not reached all at once, yet the building of Silchester must at least have shown two noble ranges of columns; and it is something to trace, and that on our own soil, the gradual developement of the type which is in truth the germ of all ecclesiastical architecture. Is there any man who can believe that, in the island, almost even in the neighbourhood, where these noble colonnades had been reared, even a Celt could be so perverse as to go back and build the rude masses of Stonehenge?

Another most remarkable discovery is that of a round temple. Two circular foundations, one within the other, may be clearly seen. It did flash across the mind for a moment that these might be the foundations of a Christian church, a British Saint Vital; for it must not be forgotten that a city which formed a part of the Empire of Honorius could hardly have been without Christian buildings. The absence of the projecting sanctuary is not absolutely conclusive against the possibility of its Christian use; still it is perhaps safer to set it down as a pagan building. It must be remembered that, if it were Christian, the outer circle of foundation would be for a wall, and the inner one for columns; in a pagan building it would be the other way.

But one relic has been found at Silchester the interest of which, from a certain point of view, is beyond all others. Among the ruins of one of the houses, one which had plainly been destroyed by fire, stowed away, it would seem, with care in a secret place, was a legionary eagle, broken away from its stem. This fact would seem to show that the Britons who withstood Cerdic and Cynric still so far looked upon themselves as Romans as to bear the ensign of Marius in their wars, and still to look on it as a sacred thing, which they strove by every means to keep from falling into the hands of the invaders. Such a piece of detail as this brings before us at once the unbroken march of history and the strange ups and downs along which that march has to be traced. We are all used to pictures of the landing of Cæsar, with the eagle brandished before the eyes of the astonished Britons. We have never seen a picture of the Briton keeping the ensigns which had been handed on to him by the conqueror who was also his teacher, and hiding them out of the sight of the conqueror who must have been, not his teacher but his destroyer. Yet it is the latter scene which most concerns us. It is because Silchester and places like Silchester were left waste without inhabitants—because those who dwelled in them were cut off by the sword or driven to save their lives in remote corners of Britain or Gaul—because for a hundred years the faith of Christ was wiped out before the faith of Woden—it is because of all this that Britain has not been as Gaul and Spain, and that we still keep the laws and the tongue which we brought from the mouths of the Elbe and the Eider. Calleva and its people were swept away that the Rædingas and the Basingas might grow up as purely English settlements on the conquered soil.

CHRISTCHURCH, TWINHAM.

1871.

THERE are not a few objects in the world which have altogether lost their original names, and have taken a name from some incidental circumstance. Thus in French the fox has wholly lost his real name of *volpil*, and has taken the new name of *renard* out of the famous beast-epic in which he plays the chief part. In England an animal of quite another kind, the little redbreast, has not wholly lost its real name, but is called by it far less commonly than by the personal pet name of Robin. Among places, the fact that the town of Kingston stands on the river Hull, and is distinguished from other Kingstons by the name of Kingston-upon-Hull, has caused the name of the river to supplant the name of the town everywhere except in formal documents. In the place of which we now speak the real name of the town has been wholly forgotten; we do not know whether it survives even in formal use, but it is quite certain that, if we spoke in ordinary talk of the town of Twinham in Hampshire, no one would know what place we meant. The dedication of the church has wholly driven out the name of the town, and the place is never called anything but Christchurch. The change is not unreasonable, for, except as the site of its minster, Twinham plays no prominent part in history. In early days it was a royal possession; as such it is casually mentioned along with its neighbour Wimborne, when the Ætheling Æthelwald rebelled against Eadward the Elder. This rebellion may pass as a very early assertion of the doctrine of hereditary right. Æthelwald, the son of Ælfred's elder brother, clearly thought himself wronged by the election of Ælfred's son. But Twinham—*Tweoxneam*, as it appears in the Chronicles—played only a secondary part in the business, while Wimborne stood something like a siege. In Domesday *Thuinam* appears as a royal lordship and as a borough, but a borough of no great account, containing only thirty houses. It is a suspicious fact that Christchurch was not represented in Parliament till the time of Elizabeth, and it is not likely that it would be represented now, had not the first Reform Bill, while docking it of a member, enlarged its boundaries. It stands, like several of the neighbouring towns, as the centre of a large parish in a thinly inhabited region of heath and wood. The great minster, standing on a comparative height, the stump of a small castle, and, more precious in its own way than either, a ruined house of the twelfth century, form altogether as striking a group as can often be found. They are indeed helped by their position, rising as they do above the Avon, the southern Avon which runs by Salisbury and Ringwood, and which is here spanned by a picturesque mediæval bridge. But the minster of course soars above all; it is so completely the all in all of the place, both in its past history and in its present being, that we can neither wonder nor complain that it has driven out the earlier name of the town.

But when we come to examine the church in detail, we feel something about it which is not wholly satisfactory. The parts taken separately are splendid, but they do not hang well together. A building of great length, not of course of the length of Winchester or Saint Albans, but of a very great length among churches of the second rank, has only a single western tower, and that one which, as the single tower of such a church, is utterly insignificant. Nowhere do we more instinctively and bitterly cry out for the central tower. It is not merely any personal or national fancy for the peculiar outline which distinguishes English and Norman minsters from those of the rest of the world; we do not miss the central tower at Bourges or at Alby, we are not sure that we miss it even at Llandaff. Bourges and Alby were designed on a plan which altogether forbade the central tower, and the question between them and the churches of England and Normandy is not a question between particular buildings, but between two rival systems of ground-plan and outline. But Christchurch, of all churches in the world, asks for a central tower and does not get it. The central tower may be best dispensed with when the church is all of a piece, built on one regular plan in which the central tower found no place; such is Bourges; such is Alby; such, to come down several degrees on our scale, is Manchester. But, when a church is, like most English churches, a jumble of dates and styles—a nave of one kind, a choir of another, transepts of a third —a central tower is above all things needed to hold them together and to fuse them into a whole of some kind. However incongruous they may be with one another, yet when they all group round the central lantern, there is something which stands in a relation to all of them, though they may stand in no relation to one another. If a great unbroken length begs for a central tower to break it, a great length broken up into bits begs still more earnestly for a central tower to keep the pieces together. There is no doubt that a central tower was designed at Christchurch; the four great arches of the lantern are there ready to bear it up; it may even have been carried up to a certain height; but, as a matter of fact, it is not there now, and the result is that the building, as a whole, is utterly incongruous. A nave whose Romanesque character is partly disguised by the clerestory windows of the next age, a nave which is the only part of the building that still keeps its high-pitched roof, transepts somewhat lower than the main body of the nave, transepts essentially Romanesque, but much altered in detail; a Perpendicular choir, with vast clerestory windows like those of Bath or

Sherborne or Redcliff; a Lady chapel of the same external height as the choir, but of course with a wholly different arrangement of windows—all these, with the further appendages of a large northern porch and a small western tower, do not form, as they stand, a harmonious whole. If the central tower were there, the several parts would at once become, if not exactly harmonious, yet at any rate not painfully inharmonious. The difference of arrangement between the nave and the choir, instead of a glaring contrast, would be little more than a pleasing variety. The transepts, instead of mere appendages to the nave, would take their proper place as independent parts of the building. The one contrast which it could not reconcile would be the contrast between the choir and the Lady chapel, and the contrast between these most violently opposed parts of the building is a contrast, not of date or style, but, we must suppose, of intentional design. The only question is as to the present western tower, which a central lantern of any dignity would of course throw into still greater insignificance. The arrangement would be the same as that at Wimborne, but at Wimborne a certain equality is kept between the two towers, by giving a slight advantage of bulk to the lantern in the middle, and a slight advantage of height to the bell-tower at the west end. Each therefore has a character and a dignity of its own, and they group well together without each being a mere double of the other. But at Christchurch, if there was to be a western tower, either alone or in company with a central lantern, it ought to have been far larger than it is.

The part of the church most deserving of detailed study is naturally the Romanesque nave. This, according to all local tradition, was the work of the famous or infamous Randolf Flambard or Passeflambard. But on this spot we have nothing to do with his infamies, but only to compare his real or alleged architectural works at two places. It was he that built the noblest work of Romanesque architecture, the mighty nave of Durham. He built it as a direct continuation in a more ornamented form of the choir of William of Saint-Calais, despising the plainer and feebler work which the monks had meanwhile done in the transepts. This is the point which gives his name a special interest in connexion with Christchurch. We need not argue as to the exact nature of his connexion with the place, whether he was ever its ecclesiastical head by the title of Dean or any other. In some character or other, it seems clear, he had authority at Twinham which enabled him to pull down and to build up. Twinham, we are told, must then have looked more like Glendalough or Clonmacnois than like anything which we are used to in England. Besides the principal church, there were nine others in the churchyard, as well as the houses of the canons. All these Flambard swept away. He built new prebendal houses, and, if we rightly understand the story, he made ten small churches give way to one great one. Of this building the nave and transepts still remain.

The first thing that strikes us in reading this history is that there is no likeness whatever between the known work of Randolf Flambard at Durham and his alleged work at Christchurch. Waltham, Durham, Dunfermline, and Lindesfarn, all hang together, but Christchurch has nothing to do with any of them. The pillars are wholly different. Instead of the vast channelled columns of Durham, we have rectangular piers set with nook-shafts, according to one of the commonest forms of the style. Both cushioned and voluted capitals, in several varieties, are freely used. The proportions are quite different from those of Durham, the arcade being much lower and the triforium much larger. In fact, there is no kind of likeness between the two. Durham is a great work of real genius. What William of Saint-Calais began, Randolf Flambard appreciated, carried on, and improved. The Romanesque church at Christchurch is good and bold; it has no glaring faults like Gloucester and Tewkesbury; but it is

ordinary work such as may be seen in a great many other
places. It has no special character to awaken any particular interest in its designer. On the whole, it looks
earlier than Durham. But Durham itself, of all places,
teaches us that a building which is earlier in look is not
always earlier in date. Did Randolf Flambard then build
the nave of Christchurch before that of Durham, before
he had been struck with the new forms brought in by
William of Saint-Calais? Or was he the builder simply in
the sense of bearing the cost without troubling himself
personally about the design?

 The lack of a central tower tends to throw the transepts into insignificance, especially as that arrangement
is followed which was so common in Romanesque minsters,
that by which very little projection was given to the eastern and western piers of the lantern, in order to make a
better backing for the stalls, the choir of course occupying
the crossing. The later change of arrangements moved the
choir, as usual, into the eastern limb, leaving the crossing
practically a part of the nave. The rood-screen of this
later arrangement is still standing, and it forms the great
difficulty in the arrangement of the church for modern
purposes. Under this we pass into the Perpendicular
choir, and the effect is singular indeed. We pass from a
minster nave into what seems to be a college chapel. For
the great importance given to the clerestory makes the
pier arches so low that they hardly rise above the canopies,
and go for nothing in the general effect. The high altar
still keeps its steps and its magnificent reredos. Less
vast than those of Winchester and Saint Albans, it shows
more real grace in its sculptured representation of the
Root of Jesse, the fellow of that which has been defaced
in Saint Cuthberht's church at Wells, and of the kindred
work in glass in the east window at Dorchester. North
of the altar stands the stately shrine, doubtless the ceno-
taph, of the martyred Margaret of Salisbury, the last of
the Plantagenets. It is basely burrowed into by modern

tablets, and balanced on the south side of the altar by one of the most grotesque instances of the monumental bad taste of later times.

The ancient foundation of secular canons, with their seal ' Sigillum Ecclesiæ Trinitatis de Toinham,' gave way, about 1150, as in so many other places, to a body of regular or Austin canons. Christchurch remained a priory of that order till the Dissolution, when, among the buildings set down as ' superfluous,' we find ' the church, a cloister, dormytary, chaptrehouse, frayter, infirmary, the subpriours lodging too the utter cloister and galery, the chapell in the same cloister, and all the houses thereunto adjoyning.' The lead of the church and cloister, besides abundance of gold and silver plate, and two of the seven bells, were reserved for the King's Majesty, five being left for the parish. This might suggest that Christchurch was an example of a divided church, and that the ' church ' referred to in the above extract means the eastern part only; but the arrangements of the interior do not confirm this idea. The rood-screen is palpably a rood-screen and not a reredos. But it is of course possible that a parish reredos may have stood across the western arch of the lantern.

Besides the minster, the twelfth-century house by the river must not be forgotten. A Romanesque minster is at least not a rarity; a house of that date and style is. This at Christchurch, though unroofed, is nearly perfect, and it would hold a worthy place among the kindred remains at Lincoln, Dol, and Bury Saint Edmunds. It is however much to be wished that it were cleared from the disfiguring ivy which hides nearly every detail.

CARISBROOKE.

1871.

THE Isle of Wight has more claim to be made the subject of a distinct history than many much larger districts. First and foremost, it is a distinct island, and not merely so many square miles of the isle of Britain. Its history has of course always stood in the closest relations of connexion and dependence towards the history of the greater island; still it is not simply part of it. It distinctly has a history, while one can hardly say that Bedfordshire, for instance, has any. Politically part of England, yet not physically part of Britain, it has been for ages included in one of the territorial divisions of England, yet it still keeps a separate being. The Isle of Wight is, for most civil purposes, part of the county of Southampton, yet no one would say of a man who lives in the Isle of Wight that he lives in Hampshire. In the early days of English occupation the island formed the centre of a small but distinct kingdom, which spread itself also over a part of the adjacent island; a small strip of what is now the mainland of Hampshire formed part of the little realm of Wight, just like the *Peraia* held by many of the Greek insular cities on the neighbouring coasts of Thrace or Asia. Indeed the phrase of 'overers,' applied by the natives of the island to immigrants from Britain, expresses pretty much the same idea as the Greek word. Wight too has another point of interest in our earliest history. It was one of the two settlements of that tribe which, though the smallest in number, formed the vanguard of the Teutonic invasion, and led the way for the greater settlements of the Angles and Saxons. For the original Teutonic settlers of Wight, like those of Kent, were of the mysterious race of the Jutes. 'Of Iotan comon Cantwara and Wihtwara,' and the Jutish name was remembered, both in the island and in its *Peraia*, as late as the days of Florence of Worcester, who places the death of William Rufus 'in Jutarum provincia.' But while the Jutish settlement in Kent was not only independent, but was the very beginning of English conquest before Angles or Saxons made any permanent settlement, the Jutish settlement in Wight always appears as more or less dependent on the great Saxon settlement on the neighbouring mainland. The first English princes of Wight, Stuf and Wihtgar, appear in the story of the first conquest as the nephews of the actual conquerors, Cerdic and Cynric, and as holding the island by their grant. As Cynric was the son of Cerdic, the words, if they are to be taken literally, would mean that Stuf and Wihtgar were nephews of Cynric and great-nephews of Cerdic. But it is more likely that the expression is somewhat lax, and that, as Asser understood the passage, they were the nephews of Cerdic and the first cousins of Cynric. We here probably find the key to the fact of a Jutish settlement under Saxon supremacy. The Jutish chieftains were doubtless the sisters' sons of the Saxon Ealdorman; for in early times it was always the sister's son, the surest kinsman of all, who was first in the affections and most closely attached to the fortunes of his uncle. Stuf and Wihtgar had played their part in the conquest of the mainland, and they were rewarded by a grant of the island after the conquest in the bloody fight of Wihtgaresburh, a name which we shall presently discuss. There the Chronicles tell us that many Britons were slain, and Asser gives some curious though meagre details of the conquest. The fight was in his eyes a final massacre of the few Britons who remained in the island, the rest

having either died in earlier fights or sought shelter
elsewhere. It is clear that he looked on the conquest
of Wight as a conquest which carried with it the utter
extermination of the vanquished.

The history of the little state thus formed records
more than one interesting revolution. Among the wars
of the seventh century, Wulfhere of Mercia overran the
island, and transferred it, or rather the allegiance of its
dependent king, from Wessex to the South-Saxon Æthel-
wealh. Fast upon this follows the pathetic story of the
conquest of the island by Ceadwalla, of the sentence
of extermination pronounced by the fierce catechumen
against the heathen islanders, and of the deliverance of
at least a portion of them by the intercession of Bishop
Wilfrith. The whole is crowned by the affecting tale of
the two young Æthelings doomed to death by the fero-
cious conqueror, but whom the good Abbot Cyneberht
obtains leave at least to teach and baptize before they
die. The story is in itself one of the most touching in
our early history; it also gives us another phase of the
ubiquitous Wilfrith, who appears as an apostle alike in
Northumberland, Sussex, Friesland, and lastly in Wight.
But the historic importance of the story is its showing
that, while the Jutes of Kent were the first, the Jutes
of Wight were the last, among the English tribes to
accept the Christian religion. The South-Saxons were
the latest converts on the mainland; the Jutes of Wight
were the last of all. Their conversion was an appendage
to the conversion of the South-Saxons; Wilfrith was
their apostle, and it might have been expected that the
island would have remained part of the South-Saxon
diocese. But the invariable rule by which ecclesiastical
divisions followed the civil divisions of the time prevailed here also, and Wight, as a conquest of the West-
Saxon Ceadwalla, has ever since remained part of the
West-Saxon diocese of Winchester.

It is a thing to be noticed that, while Kent was the

first part of England to embrace Christianity, the neighbouring land of Sussex and the kindred land of Wight should be the latest of all. The explanation perhaps is to be found in the insular position of Wight, in the position, if not insular, at least isolated, of Sussex, with its inhabited districts cut off from the rest of Britain by the great *Andredesweald*. The long heathenism of Wight is indeed more remarkable than that of Sussex. Sussex, though part of the mainland, was really more isolated than Wight, which seems designed as the highway between Wessex and Northern Gaul. It is strange to conceive Thunder and Woden being still worshipped in the island more than a generation after Winchester had become a Christian city. The fusion of Briton and Englishman in the West had begun, Glastonbury had already become a common sanctuary of the two races, while the Jutes of Wight still remained untouched by the faith which was now professed uninterruptedly from Thanet to Scilly. The further question arises, how far the plan of extermination designed by Ceadwalla was really carried out, and how far the Jutish population— save those who were spared to form the patrimony of Wilfrith—made way at this time for Saxon immigrants.

With the West-Saxon conquest the history of the island as a separate state of course comes to an end. But Wight makes its full share of contributions to English history in various ages. In the eleventh century it is spoken of over and over again, very often as a place of passage between Britain and Gaul. Æthelred tarried there on his flight to Normandy, and William appears there also at two important times in the last years of his reign. There it was that he arrested his brother Odo, who was himself using the island as a highway between England and Rome. And there it was that the Conqueror himself tarried on his last voyage from England to Normandy, while his last taxation of England was gathering in. In every expedition which touched southern England, whether it was Godwine who came to deliver England, or Tostig who came to ravage it, the Isle of Wight commonly plays its part in the course of the campaign. In later history again the island is not uncommonly mentioned. In the fifteenth century the kingdom of Stuf and Wihtgar is said to have been revived in favour of Henry Beauchamp, Duke of Warwick. But it is in the seventeenth century that the island wins its highest historical interest in the popular mind, through the captivity of Charles the First in the castle of Carisbrooke.

But the history of Carisbrooke is far from being confined to the seventeenth century. It is in fact the history of the island; its history, as recorded both in written annals and in existing remains, goes back to the earliest times when we have any notice of Wight itself. The general aspect of the place is striking. Two opposite heights of no great positive elevation, and overtopped again by loftier hills, are crowned severally by the castle and the church, of both of which we shall have to speak again. It is in the valley between the two that the remains of the earliest surviving building in the island may still be seen. These are the large remains of a Roman house, laid open not many years since, and which seems to divide the attention of visitors with the later buildings on either side of them. The position is one which sets one thinking on the different motives by which men in different ages have been guided in the choice of sites for their dwellings. In a purely warlike age a lofty site was desirable. The Gaulish settlement which so often grew into a Roman town, the castle of the Norman invader, or indeed of the military chief of any kind, was set by preference on a hill-top. But till very modern times, till the sense of the picturesque and the wish to obtain a view began to have an influence in such matters, the purely peaceful dwelling of a more peaceful time was placed by preference in spots which show that warmth and shelter were the chief objects. The Roman villa, the British bishopric, the Cistercian monastery, the mediæval manor house, all follow this same law. The Roman house at Carisbrooke is placed where no Norman baron would ever have placed his castle, where no modern seeker after the picturesque would ever think of placing either palace or cottage. It stands at the very bottom of the dell, commanding no view of any kind; but then to command a view was one of the last things which were likely to come into the mind of its builders. To special students of Roman antiquity the remains are valuable as what has been described as a first-rate example of a second-rate class. The walls remain throughout a little way above the ground; the rooms can all be traced, as well as those arrangements for warmth and cleanliness which the Romans never forgot; there is a perfect store of pavements, from the very plainest type to one of considerable richness. But to the student of English history the house has, like all other Roman remains, a higher interest than any which the study of the Roman antiquities themselves can supply. The single villa at Carisbrooke, like the desolate walls of Anderida, like the varied remains of Uriconium, stands as one of the memorials of English conquest, as one of the signs of that utter havoc and destruction which alone caused England to be England. We read in our Chronicles ' Her Cerdic and Cynric genamon Wihte ealand and ofslogon feala men on Wihtgarasbyrg.' Here we see before our eyes part of the process. In the eyes of the first English invaders a Roman house, with all the appendages of a civilization which they did not understand, was a thing to be swept away at once if the needs of warfare called for so doing. In any other case it was a thing to be left to fall to pieces of itself as it might happen. To dwell in the Roman house no more came into their heads than to adopt the Roman religion or to learn the Roman language. Had it been otherwise, had the slaughter and havoc wrought by our fathers been less complete, Englishmen would not have remained Englishmen, and Britain would never have become England.

There seems no kind of reason to doubt that Carisbrooke is the site of the battle of 530 which made Wight English. The present castle, we may fairly infer, represents the 'burh' which then yielded to the English conquerors, and which witnessed the slaughter of so many men at their hands. Nor can we doubt that the same place, whether the same exact spot or not, is meant in the entry under the year 544 which records the death and burial of Wihtgar. But what are we to make of the name which appears in so many shapes, and which seems so closely connected with that of the hero himself? We read of *Wihtgaras byrg, Wihtgara byrig, Wiht garæsbyrg, Wihtgares byri, Witgaresburcg, Witgaresbrig, Gwihtgaraburhg.* The varieties of the latter half of the name are of no impörtance, except so far as they illustrate the process by which *burh* or *byrig* has, in this and in other names, got changed into *brook* and *bridge.* The modern name *Carisbrooke* doubtless comes, by dropping the first syllable, as in the modern form of Thessalonica, from the form *Wihtgaresburh.* But the real difficulty is as to the middle part of the word. The form *Wihtgaresburh* (*Wihtgari castrum*) seems to be a later form, as it is found only in the latest manuscript of the Chronicle and in Henry of Huntingdon. This form would be perfectly intelligible, if we could only believe that the conqueror of the island bore its name. If the conqueror of Wight really was named 'the spear of Wight,' it is plain that he must have taken the name after the conquest. But in none of the earlier forms do we find the unmistakable singular genitive *es*, while in some we seem to get the plural genitive in *a*. It has been thought that *Wihtgaraburh* is a form analogous to *Cantwaraburh, Canterbury,* that *Wihtgaresburh* is a corruption, and that the hero Wihtgar has been simply inferred from this corrupted form. But *gara* is not *wara*—*Cantwaraburh* is the borough of Kentish *men*; *Wihtgaraburh* would rather be the borough of the Wightish *spears*. Mr. Earle doubtingly suggests that *gar* may be the Welsh *caer*. The addition of an English form of the same meaning would be no great wonder, if any parallel formation could be found. But surely the British form would be *Caergwiht*, not *Gwihtcaer*; nor can we remember any name in which *caer* is retained in English. Winchester is not *Wentgaraburh*. And Asser, from whom we might have looked for the British form of the name, gives us nothing nearer than *Gwihtgaraburhg*, where the *gw* is a clear attempt to give the name something of the Welsh sound, but where *caer* has left no trace at all. We must be content to leave the matter unsettled; only, while looking at the ruins of the Roman house, we would fain believe in a personal Stuf and Wihtgar as its destroyers.

The later antiquities of Carisbrooke are the church and the castle. Oddly enough, there is no distinct mention of either in Domesday, but the church probably lurks under the entry of that of *Bovecome*, Bowcombe, and the castle under that of *Alwinestone*. We can hardly doubt that it contained the 'regia aula' which beheld the arrest of Odo. The island was granted by the Conqueror to William Fitz-Osbern, but the local notion of a 'conquest' of the Isle by the Earl of Hereford comes only from a blundering cartulary, which certainly says that William Fitz-Osbern 'conquisivit insulam Vectam tempore quo dictus Willelmus Bastardus conquisivit terram Angliæ.' But the trustworthiness of the document may be judged of by its giving Earl William, instead of his real and well-known sons William and Roger, two imaginary sons John and Richard, who are made to die before their father. Most likely, 'conquisivit' was used merely in the legal sense of 'purchased,' and most likely not without a play upon the word.

The priory of Carisbrooke is always said to have been founded by Earl William, but no evidence of the fact is shown. It seems however to have been one of the churches which were granted by him to the abbey of Lire in the diocese of Evreux of his own foundation. A cell or dependent house arose at Carisbrooke, which lasted till the suppression of alien priories under Henry the Fifth. The remains are worth studying, as an example of monastic arrangements on the smallest scale. The church is purely parochial in its type, with a double nave, after a pattern common in the island. The choir was single, projecting from the northern body. It is said to have been pulled down by the famous Walsingham in Elizabeth's time, and its loss sadly mars both the appearance and the arrangements of the building. Till however it can be rebuilt in its full proportions, it is better to leave it alone than to ruin the whole thing by some imperfect substitute. On the north side stood a small cloister, which did not take up the whole length of the nave, a gateway ranging with its west wall. The tower, of Perpendicular date, is locally held to rival those of the West of England. But any one who knows either the West or the East will not set much store by it, except as a curious mixture of two types. It suggests the idea of a South-Welsh military tower, with the squarest and narrowest of belfry-windows, trying to bring in something of the more elaborate type in its buttresses and parapet. Much of singularity, something even of stateliness, is the result; but it cannot be called a good work of art.

On the whole Carisbrooke supplies several objects to examine and muse over, besides the donkey who turns the wheel, and the window where legend fixes the sticking fast of Charles the First.

MERTON PRIORY.

1873.

A MONASTIC ruin, if ruin is exactly the word in the case of which we speak, in what may now pass as a London suburb has something almost more incongruous about it than if it stood in the heart of London itself. London— at any rate the proper London with its daughter Westminster—is, after all, an ancient city; it is mainly owing to the comparatively recent fire that it does not proclaim its antiquity as clearly as Chester or York. London has been going on in one shape or another at least from the days of Aulus Plautius; many will doubtless be offended if we are not prepared to place its beginnings any number of thousand years earlier. It has gone on since that time, constantly changing, but changing in that kind of way which is the surest mark of permanence. London differs now from the London of William and the London of Constantine, as a modern city must differ from a mediæval and a Roman city. But the likeness at all those times is much stronger than the unlikeness; the London of all those dates agrees in being a city and one of the chief cities of Britain. With the suburbs of London, and with the neighbourhood of London generally, the case is quite different. No part of England changes more, and it changes at once gradually and suddenly. Till quite lately a great part of Surrey must have been one of the wildest parts of England; parts of it are so still. Large districts look as if they had been untouched by man's hand during all the time from the battle of Wimbledon—that fight of Ceawlin and Æthelberht which added Surrey to the West-Saxon realm—till people began to build villas a few years back. The passenger who goes from London to Basingstoke or from London to Reading by the Surrey route, goes through a land wilder than anything that he will see again till he gets to the New Forest, wilder perhaps than anything that he will see till he gets to Dartmoor. The incongruity of a piece of wild heath, with spick and span houses scattered here and there, is something like the process which goes on at Bournemouth, where every man cuts down so much of the wood as is needful for the site of his house, and leaves the trees growing ready made in his garden. One feature of the country not the least striking to the passer-by is that, at one stage of his journey, he goes through a district which seems to be inhabited by dead people only. Nearer again to London, at Wimbledon, Tooting, Streatham, Clapham, and in all that district, we are still struck by the unenclosed lands, the commons, some of them more or less famous. Open spaces of this kind are certainly more common round London than in most parts of England, and when surrounded by houses, they have a distinctly suburban character which is seldom seen elsewhere. Near Wakefield there is something of the kind, a large open space surrounded by houses of considerable size and considerable age, and the feeling which it at once suggests is that we have been suddenly moved into the neighbourhood of London. All this shows that the country was never fully reclaimed till it became suburban; it could never have had the look of an ordinary agricultural or grazing district; it passed from a more natural state into a more artificial one. Still here and there, among the scattered dwellings of greater size, among the respectable houses of a century back and the prim villas of our own time, we come upon remains—survivals one might almost call them—of the old villages, as they stood before they became thoroughly suburban. And among them, in a spot jammed in in a strange way by roads and railways, in a low and certainly not attractive spot, we find the remains of a house which at once suggests a long string of historic memories, the priory of Austin canons of Merton.

The name of Merton, *Merantún, Meretún*, appears in our history long before the foundation of the priory. This last dates only from the reign of Henry the First, but we first hear of Merton in the eighth century. It was the scene of that remarkable story of the death of Cynewulf which so strongly brings out the old institution of the *comitatus*, the personal tie which bound a man to his lord, and which, as in this case, was often held more binding than the common duty to the law and to the King as the common head of the state. In this story Cynewulf is killed by his kinsman, the banished Ætheling Cyneheard, and his following, and the King's death is avenged by his own following on his murderer. The King's men show all zeal and loyalty; but their feeling is evidently one of attachment to their own personal lord rather than to the head of the state. The men of the outlawed Ætheling are as faithful to him as the King's men are to the King, and each side seems to make it a point of honour to refuse all offers made by the other. Each side alike fights to the death, and on each side one wounded man only escapes with life. Of the King's men a British hostage only survives; he may well have had less loyalty than his fellows to the West-Saxon king, who had fought many fights with his countrymen. In the case of the one who escaped on the Ætheling's side the personal tie again comes in in another shape. The one man who was spared was the godson of the Ealdorman Osric, the leader of the King's party, and he owed his life to that spiritual kindred. In the next century, in 871, Merton was the scene of one of the battles of Æthelred and Ælfred, one of those puzzling stories in which we read that the Danes were put to flight, and yet that they kept possession of the place of slaughter. This seeming contradiction has some-

times been turned against the credibility of the Chronicles.
Yet it is quite possible that the Danes, every man of them
a trained soldier, who had no homes and no hope except
in keeping together, might give way before an impetu-
ous charge of the raw English levies, and yet be able
to recover themselves while the momentary victors were
scattered abroad, while some perhaps, in the blind impulse
of victory, were already beginning to go to their own
homes. When Merton was the scene of events which
stand out in our annals like these, it is remarkable that
its name is hardly ever found in the ancient charters—
only once, as far as we can find, in an alleged charter
of Eadgar which Mr. Kemble marks as spurious. The
foundation of the priory in 1117 brought the place into
more importance. One Gilbert Norman—possibly Gilbert
son of Northman—Sheriff of Surrey, is called the founder;
but in the foundation charter of Henry the First no
founder is spoken of but the King himself. This however may only be by the same courtly fiction by which
Edward the Second and Queen Elizabeth are held to have
been the founders of Oriel and Jesus College respec-
tively. In the time of its first prior, Robert, who bears
the surname of Bayle, the house of the canons of Merton
became for a while the dwelling-place of a guest and
scholar who was to win himself a name far beyond the
bounds of Merton or of England. Thomas of London,
the son of Gilbert of Rouen and Rohesia of Caen, the
future Chancellor and Archbishop, came in his boyhood
to learn the first beginnings of knowledge at Merton,
before he went on to his more matured studies at Paris,
Auxerre, and Bologna. And, according to the legend, it
was at Merton that the future greatness of the son was
revealed to the father. William Fitz-Stephen tells us
how Gilbert, coming to see his child, amazed and scandalized Prior Robert by falling down before him. The
Prior rebuked the mad old man who paid to his own son
the honour which his son should have paid to him. But

Gilbert, so the tale runs, knew better, and privately told the Prior that he bowed to one who would one day be great in the eyes of the Lord.

But it is in the thirteenth century that Merton plays its most important part in the history of England. There are no Merton Annals that we know of, but the annals of other houses contain several entries of local Merton matters, besides their notices of events happening at Merton which concerned the whole kingdom. And moreover Merton was the place of an event which was the indirect cause of great results. If Merton was the seat of the early learning of Thomas in days when Oxford was not a seat of learning at all, it was also the birthplace of a man who did more than any other to make Oxford a seat of learning. At Merton, where Ælfred fought a battle and where Walter of Merton was born, the real and the imaginary founder of the collegiate system in Oxford are in a manner brought face to face. But during this century events connected with Merton, both local and general, press fast upon us. In 1222 the Dunstable Annals tell us that the tower fell, doubtless from the same cause which brought down so many towers in those days and that of Chichester in our own. In 1230 a Bishop of Llandaff, Elias of Radnor, treasurer of Hereford, was consecrated at Merton by the obscure Archbishop Richard Grant, who covers the short time between the great names of Stephen Langton and Edmund Rich. The monks of Christ Church, as we are pointedly told, did not fail to protest against this breach of privileges of the metropolitan church. Two years later the priory of Merton finds its way into the general stream of English history. Then it was that the famous Hubert de Burgh, charged with all manner of crimes, took shelter and hid himself all trembling among the canons—' ad ecclesiam Meritoniæ fugit inter canonicos pavidus delitescens,' says Roger of Wendover. Then King Henry bade the Mayor of London to march at the head of the citizens and seize Hubert and bring him before them alive or dead. Set out they did, an army—it is called *exercitus*—of twenty thousand; but, while they were on their way, the Earl of Chester wisely suggested to the King that such a force, when once got together, might be dangerous ('si talem excitaret seditionem in vulgo irrationabili et fatuo, posset rex timere ne seditionem semel inchoatam sedare non valeret cum vellet'). So the citizens marched back again, and the rest of the history of Hubert is in no way connected with Merton.

In the course of the same century Merton was the scene of two important meetings, a great Council of the realm, and a Synod of the Church. The Council of Merton in 1236 was an assembly whose acts won the approval of Matthew Paris; and it is ever famous for the answer of the barons, which has been cut short into the phrase which has almost passed into a proverb—'nolumus leges Angliæ mutare.' The saying is perhaps sometimes quoted by people who do not remember what was the question at issue. It was no other than the proposal to make the law of England agree with the canon and civil law—that is to say, speaking generally, with the law of the rest of Christendom,—in allowing children born before wedlock to be made legitimate by a subsequent marriage. There is an extant letter of Robert Grosseteste, in which he pours forth a flood of scriptural and canonical argument on the point. But the barons were not to be moved, and this has ever since been one of the points in which English law stands by itself. The other assembly of Merton was a purely ecclesiastical one, held in 1258 by Archbishop Boniface of Savoy, who had by that time tamed down a little from the days, eight years before, when he had held his wonderful visitation of Saint Bartholomew's priory. He had now changed into a vigorous asserter of ecclesiastical discipline and ecclesiastical rights, and in the canons which he put forth at Merton the immunities of the Church are strongly stated, and the secular power in all its forms, from the King downwards, is strictly taken to task for various breaches of alleged ecclesiastical rights.

A place which has seen all this, a place which so closely connects itself with the developement and the special insular character of the English law, is certainly entitled to rank high among the historic spots of England. But we cannot say that the place is now particularly impressive. We could have wished to see some stately remains of the priory itself, some castle or royal hall, or, better still, some untouched piece of hill and plain on which we could trace out the battle-field of Ælfred. But the roads, the railways, the factories, the general atmosphere of a somewhat mean suburban village, are less favourable for research and contemplation than the hillside of Assandún or the keep and hall of Kenilworth. Yet Merton priory, a rich foundation, whose income at the time of the Dissolution was over a thousand pounds yearly, has by no means vanished without leaving traces of itself. No remains that we could see of the church or of the domestic buildings of the house are left, but the wall which enclosed the monastic precinct is still nearly perfect; we suspect that it was quite perfect till the coming of the railways. And the preservation of this particular trace of the ancient building is not without its effect. Though, as far as we can make out, there is positively nothing to be studied within the walls, yet there is something striking in finding the old precinct in this way still fenced off; it is a reminder which is quite as speaking as any mere fragment of the church or monastery could have been. And the old associations of the place are not quite forgotten. The priory, exalted as usual into an abbey, has left its name on more than one point of local nomenclature, and vague traditions still hang about of its having been the scene of events beyond the common. Still the old associations are, perhaps not unnaturally, not quite so strong as some later ones. Merton has been the dwelling-place of a modern hero. Nelson once lived there, and several names of streets and such like places remind the visitor of the fact. And after all the latest associations of Merton are not incongruous with those which are all but the earliest. If we can conceive the great king who fought at Merton feeling as it were abashed in the presence of a man whose real glory has been so shamelessly transferred to himself, the latest associations of Merton connect his name with one who really carried out a work which he began. The fictitious deeds of Ælfred may be forgotten in the presence of the real. A place which beheld the exploits, though on another element, of the first founder of the English navy was no unfit dwelling-place for the man who raised the English navy to its highest pitch of glory. On a spot where the two names of Ælfred and Nelson meet together, we may well hail one of the many cycles which bind the earliest and the latest stages of English history together.

MERCIA

LINDUM COLONIA.

[Read before the Lincolnshire Architectural Society at Grantham, June 16, 1875. I have here also worked in some matter from an earlier article in the 'Saturday Review,' October 1, 1870.]

THE last time that I was called on to speak to a gathering of this kind on a matter of local history, it was in a part of England far away from that in which we are now met. When the Archæological Institute held its meeting two years back in the city of Exeter, it fell to my lot to speak of the place of that city in the general history of England. I am now bidden to deal in somewhat the same way with the shire in which I now stand, and with the famous city which is its capital. Let no one grudge, if, in dealing with such a subject, I find more to say about the capital than about the shire at large. Let me not be thought to disparage a land which fills so great a place in our history, and whose records in the great Survey are so full of legal information and of personal interest. I will readily believe that Henry of Huntingdon, or the poet whom he quotes, spoke of the shire at large, and not of the city only, when he said :—

Testis Lincoliæ gens infinita decore.

As he makes the shire a partaker in the glories of the city and its bishopric, as he speaks of the seven provinces which are subject to the province whose head is Lincoln, I trust that no part of the shire will look on itself as being wholly shut out from anything that I may say of the city itself. The history of the shire and of its capital

cannot be separated; the shire is a body of which the
capital is the head. But to one who has studied Lincoln
city carefully through its whole length—breadth is in
this case a matter of less importance—but who has
studied no other part of the shire with the same attention,
and to whom large parts of it are altogether unknown,
the city itself cannot fail to be the foremost object in
dealing with such a theme.

Forgive me then, if, while I stand in Grantham for
the first time, my heart is still in Lincoln, where I have
lately been tarrying, not for the first time. The city too
gives me the one thread which enables me to carry back
my tale to the earliest days of recorded history, and even
to days before recorded history. With Celtic Coritani you,
Angles and Danes of Lindesey, Kesteven, and Holland,
have nothing in common save the possession of the soil
which your forefathers wrested from them. But the city
has kept up its continuous being through Roman, English,
Danish, and Norman conquests. Lincoln still in its name
proclaims itself one with Roman Lindum—that Lindum in
the isle of Britain which has a namesake in distant Kilikia
—that Lindum of the Coritani which has a namesake in
the isle of Britain at some unfixed spot among the Damnii.
But it is the ending of the English name which is characteristic of the Lindum with which we deal, an ending
which it shares with no other English town or village, and,
as far as I remember, with but one other spot throughout
the whole dominion of Rome. Our endless *chèsters* everywhere proclaim the fact of their former Roman occupation.
But they proclaim it by the mouths of English destroyers,
or restorers; they proclaim it by the name given to it by
foreign conquerors, not by any title which the place bore
while the rule of Rome lasted. It is otherwise with the
unique name of *Lincoln*. The ending of that name proclaims the rank which Lindum held among Roman cities;
it is surely enough to tell us, even if the geographer of
Ravenna had failed to set it down in writing, that

Lindum was a colony of Rome, no less than the greater city by the Rhine, the colony of Agrippina. Köln and Lincoln are cities kindred in origin and name; only, while the city by the Rhine has lost her earlier name and proclaims herself simply as the Roman *Colonia*, the city by the Witham keeps her earlier name as well as the title of her Roman rank, and proclaims herself through the whole of her long history as the Colony of Lindum.

Coming, as by some license of speech I may be said to have come, from Exeter to Lincoln, it comes naturally to me to point out some points of likeness and unlikeness between the history of the two cities and the two shires of which they were the heads. In the history of the shires there is little to be pointed out but the broadest contrasts; in the history of the cities, among many contrasts, there are some striking points of likeness. The names of the shires and the cities tell their own story. Lincoln has ever been so thoroughly the Colony that no one has ever ventured to add to it any of the common endings of the name of an English town. London herself, the Augusta by the Thames, appears as *Lundenwic* and *Lundenburh*, but Lindum never put on any such ending as *wic* or *burh*, or even *ceaster*, like the Damnonian city with which we are comparing it. *Caerloitchoit* might well have become *Lincaster*, to match *Exeter* and a crowd of others; but the name of the Colony stood its ground. The name of Exeter, in short, follows the rule, while that of Lincoln is an exception. The explanation of the difference may well be that Lincoln became English in an early stage of English conquest, while Roman memories were still fresh, and when Lindum was still remembered as the Colony. But at Exeter, an English conquest of so much later date, purely Roman memories had died away under the rule of independent Damnonian kings; Isca was, like every other Roman site throughout the land, a *chester*; but there was nothing, as there was at Lindum, to mark it out from a crowd of other *chesters.* Lindum was the conquest of heathen Englishmen in days when Britain had hardly ceased to be Roman; Isca was the conquest of Christian Englishmen after the Briton had fallen back upon his own tongue and his own national being.

If we turn to the names of the two shires, we learn the same lesson in another shape. Damnonia has never ceased to be Damnonia. The land still keeps its name under the slightly corrupted form of *Defenascir, Devonshire;* it had the privilege, shared only by kingdoms or by districts whose special character is very strongly marked, of keeping a gentile adjective. The Chronicles indeed speak of a lady of Northampton, Cnut's earlier Ælfgifu, as *Hamptonish;* but in modern English we could hardly speak of *Lincolnish.* But, as we speak of English, Scottish, Irish, and Kentish, so we speak of Cornish, and so we once spoke of *Devenish.* I am not ready at this moment with an instance of the current use of the word; but it exists as a surname, and that is enough. But while the Damnonii still keep their being, we shall seek in vain for the Coritani. They have left no trace in the name either of the shire as a whole or of any of its ridings. I trust no one will start at the word *riding,* as if I were using a word here which is in place only on the other side of the Humber. Every one who knows his Domesday must know that the name *trithing,* corruptedly *riding,* belongs by as good a right to the three divisions of Lincolnshire as to the three divisions of Yorkshire, though it is hardly in place when it is applied to the twofold divisions of Cork and Tipperary. But neither shire nor riding keeps any sign of the Briton. The later name of the shire comes straight from the English name of the city. The name which once belonged to the whole shire, but which now belongs only to its north riding, comes independently from the Roman name. *Lindesey, Lindesig,* which in Domesday alternates with *Lincoleshire* as the general name, is, I need not say, simply the island of Lindum. The name of the south riding speaks for itself: Holland, *Hollandia cismarina*, is so called for exactly the same reason as *Hollandia transmarina*, the land like to it in name and nature beyond the sea. Of Kesteven I can say nothing; I shall be glad of a local interpreter. But he must be a daring etymologist who can see in it either the Coritani or any other class of Welshmen. The utter vanishing of the British names is a sign of the utter vanishing of the British people. The British names of districts, as a rule, live on only where a large British element in the people has lived on. The exceptions are such as prove the rule. The Jutish island of Wight, Vectis, kept its name, because it was a mere island, much as rivers and great cities kept their name. Kent too, the greater Jutish realm, kept its name. And why? Kent was the first conquest. If we accept the tale which makes the English Conquest to be immediately caused by the invitation of a British prince, the invaders had had dealings with the land of Kent before their actual settlement in it. They must have been familiar with the name of the Cantii in a way in which the invaders of this part of England are not likely to have been with the name of the Coritani. And, more than this, Kent is not merely the name of a people, but the name of a district. There is the land of Cantium as well as the people of the Cantii. But, though there were Coritani, we hear nothing of any land of Coritania. The Damnonian name then lived on, because the Damnonian people were not wholly swept away. The Cantii were swept away, but they had so thoroughly given their name to the land that from the land it passed to a new race of Kentishmen, the *Cantwaru* of our own blood. The Coritani were swept away also, and their name perished with them.

To turn again to the cities, another point of difference between Exeter and Lincoln suggests itself. Lincoln is the more strictly Roman of the two. At Lincoln we may speak with perfect strictness of Roman origin, a form of words which at Exeter would be out of place. For there is every reason to think that the Lincoln that now is, the Colony of Lindum, was strictly a creation of the Roman conquerors. The Roman site was not the British site. Lincoln, as every one knows who has seen it at all, is remarkable for its position. It is, like Laon, a city set on a hill. Its minster is emphatically the visible church. It stands on a ridge of ground which forms the backbone, not only of Lincolnshire but of all eastern England, and which, though never reaching any great positive height, is still high enough to be very conspicuous in a land where mole-hills might pass for mountains. At this point it dips to the south suddenly and steeply, and rises again at a little distance. This dip is the valley of the river Witham, which flows— if the rivers of eastern England can be said to flow— at the base of the hill, and it gives Lincoln its peculiar character. As at Laon, the oldest quarters, with the minster and the castle, stand on the height; but at Laon the city has ever remained on the height, while its suburbs lie detached at the foot, and the slope of the hill itself remains uncovered by houses. At Lincoln, on the other hand, the city has spread itself continuously downwards, covering the steep sides of the hill as well as the level ground at its foot, and spreading its suburbs far beyond the sluggish stream of the Witham. The original Lindum stood wholly on the brow of the hill. Portions of its walls remain in several places, and the Roman road passing through the city to the north along the ridge of the hill is still spanned by the massive Roman arch which formed the northern gate of Lindum. But this ancient relic goes by the name of the *New*port *Gate*,—surely, if a Teutonic synonym is needed, it should be *Bar*; the ancient road too is known as the *New* Street, and outside the gate to the north may be traced the lines of an earlier settlement, which there can be little doubt marks the original British town, whose site was changed by the conquerors to a point which gave them the full advantage of the steepness of the hill. Thus the Colony of Lindum arose, and it has left, in the gate and in the portions of its wall which are still above ground, larger traces of itself than most of the Roman towns in Britain. But it is well to notice that to the north, where its remains chiefly survive, they stand now in what may pass as mere suburb, almost as open country. The city in fact has moved southwards, that is, downhill; it began to move downhill even in Roman times. The very small area of the original *chester* was enlarged by a Roman suburb, and that suburb was again enlarged ages later through great historical causes which form the most important chapter in the annals of Lincoln, and which, we are inclined to think, give Lincoln a higher interest than any other city of England.

The exact date of the English conquest of this district it is hopeless to try to fix. We have no record, such as we have of Anderida, of Bath and Gloucester and Cirencester, of the time or the way by which the city passed into the hands of the conquerors. We know not whether they at once took it as a dwelling-place, or whether, like Bath and Chester, it lay for a while ruined and forsaken. Of the process by which central Britain, the lands which went to make up the later Mercian kingdom, came into the hands of the Teutonic invaders we know next to nothing. Legend indeed has something to say about the matter. One of the stories preserved by Henry of Huntingdon makes Teutonic warriors, still in the service of the British prince, overthrow the Picts and Scots in a fight at Stamford, before they turned their arms against their employers and settled themselves in Kent. Another tale, preserved by the so-called Nennius, makes Lindum the burial-place of the British Vortemir, slain, as it would seem, in some of the Kentish battles. Of tales like these we can say nothing. Nor can we trace the course of Anglian settlement in this part of Britain so clearly as we can trace the course of Jutish and Saxon settlement further south.

The Northumbrian, Mercian, and East-Anglian kingdoms have no personal founders like Hengest, Ælle, and Cerdic. Each of them grew up by the union of a number of older and smaller Anglian settlements. Among these we can discern a kingdom of the Southumbrians, which would seem, even as late as the beginning of the eighth century, to have been sometimes ruled by a separate under-king. In 702 Coenred, afterwards head king of the Mercians, became king of the Southumbrians, and his dominions are carefully marked out by the French poet Geoffrey Gaimar, who, here as elsewhere, seems to have written from lost records or traditions:—

> Kenret regna sur Suthumbreis:
> Co est Lindeseye e Holmedene,
> Kestevene e Hoiland e Hestdene;
> Del Humbre tresk en Roteland
> Donrout cel regne, è plus avante.

And within the Southumbrian border we can discern several of those ancient tribe-names which died out before the later division into shires, and some of them have still left their traces in modern nomenclature. There were the Gyrwas, North and South, who appear more than once in Bæda; there were the *Spaldas*, whose name still lives in the town of Spalding, famous both in the real and in the legendary history of the shire. The Gainas, among whom Ælfred found a wife, have left their name to the town of Gainsburgh, where Saint Edmund of East-Anglia took his vengeance on the tyrant Swegen. But above all, we are ever meeting, in general as well as in local history, with the greater name of the *Lindesfaras*, the men of Lindesey, of whom I do not take upon myself to pronounce how often their name takes in the whole shire and how often its northern riding only. This is the most important name of all. It is not only the name that fills the greatest place in history, but it is the one name which forms a tie between the earlier and later state of things.

The English tribe took for themselves, and for their land, the name of the Roman city. The British inhabitants of the district vanished, name and thing; but, name and thing, the Roman city lived on. Its conquerors called themselves the men of Lindum, and their land the isle of Lindum. I doubt if there is another example in England of an English tribe and its district so directly taking its name from a Roman city. The southern Dorchester of the Dorsætan is the nearest case that I can think of; and even there we have not, as in the case of Lindesey and the *Lindesfaras*, a distinct name for the land and for its people. It is plain that there was no Roman town in Britain whose strength and majesty made a deeper impression on our fathers than the Colony of Lindum.

But, even if Lindum lay for a while in ruins, yet the city set on an hill could not have been hid. Its walls, which the Roman, forsaking the earlier site of the Briton, had placed on the very brow of its promontory, if they ever did stand utterly desolate, must, as they rose over the plain like the ghost of the fallen Empire, have set their mark all the more deeply on the minds of the men whose swords had left them without inhabitants. The Norman minster, the Norman castle, the mighty mounds and dykes, the work of our own people, which bear up the fortress of the stranger, had as yet no being, and even no forerunners. But the walls were there, walls speaking of the last days of Roman power, when Theodosius and Stilicho were guarding the land against inroads from the independent Celtic North, and against the more dangerous invaders of the Saxon shore. There were the gates, the massive arch which still abides, while the site of its southern fellow may be still traced on the very brow of the hill. The gate of Lindum may seem poor beside those of Trier, of Aosta, or even of Nîmes, but the gate of the colony may have made as good a show as some of the gates of Rome herself. Within the walls we may call up at pleasure the works of Roman skill, such as the researches of our own day have brought to light beneath the mould of Silchester. We may call up the forum, the basilica, changed perhaps from the heathen hall of judgement into the place of Christian worship, and the temples of Roman or British gods, either standing desolate or themselves consecrated to Christian uses. We may see the columns whose bases have been brought to light but yesterday, standing erect as no column in Britain is now left to stand. We may call up the suburb spreading itself from the southern gate of the city down the slope to the river at its foot. And we may people the land around with some traces at least of those scattered dwellings, rich with the art of bygone times, which the Roman conqueror loved to spread over the face of the conquered land. All this, at Lindum as elsewhere, must have been swept away in the first storm of heathen conquest. We have no song of the taking of Lindum, as we have, in a foreign garb at least, some fragments of the song of the taking of Anderida. We know that the work was done; of the date of the deed, of the name of the doer, we have no record.

Whatever was the fate of the city in the first moment of English conquest, it is certain that, if Lindum ever ceased to be a dwelling-place of man, its time of utter ruin was not long. The abiding Latin name of the gate, the *Nova Porta*, of itself goes far to show that there could have been no long gap between Roman or British and English occupation. While Chester lay forsaken for the three hundred years between Æthelfrith of Northumberland and Æthelflæd of Mercia, Lincoln, if it ever was forsaken, was again inhabited within a few years after the fall of Chester. Our first historical mention of Lindesey and the *Lindesfaras* sets Lincoln before us as an inhabited spot, an English and an heathen city. The first recorded fact in the history of shire and city is its conversion to Christianity in the early years of the seventh century. Paulinus, the apostle of the Northumbrians, was the apostle of the

kindred Southumbrians also. Bæda tells us how the Præ-
fect, as he calls him, of the city, Blecca his name or nick-
name, was the first to embrace the new faith. The words
used, 'præfectus Lindocolinæ civitatis,' connecting him in
such a marked way with the city, would hardly be used of
the ealdorman of the whole tribe. Are we to see in Blecca
simply the king's reeve in the town? or may we venture
to think that Lincoln had already made some steps
towards that municipal independence of which it enjoyed
so high a degree in later times? At all events, Lincoln
now became a Christian city. A church of stone—materials could not be lacking among the ruins of the colony
—was built, its site in the north-western square of the
chester being doubtless marked by that most unworthy
successor which still bears the name of its founder in a
corrupt form. In the days of Bæda that church was
roofless; but, before it thus fell into ruin, it had beheld
the consecration of the southern primate Honorius. Either
now or later, as Domesday witnesses, a church of Saint
Mary arose, the forerunner of the mighty minster of
Remigius and Saint Hugh. The district followed the
city: Lindesey became a Christian land, and crowds of its
people were baptized by Paulinus in the waters of Trent
in the presence of the Bretwalda Eadwine.

I dwell on these details, familiar as they must be
to all in the narrative of Bæda, because they have an
important bearing on the later ecclesiastical and even
political history. In the final settlement of English
kingdoms and English bishoprics, Lindesey became part
of the kingdom of Mercia and of the province of Canterbury. But north of the Humber it was never forgotten
that Lindesey had been won to the faith by a Northumbrian bishop under the auspices of a Northumbrian
king. Long after, in the days of Thomas of Bayeux,
the claim of York to spiritual jurisdiction over Lindesey
was strongly put forward, once at the very moment when
the minster of Remigius stood ready for its hallowing.

The Primate of Northumberland did not dispute the right of the Bishop of Dorchester to dwell where he would, and build what he pleased, in the far-away parts of his vast diocese. But Lindesey was part of the spiritual conquest of Paulinus; if there was to be a Bishop of Lincoln, he, the Primate of York, claimed him as one of the suffragans of his province. Nor was it always by spiritual arms only that the Northern Angles strove to make good their claim to the kindred Southumbrian land. No tale better brings home to us the identity of the Church and the nation in early times, the identity of the ecclesiastical and civil divisions, than the tale of the momentary conquest of Lindesey by Ecgfrith of Northumberland. The conqueror had won a new realm; in his eyes a new realm meant a new diocese. He at once founds a bishopric of Lindesey, and nominates a bishop, whom Archbishop Theodore consecrates without scruple. In the very next year the land is won back to Mercia by the arms of Æthelred. The newly founded bishopric lives on; but its Northumbrian bishop at once, seemingly as a matter of course, goes back to his own land, to receive a Northumbrian see from his own sovereign. Æthelred appoints a Mercian successor and the line of Mercian Bishops of Lindesey begins.

This brings us to a point of instructive likeness between the history of Lincoln and that of Exeter. Up to this stage the history of the two cities has been richer in contrast than in likeness. There never was at Exeter such a time of heathen English rule as there was at Lincoln. There is nothing in the history of the capital of Damnonia which answers to the preaching of Paulinus and the conversion of Blecca in the history of the capital of Lindesey. But there is one point in which the two cities are strikingly alike, a point which strikingly illustrates one characteristic feature of English ecclesiastical history, that custom in which we differed from continental churches, and so strangely agreed with our Celtic neighbours, the custom by which the temporal capital was often in early times not the seat of the bishopstool. As the seat of the Bishop of Damnonia was placed, not at Exeter but at Crediton, so the seat of the Bishop of Lindsey was placed, not at Lincoln but at Sidnaceaster, in that venerable church of Stow-in-Lindesey which still keeps such massive relics of early times. When England began to conform in this matter to the practice of other lands, the chairs of the bishops of what Norman writers scornfully called the villages of Crediton and Dorchester were translated to the walled cities of Exeter and Lincoln. There is thus a wide difference between cities like Lincoln and Exeter, which were chosen as the seats of bishoprics because they were already great and flourishing towns, and cities like Wells and Lichfield, which owe their whole importance to their ecclesiastical foundations, and where the town simply grew up under the shadow of the minster. In a city like Lincoln we are now tempted to look, first at the minster, then at the castle; and, when we have seen the minster and the castle, we are tempted to think that we have seen pretty well all that the city has to show us. In so doing, we pass by something older and greater than minster or castle, namely, the city itself. At Exeter as at Lincoln, the fact that a minster and a castle were in after days planted in each of them is simply a witness to the greatness of the city in days before the minster or the castle was thought of. Lincoln now suggests to us mainly the minster with its memories of bishops, the castle with its memories of kings and earls; but the cause why Lincoln ever came to have bishops or earls is because Lincoln had become great in a day when it had neither. Lincoln had played its part in history—it had risen to importance municipal and military—it had fallen into the hands of the stranger—it had its deliverance recorded in national songs—it had come to be counted as the fourth among the cities of England—before the Conqueror chose the

Roman colony as the site of a Norman castle. It was because Lincoln was already great that Remigius of Fécamp, seeking to move his see to the greatest town of his diocese, forsook the spot where such relics as the barbarism of our own times may have spared of the Roman dykes of Dorchester still look up across the winding Thames to the British fort on Sinodun. But he moved only from one seat of Roman power to another: he fixed his home on the spot where the works of all ages and races, from the rude earthwork of the Briton to the newly-rising castle of the Norman, already looked down on the land beneath them from the brow of the promontory of Lincoln.

From that height we can look forth, as it were, on the course of those great events in our early history of which the height of Lincoln was the centre. When the storm of the great Danish invasion of the ninth century burst upon England, Lindesey was one of the districts where the Scandinavian invader really found himself a home. While Damnonia saw the Dane merely as a passing ravager, while Exeter knew him, sometimes as a successful, sometimes as an unsuccessful, besieger, Lindesey became largely a Danish land, and Lincoln became preeminently a Danish city. In 874 the heathen men took their *winter-settle* in Lindesey at Torkesey. The next year we read how they passed from Lindesey to Repton, and took *winter-settle* there—how they drove out King Burhred, and how, much as Alaric gave the Roman purple to Attalus, they gave the Mercian crown to the unwise king's thegn Ceolwulf—how in 876 Halfdene divided the land of the Northumbrians, and how the next year the host came again into the Mercian land and divided some and gave some to Ceolwulf. Here we have the record of that Danish settlement which gave new lords to so large a part of England, and new names to so many of its towns and villages. Lindesey was among the parts of Mercia which the invaders *dealed* or divided among them. The name of many a Lincolnshire parish bears witness, in the Danish ending *by*, to the presence of the new conquerors, and it often preserves the personal name of the new lord to whom it passed in the division. Osbernby, Hacconby, Asgarby, Thoresby, Grimsby, Hemingby, Ormsby, Ulceby—in which two last we may see the names of men called after the worm and the wolf, the monsters of Northern legend—all live to tell us in how sweeping a way it was that the Northern invaders dealed out the land among themselves, and how truly, like men in elder days, they called the lands after their own names. Yet it was not in Lindesey as it was in two other shires, where, not mere lordships and villages, but towns of note, a local capital and a famous monastery, had to take new names from the new comers. *Northweorthig* became *Deoraby* and *Streoneshalh* became *Whitby*; but the city on the hill remained as unchanged in Danish as it had remained in Anglian hands. The Colony of Lindum was the Colony of Lindum still. In Danish hands, the city kept up its greatness in a new form, a form rich in political instruction, the form of an aristocratic commonwealth bound together with others of its fellows by a federal tie. 'Five boroughs, Leicester and Lincoln and Nottingham, swilk Stamford eke and Derby, where to the Danes erewhile, under Northmen.' So sings the poet of their deliverance by Eadmund the Doer-of-great-deeds; but the work had been already begun by his father. In the long and thrilling tale of English victory, when our annals tells us, year by year, how Eadward the Unconquered and his glorious sister went forth, year after year, winning back some portion of English ground and fortifying some new stronghold against the enemy, one only of the Lincolnshire boroughs, the frontier town of Stamford, is spoken of. In 921 Eadward fortified Towcester, and received the submission of Northampton and all the land to the Welland. One quarter of Stamford lies on the Northamptonshire side of the river; this was now his. The next year he went and fortified his new conquest, the borough on the south side of the river.

Then we read how all the folk in the northern borough bowed to him and sought him to lord. The same year he won Nottingham; Leicester and Derby had already been among the conquests of the Lady of the Mercians. Of Lincoln alone we hear nothing. Yet we cannot believe that, when all the rest of England and of all Britain had bowed to the West-Saxon king, even the proud colony could have stood apart from the rest of the island. And nineteen years later the poet of Eadmund's victory sings how he released the Five Boroughs when they were bowed low in heathen chains. We must believe that Eadward simply received the submission of the Confederate towns and secured their obedience by fortresses, without meddling with their internal constitutions; that, in short, he dealt with the Confederacy as he dealt with the Northhumbrian, Scottish, and Welsh princes. Most likely the boroughs joined in the Northumbrian revolt on the death of Æthelstan, and now Eadmund more thoroughly incorporated them with the English kingdom, and seemingly delivered their English inhabitants from Danish supremacy. Yet the *Pentapolis* still went on with more or less of federal connexion; the Five Boroughs are spoken of as submitting to Swegen in 1013, and in 1015 Sigefrith and Morkere, the victims of Eadric, are spoken of as the eldest thegns of the Seven Boroughs. The two new members of the body have been thought to be York and Chester, a theory which I can neither affirm nor deny. But, whether five or seven, they could not have been spoken of in this way if they had not kept up some strong bond of union among themselves. In this way, the history of Lincoln, and of the confederation of which it formed a member, teaches us, just as the history of Exeter does, that the tendency of the great cities of England generally was towards the same more than municipal independence, to the same kind of federal unions, which the cities of Italy won for a season, which some of the cities of Germany have kept down to our own days. The Danish Pentapolis was older than the Lombard League; it is far older than the first existing document which records the union of the Three Lands. Had these tendencies been followed unchecked, the history of England might have been as the history of the Imperial kingdoms. But other tendencies were everywhere at work, tendencies which within the Empire proved the weaker, but which in England proved the stronger. The destiny of England forbade that the patricians of Lincoln should ever be as their brethren of Rome and Sparta, of Bern and Venice.

In the renewed Danish wars, the wars of Swegen and Cnut, Lindesey plays a great part, but of Lincoln itself we hear but little. Lindesey beheld the fate of the tyrant at Gainsburgh, and the one warlike exploit of Æthelred against the tyrant's nobler son. Nor can we forget the career of the local chief, Godwine the Ealdorman of Lindesey, how he redeemed the weakness of his earlier day by dying a hero's death by the side of Ulfcytel at Assandún. The Norman came; the Conqueror became master of Lincoln in the same year in which he became master of Exeter; but we have no such record as we have in the case of Exeter of the campaign or the negotiations by which he became its master. The shire, as a whole, and its chief boroughs of Lincoln and Stamford, suffered indeed much of change and confiscation at the hands of the Conqueror; but they suffered little indeed as compared with the fate of other shires and other cities and boroughs. The witness of Domesday shows us that in no city and shire of England did so many Englishmen, by whatever means, contrive to keep large estates and high offices as they did in Lincoln and Lincolnshire.

And it is indeed a vivid picture of the Danish city which Domesday sets before us. It is plain that the conquest of the Danish Confederacy by Eadmund had not wholly destroyed the internal constitution of the commonwealth. When William came, Lincoln was ruled by a patriciate of twelve hereditary *Lawmen*, whose names speak their Danish descent. They had their common land and their hereditary jurisdictions, and we get personal details of not a few of their number. Two of them, it should be noticed, were men in holy orders, nor do the compilers of Domesday show any holy horror at the mention of the wives and children of these early clerical magistrates. The privileges of the city and of its rulers were great, and gave Lincoln almost the position of a distinct commonwealth, buying its internal independence by a simple tribute to the King. That is to say, Lincoln held, as Exeter wished to hold, very much the position of a Free Imperial City in Germany or Italy. And, as Lincoln did not submit to William till the summer of 1068, the city must for nearly two years have been practically independent, and the Lawmen must have ruled as a corporate sovereign. The city, as a commonwealth, was treated with unusual gentleness; William left its formal privileges unimpaired and its formal constitution unaltered. The Lawmen and their hereditary succession were undisturbed; at the drawing up of the Survey Danish son still succeeded to Danish father, and one Norman only had found his way into the Lincoln patriciate. But the outward aspect of the city, and its practical condition also, underwent the most important of changes. Loyal and favoured as Lincoln might be, its loyalty, like that of English towns, needed to be secured by a Norman castle. And a new ecclesiastical foundation came along with the military one. In 1070, the newly-appointed Norman Bishop of Dorchester moved his throne from the banks of the Thames to the hill above the Witham, and the church of St. Mary within the walls of Lincoln became the new cathedral church of the diocese. The church was of course rebuilt on a vaster scale, and grew into the renowned minster of Saint Hugh. The palace of the Bishop, the houses of his canons, sprang up around it. Here was change enough; the Lawmen might keep their formal rights and their hereditary succession, but their real position could hardly be the same, now that a twofold Norman garrison, military and ecclesiastical, was established within their walls. And besides this, the building of the castle and minster led to something little short of the foundation of a new town. The building of the castle is recorded to have involved the destruction of a great number of houses, and the building of the minster must have done the same. Let us add however, in justice to all men, that the new bishop from Fécamp paid for the land which he took for the building of the church and the canons' houses. But through these two processes a large number of the English or Danish citizens of Lincoln were left homeless. A place was soon found for them; at the foot of the hill beyond the river arose that lower town of Lincoln than which there are few spots in England which ought to speak with a more stirring voice to the hearts of Englishmen.

We have seen that, not only in the city, but in the shire generally, among the local landowners not a few Englishmen kept a much higher place than was common in other districts. It is for local inquirers, not for me, to know whether the blood of any of these men can be traced among the living inhabitants of city or shire. That such should be the case is perfectly possible; only, if it is to be proved, it must be proved by the undesigned evidence of genuine documents, not by the fables of a family tree. And remember too that, though it is quite possible that descendants of Harthacnut the Lawman, of Ulfkill who sold the ship to William, of Colegrim and Northman and Coleswegen, or of the married priests Leofwine and Siward, may be among my hearers to-day, yet, as none of those worthies bore hereditary surnames, they cannot have left any hereditary surnames to their descendants. As I suppose that none of us wish to be Normans, Frenchmen, or Bretons, we may hope that the forefathers of all of us were 'here when the Conqueror came.' Here and there some of us may be able to trace our descent to forefathers living at that time. Here and there a still smaller number may possibly be able to show that they hold the same lands or live in the same place as their forefathers. Only let no man flatter himself that, however old and worthy his surname, be it even the primæval Teutonic Smith, he will find forefathers bearing that surname in the pages of Domesday. But there is one among the Lincolnshire landowners in Domesday whose name and works have such a special interest, alike in the history of architecture and in the history of England, that, even at the risk of telling a thrice-told tale, I cannot hurry through the age to which they belong without stopping to pay him and them yet again a passing tribute. Coleswegen of Lincoln, a man of whom I have spoken more at large elsewhere, is a man of whom we may well wish to know more. How he came so highly to enjoy the favour of the Conqueror as to keep his lands and largely to increase them, and to have men with Norman names as his tenants, is nowhere recorded; but there is incidental evidence which shows that he was nearly connected with several persons of note both in England and in Normandy. From the Conqueror he received as a grant a piece of land beyond the river, on which at the time of the Survey, thirty houses, the beginning of the lower town, had risen. And for their inhabitants he built two churches, churches which stand high above all the other buildings of shire and city in deep and thrilling interest. Not the varied beauties of the churches of Holland—not the soaring spires of Louth and Grantham and the mighty octagon of Boston—not the works of Remigius and Alexander and Saint Hugh, and the Angels' choir itself—not the hoary relics of earlier days at Barton-on-Humber and Stow-in-Lindesey—none of these can compare with the special charm of those towers of Saint Mary's and Saint Peter's—towers whose forms would be as much at home by the banks of the Adige as by the banks of the Witham—towers which, even in the days of bondage, rose under the

To face p. 211.

hands of Englishmen, in the ancient style of Englishmen, while minster and castle, the works of strangers, were rising above their heads in the newer style which strangers had brought with them from beyond the sea. There they stand, witnesses of the days of England's ancient freedom, even more precious than if they had themselves been built in the days of freedom. While Remigius built his minster on the height in the new style of his own Normandy, Coleswegen still built his towers in the ancient style of England—the style once common to England with all Western Christendom—the style which meets us in all lands from the Tyne to the Tiber, which is at home alike on the plains of Lindesey and in the passes of the Alps and Pyrenees—the style which, when our own land adopted the novel forms of Normandy, still lived on for another hundred years in the kindred mainland. The towers of Coleswegen, begun after William entered Lincoln, finished before the great Survey was taken, still belonged to the same class which Britain and Gaul and Germany all learned from their Italian masters. They are, on their lowlier scale, the fellows of Saint Zeno at Verona and of All Hallows at Schaffhausen. What clearer evidence can we need that Englishmen had an independent Romanesque style before the Norman came, than the fact that Englishmen still went on building in their national style, while they had but to cast up their eyes and see the works of the Norman, ecclesiastical and military, rising on the hill above them?

Yet the foreign style in which Remigius rebuilt the church of Saint Mary for its new use did in some sort influence the ideas even of those who clave to the style of their fathers. That Coleswegen's towers show signs of Norman influence, that they are clearly the work of men who had seen Norman detail, only heightens their interest. They show us the old style slightly touched by the new. It adds deeper interest still that in the aisle which I saw in times past, but which I can see no longer, he conformed more distinctly to the newer model. Coleswegen or his architect was eclectic in his taste. The older style supplied the better model for towers, the later style supplied the better model for columns and arches, and he chose what was best in each. The ancient style of tower lived on in Lindesey longer than in any other district. There are not a few examples, as at Hale, as at Bracebridge, which must not only be later than the coming of William, but must be as late as the architectural improvements of Bishop Roger of Salisbury. In another building in the lower town, far later than Coleswegen's day, in the house of Saint Mary's Guild, commonly known as the stables of John of Gaunt, we see perhaps the last examples of windows which keep about them something of the character of the primitive type. The example of Coleswegen seems to have impressed on the district a conservative taste in architectural matters. But it was a taste which, if conservative, was also progressive, a taste which, as long as it could, stood fast in the old paths, but which was far from casting aside every modern improvement.

But Coleswegen is only one among many names in the Domesday of Lindesey over which we may well pause and wish for more knowledge. The body of the Lincolnshire Survey is, to those who have no local knowledge of most of the places, less interesting than the Survey of many other shires. The way in which the work was done in different districts differs widely, and the account of some shires is much richer in personal detail than that of others. In Lincolnshire the body of the report consists of little but dry statistics; the interest gathers round the minute and lifelike account of the city at one end, and round the *clamores* at the other. These last, the reports of cases when men claimed lands which were in the actual possession of others, are full of curious personal matter and of illustrations of points of law. Among other things, it is from them that we get a large part of our small amount of knowledge of one of the foremost heroes of Lincolnshire

To face p. 212.

and of England. We there come face to face with one who, like Coleswegen, won in the end the favour of the Conqueror, but who won it, first by fighting against him and then by fighting at his side. As Coleswegen did not scruple to learn from the Norman in his architectural works, so Hereward did not scruple to do service to the Norman in the war of Maine. In speaking of the hero of Ely, I assume that I need not, at this time of day, go again through the evidence which parts off his real from his legendary history. As there are still a few people who believe that the earth is flat, so there may be here and there a novel-reader or a local antiquary who takes the false Ingulf and the *Gesta Herwardi Saxonis* for true histories, and who fancies that Hereward was the son of Earl Leofric, the uncle of Eadwine and Morkere. With such I cannot argue. I can only say that, little as we really know of the true Hereward, that little is enough to make us wish to know much more. I may perhaps be allowed to sum up his story in the words in which I have summed it up elsewhere. 'He defended the last shelter of English freedom against the might of William. His heart failed not when the hearts of the noblest of the land quaked within them. Our most patriotic Latin annalist adorns his name with the standing epithet with which he adorns the name of Harold, and our native Chronicler records his deeds in words which seem borrowed from the earlier record of the deeds of Ælfred.'

But from the exploits of the hero of the fenland we must go back to the city on the hill. I will go on to note a few cases in which Lincoln comes incidentally into notice in times which are more specially my own. I speak mainly of the city and its citizens; of its bishops and earls there is much to tell; but my own thoughts dwell rather with every mention which brings into life the abiding greatness of the Roman colony, of the Danish confederate borough. We must remember that Lincoln was, in the eleventh and twelfth centuries, one of the greatest trading towns of England, rich with the commerce of foreign lands, lying open for special intercourse with the kindred land of Denmark. It was from the fortress of Lincoln that the hostage Turgot —on the soil of Lindesey he may keep his name of Thurgod —escaped to become, among endless other characters in his own and other lands, the spiritual guide of a Norwegian king, and both the guide and the biographer of a sainted Scottish queen. The citizens of Lincoln indeed seem to have had a special gift of winning the confidence of foreign princes. When, in the later days of William Rufus, the great fleet of Magnus Barefoot drew near to the coast of Anglesey, with Harold the son of our own Harold in his train, in the graphic tale which tells us of the death of Hugh of Shrewsbury, we light incidentally on the fact that the treasure of the Norwegian king was entrusted to the keeping of a citizen of Lincoln. A few years later another citizen of Lincoln is found filling higher functions in the service of a sovereign of higher rank, though hardly of greater power. When the Cæsar of the East, the famous Alexios, sent an embassy to our Henry and Matilda, the representative of Imperial majesty was not one of the great ones of the New Rome, but an Englishman born, bearing an English name, Wulfric, a man born in Lincoln city. Had he or his father fled from the Norman rule to take service in the armies of Augustus, in the ranks of those English axemen who met the Norman as manfully at Dyrrhachion as they had done on Senlac? It is a piece of the irony of history that questions like these we cannot answer; we should never have heard of Wulfric or his embassy, striking as that embassy is both in general and in local history, had not a local historian in a distant shire deemed it worthy of record, because Wulfric brought with him an arm of Saint John Chrysostom as an offering to the house of Saint Mary of Abingdon.

But, if the men of Lincoln thus flourished in other lands, men of other races than the Norman and the

Englishman also flourished in Lincoln. In the latter days of Henry the Second, we come across more than one notice of an inhabitant of Lincoln whom we can hardly call a citizen. In 1187, as the king was crossing to Normandy, part of his train was wrecked and drowned, and along with them was lost a great part of the treasure of the deceased Jew, Aaron of Lincoln. The wealth of Aaron was clearly such as to make a palpable difference to the royal exchequer. And Aaron of Lincoln, who went so proudly to the gate of Saint Albans abbey and bade its inmates know that the very shrines of their saints belonged to him, the creditor, and not to them, the debtors, can hardly be forgotten by those who have read the annals of that English abbey in their genuine shape in the *Gesta Abbatum*. In the local history he bears a name, as the reputed builder, not of the famous Jews' house, but of the other house of the same style higher up the hill, which, had it not been so much worse treated, might have preserved as much of graceful detail. Here we have, as at Saint Eadmundsbury, examples of the stately houses belonging to the favoured chattels of the King, houses to which men in those days pointed with envy as rivalling the King's own palaces. The Jews of Lincoln flourished in the same way, suffered in the same way, and had the same charges brought against them, as the Jews of other places. At Lincoln, as elsewhere, in days of enthusiasm and excitement, the race which men in common times feared, if they hated, became the victims of popular vengeance. When men were setting forth with King Richard for the crusade, the pious and valiant youth of England thought at once to add to their stock of good works and to provide themselves with treasures for their voyage, by slaying and plundering the Jews at Lincoln and Stamford, as well as at York and Lynn. And in Lincoln, as in other places, we find the ever-recurring tale of the Christian child crucified by the Jews; Saint Hugh of Lincoln, little Saint Hugh, as distinguished from the great Burgundian bishop, fills the same place in the annals of the thirteenth century which Saint William of Norwich and the uncanonized Harold of Gloucester play in the twelfth.

I pass by every-day events, fires and other accidents common to Lincoln with the rest of the world, specially common in days when houses were mainly of wood, when houses of stone were seemingly marks of the envied wealth of the detested Hebrew. But in the wars of the eleventh and twelfth centuries there are several times when Lincoln stands out as the scene of great and stirring events, events all of which have a special significance in general history, some of which may be looked on as actual turning points in the history of the kingdom. Take the great fight in the days of Stephen, which stands forth in all its vividness in the pages of Henry of Huntingdon and John of Hexham, and which is the last great event on English soil which was recorded in his distant Norman monastery by the pen of Orderic the Englishman. Read the tale for yourselves, as it was written down by men to whom the news that the King was taken captive was the last news of those stirring and evil days. Read in Orderic the tale of the stratagem of the two countesses, loyal to their husbands, if disloyal to their king, in days when every other form of good faith seems to have vanished from the earth, but when every wife was still a zealous champion of her husband. Read, not in the monk of far Saint Evroul, but in Henry the Archdeacon, an archdeacon of Lincoln diocese, the speeches, real or imaginary, in which the leaders on both sides, in their exhortations to their soldiers, are made to rake up all the fashionable scandal of the time. But, as a matter of personal and picturesque narrative, the interest of that day of battle gathers round the King, perjured perhaps in his own person, but not the less the choice of England, who lacked indeed the voice of the orator and bade another speak in his name, but who on that day wielded his weapons well, and wielded the weapons of Englishmen. We seem to be carried back to earlier days and a nobler warfare, when we see the King of the English, forsaken by his foreign mercenaries, trusting to no Norman tactics of lance and *destrier*, but standing in old Teutonic guise on the soil of his own kingdom; wielding, each in turn, the weapons of ancient English warfare; first dealing death around him with the sword of Eadmund, and then, when its blade is broken by many blows, receiving in its stead, from the hands of a citizen of Lincoln, the mightier weapon of Cnut and Harold, the Danish axe which was plied so well in English hands, alike in defence of the Colony of Lindum and in defence of the New Rome herself. We see him at last overpowered by numbers, smitten down with a huge stone, like Hektôr by the hand of Aias, seized as the most precious plunder of the day, and brought in as a prisoner within the walls of the loyal city, to see it given up to such a pitiless harrying as neither Exeter nor Lincoln had ever suffered at the hands of the great William. Six years later the tide has turned; the king is again at liberty, he is again within the walls of Lincoln. It was deemed in those days that it was unlucky for any king to set foot within those walls, and Stephen, of all kings, had every reason to put faith in such a warning. But it is set down as a sign of Stephen's stoutness of heart that he scorned all such warnings, that he kept his Christmas feast in the recovered city, and wore his crown in Lincoln, as kings did before him at Westminster, Winchester, and Gloucester. Nor was his trust misplaced; the traitor Randolf of Chester came again for a second siege; but this time his hopes were blasted; the captain of his host, whose name is not told us, but who is spoken of as one who had never before known defeat, lay dead before the Roman gate, while the Earl and the rest of his host were driven to flight, and the rescued citizens, spared from a second harrying, hastened to pay their thanks for their deliverance in the minster of

our Lady. A few years later another king wears his
crown in Lincoln, but this time not in the minster on the
height. The fear which Stephen had scorned was not
scorned by his greater successor, and Henry the Second
deemed it wiser not to set foot within the city walls. He
kept his feast in the lower suburb, not in the prouder Saint
Marys which had arisen at the bidding of Remigius, but
in the lower Saint Marys of Coleswegen. The place was
well chosen for such a rite. England was rejoicing that
the days of strife and of foreign rule were over, that the
land had come again under the rule of a king who
sprang, by the spindle side at least, of the blood of Ælfred,
Cerdic, and Woden. Henry, as much and as little English as he was Norman, the king in whom the green tree
had come back to its place and had borne its kingly fruit
—Henry, the son of Matilda the Empress, the daughter
of Matilda the Queen, the daughter of Margaret, the
daughter of Eadward, the son of Eadmund, the son of
Æthelred, the son of Eadgar, the son of the earlier Eadmund—fitly kept his feast in the suburb of the city which
Eadmund had won back for England and for Christendom,
perhaps on the spot where earlier English warriors had
first won Lindesey for England and for heathendom. The
king in whom Englishman and Norman rejoiced to see
contending races united, could hold his feast in no fitter
spot than in one of the churches of Coleswegen, in a
church reared for Englishmen, in English guise, by an
Englishman who, by whatever means, had learned to hold
his own under the rule of the Norman.

With such a day of union we might well end our survey; yet there are later events still which may pass as
links of the same chain. The siege of the city by William
of Longchamp, Bishop and Chancellor, during the days of
Richard's absence, may pass as a mere piece of military
history, save that one is tempted to rejoice as one sees the
man who did such despite to England and Englishmen
driven back even by John Lackland himself. And once

again, another fight of Lincoln, the Fair of Lincoln, as men called it, ruled that the heir of the French crown was not to reign in England. We can understand how, while John yet lived, Englishmen, whether of English or of Norman descent, may, in their despair, have deemed that the Frenchman was no worse than the Angevin, that Lewis would at least make a better king than John. But, when the tyrant was dead, when his crown had passed to a son guiltless of his crimes, our feelings change; in the partizans of Henry we see the true sons of England; in the partizans of Lewis we see her enemies. In the Fair of Lincoln we may see one stage in that long strife between France and England which stretches from the fight of Noyon to the fight of Waterloo. It was a day when nobles and commons went forth with the cross upon their breasts to drive the French out of England, wishing rather to have a king of their own land than a stranger. And it is a day the more to be remembered, along with the day when the fleet of Norman Robert was beaten back by Englishmen from the shore of Pevensey, as the last fight on any threatening scale which Englishmen have had to wage against the southern enemy within their own four seas.

My tale is now told; I have but one comment now to make. Local patriotism must sometimes have read with indignation how King Henry the Eighth spoke of the men of Lincolnshire as 'the rude commons of one shire, and that the most brute and beastly in the whole realm.' I at least venture to think that King Henry was wrong. I cannot believe that that shire was brute and beastly above all shires which made such a contribution as part of Lincolnshire certainly made to the language and literature of England. In the history of every tongue some one dialect comes to the front: it sets the standard; it becomes the written language, and the dialects which once were its equal fellows sink into forms of speech which are merely local and unwritten. Then foolish people begin to look with scorn on these less lucky dialects, to fancy that they are corruptions of the lucky one, and to call them bad English or bad French. Every one knows that what we call Spanish is Castilian, doubtless—for I do not understand Spanish—some local form of Castilian; every one knows that what we call Italian is *lingua Toscana in bocca Romana*. It is not so commonly known that what we call French is the speech of Touraine; still less is it commonly known that the tongue which we call English, while it is neither the Northumbrian of York nor the Saxon of Winchester, is the intermediate Anglian speech of Eastern Mercia. It is the speech of a district which undoubtedly takes in Northamptonshire, but also undoubtedly takes in one riding of Lincolnshire and part of another. We might not be going very far wrong if we ruled that modern English is the language of the Gyrwas. Perhaps there is some one here from Bourne eager to complain that I have robbed him of Hereward. I would bid the Bourne man enlarge his patriotism so as to take in the whole shire, for, if I have taken away Hereward from Bourne, I have certainly not taken him away from Lincolnshire. And, even if I have robbed the Bourne man of one worthy, I have another to give him instead. It was a Lincolnshire man, a Bourne man, who gave the English language its present shape. I could have been better pleased if Dan Michel of Canterbury had been the patriarch of our tongue, if we had still spoken the living Saxon of the 'Ayenbite of Inwyt.' But so it was not to be. Standard English is the speech of the Gyrwas, thrown into a literary form by Robert Manning of Bourne. Winchester, York, London, have been content to adopt the tongue of Holland and the neighbouring lands. That may be comfort enough, either for my fancied opponent from Bourne or for any man from any part of the shire whose soul is vexed at the rude language of King Harry. That shire can hardly be brute and beastly which all England has taken as its mistress. We do not speak the tongue of Ælfred; we do not speak the tongue of Waltheof; but we do speak the tongue of Hereward, the tongue in which the Chronicler of Peterborough kept on our native annals, till the pen dropped from his hand as he set down the coming to the soil of Holland of the King who wore his crown in Coleswegen's church of Wigford.

YORK AND LINCOLN MINSTERS.

1870.

EVERY ONE who travels much must be amused at almost every step with the odd local superstition which makes people in every place maintain, as a point of honour, that their own church, castle, or whatever else the local lion may be, is superior to everything else of the kind in the whole world. The native or inhabitant is offended if the impartial visitor refuses implicitly to accept the local judgement. He is glad of the opinion of the stranger as long as the stranger happens to admire; he is displeased as soon as the stranger begins to exercise any independent criticism. It will win a man a cheer at Beverley to enlarge on the exquisite grace and proportion of the choir and transepts of Saint Johns minster, and to point out the delicate ingenuity with which the later nave is adapted to them. And if you further hint that Saint John of Beverley does in these points surpass Saint Peter of York, the cheer will be louder still. But if love of truth makes you go on to say that the west front of Beverley is at once a sham in itself and a bad copy of the west front of York, the countenance of Beverley grows very black indeed. The daughter church is engaged in a somewhat undutiful rivalry with the mother, and to hint that she is not in every single point ' filia pulcrior ' is as dangerous at Beverley as it is at Caernarvon to hint that Edward the Second could not well have been born in the tower which he himself built.

Let us change the *venue* from York and Beverley to two

churches which may be more fittingly compared, namely York and Lincoln. Beverley, with all its beauty, hardly rises above the second order in point of scale. It ranges with Wells and Hereford rather than with minsters of the very first rank. But between York and Lincoln the rivalry is not only of old standing, but it is a rivalry which is perfectly fair. York and Lincoln are both of them churches of the highest rank in point of scale; their ground-plan and component parts are nearly the same; both too are buildings of essentially Gothic character, with no remains of Romanesque that are visible at once inside and above ground. Both have three towers and a double transept; in both the east end is square and of the full height of the church; each is vaulted throughout in some material or other. And if the date and style of the two differ considerably, yet in a comparison of this kind all varieties of Gothic may be fairly dealt with as one style, a style one in its general effect, though different forms of it may differ widely in details. We can hardly compare the nave of Durham with that of York, because the comparison would pretty well resolve itself into a comparison between Romanesque and Gothic; but we may fairly compare the naves of York and Lincoln, although their dates are a century or so apart.

Let us first look at the two from outside, and begin with the two west fronts. Here there can be no doubt that the palm belongs to York. And the failure of Lincoln in this repect is positively provoking, because, if the Lincoln front had only been treated simply and naturally, it would have far surpassed that of York. The western towers of Lincoln, if they only stood out from the ground, are among the very noblest towers in Christendom; no front, not those of Rheims and Abbeville themselves, could outdo a front which simply consisted of those two towers with an appropriately treated nave-gable between them. But the successive architects of this front seem to have been possessed with the notion of making some kind of western transept. Now a western transept may be very well combined with a single western tower, which thus becomes in some sort central as well as western; but it does not agree well with two towers finishing the aisles. Besides this, in the final completion of the front it was thought good both to retain fragments of two earlier Romanesque fronts and to run up a kind of screen—the merest sham—before the towers. The front thus becomes a mere blank arcaded wall, with holes cut through it to show the earlier work, and with the noble upper stages of the two towers looking over it like prisoners eager to get rid of the incumbrance in front of them. The York front, on the other hand, is at least real. It does consist of two towers and a gable between them, and its decoration is sought in the legitimate adornment of the necessary features, the windows, doorways, and buttresses. And yet there is something about the York front which is not wholly satisfactory. It does not make the most of its real size. It somehow looks like a model. We feel sure that no one, looking at the west front only, would ever take in the real height of the building at which he was looking; it is only by going round the corner that the vast bulk of the minster—visible enough from many more distant points—dawns on the near beholder. We suspect that this is partly owing to the space near the west end of the minster having been thrown far too open; people never will understand that a great church was not meant to stand all by itself, but was always designed with reference to other buildings. But it is partly owing also to the design of the front itself. The single large window placed, and placed very low down, in the upper stage of the towers undoubtedly takes away from their apparent height, and thereby from the apparent size of the whole front. This treatment seems to be characteristic of Yorkshire towers, and in some positions it is effective; but the appearance of height is certainly much better brought out by two or more windows of greater height, as at Lincoln, and as in the towers of the West of England. In short, the towers of Lincoln, simply as towers, are immeasurably finer than those of York; but the front of York, as a front, far surpasses the front of Lincoln.

As for the general outline, there can be no doubt as to the vast superiority of Lincoln. Lincoln has sacrificed a great deal to the enormous pitch of its roofs, but it has its reward in the distant view of the outside. The outline of York is spoiled by the incongruity between the low roofs of the nave and choir and the high roofs of the transepts. The dumpiness of the central tower of York—which is, in truth, the original Norman tower cased—cannot be wholly made a matter of blame to the original builders. For it is clear that some finish, whether a crown like those at Newcastle and Edinburgh or any other, was intended. Still the proportion which is solemn in Romanesque becomes squat in Perpendicular, and, if York has never received its last finish, Lincoln has lost the last finish which it received. Surely no one who is not locally sworn to the honour of York can doubt about preferring the noble central tower of Lincoln, soaring still, even though shorn of its spire. The eastern transept again is far more skilfully managed at Lincoln than at York. It may well be doubted whether such a transept is really an improvement; but if it is to be there at all, it is certainly better to make it the bold and important feature which it is at Lincoln than to leave it, as it is at York, half afraid, as it were, to proclaim its own existence. Coming to the east end, we again find, as at the west, Lincoln throwing away great advantages by a perverse piece of sham. The east window of Lincoln is the very noblest specimen of the pure and bold tracery of its own date. But it is crushed, as it were, by the huge gable-window above it—big enough itself to be the east window of a large church—and the aisles, whose east windows are as good on their smaller scale as the great window, are absurdly finished with sham gables, destroying the real and natural outline of the whole composition. At

York we have no gables at all; the vast east window, with its many flimsy mullions, is wonderful rather than beautiful; still the east end of York is real, and so far it surpasses that of Lincoln.

On entering either of these noble churches, the great fault to be found is the lack of apparent height. To some extent this is due to a cause common to both. We are convinced that both churches are too long. The eastern part of Lincoln—the angels' choir—is in itself one of the loveliest of human works; the proportion of the side elevations and the beauty of the details are both simply perfect. But its addition has spoiled the minster as a whole. The vast length at one unbroken height gives to the eastern view of the inside the effect of looking through a tube, and the magnificent east window, when seen from the western part of the choir, is utterly dwarfed. And the same arrangement is open to the further objection that it does not fall in with the ecclesiastical arrangements of the building. When a church ends in an apse, or when there is a Lady chapel of lower height than the choir, in either case the high altar holds a place of special dignity, marked out for it in the architecture of the building. But in the York and Lincoln arrangement there seems no particular reason why the high altar should be set down at the particular point where it stands rather than at any other point. From all these reasons, combined with the strange form given to the vaulting, it is certain that the general view of Lincoln choir, with all its beauty of detail, is not wholly satisfactory, while the apparent lowness of the roof is absolutely crushing. In the transepts the lack of height is more painful still; but the nave is far better; it is positively higher by several feet, and the vault is so managed as to give still greater apparent height. The pier-arches however are certainly too wide, and one wonders a little at the single tall western arch, which gives the impression of there being a single western tower, as at Ely, instead of two.

In the nave of York, looking eastwards or westwards, it is hard indeed to believe that we are in a church only a few feet lower than Westminster or Saint Ouens. The height is utterly lost, partly through the enormous width, partly through the low and crushing shape of the vaulting-arch. The vault, it must be remembered, is an imitation of an imitation, a modern copy of a wooden roof made to imitate stone. This imitation of stone construction in wood runs through the greater part of the church; it comes out specially in the transepts, where a not very successful attempt is made to bring the gable windows within the vault—the very opposite to the vast space lost in the roofs at Lincoln. Yet, with all this, many noble views may be got in York nave and transepts, provided only the beholder takes care never to look due east or west. The western view is still further injured by the treatment of the west window—in itself an admirable piece of tracery—which fits into nothing, and seems cut through the wall at an arbitrary point. But the nave elevation, taken bay by bay, is admirable. Looking across out of the aisle—the true way to judge—the real height at last comes out, and we are reminded of some of the most stately minsters of France.

In one part of the subordinate buildings York has a decided advantage. We mean in the approach to the chapter-house. The chapter-houses themselves may fight an equal fight. York pleases our eye the most, but Lincoln may put in its central pillar and the fact that its roof is real. But the approach at Lincoln is badly managed. A monastic idea is awkwardly applied to a secular building, and the entrance of the chapter-house itself is left unpleasantly open. The approach at York on the other hand is absolutely perfect. The need of turning round a corner has been most ingeniously seized on to produce, in a really small space, a wonderful effect both of dignity and of a kind of mystery. Here at least there is no lack of comparative height, and the windows, the vaulting, every detail, leave nothing to be wished for. This one small portion is really the gem of York; it is one of the gems of ecclesiastical art anywhere.

One point of difference in the history of the two churches must be mentioned, because it is the natural consequence of a difference in the history of the two cities. At York the Bishop and his church may fairly be called immemorial; at least we know nothing of York as a dwelling place of Englishmen before it had a bishop and a church. At Lincoln the Bishop did not appear till the English and Danish city had lived through some centuries of stirring history. The church of Paulinus arose on ground which may have seen Christian worship in the earlier day, but which, as far as Teutonic Christendom was concerned, was virgin soil. But Remigius fixed his bishop-stool in an existing church, and his rebuilding of the fabric did not affect the rights of the people of Saint Marys. Lincoln minster therefore remained for some ages a divided church, like a church of Austin canons, or like the church of seculars at Arundel or of Benedictines at Dunster. The presence of the Bishop and his canons in their part of the building was the novelty; the presence of the parishioners in their part was matter of immemorial right. Down to the fourteenth century they kept the nave, perhaps rather only part of it, as their parish church; then, by an agreement between parish and chapter, a distinct parish church was built, just as has been done at Carlisle in our own day, and as we believe was done at Rochester in the seventeenth century.

We have freely spoken of both these noble churches, and we have freely pointed out the faults of both. In no other way can art be really studied; in no other way can the real merits of the buildings themselves be understood. Every great mediæval church was an experiment, and the experiment commonly succeeded in some points and failed in others. But we are certainly as far as possible from wishing to depreciate either York or Lincoln. The scientific student will probably always prefer Lincoln, with its admirable outline and its exquisite beauty of work. But he will not be insensible to the vast bulk and dignity which make York so impressive to the popular mind. And the same keen and fearless spirit of criticism which makes him alive to faults which the common beholder does not observe makes him feel beauties also far more keenly.

CHESTER.

1870.

IF we were right in a former paper in saying that Lincoln is, taking one thing with another, the most interesting of English cities, we must allow that, as it has a formidable rival in York, it has another formidable rival in Chester. If we compare the City of the Legions with the Colony of Lindum, we shall perhaps be inclined to say that the mere written history of Chester surpasses in interest that of Lincoln, but that Lincoln is the most striking to visit, as its history has left more distinct traces in its present state. The position of the two cannot be compared. The Dee indeed is a far nobler stream than the polluted Witham, but the nearly flat site of Chester has no chance of producing the same wonderful effect as Lincoln on its promontory. Chester, alone among English cities, retains the perfect compass of its walls, and at more than one point of those walls the traces of Roman workmanship can be discerned. But Chester has no Roman remains *in situ* to be compared to the *New Port* of Lincoln, to say nothing of the grand fragment of Roman wall-work which lies at some distance to the west of it. The castle of Chester contains work of more ancient date than the castle of Lincoln, and its position, commanding the bridge of the Dee, is far from despicable. But it is as nothing compared with the proud steep on which at Lincoln castle and minster reign side by side. Chester again, nearly alone among English cities, can boast of two minsters—it would be only a slight stretch of language to say two cathedral churches; but Saint Johns and Saint Werburhs together could never enter into rivalry with the church of Remigius and Saint Hugh. In the matter of domestic architecture the two cities are more fairly balanced. The general effect of Chester is far more striking; the famous rows give it a character which is absolutely unique. But the real domestic antiquities of Chester are underground; what meets the eye, pleasing and picturesque as it is, is of comparatively late date, and there is nothing to set against the isolated domestic buildings in Lincoln, the Jews' House, the house of Saint Marys Guild, and the other rare fragments of the domestic work of the twelfth century. In ecclesiastical domestic work Chester has the larger store in the extensive remains of its abbey, but interesting and beautiful as they are, they hardly equal in general effect the stately ruins of the episcopal palace at Lincoln. Lastly, Chester and Lincoln alike fill a great place in the great crisis of English history, and Chester, as the last English city which held out against the Norman, fills a place above every other city. Still there is not at Chester any living witness of those times and of the changes which they wrought such as we see at Lincoln in the migration to the lower town and in the still abiding towers of Coleswegen's churches. Altogether, Chester would supply a better subject for a local history of the right kind—such an one, for instance, as Mr. Hinde has left behind him of Northumberland; while Lincoln supplies the greater store of attractive sites and objects for the musings of the historical antiquary.

The name of Chester alone proves its Roman antiquity; it also proves its importance, as having come to be known as 'the city' or 'the camp' emphatically. Still the name is historically a contraction. The Roman Deva became in later times the *Civitas Legionum*, the *Caerlleon* of the Welsh, the *Legeceaster* (in several different spellings) of the English. Both names, it will be seen, Welsh and English, translate *Civitas Legionum*, the two tongues, according to their several habits, placing the qualifying word first in the English name and last in the Welsh. And here we have to distinguish our *Caerlleon*, our *Legeceaster*, from other places which might easily be confounded with them. The name of Caerlleon on the Dee is simply the same as Caerlleon on the Usk, and Welsh writers naturally speak of Chester as *Caerlleon*. So, we presume, an Old-English writer, if he had had occasion to speak of Caerlleon-on-Usk, would have spoken of it as *Legeceaster*. In the like sort the name of *Winchester* and that of *Caerwent* in Monmouthshire are the abiding names, English and Welsh, of *Venta Belgarum* and *Venta Silurum*. The old *Venta Icenorum* survives in the form of *Caistor*, which we need not say is merely a local form of *Chester*. But there is another danger, that of confounding *Legeceaster*, which is Chester, with *Legraceaster*, which is Leicester. We do not presume to guess at the origin of this last name. In its many Old-English spellings it seems always to have an *r*, while in Domesday the *r* becomes a *d*, and it figures as *Ledecestre*. Save that Dick stands for Richard, it is hard to see how *d* and *r* can get confounded in any language but Hebrew; so this fact may be a lift for the Anglo-Israelites. It would be rash to see in Leicester a third city of the legions; for, in the passage of Henry of Huntingdon which looks that way, for *Kair-Legion* there is another reading *Lirion*, though it is fair to add that there is a like various reading *Lerion* in the case of Caerlleon-on-Usk. It is safer to be satisfied with our two Caerlleons on Usk and on Dee, and to leave the city— for in Domesday Leicester is a city—on the Soar to look after its own etymology.

It would seem likely that Deva did not receive this its quasi-descriptive name till it had already fallen, till it was no longer an existing city, but had passed for a while into the condition of a mighty and mysterious monument of past times. Let us carry our thoughts to Pevensey; let us call up the walls and towers of Anderida, the walls and towers which for so many ages have stood desolate, encompassing no single dwelling-place of man. When we look at Chester, its streets, its walls, its churches, its buildings old and new, it is hard to believe that for several ages Chester was as Anderida. The desolation and renewal of the City of the Legions are facts which admit of no doubt. We read expressly that in 894 a Danish army, followed by the forces of King Ælfred and the Ealdorman Æthelred, found shelter within its forsaken walls, and found means also to defend them during the whole winter. The way in which the Chronicler describes the desolate site is remarkable. The event happened 'on anre wæstre ceastre on Wirhealum; seo is Ligeceaster haten.' The Roman city was then 'a waste *chester*,' the future proper name, curiously enough, being incidentally used as an appellative; but the 'waste chester' still kept the memory of what it had been; it was Legeceaster, the City of the Legions, as indeed it already was in the days of Bæda. The site then in 894 was utterly forsaken; when had it become so? We can hardly doubt that its desolation dates from 607, from the great victory of Æthelfrith, when he overthrew the Welsh beneath the walls and made his famous massacre of the monks of Bangor. That victory was the last great victory of English heathendom over British Christianity; Deva was most likely the last city which was made to share the fate of Jericho and Ai. Lincoln, as we have seen, was either never destroyed at all, or else had been restored within twenty years after the destruction of Chester.

The desolation of Chester lasted exactly three hundred years. The defence of the forsaken rampart by the Danes no doubt drew attention to the capabilities of the site, and the restoration of the City of the Legions formed a part of the great scheme of fortification planned by the renowned daughter of Ælfred. In 907 Æthelflæd, the Lady of the Mercians, renewed Legeceaster, and the restored fortress at once took its place among the great cities of England.

It gave its name to a shire, and presently assumed the function so long held by its modern neighbour Liverpool as one of the chief seats of communication with Ireland. Its name constantly occurs in the history of the tenth and eleventh centuries, the most famous day in its annals being that when Eadgar, if our Scottish friends will let us believe it, was rowed by vassal kings on the Dee. At last, as its conquest by Æthelfrith marks a stage in our history as the last conquest of our heathen forefathers, so its conquest by William marks the last stage of his work also. Chester remained unsubdued till early in 1070, and, when it fell, England was finally conquered.

There is no part of the history of the Conquest which we should be better pleased to read in minute detail than the fall of the last independent English city, whose walls sheltered the widow of Harold, as the walls of Exeter had sheltered his mother. But while we do know something of the siege of Exeter, of the siege of Chester we know nothing. Chester fell, but we know not how; only the fact that Cheshire, like Yorkshire, was one of the districts marked out for special vengeance, seems to show that the resistance of town and shire must have been formidable. The city now became the capital of a great earldom, or rather of a feudal principality in which the Earl well nigh took the place of the King. Had all William's earls received the same privileges which Hugh of Avranches received at Chester, England must have fallen to pieces as Germany did, and her resurrection might perchance have given offence to jealous neighbours.

The site of Chester in early times was one well suited for the growth of a great and a strong city. It has nothing of the hill-fort about it; the slope down to the river is very inconsiderable. Its strength as well as its fitness for commerce mainly lay in the river itself, which washed the walls of the city to a far greater extent than it does now. The bridge, which, together with the walls, the men of the whole shire were of old bound to keep in repair, stands on the south side. On this side the Roman walls would seem to have been extended by Æthelflæd, who raised her mound, whose site is marked by the present castle, so as to command the bridge. To the west the water has gone back, and has left a large plain, the present race-course, between the wall and the river. The Watergate and the Water-tower no longer open immediately on the stream, but the names show that the river came up to the wall in days far later than those of the dominion of Rome. To the north the canal occupies the site of the Roman ditch, and a walk along its banks affords some most picturesque views of the wall, including some of the surviving Roman portions. To the north and to the west the wall includes green fields within its bounds, a trace possibly of the three hundred years' desolation; the modern city has grown towards the east, and on this side the wall crosses one of the chief streets of the town. Every one who has seen Chester at all knows the walk along the walls, uninterrupted through its whole course, for, though all the ancient gates have vanished, the path has been carefully carried over their sites on modern arches. Every one also knows the *rows*; the double range of shops, the like of which we know nowhere else. That it should often have been likened to the arcades at Bern only shows how many people there are who are quite unable to take in any real likeness or unlikeness.

Chester, though not an ancient episcopal see, has had, like the Oxfordshire Dorchester, the curious fate of being at different times the seat of two distinct bishoprics. At the time of the local conquest in 1070, Chester contained no monastic house; like Shrewsbury, it was a stronghold of the seculars, who possessed two important churches, one within and the other without the walls. Within the city was the church of Saint Werburh, from which the first Norman Earl Hugh, with Anselm to his counsellor, removed the secular canons, rebuilt the church, and turned it into a Benedictine abbey. A little before this,

Peter, the first Norman Bishop of Lichfield, following
the same policy as Remigius at Dorchester and John of
Tours at Wells, removed the seat of his bishopric from
little Lichfield to greater Chester. He fixed his throne
in the minster of Saint John without the walls, the church
then famous as the scene of the devotions of Eadgar
after his triumphal voyage, and which soon became more
famous as the legendary scene of the penitence of Harold
and of the Emperor Henry the Fifth. The stately Norman
work which still remains in the church is most likely due
to this bishop. For his successor, Robert of Limesey, moved
his throne again from Saint Johns to Earl Leofric's
minster at Coventry. Still the bishops were often spoken
of as Bishops of Chester, and Saint Johns kept up a kind
of vague claim to be looked on as a third cathedral church
alongside of Coventry and Lichfield. Its pretensions
however did not save it at the suppression of colleges
under Edward the Sixth, nor had they led Henry the
Eighth to make it the see of the later bishopric of Chester.
For that purpose he chose the suppressed abbey of Saint
Werburh, which became the head church of an altogether
new diocese, taken partly out of Lichfield and partly out
of York, and stretching from Cheshire into the later
Cumberland. Thus Chester may in a certain sense be said
to contain two cathedral churches, and, oddly enough,
the episcopal dwelling, formerly made out of the Abbot's
quarters at Saint Werburhs, has been lately moved to the
near neighbourhood of Saint Johns.

Neither of the two minsters of Chester can lay any claim
to be looked on as a church of the first rank, but both are
well worthy of careful study. Saint Johns is the smaller,
but it must, when perfect, have been the finer building of
the two. Unluckily it is cut short at both ends; the
Lady chapel and part of the choir are in ruins; the west
front and the central tower have vanished. The only
tower now left is a late but very stately addition, in nearly
the same position as those of Dunkeld and Brechin. Inside,

the arcades of nave and choir are examples of Romanesque, noble in their simplicity; but in the nave the triforium and clerestory have given way to a singular but effective composition of the next style. Saint Werburhs is on the whole more remarkable for the preservation of so much of the monastic buildings than from anything in the church itself. Cloister, refectory, chapter-house, Abbot's lodgings, all are there; it is one of the very best places for studying monastic arrangements. In the church but little of the Romanesque of Earl Hugh remains; the church has been rebuilt in various later styles, none perhaps of first-rate merit. West front it has none; the northern tower was swallowed up by the Abbot's house; a gigantic Perpendicular southern tower was begun but never carried up. The most striking feature on the whole is the huge south transept of the fourteenth century, used as a district parish church, and forming one of the most curious results of those disputes between the monks and the parishioners the result of which took so many different forms in different places.

PRÆ-ACADEMIC CAMBRIDGE.

1870-1874.

[I have worked in part of an earlier article in 1864 on the discoveries and buildings at Saint Johns College.]

THERE may be some who remember a memorable debate in the House of Commons some years back on the question whether it were good that Oxford should become a military centre. That debate revealed the curious fact that a large number of members of the House of Commons believed that the University of Oxford was older than the city or borough. They seem to have thought that some founder of distant times—the name of Ælfred will serve the turn as well as any other—founded an university in a wilderness, and that a town grew up round about it. Most likely they did not stop to make comparisons, but we may say for them that they thought that Oxford stood to its university in the relation which Peterborough stands to its abbey, Wells to its bishopric, and Richmond to its castle. If there had been no university, there would have been no Oxford at all. These speakers would have been amazed if they had been told that Oxford had been a military centre and a political centre, a centre in the very strictest of senses, for ages before the first germs of the university showed themselves. They would have been amazed to have been told that, instead of the city—Oxford is already a city in Domesday—growing up round the university, the university seems more likely to have grown up round the church of Saint Frithswyth. And what they thought of Oxford they would most likely have thought of Cambridge, if anything had just then put Cambridge into their heads.

To those who know anything of genuine English history it is hardly needful to say that all this is the merest superstition; but it is easy to see the origin of the superstition. If the towns did not grow up round the universities, the universities did in a great measure swallow up the towns. To see that this is not the normal result of the foundation of an university, it is only needful to cast the eye over the other universities of Britain and of Europe. Most universities will be found to have been planted in large towns, often in capitals; and, even when it is to the university that the town chiefly owes its fame, it cannot be said that the town is swallowed up by it in any sort. At Edinburgh, for instance, or Glasgow, the university does not determine the character of the city. And it is perhaps wisely ordered that in the greater, though less dignified, city, where the university might otherwise have been wholly invisible, its existence should be strongly forced on the eye by the conspicuous robes of its students. To an English eye it is hard to believe that the garb which suggests either a doctor or an alderman in full dress is simply the every-day garb of an ordinary student. On the other hand, it must not be forgotten that the students thus brilliantly apparelled hold the fate of Lord Rectors in their hands. At Saint Andrews, through the smallness of the city, the University does become somewhat more prominent; it helps to give the city its character, but it does not give it an exclusive character. The University was in old times overshadowed by the archbishopric to which it owed its being, and the present aspect of Saint Andrews is not that of Oxford or Cambridge, but rather that of a cross between Oxford and Saint Davids, with a cross, at some times of the year, of Brighton or Cheltenham. There is certainly no other place in the British dominions, we doubt whether there is any in Europe, where the University so completely determines

the character, both architectural and social, of the town
in which it is placed as it does at Oxford and Cambridge.
This difference is probably owing to two special character-
istics in the history of the English universities. First of
all, the English universities, like the English constitution,
were not made, but grew. The Scottish, the Irish, and
many at least of the famous continental universities,
were the creation of some prince, prelate, or potentate;
they grew up under the fostering shade of some minster or palace. But Oxford and Cambridge were never
founded, never planted; they were hardy plants which
sprang up of themselves, and which naturally grew to be
something greater than the institutions which needed
artificial fostering. The other cause is the foundation of
the colleges which so widely distinguish the English universities from those of Scotland and from most of those
on the Continent. The collegiate system, or some approach to it, was not absolutely unknown elsewhere,
but at Oxford and Cambridge it assumed an importance which it assumed nowhere else. The foundation of colleges was the main cause of the peculiar
architectural character of the two English universities,
as involving the erection of buildings for which there
was no need under the elder University system, and
which have gone on increasing in size and stateliness
to our own time. But the foundation and growth of the
colleges affected the relations between University and
town. There was no longer one academical corporation,
but many; and it was of the essence of the corporations
which had arisen to become owners of lands and houses as
largely as they could. This was a different state of things
from the presence of the one academic body, the University, with its members lodged as they might be in the
houses of the citizens. A large part of the soil of the town
itself was held by the collegiate bodies, and was covered
by their buildings. The University and its colleges grew
together and strengthened one another, till the two to-

gether became far stronger than the more ancient corporation from whose jurisdiction they gradually managed to withdraw themselves.

It is hard to throw ourselves back into the days before this change, and to think of Oxford and Cambridge simply as towns, just like any other towns, owing whatever importance they had to their military, commercial, or ecclesiastical advantages. And modern criticism carries down those days to a date at which men would have been aghast a few generations back. But stories of King Sigeberht will not get a hearing now, and it is to be hoped that stories of King Ælfred get no hearing except in the more convivial moments of the members of University College. The Universities must be content to look on themselves as societies which began to grow up in the city of Oxford and borough of Cambridge—such is their Domesday style —in the course of the twelfth century. And when the matter is thus brought from the land of myth into the land of history, all disputes as to the comparative antiquity of the two Universities become of very little profit. As for the boroughs, we ought to begin with Cambridge, for Roman Camboritum may fairly claim chronological precedence; but the palm of early historical importance must be granted to Oxford. But one trembles a little as to Roman Camboritum. How are we to reconcile the claims of Grant*chester*, which still keeps its name, and of Grant*bridge*, which from the days of Henry the Second has been called Cambridge? Grantchester must in the nature of things be a *chester*; it may be Camboritum; but anyhow the site of the oldest Grantbridge was a Roman site also. It was perhaps Grantchester rather than Grantbridge of which Bæda speaks as a desolate place, among whose ruins the pious sisters of Ely could find a slab of stone, a thing which in that stoneless region could be found only when the ancient conquerors had left it. But it is plain that the original Cambridge was a small settlement in what is now the least academical and the least fashionable part

of the town, lying on the left bank of the river Cam or
Grant. Not only the tower in which Saint Johns has lately
emulated Pershore, not only the tall turrets of Kings
and the more massive steeple of Great Saint Marys,
but all that is supposed to be old in Cambridge, the round
church of the Sepulchre, the minster of Saint Radegund,
the small relics which show that there once was a minster
of Barnwell, must all be wiped out of the imagination.
The present Cambridge, as a town of colleges and private
houses, had no being. The two disfigured churches
of Saint Giles and Saint Peter, the county gaol, the
mound which marks the place of the castle, these are the
buildings and sites which mark the akropolis and pry-
taneion of primitive Cambridge. And an akropolis it is.
A hill, such as hills are in Cambridgeshire, rises above
the river, and on that hill stood old Camboritum. The
Roman walls took in only a small quadrangular circuit,
whose extent it is not hard to trace, and whose boundary
in one place coincides with the boundary wall of Magdalen
College. No college has arisen within the ancient enclosure, and Magdalen, in its present shape a late foundation, is the only one which has arisen immediately outside
of it. The Roman town was no doubt utterly overthrown,
to be inhabited again only when the conquerors had themselves so far advanced as to know the value of towns and
fortresses. But before the days of Eadward the Elder the
place must have risen again, as Grantbridge was of importance enough to give its name to a shire in the new
division of Mercia. It had its lawmen, like Lincoln and
Stamford, and the privileges and customs of the borough
are fully set out in the great Survey. Like other places,
it was burned in the wars of Swegen, but a wooden town
—and towns in that part of England must have been still
more completely wooden than elsewhere—soon sprang up
again after a burning. William the Conqueror, on his
return from his first northern expedition in 1068, thought
the place to be one which needed a castle to guard it. On

the mound then, partly natural, partly artificial, which overlooks the Grant, the castle of Grantbridge, of which now no trace remains, arose at William's bidding, and played its part as a place of strength and succour for the invaders, while Hereward and the revolted English held the Isle of Ely against them. One relic only of the eleventh century remains, a small portion of the frightfully disfigured church of Saint Giles, the work of Picot the Norman Sheriff—a remorseless robber, we may add, of all men, French and English, within his bailiwick. Among his other evil deeds, he robbed the burghers of Grantbridge of their folkland, while those of Oxford keep theirs to this day. Outside the old circuit is one most remarkable work of the latter days of the twelfth century, the building so strangely known as the school of Pythagoras, and more accurately called Merton Hall. That name it takes from its owner in the thirteenth century, Walter of Merton, the renowned Bishop, Chancellor, and founder, by whose grant this house at Cambridge oddly became the property of a college in Oxford. We may believe that it is the house of a twelfth-century gentleman—we might still perhaps almost venture to say a thegn—who, without actually living in the town, found it safe and convenient to live under the shadow of its walls.

We are still on the left bank of the river, but it is from the eleventh century that we may date the extension of the old borough, the beginning of which we may call the modern academic town. The building of the castle involved a large destruction of houses, which would further involve a migration of the inhabitants to other dwellings. Probably, as at Lincoln, the expelled inhabitants of the upper town found their new abodes on the lower ground at the foot of the hill. But there was a difference between the two cases. At Lincoln the old and the new town were absolutely continuous, and there is no doubt that the two ancient churches of Saint Mary-le-Wigford and Saint Peter-at-Gowts are the churches whose building is recorded in Domesday. At Cambridge the case is less clear. The church of Saint Bene't might seem at first sight to be exactly analogous to the two lower churches at Lincoln. But surely it must be earlier than the Lincoln towers; it does not show the same signs of Norman influence. Its work is far more elaborate, but it is work of an utterly primitive and barbaric type; it is inconceivable that any one who, at some time after 1068, began to build so enriched a work, would have failed to give his details some touch of Norman character. It is far more likely that the church of Saint Bene't was the church of a distinct village, which, it must be remembered, was separated from Camboritum or Grantbridge by the river, and by the marshy ground at its banks. But it must have been now, in the Conqueror's day, that the town itself began to move to the right bank of the river. The college of canons founded by Picot in the church of Saint Giles migrated to the 'fields of Cambridge,' in the form of a Benedictine priory. Other religious foundations grew up. The town increased, and, though never walled, it was encompassed by a ditch. And the University and its colleges grew up also, till the old Camboritum, the old Grantbridge, first the Roman, then the Old-English town, sank into what we should be tempted to call an obscure suburb, were it not that, as being the seat of the local administration of justice, it still retains somewhat of the character of an akropolis.

The age of colleges has now begun, and we may profitably remark, as part of our præ-academic picture, the way in which, as the University in some sort swallowed up the town, so its colleges largely swallowed up the earlier foundations of the town. Not a few colleges, both at Oxford and Cambridge, represent more ancient monasteries and hospitals. That this kind of change took place largely at the dissolution of monasteries is not wonderful. It was an obvious thing for a pious and liberal man who obtained possession of monastic lands—who perhaps obtained

St Benets Cambridge

St Michaels Oxford.

Belfry Arch St Benets.

To face p. 244.

possession of them for that very purpose—to turn some portion of them to such pious uses as the new state of things allowed. In the universities especially it would have been strange if the monasteries and monastic colleges had not been often converted into foundations on which the new system looked with more favour. The monastic colleges in particular—those which were maintained by some monastic house or order for the reception of students of their religion—must have cried out to be restored to the nearest possible use under the new system. So in Oxford, Durham and Saint Bernards Colleges soon reappeared as Trinity and Saint Johns; Gloucester Hall, converted for a while into the Bishop's palace, was restored to academic uses, and after a while grew into Worcester College; the house of the Austin Friars, famous in early University history, appeared again under the guise of the most picturesque of the later colleges, Wadham. But it is more important to observe that the same system had begun already before the Dissolution. Both at Oxford and at Cambridge Henry the Eighth earned himself a cheap reputation for munificence by creating splendid foundations out of that which cost him nothing. At Cambridge he won for himself the credit of a founder by turning several small colleges into one large one; and he won for himself the like reputation at Oxford by suppressing his own college and his own cathedral church, and refounding them together in the guise of that anomalous society in which each element does, and cannot help doing, its very best to spoil the other. But King Henry might plead that, in all this, he only followed the example of better men. Wolsey suppressed small monasteries by wholesale in order to found his colleges, and Chichele had before founded All Souls mainly out of the spoils of alien priories. But it is more curious to notice that at Oxford Magdalen College arose on the site of an hospital, which was somewhat oddly merged in the college—that at Cambridge Bishop Alcock formed Jesus College, with its minster-like chapel, out of the decayed and half-ruined nunnery of Saint Radegund—and that Saint Johns College, the noble foundation of Lady Margaret, also arose out of a decaying or decayed society.

This last college stands on the site of an earlier hospital, which was originally founded in the twelfth century, but the exact date seems not to be certain. It appears to have had at first no ecclesiastical character at all, but to have been simply a charitable foundation for the benefit of the sick. Like Rahere's great foundation in London, it came nearer to the nature of a modern hospital or infirmary than most mediæval foundations. Most hospitals, not being actual lazar-houses, were designed, not as places of temporary relief for the sick, but as places of permanent refuge for the poor and old. Our Saint Johns Hospital, founded by Henry Frost, a burgess of Cambridge, seems to have united both objects. Soon after its foundation, a more ecclesiastical character was given to the hospital by the introduction of Brethren of the order of Saint Austin under a Prior or Master. In 1280 Bishop Hugh of Balsham attempted a curious union of objects by introducing a body of scholars into the hospital, the first attempt, it would seem, to connect the foundation with the University. As might have been expected, the secular and monastic elements did not work well together, and the Bishop wisely removed his scholars to form the oldest distinctly academical college in Cambridge—that venerable foundation of Peterhouse, the antique savour of whose name is utterly lost in its polite modern description of Saint Peters College.

It is clear from this instance that there was a wish from an early time to connect Saint Johns Hospital with the University, of which its ecclesiastical inhabitants would doubtless commonly be members. The failure of Hugh of Balsham's experiment does not show any indisposition on the part of the brethren to fraternize with the

University; it only proves that monastic and secular students did not get on well together in the same house. In the fifteenth century the society was 'admitted to the privileges of the University,' which must have given it something of the status of an academic college. Yet we are told that it had greatly decayed and nearly come to nothing, before its final change into the present Saint Johns College early in the next century.

The original hospital was built according to a pattern common in such foundations, consisting of a hall opening into a chapel at the east end. The sick and infirm inmates could thus assist at divine service without going out of doors, or, if need be, even without leaving their beds. Then the introduction of a distinctly ecclesiastical element into the foundation naturally led to architectural changes. The Austin prior and brethren were not satisfied with the little oratory at the end of the hall of the sick folk; they built them a much larger church somewhat to the south of it, following pretty nearly the usual type of Friars' churches. The infirmary with its chapel, originally the whole building, seems to have been preserved to its old use, only sinking into the subordinate position held by a monastic infirmary. Then the hospital, as a foundation, finally gave way to the college; parts of its buildings were embedded in those of the college. It is curious to see how the college, once in full possession, dealt with this relic of præ-academic Cambridge. When the whole was turned into a secular college, this later and larger church was at once ready as the college chapel. Its nave however was longer than was needed for the ante-chapel of a college; so the church was without scruple cut short at the west end, just as happened to Saint Radegunds minster when it became the chapel of Jesus College, and to Saint Frithswyths at Oxford when it fell into the hands of Wolsey. But the academic society had no need for the infirmary and its chapel; so they were freely turned to secular uses. At last, in our own day, the College found it necessary to build a larger and more splendid chapel. A new site was chosen, and the old chapel and the infirmary finally perished. The work which the good old Cambridge burgher made for the 'poor, infirm, and sick persons' of his own town passed altogether away. The thought is forced on the mind, whether, as the universities grew up in the boroughs, as the colleges grew up in the universities, some change as great as that from monasteries and hospitals to colleges may, in these days of academical revolution, be the destiny of the colleges themselves.

PRÆ-ACADEMIC OXFORD.

1870.

IT is still harder to call up an idea of Oxford in the days before its University was in being than it is to conjure up the same kind of vision in the case of Cambridge. On the one hand, the buildings of the University and its colleges have more completely given the place its architectural character than they have at Cambridge. On the other hand, Cambridge has changed its site. The academic Cambridge planted itself on ground of its own, and has made the Roman and Old-English borough into a kind of suburb. But academic Oxford arose in the heart of the earlier city; it has stamped on it a new character; it has spread itself far beyond its walls; but the old site has never been forsaken or shorn of its dignity. Setting aside a few structures of very recent date, all the main buildings, civic, ecclesiastical, and academical, and the great majority of the colleges, stand within the circuit of the ancient walls, except where the walls themselves have perished to make way for them. In this way it is harder to fancy a town which derives its chief character from a particular class of buildings, as it stood in the days before any of those buildings arose, than it is to conceive a site of the same class in the days before it was covered with any buildings whatever.

On the whole however more is left to remind us of præ-academic Oxford than of præ-academic Cambridge. While at Cambridge the chief monastic establishment has been wholly swept away, at Oxford it has been turned to account in the latter state of things by being put to a twofold use as the cathedral church of the diocese and as the chapel of the largest college in the University. Or, if it be argued that the vanished priory of Barnwell answers rather to the vanished abbey of Oseney, the comparison still remains true in another shape. For in that case the parallel must be sought between Saint Frithswyths and Saint Radegunds, and it is plain that Christ Church holds a much more important place in the general view of Oxford than the chapel of Jesus College occupies in the general view of Cambridge. Then, while the later Cambridge remained unwalled, Oxford was always a walled city, and of its walls large parts remain and the circuit can be traced throughout. Of the castle at Cambridge the mound only survives; at Oxford, beside the mound, one tower, stern and rude but picturesque, remains as the memorial of that great and historic fortress. The tower of Saint Michaels church at Oxford cannot be compared for stateliness, or probably for antiquity, with the analogous tower of Saint Bene'ts at Cambridge. But its more direct connexion with the history of the city and its defences makes it in some sort a more speaking memorial of the most stirring time in the local annals. If indeed Saint Bene'ts shows that the present Cambridge grew upon the site of an earlier English settlement, then its importance in the local history is really greater than that of Saint Michaels. But this is an importance which would be at once contested by any one who chooses to bring down the origin of Saint Bene'ts to a later date. But no one can place Saint Michaels later, and some may be inclined to place it earlier, than a date contemporary with the building of the Norman castle. On the whole then, though Oxford has no site which speaks so clearly of the older state of things as the elder Grantbridge looking down upon modern Cambridge, yet Oxford seems to have a greater aggregate than Cambridge of the remains of præ-academic days.

When we look to the early history of the two towns, a balance of the same sort may be struck between them. Cambridge, with its distinct Roman traces, has the advantage of antiquity; Oxford has the advantage of earlier and more constant historic importance. The authentic history of Oxford, like that of Cambridge, does not begin before the tenth century. Such an assertion would doubtless sound strange enough in the ears of zealous academical antiquaries of a past generation, but it is the plain truth of history nevertheless. Our first historical notice of Oxford occurs in the year 912, in the reign of Eadward the Elder. Those who believe in the spurious passage of Asser about Grimbald and the scholars with whom he quarrelled may perhaps also believe that the present crypt of Saint Peters church is Grimbald's work. The name of Oxford does not once occur in the history of Bæda. Nor does it occur in the Chronicles till the comparatively late date which we have just given. The name is not found in charters till a still later date, namely in the days of King Æthelred. There is nothing but the legend of Saint Frithswyth to connect the place with any days earlier than the days of Ælfred, and there is nothing to connect it even with the days of Ælfred, except a coin the reading of which has been disputed. But when Oxford does at last appear, it appears as one of the most important towns in England, a town fairly on a level with Exeter, Lincoln, and Norwich. In the first entry where the name is mentioned Oxford is coupled with London; these are the two great cities which King Eadward takes into his hands on the death of Ealdorman Æthelred to secure the obedience of the Mercian realm. In the new division and new nomenclature of central England it became the head of a shire, and it is not without reason that Henry of Huntingdon seems to wonder that it had never become the seat of a bishopric. We hear of it, as of other places, as destroyed and rising again in the Danish wars, and during the greater part of the eleventh

century it appears as the chosen place for holding the
most important national assemblies. It was not indeed,
as Westminster, Winchester, and Gloucester became at a
somewhat later time, one of the fixed places where the
King held his court and wore his crown at the three great
festivals of the Church; but the times when Oxford is
spoken of as the seat of great national councils point to
it as possessing a practical importance which set it in
some sort above places of higher formal dignity. When
a meeting was designed to be specially national, when
some solemn act was to be gone through which affected
Northern and Southern England alike, Oxford was the
place which was commonly chosen. Its position on the
great border stream of Wessex and Mercia made it admirably suited for such a purpose. It was at Oxford that
the Gemót was held after the restoration of Æthelred, at
which the thegns of the Five Boroughs, Sigeferth and
Morkere, were done to death by the traitor Eadric. To
this meeting a tale has been transferred which seems
really to belong to the massacre of Saint Brice. It is on
that day of slaughter that we get our first glimpse of the
minster of Saint Frithswyth, the predecessor of the present
cathedral church. Some of the threatened Danes took
shelter in the tower of the church, which was burned to dis-
lodge them. The great meeting of the early days of Cnut,
in which Englishmen and Danes were reconciled, when
both agreed in the renewal of the Law of Eadgar, was
held at Oxford. There too was that other great meeting
held in which the claims of the sons of Cnut to the
crown were discussed, and when the kingdom was again
divided. Oxford seems to have ranked as the capital of
the first Harold; it was at least the place of his coronation and of his death. Oxford was again the seat of
that great, though irregular, meeting of 1065, in which
the claims of the Northumbrian insurgents were finally
granted, and when the Law of Cnut was restored, as
the Law of Eadgar had been in Cnut's own time. In

all these cases Oxford is chosen as the place for national assemblies of special importance, where it was specially needed that both the Northern and Southern parts of England should be represented.

All these events show the great importance of the borough of Oxford in the eleventh century; but they are events which cannot be said to have left any visible memories behind them, except so far as the existing buildings of Saint Frithswyths may be looked on as representing in a figure the buildings which were destroyed and restored in the days of Æthelred. Of the next epoch we have actually existing traces. It is far from clear at what moment of the gradual conquest of England Oxford came into the hands of William; but few towns in England suffered more, whether through a capture by storm or through the oppression of William's officers. But it is certain that in 1071 the famous castle of Oxford was begun by Robert of Oily, Olgi, Ouilly —in half-a-dozen spellings. He most likely took his name from the village of Ouilly-le-Vicomte, near Lisieux. This Robert came over with several of his kinsfolk, and with his sworn brother Roger of Ivry. He was amply provided for by William, chiefly by a marriage with Ealdgyth, one of the daughters and heiresses of Wiggod of Wallingford, one of the few Englishmen who contrived to keep wealth and rank under William. This Robert and his successors have left their mark on Oxford, civic and military, to this day. Of their castle indeed the single tower that shows itself can hardly be, as it has been often called, the great keep or donjon. But in 1074 Robert, with his wife and his friend Roger, began the foundation of the church of Saint George in the castle of Oxford; and, though the upper structure has perished, the crypt of the original work still abides. It is still more interesting to read the accounts of Robert in the local history of Abingdon, in which, after allowing for some measure of pious exaggeration, some amount of truth may surely lurk. We hear there of his early sins and enormities, how he robbed rich

and poor, and specially the abbey of Abingdon; but
how sickness and visions and the influence of his English
wife brought him to a better mind, and how his latter days
were spent as a benefactor of the Church, a friend of the
poor, a promoter of works of public usefulness, and a
doer of good deeds of every kind. Amongst these is
specially recorded the building of a bridge, and the
building of a bridge was, at Abingdon at least, looked
on even four centuries later as a 'blessed business,' second
in merit only to the building of Holy Church itself. But
we are more concerned with the fact that Robert built or
repaired various parish churches both in and out of the
town, and there is very little doubt that the tower of Saint
Michaels is a surviving part of one of his buildings.
Forming, as it did, part of the fortification of the town, its
air is rather military than ecclesiastical; its type, like many
of the smaller buildings of William's reign, is distinctly of
the Primitive and not of the Norman Romanesque; but,
while it eschews all Norman ornament, it equally eschews
those earlier forms of ornament of which at Saint Bene'ts
there is no lack. It is an exact parallel in the eleventh
century to the tower of New College in the fourteenth;
their position, as forming part of a line of defence, has
stamped upon them their peculiar character.

The next century saw a still greater work arise at the
hands of members of the same family. This was the
priory, and afterwards abbey, of Oseney, a little way out
of the town, a church which under Henry the Eighth became for a moment the cathedral church of the new diocese.
The legend of its foundation is well known. The first
Robert and his English wife were childless, but in the
next generation Oxford castle was held by his nephew the
second Robert, whom we also find married to a wife
bearing an English name. Edith had been one of the
mistresses of Henry the First, and was the mother of
one of his sons, Robert, who plays a part in the wars
of his half-sister the Empress, but who must be carefully

distinguished from his more famous brother Robert Earl of Gloucester. The tradition sets her before us as singularly simple-minded and specially open to ecclesiastical influences. She was struck by the constant chattering of certain magpies, and asked of her confessor, who, it seems, knew the language of birds, what it might mean. A comparative mythologist would say that we have here again the story, not so very distant in time, of Sultan Mahmoud and the owls. But in the neighbourhood of Oxford, after the good deeds of the later days of the first Robert, ruined villages were hardly to be looked for. The confessor, Ralph by name, told her—we by no means guarantee the orthodoxy of his doctrine—that the pies were no other than the silly souls in purgatory, thus paying part of their allotted penalty. No work could better profit the lady's soul than the foundation of a monastery where they might be prayed for. Edith hearkened to Ralph, and her husband Robert hearkened to Edith, and in their joint names a house of Austin canons arose, of which Ralph became the first prior. The details of the legend we can neither affirm nor deny; but that Oseney priory was founded in 1129 by Robert of Ouilly and his wife Edith, and that the first prior bore the name of Ralph, are points about which there is no doubt. The second prior grew into an abbot, and it should be noticed that he bore the name of Wiggod, clearly pointing to the keeping up of a connexion in the Ouilly family with the nation and blood of the father-in-law of its founder.

Oxford castle, and Robert of Ouilly himself, as well as his stepson, played, as every one knows, a famous part in the wars of Stephen and Matilda. In the next century Oxford plays a greater part still as the place of the renowned Provisions. But before we reach those days, before even we reach the wars of Stephen and the Empress, we have done with that elder Oxford whose inhabitants were all either burghers, priests, monks, or soldiers. The foundation of Robert and Edith was the last act in the

history of præ-academic Oxford. Four years later we read
in the local chronicle how 'Magister Robertus Pulein scrip-
turas divinas, quæ in Anglia obsoluerant, apud Oxoniam
legere cœpit.' The faculty of divinity had now made its
beginning. Sixteen years later, Vacarius, first master—
so Gervase deemed him—of laws and lawyers, began to
teach the law of Rome in the very days of the anarchy.
Sixty years later, præ-academic Oxford came back for a
moment. In 1209 two—some say four—scholars, dwellers
in a hall of their own hiring, were hanged by the practice
of the citizens on a charge of murder, with which it was
held, by their comrades at least, that one only had anything to do, while in him the deed was only chance-medley.
All the scholars, three thousand in number, left the city,
and Oxford was again as it had been in the days before
Robert Puleyn. But four years later, Nicolas, Bishop of
Tusculum and Legate of the Holy See, put no small
penance on these heady and high-minded burghers. Præ-
academic Oxford came to an end for ever. Academic
Oxford grew and flourished, and before the end of the
century its oldest college was in being.

SAINT ALBANS ABBEY.

1871-1878.

IT needs somewhat of an effort to apply the name of 'cathedral' to the building which has been known for ages as Saint Albans Abbey. It may well keep its older name, as does Bath, where abbots so long ago gave way to bishops, and whence bishops have long practically passed away. So, among those who are behind the scenes, does Durham, where there never were abbots, as distinct from bishops, at all. It will need a long and illustrious succession of bishops of Saint Albans to make the church as famous in its new character as it has for ages been in its old. It is a church whose foundations lie deep in the early history of our land. For the abbey of Saint Albans, like the abbey of Glastonbury, is one of the ties which connect the Church of the Englishman with the Church of the Briton. But at Saint Albans the tie is much less direct than it is at Glastonbury. It is a material rather than an historical tie. At Glastonbury the British foundation itself lived through the English Conquest, and the British church still abides in a figure. At Glastonbury there is an uninterrupted continuity between the earliest days of Christianity and the days of Henry the Eighth. At Saint Albans we have to lengthen at one end and to shorten at the other; the continuity lasts from the days of Offa to our own time. A church is indeed said to have been built over the remains of the martyr almost as soon as his martyrdom happened, and the swift change from the days of Maximian and Galerius to the days of Constantine makes this tradition perfectly possible. But whatever rose on the spot in Roman times, or in the days of darkness between Roman and Englishman, was swept away in the storm of the English Conquest. Verulam, conquered by heathen invaders in the sixth century, was destroyed and forsaken. Glastonbury, conquered by Christian invaders in the seventh, was preserved and reverenced. The Roman town became a desolate ruin, and it never was, like Chester and Cambridge, restored on its old site. The abbey, founded by Offa in the eighth century on the supposed site of the martyrdom, rose at a little distance from the Roman town, and the English town of course grew up around the abbey. In site and foundation then there is no continuity whatever between Roman Verulam and English Saint Albans. But this very lack of historical continuity supplied a connexion of another kind. The choice which Offa made of a site and a patron for his new foundation implies a sentimental reverence for the state of things which had passed away, of which we have not many cases in English monastic history. The British or Roman worthy received a posthumous adoption into the Teutonic fold, and took his place, on the abbey seal and everywhere else, as ' Protomartyr Anglorum.'

But besides this historical connexion, Saint Albans and Verulam have a purely material connexion of the very closest kind. The site is changed, but the materials are, so to speak, personally the same. At Glastonbury, with all its historical continuity, we cannot point to any stone which was wrought into its present shape at an earlier time than the twelfth century. There is no physical identity between the western Lady chapel and the wooden church of the Briton. But at Saint Albans we see, though on another site, the actual bricks of Roman Verulam; possibly we see the actual bricks of the first church of the protomartyr. The forsaken Roman town appears in a twofold character in the days of the early abbots. It was a thorn in their sides, inasmuch as its ruins afforded a lurking-place for thieves and other evil persons. It was also a most useful quarry out of whose endless store of Roman bricks they dug the materials for their own buildings. We might perhaps add that it filled a third function as an occasional subject of scientific research. The eighth abbot, Ealdred, did his best to clear the ruins of their dangerous inhabitants, and he carried off such bricks and stones as were useful for the building of his church. But he also explored, for the benefit of comparative mythology, a cave which had once been dwelled in by a dragon, and he took care not to destroy the traces of its former owner: 'vestigia æterna habitationis serpentinæ derelinquens.' For the benefit of geologists too he found 'conchas, quales littus maris solet educare vel ejicere cum arenis æquoreis.' The next abbot, Eadmer, had more of the spirit of Omar about him; he burned the idolatrous books which were found in the wall, and ground to powder the altars and relics of heathendom. Out of this endless store of earlier remains the present church of Saint Albans was built by the first foreign abbot, the Lombard Paul, the nephew of Lanfranc. We say built by him, because, though much has been added and altered, the impress of the original Norman design still remains stamped on the whole building. The enormous length of its western limb must have been somewhat relieved when it had a high roof and western towers, and it is in some measure accounted for by the fact that at Saint Albans the choir was placed, not only, as was usual in Norman churches, under the central tower, but actually to the west of it, as it still is at Westminster. Yet, allowing for all this, the actual nave of Saint Albans, not reckoning the choir, is one of the vastest that we have, ranking with Ely, Winchester, and Peterborough. As the building now stands, there is something uncouth and disproportionate in its vast, long, and seemingly low body, neither lifted up, as it were, by the high-pitched roof nor yet broken by pinnacles. Yet its very strangeness and uncouthness makes it the more striking; it gives it a kind of personal character of its own, which we are not sure that we would destroy, even to have the high roof and the towers back again. The very rudeness and strangeness is somehow not out of place. We hardly judge of Saint Albans by any rules of art; it seems as if it had not been made, but had grown. Those massive Romanesque arches were actually put together by an insolent stranger of the twelfth century, who turned the English abbots out of their tombs, calling them rude and ignorant barbarians. But in so putting them together he only carried out the schemes which had been planned by the men whom he despised, and used the materials which they had collected for the work. And the materials which Englishmen had gathered together, and which the stranger made use of, may have already done duty, seven or eight hundred years earlier, as the materials of an Imperial basilica, of a heathen temple, or of the earliest church of Saint Alban himself. The use of these old Roman relics gives us a church, Norman in date, but with very few Norman details. The massive brick arches have no details at all, and in the towers and in the transepts certain baluster shafts have been used which carry us back to the earliest works at Jarrow and Monkswearmouth. These, we can hardly doubt, were at least among the materials made ready for the work by the ancient abbots, if they are not actually fragments of the church of Offa used up again. On the whole, Saint Albans, built after the Conquest by the most scornful of the strangers whom the Conquest brought into England, is still, in style, material, and feeling, that one among our great churches which most thoroughly carries us back to Old-English and even to earlier days.

The history of the fabric of the minster ought to be well known, as it is minutely recorded in one of the fullest of mediæval local histories. But there is no case in which it is more needful to proclaim the eternal precept, 'To the law and to the testimony.' Let no man think that he knows anything of the history of Saint Albans, unless he has read it for himself in the Latin. Otherwise he may be tempted to think that the Abbot bullied the Jew, when it was really the Jew that bullied the Abbot. Of the 'Gesta Abbatum Sancti Albani,' the former part, including the mythical parts—and the history even of Abbot Frithric in the eleventh century is strangely mythical—comes from no less a pen than that of Matthew Paris. Saint Albans indeed was the seat of a long-continued school of historians, who took special care to record the history of their own dwelling-place, and to notice the architectural history of their own church. How came the west front —if it still exists—to be so poor? To say nothing of later destruction and insertions, read the story of John, the twenty-first Abbot; how he began to build and was not able to finish; how he began a stately west front of most exquisite work, and how his more practical successor, William of Trumpington, carried it out in a much plainer style. Though the main limbs still keep the plan and proportions of the original building, yet the various changes have brought in a great deal of variety in style, making the church a text-book of mediæval architecture from its beginning to its ending. One thing specially to be noticed is that, though but little of the ancient fittings remains, few churches retain the ancient arrangements more distinctly marked. The great Saint Cuthberht's screen still spans the western limb; not a mere rood-screen, but, as its two doorways show, the reredos of the people's high altar at the eastern end of the nave. With this before our eyes, it is well to remember that the great East-Anglian churches of Wymondham and Binham, two of the best examples of the double arrangement, were both of them cells of Saint Albans. So was Tynemouth, in the far north, where we also know from Matthew Paris that the same arrangement was made, and where it is still to be seen, though both churches are in ruins. The favourite arrangement of the Austin canons is here adopted by Benedictines. But we will not venture to say whether the mother church was divided in property, as it clearly seems to have been in use. At the east end again, behind the monastic high altar, we still see the great reredos, the fellow of that at Winchester, and beyond that now again stands the shrine of the protomartyr. Now that Saint Albans has become the seat of a bishopric, it is well to remember that it is really two churches under one roof. It is not a case like Hereford or Lichfield, where there could be no doubt as to throwing down all encumbrances, and making the church one whole. The vast size of Saint Albans, and the ancient division which made two ritual churches out of what was architecturally one, make this a special case. When the chapter is fully organized, we shall have, as once was at Carlisle and Lincoln, the church of the canons and the church of the parish ready made to hand.

NORTHUMBERLAND

POINTS IN EARLY NORTHUMBRIAN HISTORY.

1876.

[Read before the Royal Institution of Kingston-on-Hull, February 22, 1876. I must here, as in some other cases, make my apology to Jovius for speaking of him as 'the great persecutor of the Christian name.' I may mention that the formal ceremony of laying aside the Empire was done, not at Salona, but at Nikomêdeia.]

I HAVE been asked to come once more among you, as I have done more than once in other years; and I have been further asked to take as my subject something bearing on the early history of your own part of England. Perhaps, if I had been left wholly to myself, I might not have chosen such a theme. Out of the abundance of the heart the mouth speaketh; and my mouth would be best obeying the dictates of my heart if I were now to tell you what I have seen among the stony hills of Herzegovina, among the mountain plains of Montenegro, and among the hills and islands of the Dalmatian shore. I have come back thence to my own Wessex; I have passed thence to your Northumberland; yet I must confess that my heart is neither in Northumberland nor in Wessex, but that it lingers still in the lands beyond the Hadriatic. And yet even in those lands there have been points and moments when my thoughts have been carried, by no slow, by no direct or unnatural process, to Britain, and in Britain to its Northumbrian regions. From the most wondrous spot on the Dalmatian shore the path is easy to the metropolis of Northern England. There, on one of

the many peninsulas of that broken coast, with the sea in
front, with the mountains at its back, with lesser hills
rising like watch-towers on either side, with islands like
guard-ships anchored off the haven, did Diocletian, weary
of empire, choose the place of rest for his later days.
There, hard by Salona, once one of the great cities of
the world, now lying ruined and desolate, he built for
himself the mightiest house that ever arose at the
bidding of a single man. He reared the palace of Spalato, the house which became a city, the house whose
walls sheltered the fugitives of fallen Salona, and which still
flourishes as a city of men, as a haven of the sea, while
the older dwelling-place of man is forsaken. There the
great persecutor of the Christian name reared the temple
of his gods, the mausoleum which was to receive his own
ashes. And there, as the centre of his work, he reared
the long rows of columns and arches which, after thirteen
hundred years, still claim our undiminished admiration
as the parents and models of every later effort of the
building art. A few years passed away; the crown of
Diocletian rested on the brow of a Cæsar yet more famous
than himself; and the buildings of the bitterest foe of the
Christian faith became the models of the first temples
which the lords of the world dedicated to the use of
Christian worship. And he who wrought this change
was one whom you who hear me may claim, if not as a
countryman, at least as a guest. It was from your land,
from our own island and from your special part of it, that
the man went forth who was to give another face to the
Roman dominion and to stamp his impress on all the later
history of the world. The birthplace of the first Christian
Emperor has been disputed between Illyria and Britain,
between the mainland which opens to the sea at Diocletian's Spalato and the mainland which opens to the sea
at Edward's Kingston-upon-Hull. Few scholars now
doubt that Illyria has the better claim; but no man has
ever doubted that, if Britain did not see the first days of

his life, she at least saw the first days of his empire; no man has ever doubted that the crown which Diocletian laid aside at Salona was placed upon the brow of Constantine at York. And the work which the one began the other finished. The organization of the Roman power on a new and firmer basis, the true creation of that long Imperial line whose fall living men can still remember, was a work which was begun by the man who withdrew from empire within the walls which we still may gaze on at Spalato; it was brought to perfection by the man who was called to empire within the walls which we still may gaze on at old Eboracum. And as it was with the political, so it was with the artistic work. The forms of beauty which, at the bidding of the heathen persecutor, had risen in all the freshness of the new birth of art, were turned, at the bidding of the Christian founder, to adorn the holy places of the faith which Diocletian boasted that he had swept away from off the earth. The arcades of Spalato were the models of the arcades of the earliest and noblest of Roman churches, of Saint John Lateran and Saint Paul without-the-Walls. They were the models of Ravenna and Lucca and Pisa, the more distant models of the nave of Southwell and the nave of Selby, the more distant models still of Canterbury and York, of Ripon and Howden, of Rievaux and Fountains, of Hedon and Patrington, of Beverley and Hull. It is then, I deem, by no strained process of thought that from the resting-place of Diocletian the mind makes its way to the crowning-place of Constantine. It is by no crooked path that from Dalmatia the thoughts wander to Northern Britain, that the walls and towers of Spalato call up the memory of the walls and towers of the capital of your shire, the metropolis of your province. And there is one analogy which may bring us nearer still to the spot on which we are now met. The origin of some of the cities of the earth is shrouded in darkness; of others we know the names of the personal founders. No man can tell when or under whose guidance Salona and Eboracum first became dwelling-places of man. But we know who called into being the haven of Spalato and the haven of Kingston. And the founder of Kingston holds a place in the history of England at least equal to the place which the founder of Spalato holds in the history of Rome. As Diocletian was the organizer, the second founder of the Roman Empire, so Edward was the great organizer, the last of the many founders, of the English kingdom. And if the persecuted Christian had cause to curse the rule of Diocletian, the banished Hebrew had only less cause to curse the rule of Edward. But the creation of Edward had a worthier beginning than the creation of Diocletian. Diocletian, weary of dominion, built himself a house, and, in the chances of after times, his house grew into a city. Edward, in the fulness of his power, in the far-seeing keenness of his wisdom, marked out a spot, not for himself but for his kingdom; and there sprang into being at his word one of the great seats of that seafaring enterprise, that commercial wealth, of England which were among the objects which the great king had nearest to his heart.

I have thus, I hope, shown that the road from Dalmatia to Deira, that the special road from Spalato to Kingston-upon-Hull, is somewhat less long, somewhat less crooked, than you might at first sight have thought. But, having made the journey, I must not forget at which end of it my immediate duty lies. I have to speak of Deira, not of Dalmatia. I must remember that my business lies on the banks of the Humber and on the shores of the German Ocean, not among the gulfs and islands and peninsulas of the Hadriatic. I have to trace out, broadly and hastily, but, if I can, truly and clearly, some of the leading features of the history of your part of England and of Britain in its relations to the wider history of England and of Britain in general. In so doing, I must make some geographical distinctions. We in the South often talk of the North of England, as you may perhaps sometimes find occasion to talk back again of the South. But I am not sure that the words 'North of England' always mean exactly the same extent of country on the map. It means rather different things to the political inquirer and to the picturesque tourist. If we were now to begin to talk politics, and to discuss the distribution of seats in the House of Commons, we should not get on very far without using the words 'North of England.' But we should use them in a sense which would not take in the whole of the North of England; we should use them in a sense which would most likely leave out the most northern part of all. We should mean primarily Yorkshire and Lancashire—perhaps, if we meant to be very accurate, certain parts of Yorkshire and Lancashire. To most people in the South, the North of England would, in such a discussion, mean Yorkshire and Lancashire, and not much else. Those who knew something more of the North might go on to take in the coalfields of Durham and of the southern part of Northumberland in the modern sense. But, in such a discussion, no one would take in, because there is no reason why he should take in, Cumberland, Westmoreland, or the northern part of Northumberland. To the picturesque tourist, on the other hand, the North of England would mean mainly Cumberland and Westmoreland, the Lake district in short—in ignorance perhaps of the rich stores of natural beauty to be found in Yorkshire, in further ignorance perhaps that no small part of the Lake district itself lies within the borders of Lancashire. This last is a grievance which the Cartmel part of Lancashire has to share with some other parts of the world. It is a hard task to convince mankind that Mont Blanc is not, and never was, in Switzerland. So in my own part of our island, our local feelings are often trampled on by tourists who calmly set down the finest scenery in Somerset as being part of Devonshire. My local back was not a little put up when I once read in a tourist book that the Barle,

a river which no one here is likely ever to have heard of,
but every inch of whose course lies in Somerset, was the
best trout-stream in Devonshire. 'West of England' is
a phrase just as vague as North. That phrase takes in
Gloucestershire, at all events when cloth is the matter in
hand; yet the city of Gloucester is a good deal nearer to
the North Foreland in Kent than it is to the Land's End
in Cornwall. Bath, which is more undoubtedly part of the
West of England, stands about equally distant from the
eastern and western ends of the island. I mention these
facts, because difficulties of the same kind as those which
meet us in our common modern speech meet us also in
dealing with the early history of our country. If I were to
speak of the early history of Northern England, I might be
fairly asked to define my meaning a little more exactly.
There is a history of Northern England which would take
in a very wide range indeed, which would have a good
deal to say to the history of Scotland, of Wales, and of
central England. Within that history there is, what the
mention of Northern England in early times would most
naturally suggest, the history of Northumberland in the
widest sense, sometimes as a single kingdom, sometimes
as the two kingdoms of Deira and Bernicia. Within this
history again there is, what more immediately concerns
you here, the special history of Deira or Yorkshire. Now
each of these greater and smaller regions really has a
history of its own in the strictest sense. And what I am
trying to do now is, not to tell you the history of any one
of them in detail, but to point out some of the special
features of each in relation to the history of the others,
and to the history of England in general.

The main characteristic feature in the history of
Northern England may be said to be this. Northern
England has over and over again had the chief place in
the island set before it; it has grasped at it; it has held it
for a while; but it has never permanently kept it, till, in
quite modern times, it has certainly both grasped it and

kept it from one point of view. Politically and commercially, Northern England, that is, in this sense of the words, chiefly Yorkshire and Lancashire, now holds, as you know much better than I can tell you, the first local place in our island. I say the first local place, because, after all, the greatest city of the island, the capital of the whole kingdom and of the whole British dominions, is not within your borders. But the importance of London is not a local importance, like the importance of Manchester and Liverpool, of Leeds and Hull. London became the capital of England, because, among the great cities of England, it was at once the greatest and, in a certain sense, the most central; perhaps we may add that London earned its place by gallant resistance to the Scandinavian invader. But the modern importance of London is wholly that of a capital, not that of a local city. The importance of Liverpool and Manchester is the importance of Liverpool and Manchester in themselves; the importance of London is not the importance of London in itself; it is the importance of the place which is the seat of the common government of the whole land, the centre and meeting-place of people from every part of the whole land. In that vast range of buildings which is popularly called 'London' and vulgarly called 'the metropolis,' there is, unless haply within that ancient and illustrious city round which that range of buildings has grown, no real local love for the place itself. People who cannot live save in London, who despise everything out of London, who unconsciously fancy that London is the whole world, have not the same local patriotism for London which a man of one of your great towns has for his own town. It is not London as London, it is the capital of England and of the British dominions, which your man who cannot live out of London really cherishes. For strictly local importance—for the personal importance, so to speak, of the place itself, as distinguished from what we may call the official importance of the capital—Northern England now undoubtedly stands first. It stands first, all the more unmistakeably first, because it is not the seat of actual dominion. If York had become, as it very well might have become, the abiding capital of England, the other towns of Northern England could hardly have risen to the importance to which they have risen. The history of Northern England may therefore be said to come to this, that, after several struggles for dominion, we may say after several periods of dominion, it has at last come to the front in another and a better form than that of dominion.

In this sense the history of Northern England begins before it became Northern England, before any part of Britain became England at all. York—not indeed Anglian and Danish Eoforwic, but the older Eboracum which the Anglian and Danish city locally continues—holds a place which is unique in the history of Britain, which is shared by one other city only in all the lands north of the Alps. York, and York alone among the cities of Britain, has been the dwelling-place of the Cæsars of Rome. London was even then the great seat of commerce, but York was the seat of Empire. York saw the last days of Severus in one age and of Constantius in another; and from York, as I have already said, Constantine went forth to change the face of the European world for all time. And he went forth first of all to what we may call the sister city of Eboracum, to Augusta Treverorum, to Trier upon the Mosel. York and Trier are the two Imperial cities beyond the Alps; the love of Julian, and of Julian alone, for his dear Lutetia does not entitle Paris on the Seine to rank in Imperial history alongside of the cities on the Mosel and the Ouse. Yet the history of Paris supplies a certain not uninstructive analogy with the history of York and of Northern England. Let no man beguile you into thinking that Paris has been from all eternity the one inevitable capital of Gaul. But it is none the less true that Paris saw the headship of Gaul dangled before her over and over again before the time when she actually grasped it. Under Julian, under Chlodwig, perhaps under Pippin, certainly under Charles the Bald, things looked for a moment as if Paris was going to be the head. But it looked so only for a moment, till the day came when Paris, her prince and her citizens, proved, like London and her citizens, their worthiness for the post in the great siege at the hands of the Northmen. In the like sort this your land and its ancient capital had a glimpse of Empire, in days when Empire meant dominion far beyond the bounds of the Isle of Britain. And when our forefathers had come into the land, when so large a part of Britain had become England, this northern portion of the land seemed to be more than once on the full march to the supremacy over the whole. These glimpses of dominion form the early history of Northern England as Northern England; but before I speak of them I must give a few words to the process by which the land of Eboracum became Northern England.

Of the whole story of the English Conquest no part is more obscure than the history of the English settlement in Deira. Do not, because Deira and Bernicia were presently joined together under the great name of Northumberland, mix up the settlement of Deira and the settlement of Bernicia. Of the settlement of Bernicia, the land from the Tees to the Forth, we know something. It is not much that we know, but it is something. A number of scattered English settlements were gathered together under Ida, the patriarch of Northumbrian kingship, him whom the quaking Britons spake of as Ida the Flamebearer. But his throne was not planted within the walls of Imperial York; his dominion did not spread over the hills of Cleveland or over the flats of Holderness. From a rock overhanging the German Ocean, he ruled on the estuary of the Forth, but not on the estuary of the Humber. On the height of Bamburgh a hedge—a palisade—fenced in his royal city; the hedge gave way to a wall of earth, and in later days the site of the royal city was covered by the defences of a single castle. Few spots in Britain have beheld more stirring events than the fortress which sits so proudly on that stern basaltic rock. But we might freely give up the tale of one of the many sieges of Bamburgh, could we get in exchange a single ray of light to throw on the struggle which made Eboracum English. Not a detail have I to set before you of the way, of the time, when the city of Severus and Constantius, the head of all the Britains, came into the hands of the Anglian invaders. There is indeed an uncertified British tale about an archbishop of Eboracum withdrawing from the conquered city; but we have not a word from the other side. We have no fragments of a song of Eboracum, as we have fragments of the song of Anderida; we have no such living and speaking witnesses of the day of victory as the earth has given up to the research of our times within the walls of Silchester. There we may still see the very eagle which yielded to the arms of Cerdic; we have no such memorial in the capital of the North. Yet no prey in the whole land could have been richer. Roman York must have been a great and mighty city. The inhabited space had spread far beyond the walls of the first Roman enclosure, those walls of which so stately a fragment still strikes the eye of every visitor in the space between Saint Leonards hospital and Saint Marys abbey. We are sometimes inclined to wonder at the small extent of the Roman enclosure in the case of famous cities like York and Lincoln, and to contrast it with the far greater space which lies within the walls of a place like Silchester, which could at no time have been a real rival either of the Imperial dwelling-place or of the colony of Lindum. The cause doubtless is that the settlement of Eboracum and Lindum belongs to the earlier days of Roman occupation. The oldest town represented simply the original camp, and that small enclosure spread out into spacious suburbs while the Roman still ruled in the land. Roman York, if under that name we take in the whole inhabited circuit which had gathered round the first camp, stretched beyond the Ouse just as modern York does. And the land round the capital was full of smaller towns and detached houses, rich with the culture and splendour which the Roman carried with him into the furthest points of his dominion. I have gone over but a small part of your wide shire; but I have seen the lines of the camp at Malton; I have seen the ground thick with the rich mosaic pavements which lurk under so many houses in what once was Isurium, what now is Aldborough. Mark the name; Isurium did not live on by its old name; it did not, like Tadcaster and Doncaster, keep up the memory of the Roman *castrum* in its new name. The Roman town perished; it stood void; when men again dwelled on the site, the memory of Roman habitation had passed away; the Roman walls stood as a mysterious relic of past times, like the huge stones, reared in unrecorded days by forgotten hands, which stand at no great distance. The new inhabitants had no better, no more distinctive, name than the Old Borough—the fortress built long ago, they knew not when or by whom—to give to the relics of the once flourishing city of men which the sword of their conquering forefathers had made a wilderness.

But if it thus fared with the lowlier settlement of Isurium, how fared it with the city of the Cæsars? Was there any time when the walls of Eboracum stood empty with no dwelling-place of man within them? I cannot answer the question with any certainty—I know not whether local research can throw any light upon the question. The general history of Britain leaves the question, like most questions touching the English settlement of Deira, shrouded in utter darkness. Yet one might almost venture the guess that so great and strong a city might be able to hold out long after the surrounding country, and that Eboracum may not have fallen before the English arms till Englishmen had ceased to be utter destroyers, and had learned to dwell in the cities which they subdued.

At any rate, if York ever stood desolate, its day of desolation could not have been long. Early in the seventh century it was again a city, and a royal city, the capital of the Bretwalda Eadwine. Nay, by that time the second period of dominion had begun for the city and for the land of which it was the head. Our first glimpse of the city on the Ouse, after it had changed from Roman Eboracum into English Eoforwic, shows it to us as a city not only royal, but more than royal, as the seat of a supremacy acknowledged by all the Teutonic kingdoms of the island, save Kent alone.

Over the settlement of Deira then a dark veil hangs; but towards the end of the sixth century the veil is in a measure lifted, and we see something of the mighty realm that was formed by the union of Bernicia and Deira. The great name of Northumberland is now heard for the first time under kings who went forth conquering and to conquer. We can see that the land between Humber and Forth is disputed between two rival kingly houses, each sprung of the stock of Woden by different lines, one representing the kingship of Bernicia and the other the kingship of Deira. Each line alike gave kings to the united realm, kings under whom the Northumbrian name rose to the first place among the Teutonic settlements in Britain. Under Æthelfrith grandson of Ida the Northumbrian arms won one of those victories which form landmarks in the history of our folk, one of those great days which helped to make England England. Like many a man of Northumberland after him, Æthelfrith smote the Scots with a mighty overthrow; but in his day warfare with the Scots was still of less moment than warfare with the Briton. Call up before your eyes the map of our island as it stood in the third quarter of the sixth century. From Kent to the Forth the whole Eastern coast is English; Canterbury, London, Lincoln, York, are English and heathen cities; but neither Angle nor Saxon has yet made his way to the Western sea. The unbroken British land still stretches from the Land's End to Dunbarton; Isca, Aquæ Solis, Glevum, Uriconium, are still British; they have not yet changed into Exeter, Bath, Gloucester, and fallen Wroxeter. And, if I may venture to tread the narrow debateable land which parts off history from fable, I would add that monks of his own race still—or shall we rather say already?—raised their song over the tomb of Arthur in the isle of Avalon. But beyond all these, at the very angle, the very turning point, of Northern and Southern Britain, Deva, the City of the Legions, still stood untouched on its *Wirhæl*, the link which bound the Briton of Strathclyde to the Briton of what we now specially call Wales. It was clear by this time that the English had won a hold on Britain from which they could never be dislodged. But it was still far from clear whether their power was destined to any further advance. It had still to be settled whether the fate of the island was not to be divided lengthways, with its western side as the lot of the Celt and its eastern side as the lot of the Teuton. The generation which saw the beginning of English conversion to Christianity saw also the warfare which was to settle for ever which was to be the ruling race in this island. Through the still unbroken mass of unconquered land which formed the western side of Britain, West-Saxon Ceawlin was the first to pierce his way, and to carry the English arms to the shores of the Severn sea. Wales in the modern sense was thus for ever cut off from the West-Welsh peninsula, the land of Devonshire and Cornwall. But to break through at another point, to cut off Wales from Strathclyde as well as from Cornwall, to carry the English arms to the Irish sea, was a triumph which was destined not for West-Saxon but for Northumbrian prowess. That Ceawlin strove after the great prize of Deva there is little doubt; but he failed to win it; he made Uriconium a desolation, but he never reached the north-western sea. That was the work of Æthelfrith; the grandson of the Flame-bearer smote the Britons beneath

the walls of the City of the Legions, and left those walls to
stand void till Chester again rose as a city at the bidding of
the daughter of Ælfred. You will all have heard the tale,
many of you will know the mournful melody, of the monks
of Bangor. And it is not unnatural that the feelings of
those who hear the tale should go with suffering Christians
against heathen invaders. Yet we should not forget that
those heathen invaders were ourselves. We were the
Turks, and worse than the Turks, of those days; the sword
was our only argument; the persecuted Briton had not
even the chance of Koran or tribute. But simply because
we carried slaughter and havoc to a more fearful pitch
than any Turk ever carried them, for that very reason our
conquest carried with it the hopes of better things. We
stood on the ground which we made without inhabitants,
to grow up, not as a mere conquering caste, but as a new
people of the land. We stood ready to receive a new faith
and a higher civilization. The teaching which we cannot
say that we refused at the hands of the Briton, because
the Briton never offered it to us, we stood ready to receive
from the Roman and the Scot. The victory of Æthelfrith
at Deva was, as I said, one of those great blows which
made England England. The British power was now
broken in pieces; the long unbroken Celtic land was split
into three fragments, each standing ready to be conquered
in detail. Northumberland, Mercia, Wessex, had now
each her special portion of British territory to deal with.
We may weep for the monks of Bangor; but the day of
their massacre was none the less one of the great days in
the growth of the English nation. And the victory of
Æthelfrith was the last great victory of the heathen English; Deva was the last city which was taken only to be
left desolate. When Æthelfrith slew the British monks,
part of England was already Christian. Our first picture
of Northumberland is the picture of her first Christian
king. And before that same seventh century had passed,
Northumberland had become the brightest part of the

whole island, the special home of learning and holiness, the cradle of the history of our people, the cradle of the poetry of our tongue.

The conqueror of Deva fell in battle, and his dominion passed away to another house; but the greatness of the Northumbrian land was not thereby touched. Æthelfrith of Bernicia gave way to Eadwine of Deira; and we now see the supremacy of Northumberland distinctly acknowledged. Its king holds the rank of Bretwalda, accompanied, it would seem, by a more widely extended dominion than had been held by any of the earlier princes who bore that title. Mark too that we now distinctly see the old Imperial city standing out as the capital of the newly united realm. But mark too how gradual a thing the progress of English conquest was, how often little scraps of territory in favourable positions were held by the Britons long after the neighbouring land had passed into the hands of the invaders. Eadwine ruled in York; but, even after Deva had fallen before Æthelfrith, spots much nearer to York than Deva were still British. Every one knows the name of Leeds; every Yorkshireman ought to know the name of Elmet. The district still keeps its British name, and so, besides Leeds, do one or two other places in it. That was Eadwine's own conquest; while he was spreading his external supremacy over so large a part of the island, he had still to win this little land close at his own door to form part of his immediate kingdom.

Of Eadwine, in his character as the first Christian king in Northumberland I need hardly speak. Every one surely knows the tale, if not in Bæda's own text, yet at least in some of the endless translations and followings of his tale, to the number of which I must confess to have myself added. But the tale gets fresh clearness and fresh interest from a sight of the places which figure in it. I suspect that most people fancy—I am sure that for a long time I fancied so myself—that the famous debate among the Northumbrian Witan, the old thegn's parable of the swallow, the worldly-wise argument of Coifi, all happened at York. But when the story gets more life by going over the ground, it is plain that the council was not held in the city, but in some rural hall of the king. The most likely place is that spot by the Derwent which had been Derventio, which was to be Aldby, not far from the battle-field of Stamfordbridge. And one who has stopped at the Market Weighton station, who has walked along with the church of Godmundingaham on the high ground above him, who has marked the church itself on its knoll, who has found—I was not sharp-sighted enough to find—the earthworks which are said to surround it, who has further stood among those strangely irregular masses of ground at some distance, about which the learned dispute—and I am sure I will not take upon me to decide—whether they are the work of nature or art—he who has gone over all this ground for himself will go away with a more vivid picture of the times when the temple of the old gods stood in the enclosure which is now the churchyard; he will more easily call up before his eyes the headlong ride of Coifi, and the amazement of men as the priest of Woden hurled his spear against the holy place of the creed which he cast away. I have myself seen but a few of the historic spots of your great shire; but I have seen quite enough of them to carry away an idea of the events of old Northumbrian history such as I could never have formed if I had simply looked at it through the spectacles of books. It is something to have trodden even part of the ground which Bæda and others since Bæda have made famous. York of course and its minster every man has seen; but I know not what proportion of those who have seen them have made their way into the inner lurking-places of the crypt, to trace out, among the richly channelled columns of Archbishop Roger, the few rough stones which remain of the church of Eadwine and Paulinus.

But the church of Eadwine and Paulinus suggests another thought which is closely connected with that aspect of Northumbrian history which I am throughout keeping in my eye. Look at the ecclesiastical map of England: you are at once struck with the strange inequality in geographical extent between the two archiepiscopal provinces. Turn over the records of ecclesiastical history, so largely the records of ecclesiastical disputes, and you will find that in our own land there was no more fertile source of disputes than the claims of the archiepiscopal see of York to equality with, sometimes to precedence over, the archiepiscopal see of Canterbury. It sometimes strikes us as strange how there could be a dispute of this kind between the Archbishop of York, who for a long time had but a single suffragan bishop, and the Archbishop of Canterbury who had a dozen and more. But here you have, in an ecclesiastical shape, one of those glimpses of dominion which were given to the Northumbrian kingdom, and, along with it, to the Northumbrian archbishopric. Look again at the map, and take in, not only all England but all Britain; conceive a province stretching from the Humber to Cape Wrath, and the island is not unequally divided between such a province and the other province stretching from the Humber to the English Channel. And this is what the ecclesiastical province of York was meant to be. All Britain, Celtic and Teutonic, was to be divided between the two English primates. Wales and Cornwall were thrown into the lot of Canterbury; Scotland, a tougher morsel, was thrown into the lot of York. Canterbury did make the spiritual conquest of Wales and Cornwall; but the claims of York to spiritual jurisdiction over Scotland were always somewhat shadowy. Still there were such claims; they were asserted, and they were, ever and anon, partially enforced, fully down to the thirteenth century. And a memory of the old arrangement lived on in the fact that, though the churches of Scotland threw off their submission to York, they had no archbishop of their own, till the claims of York had utterly passed away in the Scottish war of independence. On the other hand, as the Northumbrian kings sometimes extended their power south of the Humber, so the Northumbrian primates ever and anon laid claim to jurisdiction over more than one diocese south of the Humber also. But it is only within much later times that the spiritual greatness of the North, like some aspects of its temporal greatness, has made palpable advances. Instead of the one suffragan of York in the eleventh century, her two suffragans in the twelfth, she now has six; and three of them are distinctly badges of conquest. The sees of Chester and Manchester have arisen on ground won from Canterbury, and Man is a conquest from Norwegian Trondhjem.

The greatness of Northumberland goes on all through the seventh century and part of the eighth. It goes on through momentary defeats, defeats which almost rise into momentary conquests, through revolutions, through divisions and unions and transfers of the crown from one branch of the stock of Woden to another. Eadwine died in battle, and Northumberland was overrun, not only by Mercian, but by British enemies. Oswald the sainted king died in battle also, and heathen Penda again overran the land. But misfortunes of this kind were only momentary; Eadwine and Oswald were both Bretwaldas; so was the more lucky Oswiu, in whom the kingship of all Northumberland finally came back to the house of Ida. If Penda carried fire and sword as far as Ida's fortress by the Ocean, the fight of Winwæd cost him his power and his life, and took away from the older gods all hope of winning back the folk of England to their altars. Through the greater part of the seventh century, Northumberland is incontestably the first power in Britain, a power ruling far away to the west and north, over lands which for ages we have been taught to look on as if they had been Scottish from all eternity. At last, at Nectansmere the Celt had his day of vengeance, and the north-western dominion of the Northumbrian Angles was cut short on the field on which Ecgfrith fell. Still the North kept for a while her religious and intellectual supremacy, as the cradle of the second youth of English genius, of the first birth of English learning. Do not forget that the English tongue, that the earliest compositions in the English tongue, are more ancient than the migration which brought Englishmen to the shores of Britain. The first poets of the English race belonged, not to this our island England, but to the older England on the mainland. Had their tongue been Greek instead of English, their fame would have sounded from one end of heaven to the other. But the poets of our Homeric epic and of our Homeric catalogue, the gleemen who sang the tale of Beowulf and the Song of the Traveller, being English, are nameless. But of the first Christian English minstrelsy, of the first recorded English minstrelsy on British ground, the land of Northumberland, the land of Deira, is the parent. Yours is Cædmon, the bard of the Creation, the bard of the battles of the patriarchs—he who, a thousand years before Milton wrote, had forestalled Milton alike in his daring subject and in its majestic treatment—he who sang how Abraham went forth to the slaughter of the kings in the same strains and with the same living strength as he might have sung how heathen Penda fell before the sword of the Lord and of Oswiu. And if Whitby—in those days Streoneshalh—claims, as the home of Cædmon, the firstfruits of English sacred song for your own Deira, so Jarrow, the home of Bæda, claims the firstfruits of English learning, of English written history, for your neighbours of Bernicia. Each of the lands which made up England has had its share in building up the tongue and the literature of England. From Northumberland came her first poetry and her first learning; from Wessex came the beginnings of her prose literature, her Chronicle written in our own tongue. And, to make all equal, the speech which has become the written English of the last five hundred years is neither the tongue of Cædmon of Northumberland nor the tongue of Ælfred of Wessex, but the tongue which lies between the two, the tongue of that side of Mercia which stretches towards East-Anglia. Each part of the land then owes something to each other part; but that Northumberland led the way, alike in poetry and in history, alike in English and in Latin composition, is a fact which no Mercian or West Saxon can venture to deny.

Here then, in the seventh century, we see Northumberland incontestably the first state of Britain, first in arms and first in arts. But neither the political nor the literary supremacy of Northumberland was lasting. As the Imperial position of York in Roman days was but a glimpse, so the great position of York and of all Northumberland in the second stage of English settlement in Britain was but a glimpse also. The power of the Northumbrian Bretwaldas, the lore of the Northumbrian poets and scholars, passed away to other parts of England. In the course of the eighth century Northumberland was utterly weakened by internal strifes, by the endless setting up and pulling down of momentary kings. In the early years of the ninth century, it submitted, along with the other English kingdoms, to the supremacy of West-Saxon Ecgberht. Mark that I say merely the supremacy; I fancy that some people still fancy that Ecgberht and Ælfred were immediate kings of all England. I suppose those at least do so who believe that Ælfred founded the University of Oxford or some college in it. But such old-wives' fables may be left to the sect which cherishes that curious belief. Those who know English history know that that stage of the West-Saxon supremacy which is represented by Ecgberht in no way interfered with the separate being of the kingdoms of Northumberland, Mercia, and East-Anglia. The external supremacy—in the next century it was called the Imperial supremacy—of the head kings was a supremacy purely external. What Ecgberht did was simply to transfer to Wessex, more thoroughly, more permanently, that same kind of external supremacy which several Northumbrian kings had held over Wessex itself.

And now we come to a third glimpse of dominion again held up before the eyes of the Northumbrian realm and the great Northumbrian city. The land and its capital had been great under the Roman, and the Roman had utterly passed away; they had been great under the Angle, and the power of the Angle had passed into the hands of the Saxon. Then came the great invasion of the Danes, an event which must have changed the whole face of Northern England, and the traces of which in speech and in nomenclature abide to this day. Under a new race of conquerors Northumberland again lifted its head. I will not go here into ethnological speculations, and I must give one word of warning against the way in which some people see Danes and Northmen everywhere, and attribute to direct Scandinavian influence everything which Dane and Englishmen have in common as nearly allied members of one great race. People who talk in this way are in much the same state of mind as those other people—or perhaps the same—who think that the object of comparative philology is to show that Greek is derived from Sanscrit. And those who talk in this way commonly talk so fiercely, and with so wild a rush of words, that I have sometimes ventured to call them the Berserker school. But laying aside this Berserker madness, the effect of which of course is to tempt us to underrate the real amount of Danish influence in England, let us see what that amount really was. It is clear that a great part of Northumberland and of north-eastern Mercia received Danish rulers. It is clear that, with their Danish rulers, they received Danish settlers in numbers large enough to hold the chief landed estates in the country and to form the ruling class in the chief towns. A crowd of places changed their names, and were called afresh after their new Danish lords, with the Danish ending *by*. That ending pretty well enables us to trace the extent of actual Danish settlement in Northumberland and Mercia. I say in Northumberland and Mercia; because in East-Anglia, though that land was undoubtedly conquered by the Danes and became the seat of a Danish dynasty, local nomenclature was not changed in the same way. In Northumberland and Mercia, the *by* ending stretches from Whitby on one side and Allonby and Kirkby Kendal on the other, through Yorkshire, Lincolnshire, Leicestershire, in all which shires the ending is common, on through Northamptonshire, where it is rare, into Warwickshire, where it dies out at Rugby. But in East-Anglia the *by* ending is not in this way spread over the whole country; there is a group of *by*'s all by themselves in one part of Norfolk, and that is all. The Danish conquest then, though its effects have been a good deal exaggerated, was a very important event and wrought very great changes. Without working such changes as the English Conquest of Britain, it must, within those districts which it touched at all, have wrought a greater immediate change than the Norman Conquest of England. I say a greater immediate change; because it certainly did not work so great a lasting change. On the one hand, the Danes were the kinsmen of the English, kinsmen nearer, it would seem, to the Northern English than to the Southern. On the other hand, the Danish Conquest, like the earlier English Conquest, was a heathen conquest, and in this respect it must have been at the time a far greater change than the later Norman Conquest. But the Dane, when once settled in England, among a people whose language, habits, and feelings had much in common with his own, soon adopted their religion also. The Christian Dane soon became the countryman of the Christian Angle; but it was not till after a time in which the Christian Angle was glad to welcome Saxon conquerors as deliverers from his heathen masters. Here then was the weakness of the Danish rule; here was the hindrance which made the third period of Northumbrian greatness still more truly a mere glimpse than the two which went before it.

I said just now that, by help of local nomenclature, we are able to trace the extent of the Danish settlement in Northumberland and Mercia. Now this leads us to a fact which I fancy is not always taken in as it should be, a fact which at any rate cost me some time, some reading, some journeying, and some thought, before I fully took it in. This is the fact that all Northumberland did not become Danish in any sense. I would not rashly say even that all Deira, that all Yorkshire, did. Deira, even after it had taken its modern name of Yorkshire, stretched, as Domesday will show, far beyond the present bounds of the three ridings. It reached from sea to sea, and took in much that is now Lancashire, Cumberland, and Westmoreland. It took in, in short, so much of Cumberland and Westmoreland as was English at all. You will see the exact boundaries by looking to the ecclesiastical divisions—which always represent older secular divisions—as they stood before modern changes. The diocese of York, as it stood down to Henry the Eighth, will show you the western and northern boundaries of the kingdom of Deira, the Yorkshire of Domesday. The phænomena of north-western England are exceedingly puzzling; I should not like to be bidden accurately to map out the exact extent of Scandinavian settlement on that side. Standing here in Hull, I would ask to be allowed to keep myself in the safer region which is washed by the German Ocean. Here we can trace our Danes easily. They go up all through Lincolnshire and Yorkshire; but where Yorkshire ends, they end too. Yorkshire or Deira, or at any rate all its central and eastern part, became Danish, so far as any part of England became Danish. Danish kings reigned in York; Danish lords divided the surrounding lands among them. But beyond the Tees in Bernicia, in the diocese of Durham, to give it its later ecclesiastical name—that is, not only the temporal *bishop-*

ric of Durham, but the whole ecclesiastical diocese—the Danes conquered in a sense, but they did not settle. Nomenclature proves it: the nomenclature of that district opens several very curious questions; but I will mention only the one point which immediately concerns me. The *by* ending, so common in Deira, dies out in Bernicia. That alone proves that the land was not occupied as Deira was. And we know that English princes went on reigning at Bamburgh, most likely under Danish supremacy, while the Dane himself reigned at York, and threatened to make York, as it had been under the Roman and under the Angle, once more the head of Britain.

This time I say 'threatened' rather than promised. Whatever may be any man's feelings with regard to any earlier or later time, I presume that every man, even in the most Danish parts of the Danish land, must feel his heart go forth with the West-Saxon champions of England and of Christendom in the great struggle of the tenth century. Such at least was, in the tenth century itself, the feeling of the English inhabitants of the Danish Five-Boroughs, when Eadmund the Doer-of-great-deeds set free those who had so long pined in heathen bondage. And, if such was the feeling at Lincoln and Nottingham, at Derby and Leicester and Stamford, we may guess that it was the same at York also. Yet, looking at things from a purely local and Northumbrian point of view, the warfare of the children and grandchildren of Ælfred, the warfare of Eadward and Æthelflæd, of Æthelstan and Eadmund and Eadred, was a warfare which did more than anything before or after to weld England into a single kingdom, but which did that work only at the cost of a more distinct subjection of Northern to Southern England, of the Dane and the Angle to the Saxon, than had been wrought by the Bretwaldaship of Ecgberht. Deira, under her Danish kings, stood forth again as a rival power with Wessex; York stood forth again as the rival of Winchester; but this time it was the rivalry of a foreign and heathen power. A new Penda threatened England from the throne of Eadwine, and the part of Oswiu had now to be played by the conqueror from the South. But it needed campaign after campaign, submission after submission, revolt after revolt, before the stubborn Dane finally bowed to his West-Saxon lord. The Dane rises under his native chiefs; he calls in his kinsfolk from Denmark and from Ireland; he leagues with the Scot to fall at his side at Brunanburh; again and again he wrests half the kingdom from his momentary conqueror. At last, after four reigns, the struggle is over, the kingship of Northumberland passes away, and Deira and Bernicia are ruled, sometimes by a single earl, sometimes by two, lieutenants of the West-Saxon prince who has grown into King of the English and Emperor of Britain. For the Imperial style now lives again; but the seat of Empire has finally passed from York to Winchester, to pass again from Winchester to London. But the Northumbrian spirit was not dead; in Bernicia the line of the ancient princes still ruled as earls on the rock of Bamburgh; and Northumberland as a whole, Dane and Angle, Deira and Bernicia, could at least turn the scale between rival kings of the West-Saxon house. Eadgar the Peaceful was called to the throne by the voice of Northern England; and in the Guildhall of your metropolis he stands side by side with Constantine, as the prince who confirmed the men to whom he owed his crown in the possession of their local laws and their ancient freedom. The third chance of Northumbrian dominion had passed away; but it passed away by the process through which Northumberland and Wessex alike became parts of England.

It might perhaps have seemed that yet another chance of dominion was offered to Northern—to Danish—England when all England passed under the dominion of a Danish king.. But the conquest of all England by Cnut was an event of quite another character from the earlier settlement which made Deira so largely Danish. It was a personal conquest far more than a national settlement. A king of Danish birth was set on the West-Saxon throne; but his dominion remained West-Saxon. The reign of Cnut was in fact the highest point of West-Saxon greatness. Winchester was the Imperial city of Northern Europe, where the Emperor of six kingdoms, the lord of the Ocean and the Baltic, wore his crown in the city of Ælfred as the home which he had chosen out of all his realms. Under Cnut Northumberland must have flourished; for the laws of Cnut were, in the usual formula, looked back to in after days, as marking the good old times, the times of peace and good government. But at no moment in English history was there less sign of Northumberland being the ruling land, or York the ruling city, of England. Even when the kingdom was again for a moment divided between the sons of Cnut, it was Mercia rather than Northumberland which came to the front; the capital of the first Harold was not York but Oxford. Northumberland still continues to play a great part in English affairs; but we can hardly say that she ever had a fourth chance of dominion to be put on a level with her three earlier chances. The land often stands apart from the rest of England; it seems often to aim at local independence; but there is no distinct sign of its aiming at dominion. Northumberland rose in the days of the Confessor; but the insurgents were won over by the acknowledgement of the earl of their own choice. Northumberland refused to acknowledge Harold the son of Godwine; but the malecontents—they did not reach the stage of insurgents—were won over by the presence of the new king and by his marriage with the sister of their new earl. What changes might have happened had Harold of Norway been victor at Stamfordbridge we can only guess. He might have reigned at York; but he assuredly would not have been satisfied with a mere Northumbrian kingdom, and London and Winchester might have had the same charms for him which they had for Cnut. The conduct of Eadwine and Morkere at the moment of the Norman invasion seems to point to a hope of holding Northern England as a separate earldom or kingdom, and of leaving Harold or William, as the case might be, to rule in Wessex as he thought good. So again, we can only guess at the schemes of those who so often defended the Northern land against the Norman, and who so often called in the kindred Dane to their help. Most likely those who sought, now for West-Saxon Eadgar, now for Danish Swegen, to rule over them, dreamed of driving the Norman out of all England, if it could be done, and, if that hope failed, of holding York and Northumberland as a realm independent of him. But vague schemes of this kind hardly amount to a fourth chance, to a fourth glimpse, of Northumbrian dominion.

One thing at least is certain, that the Norman Conquest crushed all hopes of Northumbrian dominion, as dominion, for ever. In this sense the Norman Conquest was in very truth a Saxon Conquest. It ruled that England should be for ever an united kingdom; and it further ruled that the seat of dominion of that united kingdom should be placed in its Southern, and not in its Northern part. Yet Northern England may at least boast thus much, that in no part of the land did the Conqueror meet with stouter resistance, that on no part of the land did his avenging hand fall more heavily. We read in the writers of the time of the harrying of the northern shires, of the fields laid waste, of the towns left without inhabitants, of the churches crowded by the sick and hungry as the one place of shelter. We read in the formal language of documents how men bowed themselves for need in the evil day, and sold themselves into bondage for a morsel of bread. We read how the weary and homeless met with such shelter, such alms, as one monastery and one town could give at the hands of good Abbot Æthelwig of Evesham. And, perhaps more striking than all, we read in the calm pages of Domesday the entries of 'waste,' 'waste,' down whole pages, the records which show how lands which had supplied the halls of two or three English thegns could now yield hardly a penny of income to their foreign masters. To most of us all this is mere book-learning; it was mere book-learning to me a few months back. But tales like these put on a new and fearful truth, they are clothed with a life which is terrible indeed, to one who has seen the like with his own eyes. Let me go back once more to the lands from whence I set forth at the beginning of this lecture. The harrying of Northumberland has ceased to be a mere name to one who has seen somewhat of the harrying of Herzegovina. The churchyard of Evesham, crowded with the refugees who had fled from their wasted homes, becomes a reality in the eyes of one who has looked on the same sad sight in the *lazzaretto* of Ragusa.

With the Norman Conquest then all chance of Northumberland maintaining itself, either as the dominant part of England or as a state distinct from Southern England, came to an end. But the history of the land, as still a great and important part of England, went on unbroken. The men of the North overthrew the invading Scot at Northallerton and at Alnwick; the barons of the North were foremost in wresting the Great Charter from the rebel king. And in one special aspect of the ecclesiastical and artistic life of England, the shire that was Deira stands foremost among all the shires of England. The same Walter of Espec who led the men of Yorkshire to victory under the banners of the older saints of York and Beverley and Ripon was also among the first to enrich the dales of Yorkshire, their woods and their rushing streams, with the holy places of the new-born order of Citeaux. It was from a foreign house that the Cistercian took his name; but it was English Harding who received at his hands the homage of a founder. On later times I will not enter; I need not read in your ears the long bede-roll of the worthies of your shire, or the bede-roll—not a short one—of the worthies of your own borough. Among the worthies of Northern England I will speak of but one, the latest but not the least. It is by no unfitting cycle that the list of the great historians of England, which began with a man of Bernicia, ends as yet with a man of Deira. The line which began with Bæda goes on through Simeon of Durham and Roger of Howden and other worthy names, till in our own day, the same Northern land has sent forth the most life-like portrait-painter of English kings, the most profound expounder of the English constitution. From one who lived at Jarrow and who sleeps at Durham the torch has been handed on to one who has come forth from Knaresborough and Ripon, to make the form of the second Henry stand before us as a living man, to make the legislation of the first Edward stand before us as a living thing.

KIRKSTALL.

1872.

THE great Cistercian movement of the twelfth century has left its mark in a singular way on the taste and speech of the nineteenth. The companions of Saint Bernard are the men who, if they have not, like Sultan Mahmoud, supplied us with ruined villages, have at least supplied us with ruined abbeys. We believe that there is a class by no means small among articulate-speaking men with whom the word 'abbey' simply means 'ruin,' except perhaps when the name is transferred to houses built 'in the abbey style,' which commonly means that they have pointed windows without any tracery. What is thought of 'abbeys' in such an exceptional state as those of Westminster and Bath it is not for us to guess. It is so distinctly understood that an abbey, to be an abbey, must be unroofed and have its walls broken down, that it is not unnaturally inferred that every building in such a state must be an abbey. A castle is perhaps an exception. We do not remember to have heard of Caernarvon or Chepstow abbey. Otherwise abbeys are ruins and ruins are abbeys. What people think the abbeys were before they were ruined, or whether they think that they were, like some freaks of modern caprice, built as ruins from the beginning, is a mystery too deep to be pried into.

All this mainly comes of the Cistercians. A ruined abbey is commonly a Cistercian abbey. The rule is not universal, but it is general enough to make it a presumption that a monastic ruin of the regulation kind is Cistercian.

The older houses, the Benedictine houses, for the most part either arose in towns, or else towns rose around them. Now in a large town a genuine picturesque ruined abbey can hardly be. The practical necessities of town life cannot afford to devote any large space of ground to the pious contemplation of ruins. And the picturesque associations of the genuine 'abbey' are hardly possible in the midst of a busy centre of men. The great mass of the Benedictine churches have therefore either utterly perished or else exist, wholly or partially, as cathedral or parochial churches. The large class of churches which were divided between the monks and the parishioners, those which supply that class of mutilated buildings where the nave is standing and the choir has perished, were sometimes Benedictine, but more commonly belonged to Austin canons. But a Benedictine church, neither destroyed nor preserved nor cut in half, but surviving in the form of a picturesque ruined abbey, though not altogether unknown, is certainly far from common. It was the Cistercian movement of the twelfth century which covered the vales and river-sides of England with those religious houses which still exist in the form of the 'ruined abbeys' of popular speech. That movement in England was the counterpart of the Benedictine movement in Normandy a hundred years earlier. Then we read that no Norman noble thought his estate perfect unless he had planted a colony of monks in some corner of it. So it was in England, especially in Northern England, in the days of the Cistercian reform. The causes which gave the movement a special vogue in Northern England are obvious. Northumberland was left almost without monks through the whole time between the coming of the Danes and the coming of the Normans. A few Benedictine foundations arose in the period of the Conquest itself. The hut of a wanderer from Auxerre grew by William's own help into the great minster of Selby. Ealdwine and his companions from Winchcombe revived the monastic life at Jarrow and Monkwearmouth, and from them the Bene-

dictine rule spread to the great church of Durham itself.
The metropolitan church at York always remained secular;
but, just beyond the walls of old Eboracum, Earl Siward's
church of Saint Olaf of Galmanho grew into the abbey of
Saint Mary. This was about all that could then be found
between Trent and Tyne. The land indeed lay open as the
chosen field for the new monastic movement. Yorkshire,
with its hills and dales and rivers, its natural wastes and
the artificial wastes created by the stern policy of the
Conqueror, was ready made to be occupied by Cistercian
settlements. The monks of the new rule deliberately
shunned the haunts of men. Whether they deliberately
sought for scenes of natural beauty may be doubted; but
at all events they stumbled upon them. When men set
out to seek uninhabited places where the two great necessaries of wood and water are to be found in plenty, the
chances are that, whether they design it or not, the sites
which they light upon will turn out to be highly picturesque. The Cistercians occupied wildernesses, and they
carried with them agriculture and the arts. But it rarely
happened that a Cistercian abbey became the nucleus of a
town, like the more ancient houses of Peterborough and
Crowland. The growth of modern towns has sometimes
invaded the Cistercian retreats, but while the monasteries
lasted, the Cistercians probably discouraged the growth
of younger towns, just as they avoided choosing the older
towns as dwelling-places. Hence it follows that the
Cistercian monasteries have seldom been, like the Benedictine, either wholly swept away or preserved, wholly
or partially, as existing churches. Sometimes they have
become private dwelling-houses, as at Woburn and Newstead. But more commonly their skeletons or ghosts
survive in the form of ruined abbeys. They have been
unroofed and dismantled, but it has seldom been the
interest of any one wholly to pull them down. For the
same reasons, the ruined Cistercian abbey commonly preserves its monastic buildings in a more perfect state than

any other. When a Benedictine monastery survives as a parish church, its domestic buildings have for the most part utterly vanished; now and then some fragment is turned to lay uses. When it survives as a cathedral church, the monastic buildings have been cut up into canons' houses. The Cistercian houses commonly still keep their refectories, dormitories, and the rest, neglected, ruined, mutilated, it may be, but at least not turned into prebendal drawing-rooms and nurseries.

The result of this peculiar destiny of the Cistercian houses has been that they have won a higher place in popular estimation than in strictness they deserve. Few Cistercian churches were absolutely of the first rank. Fountains stands almost alone in having any claim to stand alongside of Benedictine churches like Gloucester, Peterborough, and Glastonbury. But, while they attract the common observer by their picturesque sites and by the vague charm which seems to attach to their ruined state, they supply the scientific inquirer with better opportunities than can be had anywhere else of studying the domestic arrangements of a monastery. And the churches themselves, though not rivalling the vast scale of the episcopal and greater abbatial churches, constantly present forms of the highest architectural beauty. A large proportion of them are built in the purest form of the graceful style of the thirteenth century. Others belong to a somewhat earlier time, in cases where churches have been preserved which date from the first foundation of the monasteries in the twelfth century. As belonging to the later days of Romanesque, they supply excellent studies of the stages by which that style gradually gave way to the fully developed forms of Gothic art.

Among this earlier class a high place must be given to the well-known abbey of Kirkstall. Its picturesque site on a hill-side gently sloping to the Aire is now hardly clear of the smoke of Leeds and its suburbs; at the time of its foundation the place must have been a wilderness.

It was chosen, like so many other monastic sites, as being rich in the two great monastic necessaries. It is described in the local history as ' locus nemorosus et frugibus infecundus, locus bonis fere destitutus, præter ligna et lapides et vallem amœnam cum aqua fluminis quæ vallis medium præterfluebat.' But, as at Bec and in so many other cases, the site on which the monastery was finally fixed was not that which had been first chosen. The history, which will be found in the fifth volume of the Monasticon, is well worth reading, as an example of the difficulties and vicissitudes which seem always to have beset the early years of a newly founded monastery. For our purpose it is enough to say that the existing buildings of Kirkstall abbey, of the foundation of Henry of Lacy, a grandson of the famous Ilbert of Domesday, were begun in 1152 by the first Abbot, Alexander, who had been Prior of Fountains, and who led his spiritual colony from that monastery, itself then a foundation of only about twenty years' standing, to their new home at Kirkstall. Abbot Alexander sat for thirty years, and we read that within that time he carried on architectural works with remarkable zeal and success. He was able during his lifetime to build all the chief buildings of the monastery in a permanent form. He built the church, cloister, chapter-house, two dormitories, two refectories, and the other buildings that were needed. In the words of the history :—

> In diebus illis erecta sunt ædificia de Kirkestall ex lapide et lignis delatis. Ecclesia videlicet et utrumque dormitorium, monachorum scilicet et conversorum, utrumque etiam refectorium, claustrum, et capitulum et aliæ officinæ infra abbatiam necessariæ, et hæc omnia tegulis optime cooperta.

The Abbot was unusually lucky in being able to carry out such great works during a first incumbency. Few first abbots of any order lived, like Alexander and the more famous Herlwin of Bec, to see their societies so thoroughly organized and possessed of such a perfect and elaborate set of buildings. And we may count him lucky also in that so large a portion of his work still exists for our own study. The church of Kirkstall, as it arose between 1152 and 1182, has never been rebuilt, nor has it been either greatly altered or greatly mutilated. The ground-plan remains as its founder designed it. The chief later changes were the insertion of some Perpendicular windows, especially a great one at the east end, some of the usual tampering with the gables, and the raising of the single central tower. This last addition was most likely the cause of the only important mutilation. About 1792 a large part of the tower fell, leaving the tower itself in a strangely shattered state, and of course crushing a great deal of the central part of the church. Otherwise it would seem that the church had hardly suffered at all beyond the process of unroofing, which, we suppose, is of itself enough to raise any building to the rank of a ruin. The church is therefore nearly perfect, and it bears in all its fulness the impress of the date and circumstances under which it arose. It is just such a church as we should expect to be built by a brotherhood of a young order whose zeal was still warm. It is plain and stern, but in no way rude or unfinished. The simplicity of the ground-plan is thoroughly Cistercian. The eastern limb is short, the choir having occupied the space under the tower and the two eastern bays of the western limb. There are no choir-aisles, no surrounding chapels, no projecting Lady chapel or procession path in any shape, nothing but three chapels projecting from the east side of each transept, divided from one another and from the eastern limb by solid walls, and giving a dark, stern, and cavernous look to the whole eastern part of the church. Allowing for the few later insertions, the style of architecture throughout the church, and through a large part of the domestic buildings, is altogether uniform, and is plainly the unaltered work of Abbot Alexander. It shows that stage of the transition when the pointed arch had come into general use for constructive purposes, but when it had not yet been applied to the arches of smaller and decorative openings. Throughout the church of Kirkstall all the constructive arches, the pier arches and the arches of the vaulting, are, without a single exception, pointed. The arches of the doors and windows and the other smaller arches, equally without exception, remain round. This rule, so strictly followed in the church itself, is not quite so strictly followed in the contemporary conventual buildings, but it may fairly be looked upon as prevailing throughout. The same plainness and severity which we see in the ground-plan we also see in the side elevations. Each bay consists simply of the pier arch and of a single clerestory window pierced in the wall above. There is no triforium-stage between the arcade and the clerestory, nor are the clerestory windows provided with any subordinate arches, nor is any passage made among them. But, on the other hand, though the triforium is wanting, we do not find that bare space between the arcade and the clerestory which we find in many churches of the German Romanesque, and at home in the later Cistercian church of Tintern. Such an arrangement, unless it is filled up with the mosaics of Ravenna, always looks bare, unfinished, and inharmonious. It always shows a lack of design, while at Kirkstall there is no lack of design, though there is throughout a seemingly intentional lack of ornament. The aisles, the small chapels, and the eastern limb, were vaulted; the nave was not; the fact that the eastern limb is vaulted shows that the lack of vaulting in the nave is intentional, and not owing to want of skill or daring to vault so wide a space. While the first fervour of Cistercian zeal was still warm, it was probably deemed a duty to do well whatever needed to be done at all, but a vault and a triforium were most likely looked on as needless luxuries.

The domestic remains at Kirkstall are very large, and in some points puzzling. As far as we can make out, they have never been thoroughly examined and mapped out as they deserve to be. If they have ever so been done, we shall be glad to learn the fact and to see the book in which it is done. The two dormitories of Abbot Alexander are plainly to be seen, that of the monks attached to the south transept, and that of the *conversi* parallel to it on the west side of the cloister. The double refectory may also be seen on the south of the cloister, parallel to the nave. But there seem to have been a good many changes in this part of the buildings, changes not only due to alterations of later date, but to changes of design while the work was going on. The minute examination of these changes would be a worthy work for local inquirers or for inquirers from any quarter. It would have been not unworthy even of the hand which walled up again the domestic buildings of Christ Church, Canterbury.

[I leave the passage about the refectories and dormitories as I wrote it eleven years back. I have not been at Kirkstall since. The usual Cistercian arrangement was to make the refectory, not parallel to the nave, but at right angles to it. Such was the original arrangement at Old Cleeve in Somerset; but it was afterwards changed to a refectory parallel to the nave, as in a Benedictine house. Something of the same kind may have happened at Kirkstall.]

SELBY.

1875.

To those of whom we heard at Kirkstall, those who hold that every abbey must be a ruin and that every ruin must be an abbey, it may seem strange to claim the first place among the abbeys of Yorkshire for Selby. That great church has had the luck, good or bad, to be preserved in an almost perfect state, and for that cause it is not unlikely that there are many to whom its name would not occur at all in running over a list of Yorkshire abbeys. That Selby ought actually to hold the very first place among the monastic remains of the land richest in monastic remains we will not dogmatically affirm. Such a classification depends on many questions, questions to be looked at from many points of view, and it allows wide room for fair differences of taste. It is hard, for instance, to compare Selby and Fountains. At Selby the church is nearly perfect, but the adjoining buildings have utterly perished; at Fountains the series of monastic buildings, church and everything else, are, as a whole, more perfect than anywhere else, but they are all ruined, or at least roofless. If by an 'abbey' we understand, not the church only, but the whole monastery, Fountains may surely claim the first place in Yorkshire and in England. But if the church of Fountains stood, like the church of Selby, roofed and in use, with only a comparatively small mutilation, we may doubt whether, of the two churches taken alone, Selby would not commonly be allowed to claim the higher place. The difference is between a Benedictine abbey, which has become the parish church of a considerable town, and a Cistercian abbey, which, like other Cistercian abbeys, was planted in a wilderness and remains only as a ruin.

The monastery of Selby was a foundation of the Conqueror, and Selby itself was, according to a tradition which its very unlikelihood makes likely, the birthplace of his one English-born child. Selby and Yorkshire may indeed count it something if the Lion of Justice, the mighty Henry, was born among them. But the tale rests on no more certain authority than tradition. The king who made peace for man and deer was undoubtedly by birth an Englishman; we cannot say for certain that he was a Yorkshireman. The chief difficulty in the story is to reconcile the statement of Henry's birth at Selby with the other traditions of the place. The name *Selby*, with its Danish ending, whether we hold that the place is really called from the *phoca* or sea-calf or not, would seem to imply that there was there a town or village or human settlement of some kind, before the days of the Conqueror and his son. But, if we accept the received legend of the foundation of the abbey, it is hard to understand whereabouts at Selby any one, not to say an Ætheling, could just then have been born at all. For, according to the story of the abbey, the first building at Selby was the monastery, and the monastery was then at most only just rising. Selby, in short, was one of the latest of those cases where the cell of an anchorite grew into a monastery, and round the monastery there gradually sprang up a town. Benedict of Auxerre, charged with a finger of his patron Saint German, fixed his cell by the Ouse as a lonely hermit, and lived to be abbot of a rising monastery. Such an origin must be carefully distinguished from the usual origin of a Cistercian house. The Cistercian houses were strictly founded from the beginning; Benedictine houses of the class of Selby began of themselves and were founded afterwards. And, though the Benedictine house might

begin on a spot as solitary as the site of the Cistercian
houses, it scarcely ever remained solitary; if a Benedictine house was not founded in a town, a town presently
grew up around it. A town therefore grew up at Selby;
no town ever grew up at Fountains. Such at least is the
story; but we are met by the difficulties both of the name
of the place and of the tradition, whatever it may be
worth, about the birth of Henry. That tradition must be
taken for whatever a mere tradition is worth; the fact
that at Selby, as at a crowd of other places, a building of
impossible date used to be shown as the birthplace of the
local hero, as it proves nothing for the tale, really proves
nothing against it. But, if Henry was born at Selby,
unless his birth there was the result of the merest chance,
there must have been some place for him to be born in
other than the cell of an anchorite. And, as we have hinted,
the fact that the place bears a name which was much
more likely to be given to it before 1068 than after that
year does look as if there might have already been some
human dwelling-place at Selby besides the hermitage of
Benedict of Auxerre, even if we can conceive him to have
got to Selby so soon as the time of Henry's birth. There
is something therefore to be said both ways; but, if Henry
was not born at Selby, we can see an intelligible reason
why he should be born at least in that neighbourhood.
His birth, if not specially at Selby, yet at all events in
England and in Yorkshire, would exactly answer to the
birth of Edward the Second at Caernarvon; for we need
hardly repeat that Edward the Second was born at Caernarvon, though not in the tower of his own building. If
the Conqueror took care that the one son who was born
to him as a king should be born, not only in his kingdom,
but in that part of his kingdom which it had cost him
most trouble to win—and this would be true of York
even in 1068, though it became truer still in 1069—his
policy would be exactly the same as the policy by which
Edward the First took care that the son whom he

designed to be Prince of Wales should be born upon Welsh soil.

The early history of Selby is therefore hard to put together; we have to make out what we can between two legendary tales, neither of which rests on any direct or trustworthy evidence. But it is in any case certain that we have at Selby a foundation of the Conqueror, which grew up into a high position among the monastic houses of England, to a specially high position among the monastic houses of its own district, where it could have had no rival of its own order except the house of Saint Mary at York. The earlier monasteries of the North had been swept away in the Danish invasion. The four great churches of the diocese, the metropolitan church and its three satellites, the three churches which sent forth their banners to the battle of the Standard, Saint Peter of York, Saint John of Beverley, Saint Wilfrith of Ripon, together with the more distant church of our Lady at Southwell, were all of them, in their later estate at least, secular foundations. The other houses which have made Yorkshire famous as a specially monastic district are of the Cistercian or other later orders. Selby and Saint Marys at York stand alone in their own region as Benedictine houses of the first rank, and of these two Selby stands alone as having its church preserved in an all but perfect state. This rarity of great Benedictine houses of any date, this absolute lack of monasteries which went on uninterruptedly, or nearly so, from the earliest times, distinguishes the monastic history of Yorkshire from the group of great monastic houses in the fenland and from the other great group in the diocese of Worcester, the diocese from which Ealdwine set forth to revive the monastic life in Yorkshire, and which so long kept up a close connexion with the see of York. In that land we have Worcester, Gloucester, Tewkesbury, fallen Winchcombe, and the lesser houses of Malvern and Deerhurst, all near together; so in the other land there was that great gathering of mighty abbeys of which Ely and Peterborough still remain as two of our noblest episcopal churches, while Crowland and Thorney, if sadly mutilated, have not wholly vanished like Ramsey. But these districts, so rich in their own way, have nothing to set against the Cistercian remains of Yorkshire. We can hardly conceive Cistercians within the range of the Bedford Level. There would be rivers indeed for them in plenty, but where are the hills and valleys? A Rievaux by the Ouse or the Nen is a thing which no imagination can conjure up, and even the other more favoured land could hardly supply exactly the same kind of sites as those supplied so abundantly in the land of Northern monasticism. The Cotswolds and the range of Malvern would supply plenty of heights and hillsides, but they would supply but few distinctly Cistercian valleys. In the eastern and the western districts then we find great and ancient Benedictine houses, either founded in already existing cities, or else surrounded by a town, greater or smaller, which has grown up under their shadow. Therefore, as a rule, they still survive in a more or less perfect state. In the North—the comparative North; for the furthest North presents other features—we find the churches of the later orders standing solitary and in ruins. Selby and Saint Marys, exceptional in their own district, form a link between the two; they are, together with several other houses in other parts of the kingdom, the fruit of the zeal of the days immediately following the Norman Conquest, before the specially Cistercian reform had reached England.

We have thus, by a kind of process of exhaustion, marked out the abbey of Selby as holding an unique position as the one great Benedictine monastery of Northern England surviving as a parochial church. But we must remember that Selby became a parochial church only after monks had passed away, indeed as late as the days of James the First. The church of Selby never was divided. As at Malvern, the minster became the parish church, and the elder parish church was forsaken. And the minster of Selby is in truth a building worthy to have lived on through all changes. In outline it is certainly lacking; the western towers were never carried up; the south transept is gone—the only mutilation of the church itself, as distinguished from the utter sweeping away of the conventual buildings which joined it on the south side. And even this mutilation was negative rather than positive. The ancient central tower fell in the year 1690, and crushed the south transept. The tower was rebuilt in the mean style of the time; the transept was not rebuilt at all; down to that time the whole of the building must have been perfect. As we see it now, the general aspect of bulk and stateliness, which is the impression which the church gives at the first glimpse from the railway, is not belied upon a nearer examination. In the lantern and the surviving transept we have the remains of the original Norman building. The nave, in its full length, is one of the richest and most varied examples of the Transition; its distinguishing feature is one which is shared by some other churches of the same region; in no single bay do the south side and the north agree. Some difference or other seems to have been studiously made between each arch and the arch opposite to it. It is this part of the building which supplies the greatest study of remarkable architectural forms. It is one which it would be instructive to compare with the contemporary nave of Worksop, in the same diocese, though not in the same shire. But in most eyes the glory of Selby will be its choir, ending in a window, which may claim at least the second place of its own class in England, and therefore in the world. Like York, Lincoln, Ely, and Carlisle, Selby has neither apse nor low chapels spreading beyond the main building. The ends of the choir and its aisles form the grand and simple east end of a type exclusively English. Within, the choir may be thought to suffer somewhat from the common English fault of lowness. A somewhat larger triforium-range would have made the difference. The vaulting of wood is clearly the right thing, if the walls and pillars were found unable to support a vault of stone. A wooden vault is of course a mere makeshift, but it is an allowable and necessary makeshift. The wooden vault of Selby is thoroughly good of its own kind, and it is a special relief to one who comes to it from the paltry roofs of its metropolitan neighbour at York.

Altogether, while we must leave it uncertain whether the one English-born son of the Conqueror really was born at Selby, we must allow that Selby has at least grown into a birthplace worthy of him. And one would the more gladly believe the tale because though, as we have seen, the architectural history of Selby is spread over several centuries, its history, as distinguished from its architecture, belongs, save one not very important fight in the seventeenth century, wholly to the age of Henry's birth.

NOTES IN THE NORTH RIDING.

1875.

THE North Riding of Yorkshire contains two remarkable spots which may be easily visited in a day's journey, namely Kirkdale, precious alike to antiquaries and to palæontologists, and Lastingham, which, except so far as the geologist is at home everywhere, the antiquaries have, we believe, wholly to themselves. Certain it is that the idea which is first suggested by the name of Kirkdale is that of a cave full of hyænas, while the idea which is first suggested by the name of Lastingham is, what may pass in some sort for an artificial cave, the crypt of the church. But the two stand as members—Lastingham perhaps as the furthest outpost—of a group of spots of singular and varied interest. A good day's ramble will take the traveller through many varieties of scenery, and through places whose antiquarian associations pretty well cover the whole field of British history. We may start from the Roman camp at Malton; we may go on among the hills through which the Conqueror struggled back with so much pain from his Northern conquests, by the great foundation of Walter of Espec, by the two places which the verse of the satirist has inseparably joined to the name of the second duke of the house of Villiers. Lastingham meanwhile carries us back to the saints of Bæda, and Kirkdale in its church commemorates the days of the Confessor, and in its cave carries us back to days before the Briton himself. We are in a land of hills and streams, streams which make up that Derwent which flows by

Stamfordbridge, hills which give us every variety of hill scenery, from the bleak moor of Lastingham to the wooded vale where the votaries of the religion of Citeaux fixed themselves by that Rye which gives its name to Rievaux. Some spots are richer in earlier, some in later, associations, but all have something to offer. Helmsley, which, and not the geographically impossible Hexham, was doubtless William's resting-place after his hard march through the Hambledon hills, forms a good centre for many places. The name of Helmsley must be familiar to many who never were there through the two famous lines of Pope, which tells how

> Helmsley, once proud Buckingham's delight,
> Slides to a scrivener or a city knight.

Lord Macaulay's readers know how 'the once humble name of Duncombe' got transferred to the lands which had once been the reward of Fairfax; and students of local genealogy may know how the name passed, not only to the lands—the lands which the House of Commons proposed to confiscate as a punishment of their owner's fraud—but also to their later possessors. Now, if Brown chooses to call himself Duncombe, or if Duncombe insists that Brown shall call himself Duncombe, no great harm is done to any one, and Brown most likely is pleased. But when the lands of Helmsley were made to take the name of Duncombe, a real wrong was done to geography. The student of local nomenclature, careless of pedigrees of yesterday, is indifferent alike to Browns and Duncombes. 'Brown Park' would cause him no perplexity; but when he hears of 'Duncombe Park' as the name of a place, he naturally asks, How came a *combe* in Yorkshire? The thing is a fraud on nomenclature as great as any of the frauds which the first Duncombe, 'born to carry parcels and to sweep down a counting-house,' contrived to commit on the treasury of the nation. It is as though a Kirby or a Thoresby should come down into the south and bring his name with him, and should thereby set inquirers wondering how a Danish 'by' got into Sussex or Dorset. But, whether Duncombe or Helmsley, the castle is still there, and we may thank the fraudulent scrivener that he had at least the grace to build his palace away from the ancient castle and to leave it as castles may best be studied. Helmsley has at least escaped the fate of Alnwick. We may still trace the vast ditches, the keep— the work it well may be of Walter of Espec, the hero of the Standard, the Norman patron of English learning— and side by side with it the work of later times, the delight of the proud Buckingham. The castle is at Helmsley the main attraction; the church contains some original work of the twelfth century; but the greater part is in the modern Norman style, a style which always awakens a certain desire to laugh, and which awakens it the more strongly as the new work more closely imitates the old.

But Helmsley, besides its merits in itself, is the centre for many other places. From the castle of Walter of Espec we naturally turn to his abbey, to Rievaux in its lovely valley, where in the transepts the work of the founder himself remains ingeniously preserved and adapted in the enlargement of the building in the next century. As we look down on the famous ruin from the terrace above, the strange departure from the common law of orientation, combined with the great size of the choir, may well lead the spectator astray at the first glimpse. He may easily take the main surviving part of the building for the western limb, instead of what it is, at least conventionally, the eastern limb. But it is less needful to dwell on a building so well known as Rievaux than it is to point out the importance of two places which lie on the other side of Helmsley. First we reach Kirkdale, in the solitary *Kirk-dale* itself, watered by its *beck*, the good old English name which carries us far away to Normandy, to Herlwin, to Lanfranc, and to Anselm. The Hodgebeck joins its waters with those of a Dove less famous than its

more southern namesake, the Dove which itself joins the
Rye, and the Rye the Derwent, so that the waters which
flow by perhaps the only stone which bears the graven
name of Tostig find their path into the Ocean by way of
Stamfordbridge. There, in the little church standing
apart from the dwelling-places of man, we find portions as
precious in the eyes of the architectural antiquary as the
neighbouring cave is in the eyes of the palæontologist.
We have here a dated example of work of the moment
when the newly introduced Norman style was displacing
the earlier Romanesque forms common to England with
all Western Europe. It is part of the same chain as
Coleswegen's towers at Lincoln, but it is an earlier link.
The inscription on each side of the sundial at Kirkdale tells
us how Orm, the son of Gamel, bought Saint Gregorys
minster when it was 'all tobroken and tofallen,' and made
it new from the ground in the days of Eadward the King
and Tostig the Earl. The rebuilding of Saint Gregorys
minster—mark the use of the word 'minster' here, as at
Assandún, for a church of the smallest scale, and which
we can hardly conceive as maintaining more than a single
priest—came between the years 1055 and 1065. Within
those years Eadward was busy in building his church at
Westminster in the new style, and the influence of the
new models made their way even to Kirkdale. Both in
the west doorway and in the chancel arch, the work,
though very rude, is quite unlike the forms of Primitive
Romanesque, and shows a distinct, though not very successful, attempt to imitate the foreign forms which were
creeping into use. This small, plain, and solitary church,
in a feature which it takes some trouble to find when we
have got there, is in fact a most important link in the
progress of architecture in England. At Deerhurst—a
church of far greater pretensions, but built earlier in the
days of the Confessor—there is no approach to Norman
work whatever. At Kirkdale the approach may be seen
distinctly, though seen only in the very rudest form.

We pass from Kirkdale to Kirkby Moorside. Both places have names taken from the church, and both therefore of comparatively late origin. They stand therefore in contrast with the venerable gentile name of Lastingham. In that name some have seen the 'lasting home' of its inhabitants, while one ingenious man, hearing that Lastingham was the home of Lastingas or Lastings, wrote to say that he had looked in the parish register and could find no such family as the Lastings there. Very modern ideas, it seems, may dwell in very ancient spots. But we have not yet reached Lastingham, and on the way we must give a moment to that Kirkby Moorside where the best-known lord of Helmsley has been said, with a good deal of exaggeration, to have died 'in the worst inn's worst room.' Thence either of two roads, both of them leading over hill and dale, but one of them specially leading over many hills and dales, will lead to what is in some sort the most remarkable building of the neighbourhood—the strange, incongruous, unfinished, mutilated, disfigured, and yet in some sort stately, church of Lastingham. The place, deep in a hollow on the moorside, was a savage wilderness in the days of Bæda. But for the church and the village which is gathered round it, it would be a wilderness, solitary, if not savage, still. With valleys bearing the attractive names of Ferndale and Rosedale on either side of it, Lastingham itself, though approached on every side from ground higher than itself, can hardly be called a dale. The air of the whole place is strange and un-English, and the un-English effect is increased by a tall cross on a height above the church and village, though the cross actually commemorates nothing more ancient than the beginning of the present reign. Yet the monument is not inappropriate, looking down as it does on one of the first spots where the cross was planted in this part of England. Within less than a generation from the day when Coifi led the way to the overthrow of the heathen temple at Godmundingaham,

Lastingham became the site of one of the earliest of Northumbrian monasteries, the seat of the holy Cedd, the brother of the more famous Ceadda of Lichfield. There he was buried, and there his memory is still preserved in local reverence. His well by the neighbouring stream has been repaired and adorned in quite modern times. But though the history of Lastingham thus carries us back four centuries earlier than the days when Orm rebuilt Saint Gregorys minster, the building itself does not carry us quite back to the days of Eadward and Tostig. In Domesday Lastingham appears as having been held by Gamel, who can hardly be the father of the founder of Kirkdale, nor yet his son who was slain by the practice of Tostig; he must rather be that other Gamel who avenged his blood by being one of the foremost in the revolt of Northumberland. From him it had passed to Berenger of Toesny, and of him it was held by the then newly-founded monastery of Saint Mary at York. According to one story, Lastingham was actually for a while the dwelling-place of the brotherhood, on their road from Whitby to York. Then it was doubtless, in the days of the Conqueror, that there arose that tall apse, stately in its very plainness and sternness, whose outside displays its plainness and sternness untouched, but which within has been disfigured above all apses, above almost all buildings of any shape. How far human perversity, not without a certain kind of ingenuity, can go in the way of disfiguring a venerable building, no man fully knows till he has been to Lastingham. As a study of human nature, it is worth any one's while to see how the apse of Lastingham has suffered within. From any other point of view it is better to shut one's eyes within the choir, and to study only the simple grandeur of the outside and of the crypt beneath, with its short and sturdy columns supplying a perfect study of capitals of the earlier Norman type. To make out the exact history of the rest of the building would almost need the gifts of a Willis. At first

Lastingham

Lastingham Crypt.

To face p. 314.

sight the stately apse of the eleventh century seems to have come into strange union with a commonplace parish church of the fourteenth and fifteenth centuries. But, both within and without, it is easy to see signs that a large church, much longer and higher than the present one, was at least begun, but possibly never finished, about the end of the twelfth century. The piers and their arches are there, but the upper part is gone or never was built, while there are piers and the beginnings of arches to the west of the present tower. To the exact nature of the process we will not commit ourselves, but it is certain that a church on a great scale was begun, but was either never finished, or else was strangely and recklessly mutilated at a time long before the dissolution of monasteries gave the general signal for such mutilations.

Not exactly in the same district, but still within easy reach of Helmsley, is another strange case of destruction, though wrought in this case at the usual time. The priory church of Old Malton, approached by a pleasant walk from the Roman camp of New Malton, besides the usual loss of its monastic eastern portion, has had its nave in the like sort cut short both in height and length. But at Lastingham the west end, whatever it was, has utterly perished; while at Malton, though one of the twin towers is gone, there is enough to bear witness to the former being a thirteenth-century front of a high order. Malton, in short, has a good deal to show both in the Roman and in the mediæval way; only it must not, any more than Brihtnoths Maldon far away, set itself up to be Camelodunum.

THE PERCY CASTLES.

1875.

WHEN the student of early English history crosses the Tees, a frightful thought at once presses itself upon him. He is in the land which is not set down in Domesday. He feels himself at the mercy of pedigree-makers. If a man chooses to say that his forefathers lived at such a place before the Norman Conquest, the historian looks incredulous, but the pretender cannot always be at once sent to the right-about, as he can at any point between Carisbrooke and Northallerton. There is not always the means of at once turning to the law and to the testimony to see whether these things are so. To be sure sometimes the Survey itself will help us, even in the lands which it does not directly describe. When the Chronicle of Alnwick tells us of a certain William Tison who died fighting by the side of Harold at Senlac, we hardly need to turn to any further authority to set aside a story which is fully set aside by the evidence of its hero's Norman name. Yet it is something to be able to point in Domesday to the name of Gilbert Tison, and to his estates, the spoil of several patriotic Yorkshiremen. We see how calmly the local romancer has borrowed a name from the other side, and we see also that, whenever he wrote, people were already beginning to think that to have been settled in a place 'before the Conquest' was even grander than to have 'come over with William the Conqueror.' But if in the Bernician shires we are in a land where we have lost our greatest safeguard of all, its place is supplied, as well as may be, by lesser safeguards of no small abundance and value. For the genealogical antiquities, as for the antiquities of all kinds, of the shires beyond the Tees, of the palatine bishopric and the border earldom, the materials are rich, and no materials have ever been more diligently and more acutely handled by local inquirers. Indeed the great monuments of Northumbrian research, the Surtees Society and its publications, have more than a local character. They rank among the most valuable contributions to early English history. Northumberland too has been made the subject of the model county history, one of the few whose authors have remembered that the main object of writing the history of a county is to throw light on the history of the whole kingdom. Foremost in interest among the monuments of Northumberland in the narrower sense, of the earldom beyond the Tyne, stand the castles, the castles of every size and shape, from Bamburgh where the castle occupies the whole site of a royal city, to the smallest pele-tower where the pettiest squire or parson sought shelter for himself in the upper stage and for his cows in the lower. For the pele-towers of the Border-land, like the endless small square towers of Ireland, are essentially castles. They show the type of the Norman keep continued on a small scale to a very late time. Perhaps many of the 'adulterine' castles which arose in every time of anarchy and which were overthrown at every return of order, many of the eleven hundred and odd castles which overspread the land during the anarchy of Stephen, may have been of much greater pretensions. At any rate, from the great keep of Newcastle—were we not in Northumberland, we should speak of the far greater keep of Colchester—to the least pele-tower which survives as a small part of a modern house, the idea which runs through all is exactly the same. The castles and towers then, great and small, are the most marked feature of the country. They distinguish it from those shires where castles of any kind are rare; and the use of the type of the great keeps on a very small scale distinguishes it from the other land of castles. In Wales the Norman keep is not usual; the castles are, for the most part, later in date and more complex in plan; and the small square private tower, the distinctive feature of the North, is there hardly to be found. Northumberland has much to show the traveller in many ways, from the Roman wall onward, but the feature which is specially characteristic is that it is the land of castles.

In speaking of Northumbrian castles it is curious to see how in most minds their mention at once suggests the name of one particular family. Romancing about Tison has gone out of fashion; but the fashion of romancing has gone on with another name. In any matter which has to do with castles, and with what have happily been called 'castle times,' the name of Northumberland at once calls up the name of Percy. Yet, when we come to look a little more narrowly into matters, we shall see how little Northumberland and Percy really had to do with one another. If one chose to be very precise, it would not be wrong to say that no real Percy ever had anything to do with Northumberland at all, except in that elder sense of words in which Yorkshire is a part of Northumberland. As there never was a Duke, so there never was even an Earl, of Northumberland sprung from the male line of the Percy of Domesday. The Northumbrian castles which we instinctively think of as Percy castles were never held by the first, the only true, line of Percies. The Percy of Domesday belongs not to the later Northumberland, but to Yorkshire. The Percies of Northumberland, the descendants of Jocelyn of Louvain, had in truth more claim to rank as Karlings than as Percies. But while surnames were still territorial, while they still marked possession of this or that place, rather than descent from this or that man, for the husband of the heiress of Percy to call himself Jocelyn of Percy was not quite the same thing as when Sir Hugh Smithson took the name of his wife's grandmother simply because it was thought to sound finer than the good old Teutonic name of his own forefathers. But the fact is that the great Northumbrian castles which have become specially suggestive of Percies are no more the work of the Karling Percies than they are of the Smithson Percies. At Alnwick almost the only feature of beauty or interest which the hand of the destroyer has spared is the one fragment which belongs to the days that give Alnwick its place in English history. The noble gateway of the ancient keep belongs to days long before the coming of Percies; it is the work of the older lords of Alnwick of the house of Vescy. So it is at Warkworth; so it is at Prudhoe. The Percy of the true line never was there at all; the Percy of the second line came in as one who dwelled in goodly houses which other men had builded. It was perhaps in some desperate effort to carry back the possession of its later lords to an earlier time, that some daring genealogist, forgetful that Percy was the name of a real spot of Norman ground, devised the tale of the soldier who pierced King Malcolm's eye at Alnwick and so took the name of *Pierce-eye.* The tale is much of a piece with other genealogical tales; only unluckily it cut two ways. It exalted the Percy of Northumberland by taking him to Alnwick before his time; but it lessened the antiquity of the Percy of Normandy and Yorkshire. For once therefore truth got the better of error; people who believe that Bulstrode came riding on a bull to meet the Conqueror do not believe that the first Percy pierced the eye of Malcolm of Scotland.

Yet the place of the house of Percy in English history, the place to be sure rather of the second line than of the true Percies, is one which nothing but flattery can ever lead us to forget. Its last age is perhaps the most honourable. The last Percy but one took his place alongside of Manchester and Essex. One version of the contemporary career of the first recorded Smithson may be read in Tait's

History of Alnwick, one of the few books of the kind which are not written in a spirit of cringing. Another version, carrying Smithson, or haply Smithton, up into Domesday, may be seen in the peerages. Which is true, or whether either is true, is a matter of perfect indifference to English history. The earlier history both of the Percies and of their castles may be studied in the volume which was published by the Archæological Institute after its meeting at Newcastle, the work of the late Mr. Hartshorne, the best inquirer into such matters till the appearance of Mr. Clark. Only one cannot help being amused at the fervour of zeal into which Mr. Hartshorne lashes himself at every mention of the name of Percy. He works very hard to make out a case even for the double traitor who first betrayed Richard to Henry, and then rebelled against Henry in turn. Rather than own a Percy to have been in the wrong, the vulgar names of usurper and the like are showered on the deliverer to whom the Lords and Commons of England gave the crown which was theirs to give. With Mr. Hartshorne reverence for the Percies extends to the modern occupiers of their name, and he has his bursts of admiration even for the modern works to which the glories of Alnwick have given way. Yet, after all the daubing of flatterers, Percy remains a great historic name, and the castles in which the second line of Percies dwelled have an interest in themselves, an interest deep and lasting, independent either of genealogical fables or of genealogical truths. And Mr. Hartshorne's book, in spite of its Percy-worship, is a good and useful book, and guides us to several spots which never had anything to do with Percies at all.

Of the chief Percy castles, the historical importance of Alnwick belongs to its præ-Percy times. The popular belief seems to be that Dukes of Northumberland of the name of Percy have reigned uninterruptedly at Alnwick from the days of the Conqueror or earlier down to our own time. We have seen the travels of an American professor, who sets down with charming simplicity the story which he was told at Alnwick about the Duke of Northumberland's dealings with King Malcolm, in which the appearance of the Duke's daughter, Lady Something Percy no doubt, added to the charm of the legend. Yet at Alnwick in the eleventh century, even in the latest years of the century, there was neither Duke nor Earl, neither Smithson nor Percy; it is not clear that there was any castle at all. Still it was undoubtedly at Alnwick that Malcolm and his son Edward lost their lives in the days of Rufus; at Alnwick it was that, eighty years later, William the Lion was taken captive, to yield to the English overlord a more full submission than any King of Scots had yielded before him. The place of the ambush by which the earlier king died is still shown, marked by the traditional name of Malcolm's Cross, and by a ruined chapel of Romanesque date hard by. The place is a height looking out on another range to the south, while between them flows the Alne, with the lower height crowned by Alnwick castle and town rising above it. When William came, Alnwick had a castle, the work of Eustace Fitz-John, son-in-law of the first Ivo of Vescy, who seems to have set the fashion to the place of handing on the names of mothers and grandmothers rather than those of fathers. The capture of the Lion king chiefly suggests the remembrance of the special engagements by which he regained his freedom. Hitherto, though the Scottish king had been the man of the English overlord, no Scottish subject had been bound by the like allegiance, no Scottish castle had been held as a pledge of the faith of its prince. The treaty of Falaise imposed these new burthens, and it was from these new burthens, not from the obligations of the old commendation, that the Lion of Poitou released his brother Lion of Scotland. Another Scottish king, early in the next century, did his homage at the same place. Then, in 1309, the first Percy of Alnwick crept in unawares, through a grant or sale from Bishop Anthony Bek, who seems to have played the last

Vescy a rather shabby trick. Since then Alnwick appears now and then in history; it has stood a siege or two and seen a king or two, but it has not been the scene of great national events, like the slaying of Malcolm and the homage of William.

At Alnwick then the main interest of the place is in its memories, memories of days before the name of Percy had been heard there. Warkworth, of less historic fame than Alnwick, is in itself a more pleasing object of study. Bating two or three rooms in the later keep, it stands, as a castle should stand, free from the disfigurement of modern habitation. This keep, a work of the Percies of the second line, is a good study of the process by which the purely military castle gradually passed into the house fortified for any occasional emergency. Placed on its peninsular hill rising above the Coquet, few military or domestic buildings surpass its picturesque outline. The later chapel, as well as the later hall, is in this keep; but the older chapel and the older pillared hall are still to be traced in their foundations. But the chapel was to have been more than a chapel. According to a practice found in several royal and in a few baronial dwellings, it was to have been a small minster, a cross church with an attached college, within the castle walls. In a hill-side on the other bank of the river, approached by a wooded dale, is the famous hermitage, so well known in legend, but whose history Mr. Hartshorne is driven to guess at. The chapel hewn in the rock carries us to the rock-hewn churches of Brantôme and Saint Emilion. Here in England the sight of architectural details cut in the rock, an apparent vault with apparent groining and bosses, is strange and unusual. Mr. Hartshorne looks on the hermitage as the work of the third Percy of Alnwick, the second of Warkworth, Henry by name, in the time of Edward the Third. That it is a Percy work can hardly be doubted; but it must not be forgotten that Warkworth contains, both in its castle and elsewhere, important remains of præ-Percy times.

Bywell. Trinity Church, Colchester.

To face p. 322.

The oldest parts of the castle may have seen the coming of the Lion of Scotland, and the parish church is a large and, allowing for modern restoration, a well preserved building of Romanesque date. At Prudhoe, the castle where Percy succeeded Umfraville, the ugly house within the walls is perhaps less offensive than the turning of the ancient building itself into a modern dwelling-place. But we admire the pile as it stands above the Tyne; we admire the entrance-tower, with its chapel containing the earliest known oriel window, one of the simplest and most graceful pieces of work of its kind. There is the shattered keep, which withstood the Scottish assaults when Warkworth fell before them, where its founder, Odenell of Umfraville, kept at bay the host of the Northern king till Randolf of Glanville, the warlike Justiciar, the author of our first legal treatise, came to his help. At Prudhoe there are no Percy memories, no Percy buildings; all belongs to an elder day. The keep of the twelfth century leads us back by easy steps to a yet more venerable monument on the other side of the river. There the church tower of Ovingham, of the purest præ-Norman Romanesque, recalling Monkwearmouth itself on a scale of greater bulk and stateliness, carries us back to days when Percies were not, and when, if we may trust one of the most venerable of Northern sagas, the son of Smith would have been as little likely as the son of Karl to be ashamed of his own name.

BAMBURGH AND DUNSTANBURGH.

1875.

WE lately spoke of some of those castles of the great Border earldom which derive their chief reputation in popular, though not in historical, belief, from their comparatively modern connexion with the second house of Percy. But there are other castles in the same land which play but little part in the hands of the genealoger or the romancer, but which really have, in one way or another, a higher interest than any of those castles whose names are to most ears more familiar. Two castles of the Northumbrian earldom stand out, each, in its own way, pre-eminent among all their fellows. One is, in its memories, if not in its fabric, the most historic of all, and if its fabric is sadly disfigured by adaptation to modern uses, it yet stands, with its main outline at least hardly marred, on a site which is all but the noblest by nature, and which surpasses the sites of all other northern fortresses in ancient and abiding historic interest. The other plays but little part in history, but it surpasses all in the natural grandeur of its site, and it alone abides, as a castle should abide, in all the majesty of a shattered ruin. These are the two fortresses of Bamburgh and Dunstanburgh, each standing far away alike from the busy dwelling-places of man and from the softer scenery of inland hills and dales. Utterly unlike the keep of Newcastle in the midst of its thronging streets, utterly unlike Alnwick and Warkworth and Prudhoe, looking down from their gentler heights on their rivers, are these two stern rock-fortresses overhanging the German Ocean. Among buildings of their own class, they are the very glory of the old Bernician realm. Of the two shires into which the still English portions of that realm are divided, each, by a kind of equitable arrangement, contains the spot of deepest importance in its own line. Northumberland contains the immemorial dwelling-place of its kings and earls. Durham contains the no less proud dwelling-place of the princely bishops from whose church the palatine shire has taken its name. With Bamburgh in the land beyond the Tyne, with Durham in the land on this side of it, it is an insult to those two great and historic shires to speak of them, as is done in Murray's Handbook, as if mere ballads and popular traditions were the chief things to be thought of in them. Ballads and popular traditions are well enough in their place, and, in their place, they will never be despised by any rational inquirer. But it is not of ballads and popular traditions that we chiefly think when we see the whole volume of English history unfolded before us around the mighty keep of Bamburgh, or when we trace the fates of the great Bernician bishopric, in its wanderings from the cell of Aidan on his hermit island to the lordly home of William of Saint Calais and Hugh of Puiset.

We have said that, among the objects of historical interest in Northumberland, the castles claim the first place as the distinctive historic feature of the country. When we look on such a fortress as Bamburgh, and think of all the events whose memories dwell around it from the earliest days of English history, we may be tempted to say that, in purely historical interest, as a monument of recorded men and recorded acts, it surpasses even the great wonder of the northern land, the Roman wall itself. In truth the interest of the wall and that of the castles are of two wholly different kinds. The wall is there, less mysterious indeed now than it was to Procopius in days when, comparatively new as it still was, it had passed away into the shadowy wonders of an unknown cloudland.

But, diligently as it has been studied, rich as has been the return which it has yielded to those who have studied it, the Roman wall, whether we call it the wall of Hadrian, of Severus, or of Theodosius, still remains a work shrouded in a certain degree of mystery. It is a monument of ages which have utterly passed away, a monument which might be almost said to have been already an antiquity when the first Englishman gazed on it in wonder. Whatever part the great wall played in history in days when strife within this island was still a strife between Celt and Roman, it has played no part since English history began; it has not even, like many meaner works, served as a political frontier. It might be hazardous to say that it has never at any time formed the boundary of shire or kingdom; but it has certainly not served as such for any great time or through any great part of its length. The wall is a monument of the past which has utterly vanished, a monument of the fortunes of those who came before us in the possession of the land which is now ours. The castles are also the monuments of a past which is gone for ever; but it is a past which is our own past, a past which is connected by a tie of unbroken continuity with the present.

But at Bamburgh above all we feel that we are pilgrims come to do our service at one of the great cradles of our national life. It is the one spot in northern England around which the same interest gathers which belongs to the landing places of Hengest, of Ælle, and of Cerdic, in the southern lands. It is to the Angle what those spots are to the Jute and the Saxon. The beginnings of the Anglian kingdoms are less rich in romantic and personal lore than are the beginnings of their Jutish and Saxon neighbours. Unless we accept the tale about Octa and Ebussa, we have no record of the actual leaders of the first Teutonic settlements in the Anglian parts of Britain. The earliest kingdoms seem not to have been founded by new-comers from beyond the sea, but to have been formed by the fusing together of smaller independent settlements. Yet round Bamburgh and its founder Ida all Northumbrian history gathers. Though its keep is more than five hundred years later than Ida's time—though it is only here and there that we see fragments of masonry which we can even guess may be older than the keep—it is still a perfectly allowable figure when the poet of northern Britain speaks of Bamburgh as 'King Ida's fortress.' The founder of the Northumbrian kingdom, the first who bore the kingly name in Bamburgh, the warrior whom the trembling Briton spoke of as the 'flame-bearer,' appears in the one slight authentic notice of him, not as the leader of a new colony from the older England, but rather as the man who gathered together a number of scattered independent settlements into a nation and a kingdom. And, when we find ourselves in a land, no longer of *casters* but of *chesters*, we begin to ask whether Octa and Ebussa do not mean something, whether some of these settlements were not Jutish or Saxon rather than Anglian. The Chronicler records of Ida that in 547 he 'took to the kingdom' ('feng to rice'); but nothing is said of his coming, like Hengest or Cerdic, from beyond sea. And all the other accounts fall in with the same notion. Henry of Huntingdon, though he has no story to tell, no ballad to translate, was doubtless following some old tradition when he described the Anglian chiefs, after a series of victories over the Welsh, joining together to set a king over them. And all agree in speaking of Bamburgh, called, so the story ran, from his queen Bebbe, as a special work of Ida. Whatever may be the origin of the name, it suggests the kindred name of the East-Frankish Babenberg, which has been cut short into Bamberg by the same process which has cut short Bebbanburh into Bamburgh.

But Bamburgh was a fortress by nature, even before Ida had fenced it in, first with a hedge and then with a wall. That mass of isolated basaltic rock frowning over the sea on one side, over the land on the other, was indeed a spot marked out by nature for dominion. Here then was the city of Bebbe, strong but small, the royal city, reached only by steps, with a single entrance cut in the rock, and whose whole circuit did not exceed that of two or three fields. That is, the whole length and breadth of the royal city of Bernicia was no greater than that of the present castle. Its highest point was crowned, not as yet by the keep of the Norman, but by a church which, according to the standard of the eighth century, was a goodly one. This church contained a precious chest, which sheltered a yet more precious relic, the wonder-working right hand of the martyred king Oswald. We read too how the city, perched on its Ocean rock, was yet, unlike the inland hill of the elder Salisbury, well furnished with water, clear to the eye and sweet to the taste. Here was the dwelling-place of successive Bernician kings, ealdormen, and earls; here they took shelter as in an impregnable refuge from the inroads of Scot and Dane. Here the elder Waltheof shut himself up in terror while his valiant son Uhtred sent forth and rescued the newly founded church and city of Durham from the invader. But by the time that we reach the event in the history of Bamburgh which is told to us in the most striking detail, the keep had already risen; the English city had become the Norman castle. In the days of Rufus, when the fierce Robert of Mowbray had risen a second time in rebellion, the keep of Bamburgh, safe on its rock and guarded by surrounding waves and marshes, was deemed beyond the power even of the Red King to subdue by force of arms. The building of the *Malvoisin*, the Evil Neighbour, the $ἐπιτειχισμός$, as a Greek would have called it, was all that could be done while the rebel Earl kept himself within the impregnable walls. It was only when he risked himself without those walls, when he was led up to them as a captive, with his eyes to be seared out if his valiant wife refused to surrender, that Bamburgh came into the royal hands.

Yet, simply as a spot to gaze at, the castle of Dunstan-

burgh, which has hardly any history, may claim a rank
higher even than royal Bamburgh. Neither history nor
tradition tells us how the fortress came by its name; yet
Dunstan was a Northumbrian as well as a West-Saxon
name, and Dunstan the son of Æthelnoth appears among
the Northumbrian chiefs who rose up against the tyranny
of Tostig. But be its founder who he may, though the
castle itself plays no part in history, it has been the possession of two memorable lords. It was for a while the
property of Earl Simon; and it had passed to him from a
lord who, whatever may have been his pedigree, bore the
glorious name of Hereward. After the fall of the great
Earl, it passed to Edmund of Lancaster, him who had
once borne the name and garb of a Sicilian king, and
from him it passed to his son, that Thomas of Lancaster
whose name was by the voice of the English people placed
on the roll of saints alongside of Simon himself. To Earl
Thomas there is every reason to attribute the present
building. In Mr. Hartshorne's collection we find him
receiving a licence to crenellate, combined with a full
official account of the works. There those works stand as
they should stand. At Alnwick, at Warkworth, at Prudhoe, at Bamburgh itself, the historic sense is grated on
by modern habitation in various forms. At Dunstanburgh happily all is ruin. Its isolated hill stands yet
more nobly than the isolated hill of Bamburgh; the waves
dash more immediately at its feet, boiling up in a narrow
channel close under its walls, as if art and nature had
joined together to make the fortress of Earl Thomas
grim and awful above all other fortresses. Nothing can
well be conceived more striking than the Lilburn tower,
a Norman keep in spirit, though far later in date,
rising on the slope of the wild hill with the tall basaltic
columns standing in order in front of it 'like sentinels of
stone.' Yet, simply as a building, one is almost more
struck if one approaches from the opposite side, and if the
vast gateway, with its two huge circular towers, is the

first feature to burst upon us. It doubtless has its rivals in other places where we more naturally look for some of the great works of human skill. In that desolate wilderness the gateway and the whole castle have an effect which is sublime beyond words.

SUSSEX

THE CASE OF THE COLLEGIATE CHURCH OF ARUNDEL.

1879-1880.

[This paper was first written in 1879, at the time of the first trial. I had not then seen the documents in full. I afterwards recast it by the light of the two trials and of a study of the documents. It was satisfactory to find that such a study thoroughly confirmed the conclusion which I had come to by the mere use of the comparative method.

I have added, as an appendix to the paper, part of an article from the Saturday Review, September 11, 1875, describing two of the best examples of the class of churches referred to, one of which is mentioned in the paper itself.]

THE question which, after two trials, has lately been decided in favour of the Duke of Norfolk against the Vicar of Arundel is one which involves many points of historical and antiquarian interest. The point in dispute was whether the building forming the eastern limb of Arundel church was simply the chancel of the parish church, or whether it was in strictness a separate church, formerly belonging to the suppressed college, and now forming, with the other property of that college, an absolute possession belonging to the duke. In the former case the duke would have simply the rights and liabilities held by an impropriate rector over the chancel of a parish church. In the other case the building would be absolutely at the duke's disposal, as much as a house or a barn that belonged to him. Much that was said at the two trials by counsel, and even by judges, much that has been said in the way of newspaper comment, sounds very wonderful to those to whom the case of Arundel church seemed only a very simple instance of a class to which they were well accustomed. It may therefore be useful to compare the case of Arundel at some length with a number of other cases which have more or less of analogy with it.

It was even doubted at the trial whether there could be in strictness two churches under one roof, that is, whether a building which forms one architectural whole and which in artistic and in ordinary language would be spoken of as a single church, could really contain what, in point of property and use, are two distinct churches. I confess that I was surprised that there could be any doubt upon the subject. The arrangement is a very common one, and it is one which I have always carefully noticed whenever I have come across it. I have myself spoken of it in several monographs in various periodicals and local proceedings, and it must surely be familiar to any one who has studied the different classes of monastic and collegiate churches. The case of Arundel seems singular, simply because both churches are standing, though one is disused, while in most cases one of the two has been pulled down. That is to say, the successive Earls of Arundel have forborne to exercise the right of destruction which the law gave them. In most cases that right has been unsparingly exercised; Arundel is one of the small class of cases in which it has not.

In some collegiate churches, in perhaps the majority of monastic churches, there was no connexion with any parish. The inhabitants of the place where the college or monastery stood had no proprietary rights in the monastic or collegiate church; they had their own distinct parish church, standing quite apart. In other cases the parish church and the monastic or collegiate church stood close together and formed one architectural whole. That is to say, a building which formed architecturally a single church was, as far as use and property were concerned, divided into two churches, one belonging to the parish, the other to the monks or canons. I must here add an interpretation clause for my own article. To avoid endless repetitions and explanations, I shall use the word *monks* to denote all members of religious foundations, and the word *canons* to denote all members of secular foundations, whatever was their title in each particular case. The members of the secular foundations bore various titles —canons, prebendaries, fellows, chaplains, and others; at Arundel the original name was chaplains, for which the name of *fellows* seems to have been a later alteration. But the nature of the foundation was the same, whatever was the title of its members. In these cases of divided churches, the eastern part of the building commonly belonged to the monks or canons, the western part to the parishioners. Most commonly, in the usual case of a cross church, the parishioners had the nave, while the monks or canons had the choir and transepts. Thus the building, while it formed architecturally a single church, formed in point of possession two churches, which, wherever legal precision was needed, were spoken of severally as the 'parish church' and the 'abbey church,' 'priory church,' or, as at Arundel, 'collegiate church,' according to the nature of the foundation, But neither now nor then was such legal precision likely to be always attended to in ordinary speech. A building which, for all architectural and artistic purposes, was one building, was constantly spoken of as one building. The two churches under one roof, forming one architectural whole, were constantly spoken of as one church. Men spoke then, as we should speak now, of 'Arundel church' as a whole. And as one part was collegiate, another part parochial, it is not wonderful if the whole was often spoken of, sometimes as 'collegiate church,' sometimes as 'parochial church.' But whenever legal precision was of importance, the two parts of the building were carefully distinguished by their proper names. And never was the distinction more needed than when one part of the building changed owners. Such a

time came amid the changes of the sixteenth century.
When the monasteries were suppressed under Henry the
Eighth, and the colleges, partly under Henry the Eighth,
partly under Edward the Sixth, that part of the building
which formed the monastic or collegiate church came into
the hands of the king with the rest of the monastic or
collegiate property, and was dealt with by him or his
grantee according to their pleasure in each particular case.
It was dealt with precisely as those suppressed churches
were dealt with which stood apart from any parish church.
Its architectural connexion with the parish church made
no difference. But, whatever happened to it, the right of
the parish in its part of the building was not touched.
That was no more interfered with by the suppression of
the monastery or college than it was when the two
churches stood altogether apart. The monastic or collegiate church was in most cases altogether pulled down.
In others it was dismantled and left as a ruin. In others
it was allowed to stand whole, but was disused; in a few
cases it was bought by the parishioners or given them by
some benefactor, and was added to the parish church.

I shall speak throughout of monastic and collegiate
churches together, because I cannot see that it makes
any difference whether the corporate body which divided
the church with the parish was regular or secular. The
rights and relations of the corporation towards the parish
would be the same in either case. The abbot and monks
in one case, the dean and canons or other collegiate body
in the other case, might be simply the corporate rector
with the rights and liabilities of any other rector, or they
might be something more, namely the absolute owners of
the monastic or collegiate part of the building. It makes
no difference that in the majority of collegiate churches
the canons seem to have been simply a corporate rector,
while in the vast majority of monastic churches the
monks were absolute owners, either of the whole church,
if there was no parish attached, or, as has been already

said, of part of it when there was a parish attached. The reason is plain; the monks had much more reason to seek for a complete separation from the parishioners than the secular clergy had. In fact, in many collegiate churches the evident object was simply to provide for the better performance of divine service in the parish church. The canons or other clergy were simply a multiplied rector; when the college was suppressed, the rectory passed with the other college property to the king's grantee; but this gave him no rights over the chancel beyond the ordinary rights of a rector. It was his duty to keep up; he had no power to pull down. But where the absolute property of any part of the building was vested in the corporate body, whether monks or canons, the power of destruction passed into the hands of the grantee, and he most commonly put it in force.

On the other hand, it is equally clear that there were, or had been, monastic churches which were also parochial, and in which the monks had simply the rights of rectors. This I conceive was the case with a number of small monastic churches, chiefly in Wales—I mention that of Penmon in Anglesey, as the last which I have seen—where the whole church is standing, and where there is no sign of any division having been made. Here, I conceive the monks were simply a corporate rector, so that the dissolution did not affect the rights of the parishioners in the chancel. In other cases the church was in the same way originally held in common by the monks and the parishioners; but disputes arose, as was but natural; and it was agreed to divide the building, the monks taking the eastern part and the parishioners the western. The cases of this kind where the history is recorded give us the key to a number of other cases where the history is not recorded—where at least it is not accessible to me—but which present the same appearances as those whose history is known. When we see a church, known to have been monastic or collegiate, whose western part is standing and is used as a parish church, but whose eastern part is pulled down, ruined, or disused, we may, in absence of proof to the contrary, presume a division of the building between the parish and the monks or canons. It does not follow that the division was in all cases the consequence of a dispute. The church may have been in some cases so divided from the beginning; but it is naturally in those cases where there was a dispute that we get the history in the fullest detail.

It must further be remembered that, if any distinction could be established in this matter between monastic and collegiate churches, a distinction for which I do not see the slightest ground, still that distinction would not apply to Arundel. For there, as the grantee took the place of the college, so the college had before taken the place of the suppressed alien priory. The rights with which the new foundation was clothed would not be smaller than those which had been held by the earlier body; they might conceivably be greater.

I now come to the examples[1] which show that it was a common practice for a church to be divided between a parish and a monastic or collegiate body, and that in such cases the two parts were formally spoken of as the 'parish church' and the 'priory church,' or whatever else might be the proper description in that particular case. But we must not look for strict consistency of usage on this point. The church, though divided for purposes of possession and use, still, as a building, formed one whole. When there was no particular necessity to insist on the fact of division, people would naturally speak of the two

---

[1] I keep to English examples, as I have not given much attention to the matter out of England. But I stumbled on a case of the kind in 1879 at Château du Loir in Maine, where the *curé* kindly volunteered a bit of local history proving the division, not knowing that it would be specially acceptable.

The double choirs, capitular and parochial, of the great German minsters are the same in principle as the arrangement of which we are now speaking; but the artistic effect is quite different.

parts together as a single church. It was only when it was specially needful to insist on the division that the parts would be spoken of severally as the 'parish church' and the 'priory church' or 'collegiate church.'

I will begin with a case in which the history of the division is minutely recorded, having been brought about by a dispute as to the right of visitation. This is the church of Wymondham in Norfolk, first a dependent priory of Saint Albans, afterwards an independent abbey. It was also a parish church, and in 1249 a dispute arose as to the right of the archdeacon to visit in it. The question was settled by papal authority in favour of the archdeacon, so far that his right of visitation was established within the parochial part of the church, which is distinctly distinguished as the 'parish church.' The document is printed in the Gesta Abbatum Sancti Albani, i. 355—360. The description of the church, as given in the archdeacon's pleading, is explicit.

Cum enim ecclesia de Wydmundham, de qua agitur, sit parochialis ecclesia, et non cella, ad quam per priorem et conventum vicarius Norwicensi episcopo præsentatur, et curam animarum recipit ab eodem, et ad ipsam parochiani confluunt pro divinis, et a vicario ecclesiastica recipiunt sacramenta, monachis ipsius cellæ facientibus intra chorum; ad quam etiam parochianis per publica strata patet ingressus, ipsis vero monachis ad chorum datur aditus aliunde; licet parietes parochialis ecclesiæ, et chori in quo per monachos deservitur, continui sint, ipsosque sit protegens idem tectum, hujusmodi tamen ecclesia infra cellæ ambitum non consistit, nec ad ipsam indulgentia se extendit.

The decision of the papal court runs as follows:—

Ut memoratum archidiaconum permittant uti juribus supradictis in dictis ecclesiis pacifice et quiete : nomine autem ecclesiæ de Wymundham parochialem intelligimus ecclesiam, cum vicario, et plebe quæ pertinet ad eandem.

Here we have described, as distinctly as words can describe anything, two churches forming one building under one roof and with continuous walls, which were yet so distinct in point of possession and use that the archdeacon had jurisdiction in one part of the building and not in the other. But the 'prædictæ ecclesiæ' in the last extract do not mean the monastic and parochial church, but the two churches of Wymondham and Binham, both of which were concerned in the dispute.

For the later very important history of Wymondham I have not any original document to refer to. I must be satisfied with the account in the Monasticon (iii. 328), and in Mr. Petit's paper on Wymondham, in the volume of the Archæological Institute at Norwich for 1847, p. 117. Both refer to Blomefield's History of Norfolk, which I have not at hand. It appears that the second dispute arose about 1410, this time between the parishioners and the monks, and it was settled by Archbishop Arundel. The way in which the constructive division was made was singular. The monks took the choir and transepts, with the tower which stood immediately west of the crossing, together with the south aisle of the nave. The parishioners had the nave and the north aisle; they also built a tower at the west end. The abbey tower in the middle formed a complete barrier, with a dead wall, between the eastern and western parts of the church. At the dissolution, the parishioners bought the south aisle and the abbey tower. They did not buy the choir and transepts; these therefore were destroyed, and only some ruins are left.

The church of Binham, another cell of Saint Albans, was, as I have said, concerned in the same dispute as Wymondham. The western limb is now standing, and forms a complete parish church, with a chancel marked off in its eastern part. It was evidently cut off from the monastic church by a solid wall, forming a reredos to the parish high altar, and pierced with the two doors usual in a reredos.

Another cell of Saint Albans was Tynemouth, where also in 1247 a dispute arose between the church of Saint Albans and the Bishop and church of Durham, about the right of visitation. This is recorded by Matthew Paris (Chronica Majora, iv. 609, ed. Luard). The words are— 'super visitatione facienda in ecclesia parochiali, quæ est in monasterio monachorum de Thinemue.' In the decision of the question (iv. 615), the dispute 'super visitatione ecclesiæ parochialis de Thinemue' is settled by ruling that the bishop and his officials shall have jurisdiction

in illa parte ecclesiæ de Thinemue in qua parochianis divina celebrantur, sine onere procurationis, ita quod de monachis seu alia parte ecclesiæ sive etiam de ipsa cella se nullatenus intromittant.

Here the 'ecclesia parochialis' is defined to be a part of the general 'ecclesia' or 'monasterium' (*minster*) of Tynemouth.[1] And, though the whole is now in ruins, the distinction is still clearly marked. The reredos of the parish high altar, plainly set up at the time spoken of by Matthew Paris, is still to be seen across the western arch of the crossing.

The further history of Tynemouth, as given in the Monasticon (iii. 309-310),[2] shows that in the time of Elizabeth, the 'parish kirk,' which was then still in use, was distinguished from the 'abbey kirk,' to the east of it, which was in ruins. A new parish church, apart from the priory, was begun in 1659, and by the end of the seventeenth century the old parish church was unroofed.

In these cases we have part of the building distinguished in legal language as 'ecclesia parochialis,' while, in one case at least, the two parts were popularly distinguished as 'parish kirk' and 'abbey kirk.' We find the same language in use at Leominster, a church which I

[1] It must be remembered that, besides the use of *monasterium* to mean *monastery*, it also often means *minster*, that is, the church as distinguished from the other buildings, and that whether the church was monastic or secular. The Waltham charter says, with perfect accuracy, that Harold '*construxit* monasterium;' it would have been inaccurate to say that he '*fundavit* monasterium.'

[2] Many more details will be found in the late Mr. W. S. Gibson's History of Tynemouth; but, amidst much declamation, he fails to grasp the history of the divided church.

have studied very minutely, and of which I wrote an account in the Archæologia Cambrensis, and also in the local History of Leominster by the Rev. G. F. Townsend, p. 209. Here we have the witness of Leland (see Monasticon, iv. 55). He says :—

Ther is but one paroch chirch in Leominster, but it is large, somewhat darke, and of antient building, insomuch that it is a grete lykelyhood that it is the church that was somwhat afore the Conquest. The chirch of the priorie was hard joyned to the est end of the paroch chirch, and was but a small thing.

The parish church, though certainly not 'somewhat afore the Conquest,' contains the greater part of the twelfth century minster, namely, the nave and north aisle. The south aisle was widened into a large building, with the parish high altar at the east end. The choir and transepts which formed the priory church had plainly been pulled down before Leland's visit. Their foundations were dug up some years back. But the evidence for the distinction at Leominster does not merely rest on the English of Leland. It occurs also in the formal Latin of the will of Philip Bradford in 1458, printed in Mr. Townsend's book, p. 41 :—

Lego . . . corpus meum ad sepeliendum in capella sanctæ Annæ infra ecclesiam parochialem Leomynstriæ. Item, lego altari S. Petri in ecclesia monachorum ijs. Item, lego altari Sanctæ Trinitatis in ecclesia parochiali ibidem xijd.

This last document gives us another clear case of distinction between the 'ecclesia parochialis' and the 'ecclesia monachorum,' existing as separate churches within what, speaking architecturally of the building, we should call a single church. This leads us to an entry in Matthew Paris (Chronica Majora, iv. 227, ed. Luard), where, under the year 1242, he records the consecration of 'ecclesia conventualis canonicorum de Waltham.' No one who knows the earlier and later history of Waltham abbey can doubt as to his meaning. The present church consists of the nave only; the choir, transepts, and central tower are

Wayborne.

To face p. 343.

gone. The solid wall which ends the church to the east is clearly a carrying up of the reredos of the parish high altar; the doors may be traced. Within this parish church or constructive nave it is alleged that two or three of the eastern bays still form the parish chancel, and that the impropriate rector, and not the parish, is bound to repair those bays. I do not profess to know whether this claim is good in law; but the mere belief is enough to show historically that the present church of Waltham was a complete parish church with its chancel, distinct from the monastic church to the east of it. That eastern church was the 'ecclesia conventualis' of Matthew Paris. It was no doubt rebuilt on a larger scale in the thirteenth century, and consecrated afresh, while the parish church to the west of it remained untouched. It is hardly needful to say that the 'canonici de Waltham' in Matthew Paris' entry are the Austin canons put in by Henry the Second, not the secular canons of the elder foundation of Harold.

In all these cases the monastic church is gone. The grantee exercised his right of property by pulling it down or leaving it in ruins. With these before us we can better understand a crowd of other cases, where we see the same appearances, but where I at least do not know the documentary history. Such are the monastic churches of Worksop, Blyth, Bridlington, Usk, Chepstow, Margam, Deerhurst, Lanercost, Monkton in Pembrokeshire, the collegiate church of Ruthin in Denbighshire, and many others. I speak only of monastic and collegiate churches; they must not be confounded with another class, chiefly found in Norfolk, where the chancels of purely parochial churches have been—illegally, as I conceive—pulled down or allowed to fall into ruin by their lay rectors. The monastic or collegiate church commonly lay to the east of the parochial church; but there is a very singular and puzzling building, the priory of Waybourne in Norfolk, where the two lie in an irregular way side by side. To this point I shall have to come back.

But the grantees did not in all cases exercise their right of pulling down the monastic or collegiate church. In some cases it was added to the adjoining parish church. These cases must be distinguished from those in which the parish at the dissolution became possessed of a monastic church which had never been parochial at all. At Great Malvern, for instance, and at Selby, the parishioners bought the monastic church, and forsook and pulled down the old parish church which stood quite distinct. I am speaking only of cases in which, in a divided church, the monastic part was added to the parochial part. There are good instances of this at Dorchester, Tewkesbury, and Sherborne. At Dorchester Richard Beauforest, in his will, dated 1554 (printed in Addington's Dorchester, p. 98), says—

I bequeth the Abbey Churche of Dorchester, which I have bought, and the implements thereof, to the Paryshe of Dorchester aforesaid, so that the said Parishioners shall not sell alter or alienate the said Churche Implements or any part or parcell thereof withoute the consente of my heires and executors.

Now that this does not mean the whole of the present church of Dorchester, but only a part, is plain from other items in the same will, where the testator bequeaths twenty shillings 'to the reparations of my parishe church.' He is described as 'of the towne of Dorchester;' so 'my parish church' can only mean the parochial part of Dorchester church. Leland, too (see Addington, p. 105), says distinctly—

The Body of the Abbay Chirch servid a late for the Paroche Chirch. Syns the Suppression one (Beauforest) a great riche Man, dwelling in the Toun of Dorchestre, bought the Est part of the Chirch for 140. Poundes, and gave it to augment the Paroch Chirch.

Here we clearly see the distinction between the abbey church which Beauforest bought and gave to the parish, and the parish church to the repairs of which he made a bequest. And we may mark the various forms of language which naturally grew up in speaking of buildings of this kind. Leland, describing what he saw without any legal precision, calls the whole building the 'abbey church;' the parochial part he calls indiscriminately, 'the body of the abbey church,' 'the west part of the church,' and 'the parish church.' But in Beauforest's will, as a legal document, more careful language is used. Here the two parts are distinguished as 'the abbey church,' and 'the parish church;' and it strikes me, though I do not feel positively certain, that he uses the words, 'church of Dorchester' to take in both. For he leaves his body 'to be buried in our Lady Ile within the church of Dorchester.' Every one at Dorchester would know whether 'our Lady Ile' was part of the abbey or of the parish church. At Tewkesbury again, in the inventory of the property of the monastery drawn up by Henry the Eighth's commissioners (Monasticon, ii. 57), among 'buildings deemed to be superfluous' comes 'the church.' That this again means only part of the building appears from what follows. I quote the Monasticon.

Rudder says, 'It appears by an ancient deed transcribed into an old council book, that before and at the time of the dissolution, the body of the abbey church was used as the parish church, and that the parish purchased of the king the chancel, steeple, and bells, with the clock and chimes for 483l.'

Here again the local historian does not speak with strict legal precision; but the commissioners do. 'The church,' in a list of the possessions of the monastery, would be understood only of that part of the building which belonged to the monastery. This the parishioners bought of the king, and added it to what was their own already, 'the body of the abbey church,' that is, the western limb of the minster, which formed the parish church.

The history of Sherborne is given in the Monasticon, i. 335. It appears from Leland's account that there also the parishioners had their parish church in the western limb of the cruciform minster. 'The body of the abbay chirch dedicate to our Lady, servid ontille a hunderithe yeres syns for the chife paroche chirch of the town.' The parishioners had also a building to the west of this, known as All Hallows. A violent quarrel, or rather fight, between the monks and the parishioners in the fifteenth century, led to a settlement, by what authority Leland does not say, by which the parishioners had to withdraw wholly from the minster (Saint Mary) and kept only All Hallows. 'Postea vero, omnium sanctorum ecclesia, non autem Dominæ Mariæ, tanquam parochialis ecclesia usurpabatur.' At the dissolution 'the church, steeple (campanile), and churchyard of the monastery' passed to a lay grantee, from whom they were bought by the parish. All Hallows must then have been forsaken, as it now remains a ruin, while the minster forms the parish church. I said something about this matter in the Somerset Archæological Proceedings for 1874, where I refer to Professor Willis' paper on Sherborne, in the Archæological Journal, vol. xxii. p. 179. The plans are in the same volume, p. 196, and in the Bristol volume of the Institute, p. 200.

These cases of Dorchester, Tewkesbury, and Sherborne further help us to understand another class of cases in which the usual arrangement seems to be reversed, where the eastern part is used as the parish church, and where the western part is destroyed. This is the case at Pershore and Boxgrove. I can find no documents in the Monasticon to explain the reason, but I imagine it to be this. The parishioners became possessed of the monastic part of the church, and as that was often the larger and finer of the two, they did not care to keep up their former parish church to the west of it. At Boxgrove there are distinct signs that there once was a separate church in the ruined nave, as there is the usual reredos, with its doors, carried up so as to make a partition wall. I take this also to be the explanation of the very extraordinary appearances at Llantwit Major in Glamorganshire, where to the west of the present church is a building, roofed but disused, which is known as 'the old church,' though it is certainly later in date than the part now in use. I can only take this to mean that it is the former parish church, which was disused when the parishioners obtained possession of the larger monastic church to the east of it.[1]

We may now come to another exceptional case where the parish church was not at the west end of the monastic church, but at one side of it. I have remarked one very anomalous case at Waybourne; there is one easier to understand at Romsey. There the abbey church is now the parish church. I cannot find anything in the Monasticon about the way in which it became so; but I distinctly remember reading, probably in some local book, a deed of Bishop William of Wykeham, by which it appeared that the parish church of Romsey was then in the north aisle of the nave of the abbey church. The parishioners obtained leave to enlarge their church; the building bears witness to the way in which this was done. They built a double aisle to the north, which has since been pulled down. One can hardly doubt that, when the parishioners became possessed of the whole of the abbey church, they no longer cared to keep up this small addition, and so pulled it down.

But in cases when a church was divided between the parish and a monastic or collegiate body, it sometimes happened that the corporate body dispossessed the parishioners. We have seen one case something to this effect at Sherborne. In the preface to the seventh volume of the edition of Giraldus Cambrensis in the Chronicles and Memorials (pp. lxxx—xcix), I have collected the evidence for the fact that no less a church than Lincoln minster was, from its foundation in the time of William the Conqueror to the fourteenth century, a divided possession between the bishop and his chapter and a body of parishioners. Remigius founded his cathedral church in an

[1] See Archæologia Cambrensis for 1858, p. 37.

existing parish church, exactly as the cathedral churches of Truro and Liverpool have been founded in our own time. He of course rebuilt the church on a great scale, but the parishioners kept their right, and occupied the nave of the minster, or part of it. In the fourteenth century a dispute arose between the chapter and the parish, which was ended by common consent by the parishioners leaving the minster, and withdrawing to a separate parish church which was built for the purpose. This case of real divided possession in a cathedral church must be distinguished from cases like those of Ely and Norwich, where a parish has been allowed to occupy part of a cathedral church by some later arrangement. But I believe, though I cannot bring my evidence at this moment, that the occupation of the nave at Carlisle as a parish church was not a case of this last kind, but was a real case of divided possession. At Rochester again, I believe the parish held the nave, and that the parish church hard by was built instead, as at Lincoln. At Llandaff, Saint Davids, and Bangor, the cathedral church is also parochial. I do not know how the case stands legally; the architectural arrangements have differed at different times.

In other cases again the monastic or collegiate church was neither destroyed nor ruined nor added to the parish church. It was simply disused. Here comes the typical case of Dunster, the account of which is given in Collinson's History of Somerset, ii. 18, and of which I have said something in the Transactions of the Somerset Archæological Society (1855, pp. 2–12). The church is a cross church with a central tower. Westward of the tower was a perfect church, with chancel and rood-screen, the latter reaching, according to local custom, right across the church, and approached by a turret in the outer wall of the south aisle. East of the tower was a second choir, fenced off by a second screen. To this the transepts and crossing formed a kind of ante-chapel. Nowhere in short were the arrangements of the class of churches so easily studied as at Dunster, up to the time of a very recent 'restoration.' The two churches, parochial and monastic, west and east of the tower, were absolutely perfect. The parish church, a perfect parish church, with its screened chancel, remained untouched, with its high altar under the western arch of the tower. The tower with the transepts on each side of it, formed a neutral space between the two choirs. 'Restoration' has had its usual effect of wiping out history. The two churches have happily not been thrown into one, but the ancient arrangement has been altogether confused by taking the neutral space under the tower into the parish choir, and removing the parish high altar to the eastern arch of the tower instead of the western. There is thus no space left between the two choirs. The former arrangement, so lately destroyed, was the result of a dispute between the parishioners of Dunster and the monks of the priory there, a cell to the cathedral monastery of Bath. This dispute was settled in 1498 by a composition decreed by three arbitrators, Richard Bere, Abbot of Glastonbury. Thomas Tremayle, a judge, and Thomas Gilbert, a doctor of canon law. The parishioners were to make themselves a separate choir, taking, it would seem, the existing altar of Saint James just outside the roodloft as their high altar. This implies that, up to that time, the monks' choir had been the chancel of the parish church. But now the monks and the people made themselves separate choirs, east and west of the tower, leaving the tower itself free between the two. The words which concern us are :

Quod vicarius modernus et successores sui vicarii habeant chorum separatum a dictis priore et monachis sumptibus et expensis parochianorum faciendum et erigendum, factum et erectum separandum, et quotiens opus fuerit de novo construendum, in nave ecclesiæ ad altare sancti Jacobi apostoli quod est situatum ex australi parti hostii quod ducit a choro monachorum in navem ecclesiæ.

Some regulations follow about processions, in which the two choirs are distinguished in a marked way;

Cum dicti prior et confratres per medium chori sui euntes egredi incipiant hostium ex parte boreali chori vicerii et parochianorum.

There is much that is curious in the history of Dunster church which I leave to Mr. Maxwell Lyte. The above is enough for my purpose, to establish it as one of the best, till late changes the very best, example of a divided church.

Dunster, of which we have the history, gives the key to the church of Ewenny in Glamorganshire. Here, unlike Dunster, part both of the monastic and of the parochial church has been destroyed; but enough is left to show the distinction in the most marked way. The western limb of a cross church forms the parish church, fenced off by a solid reredos across the western arch of the tower. The monks' choir is fenced off by another open screen across the eastern arch, just as at Dunster. The transepts and the crossing are, as they once were at Dunster, neutral. Since the 'restoration' of Dunster, Ewenny, unless that too has been 'restored' out of its historical value since I was last there, remains the most perfect example of churches of the class.

In arguing this matter, I have been met at every stage with the objection that my instances are drawn from monastic churches, and that we cannot argue from them to churches of seculars. I must repeat that, for the purposes of the present argument, I cannot see any difference between the two. The relations between the parish and the corporate body differed in different places, whether that corporate body was regular or secular. As I before said, disputes and divisions were far more likely to arise in the case of regulars than in the case of seculars. We must therefore be prepared to find our monastic examples many, and our collegiate examples few. But I can see no difference of principle between them. Nor are we wholly without collegiate examples. I have already quoted the case of Ruthin, where the choir has been destroyed, while the nave remains as the parish church, exactly as in divided monastic churches. Here is at least a presumption of divided possession between the college and the parish. The history of the collegiate church of Howden would, I suspect, throw some important light on the present matter. The choir is in ruins; I can find nothing about it in the Monasticon; but I distinctly remember having read—again most likely in some local book—that a case which must have been very like the case of Arundel was argued in a court of law in the reign of Elizabeth. The parish called on the grantee of the college property to repair the choir; this claim could have been made only on the ground that the college choir was the chancel of the parish church. The grantee refused; I can conceive no ground for his refusal, except that the choir was not the chancel of the parish church, but that it was an absolute possession of the college which had passed to him as the grantee of its property. Here was a question of fact, on which it would be dangerous to say anything without knowing the evidence on both sides. Either relation would be perfectly possible; the question was which was the actual relation in this particular case. My story adds that, while the suit was pending, it was practically settled by the choir falling in, after which neither side thought it worth while to continue the litigation. I tell this only from memory; but it is a point on which I am likely to remember accurately, and the records can doubtless be found somewhere.

Another case which helps us is that of the collegiate church of Fotheringhay. Here in 1412 Edward Duke of York founded a college, endowed, as at Arundel, with the estates of alien priories. The choir seems to have been built by his father, Duke Edmund, who had designed the foundation of the college, but had not actually carried it out. In 1435 Duke Richard rebuilt the nave. The contract for the building is preserved, and the language used in it seems distinctly to show that the nave formed a parish church distinct from the collegiate choir. William Horwood, freemason, 'graunts and undertakes to mak up a new body of a kirk joyning to the quire of the College of Fodringey, of the same hight and brede that the said quire is of.' And throughout the contract the old building is spoken of as 'the quire' and the new building as 'the church.'[1] The college property was granted in 1553 to John Dudley, Duke of Northumberland; the choir must have passed with it, for it was in ruins when Fotheringhay was visited by Queen Elizabeth. She, finding the tombs of the Dukes of York neglected among the ruins, caused their bodies to be removed into the church and new tombs to be made.[2]

These cases bring us to the immediate case of Arundel. I should myself, on seeing the choir stand perfect but disused, and knowing that the church had been collegiate, have inferred the history from the appearances. I should have inferred, without documentary proof, that the collegiate choir had been the absolute property of the college, and that it had, as such, passed to the grantee. I should have argued that the case spoke for itself, that the collegiate part of the church, which would most likely have been destroyed if it had been granted to a stranger, had been preserved because the grantee was himself the Earl of Arundel, the representative of the founder, who naturally cared for the tombs of his forefathers and for the buildings which they had raised. That is to say, I should, simply from the analogy of other cases, have assumed the claim which was actually made by the present Earl of

---

[1] This argument would not be enough by itself, as in parish churches the 'church' often means the nave, as opposed to the chancel. But the phrase, 'quire of the college,' seems to mark distinct possession, and the destruction of the choir proves the case.

[2] See the account of Fotheringhay, published by the Oxford Architectural Society, p. 9.

Arundel and Duke of Norfolk. Without looking at a single document, the circumstances of the case, as compared with other cases of the like kind, were consistent with that view, and were not consistent with any other. I cannot understand how a parish chancel could come to be disused, unless it were liable to be destroyed. If the Earls of Arundel had been no more than ordinary impropriate rectors, they could have had no right to cause the disuse of the chancel. Their business would have been to keep it in repair for use. On this theory a monstrous wrong had been done for three hundred and thirty years, seemingly without any protest. The 'onus probandi' undoubtedly lay on those who denied the duke's right.

But the documents which were produced at the trials placed the matter beyond a shadow of a doubt. They start from the foundation of the college of Arundel by Richard Earl of Arundel in 1387. This I may call the second college. It appears from Domesday[1] that at the time of the survey there were secular clerks in the church of Saint Nicolas at Arundel, who had certain dues in the port of Arundel and property elsewhere. These clerks must have given way to Benedictine monks at some time between 1086 and 1094. For the priory was a foundation of the famous Roger of Montgomery, Earl of Shrewsbury, lord of Arundel and Chichester, who made the new foundation a cell to the abbey of Seez of his own foundation. After the French conquest of Normandy, Arundel, as a dependency of Seez, became an alien priory, and underwent the usual ups and downs of such foundations. It was suppressed earlier than the most of its fellows, falling under Richard the Second and not living on to Henry the Fifth. Then the seculars came back in the form of the master and chaplains of Earl Richard's college. His deed of foundation sets forth that the late Earl Richard, his father, had

---

[1] P. 22. In the first column we read of the tolls of the haven, 'de hiis habet S. Nicolaus xxiiii solidos,' and in the second column is the name of Hertinges, 'de hoc manerio tenent clerici de S. Nicolao vi hidas.'

designed to found three chaplains in Arundel church—' in ecclesia parochiali Arundell prioratu monachorum ordinis S. Benedicti, cella subjecta abbathiæ de Sagio alienigenæ in partibus Franciæ.' The deed also speaks several times of the ' ecclesia parochialis,' ' parochialis ecclesia per quinque monachos monasterii de Sagio solita gubernari,' &c. The elder Earl Richard then changed his mind, and designed to found a college of priests and clerks in his own chapel in the castle. Neither purpose was ever carried out when he died. His son, the younger Earl Richard, was hindered by some difficulty not described from making the foundation in the castle chapel ('quum idem collegium perpetuò dictà capellà infra castrum nequeat stabiliri'[1]). Considering then the desolate state ('desolatio,' 'viduitas') of the parish church, now that the monks from Seez had, on account of the wars, gone back to their own country, he determined to make his foundation in the parish church. Then arose the college of Arundel, 'Collegium S. Trinitatis Arundell,' instead of the priory. It consisted of thirteen chaplains, of whom one was Warden or Master (' Custos sive Magister perpetuus '), one Vice-Master (' Sub-magister '), a third Sacrist and Subchanter (' Sacrista et Succentor '). A Subchanter without a Præcentor seems a little anomalous. There were also some inferior members.

There is nothing in the deed of foundation to imply a division of the fabric, or to settle anything as to rights of ownership on the part of either college or parish in different parts of the church. The church is spoken of as one, 'prædicta ecclesia;' we hear of 'cancellus,' 'magnum altare,' and the like, just as we should in an undivided church, but also just as we might in a divided church, if there was no special reason for insisting on the fact of division. There is nothing about the repair of the fabric at all. And, with a collegiate body, the question

[1] Was this any question as to the position of the chapel, which may well have hindered consecration ' de solo ad cælum ' ?

of divided or joint ownership might very likely not be stirred at all till some question arose about the liabilities to repair. In course of time such disputes did arise, and the next document distinctly shows that, at all events by the year 1511, Arundel had passed into the class of divided churches.

The document of that year is in some respects the fellow of the Dunster document of 1498, with this difference, that the Dunster document orders the division to be made, while the Arundel document rather implies that it is made already. This is an arbitration by which the two arbiters, Thomas Earl of Arundel and Robert Sherborn Bishop of Chichester, decide a dispute between the college and the parish ('major et burgenses ceterique parochiani villæ de Arundel') as to the repair of part of the church described as 'þe crosse partes.' These 'cross parts' are the transepts and central tower. The dispute was

de et super reparatione et sustentione illarum partium ecclesiæ ibidem quæ vulgariter dicuntur 'þe cross partes,' ducentes ab austro per mediam inter chorum et navem ecclesiæ usque ad boream una cum eodem medio et campanili supra illud mediam erecto campanisque ac ceteris omnibus et singulis rebus in eisdem existentibus et ad eadem pertinentibus.

Here the eastern limb is 'chorus,' the western is 'navis.' But the architectural 'chorus' is not in 1511 the chancel of the parish church, whether it was so or not in 1387. Just as at Dunster, just as at Binham, there is a distinct parish chancel, only occupying a somewhat singular place, one different from that which it occupied at Dunster and Binham, but not very different from that which it occupied at Leominster and Blyth. When I was at first at Arundel in 1853, the parish church with the parish altar was in the south transept. That this was no modern arrangement springing out of the dissolution of the college, appears from the document which we have now in hand. The arbiters decree—

Quod onus sustentationis ac reparationis insulæ [1] australis dictæ ecclesiæ, *quæ cancellus parochialis vulgariter nuncupatur*, pertineat solum et insolidum ad præfatos magistrum et socios [2] et eorum successores in perpetuum. Et quod onus sustentationis ac reparationis alterius insulæ borealiter situatæ simul cum navi ecclesiæ et insulis ejus ad præfatos majorem, burgenses, et parochianos qui pro tempore fuerint, in perpetuum pertineat. Et insuper quod onus sustentationis ac reparationis illius mediæ partis quæ campanile vocatur, in pavimentis, muris, columnis, singulisque dicti campanilis appenditiis tam intus quam extra, subtus quam supra, perpetuis futuris temporibus per dictes partes æqualiter supportetur et sustineatur.

Nothing can be plainer. There is a perfect parish church with its chancel, wholly apart from the choir of the college. The parishioners, according to universal custom, repair the nave and its aisles. The college, as rectors, repair the parish chancel; its unusual architectural position makes no difference; wherever placed, it is equally the parish chancel, the repair of which is borne by the holders of the rectorial tithe, that is, in this case, by the college. The north transept the arbitrators adjudge to the parish; the tower they make a common possession. One would like to know what the exact nature of the dispute was, and on what grounds the earl and the bishop came to their decision. In most cases, where the eastern limb has perished, the transepts have perished with it, showing that they formed part of the suppressed church. Here at Arundel the case was clearly otherwise. But this peculiarity does not touch the main point. Westward of the 'chorus' or eastern limb there was in 1511 a complete parish church, following the ordinary law of parish churches, its nave repaired by the parish, its chancel by the rectors. Of the 'chorus' itself nothing is said; it was out of the reckoning; whatever it was in

---

[1] The Latin *ala* became *isle*, or *ile* the older spelling; *aisle* is modern. *Isle* or *ile* is here translated back into *insula*.

[2] The *capellani* of 1387 seems by 1511 to have grown into the higher rank of *socii*. In the later documents both names are used.

1387, in 1511 it had become a separate church belonging to the college, with regard to which the parishioners had neither rights nor burthens.

The force of the document of 1511 is rather to assume the division as something existing than to ordain it as something new. We may either take it as explaining the vaguer language of 1387, or else we may infer that the division took place at some time between the two dates. The main point is that in 1511 Arundel was a divided church, containing two choirs, in one of which, placed in the south transept, the college had the ordinary rights and duties of rectors, while the other, forming the eastern limb, the architectural choir, was the choir, the collegiate church, of the college, apart from the parish.

Each of the documents explains the one which comes after it. We now come to the document of 1545, bearing date December 12 of that year. This followed very closely on the Act of Parliament of that year, the first act for the suppression of colleges, that which simply gave the king power to suppress, while the act of Edward the Sixth two years later absolutely suppressed those colleges which escaped under Henry. The college by this deed gives up to the king all its possessions of every kind. They are thus described, as far as concerns us now:—

Reddimus . . . . totam cantariam sive collegium nostrum prædictum. Ac etiam totum scitum, fundum, circuitum, ambitum vel præcinctum, ac *ecclesiam, campanile, et cimiterium* ejusdem cantariæ sive collegii, cum omnibus et omnimodis domibus, edificiis, ortis, pomariis, gardinis, terra et solo, infra dictum circuitum et præcinctum cantariæ sive collegii prædicti.

Fourteen days later, December 26, the king grants all this to Henry, Earl of Arundel, in consideration of good services and of the sum of 1000 marks. The words which concern us are:—

Damus et concedimus eidem comiti totum scitum, fundum, ambitum, circuitum, et precinctum, nuper ecclesiæ collegiatæ sive collegii Sanctæ Trinitatis de Arundell in comitatu nostro Sussexiæ,

alias dictæ nuper collegii sive cantariæ Sanctæ Trinitatis de vel in
Arundell in comitatu nostro Sussexiæ, modo dissolutæ, ac etiam
campanile et cimiterium ejusdem nuper collegii sive cantariæ. Ac
etiam omnia et singula mesuagia, domos, edificia, structuras,
horrea, grangeas, columbaria, ortos, pomaria, gardina, stagna,
vivaria, terram, fundum, et solum, nostra quæcunque infra scitum
ambitum circuitum et procinctum dictæ nuper ecclesiæ collegiatæ
collegii sive cantariæ prædicta existentes, aut dictæ nuper ecclesiæ
collegiatæ collegio sive cantariæ aliquo modo dudum spectantes
sive pertinentes, ac parcellam possessionum et reventionum ejusdem ecclesiæ collegiatæ collegii sive cantariæ dudum existentes.

Nothing can be plainer than that the college here
surrenders to the king, and that the king grants to the
earl, something which is described as a church, 'ecclesia,'
and which is further defined in the second grant as the
'collegiate church,'—'ecclesia collegiata.' What was the
building which was thus granted? Clearly not the whole
building which was doubtless, then as now, commonly
spoken of as 'Arundel church,' and which might be even
spoken of either as 'the parish church' or as 'the collegiate church,' one of those names in strictness belonging
to part of the building, and the other to another part.
The college could have no right to surrender to the king
those parts of the building which belonged to the parish,
the nave, nave aisles, and north transept, nor yet the
south transept or parish chancel, within which they had
simply the rights and duties of rectors. The 'collegiate
church' which they surrendered could have been only
those parts of the building which are left untouched in
the award of Earl Thomas and Bishop Sherborn, those
parts in which they had an absolute property, that is the
eastern limb, the 'chorus' of that document, the constructive choir namely, and the Lady chapel to the north
of it. As a matter of fact, that is what they did surrender.
These parts have ever since been the possession of the
successive Earls of Arundel, who have dealt with them as
they thought good. As a matter of fact, those parts of
the building did become their possession, a possession

which was dealt with in quite another way from the
parish chancel in the south transept. There the earl
succeeded to the college in the ordinary position of a
rector, a position involving a duty to keep up, but giving
no right to pull down. But the 'chorus,' the 'ecclesia
collegiata,' the grantee had a full right to pull down,
a right which most grantees exercised freely. We may
be sure that, if Earl Henry had done like most other
grantees, if he had done as John Duke of Northumberland
did at Fotheringhay, and had pulled down everything east
of the tower, there would have been no dispute. It is simply
because Earl Henry was less destructive than most of his
class that any dispute has arisen. The course which he
chose to take was the rarest of all. The commonest
course was to pull down the monastic or collegiate part
of the church altogether, but to sell or give it to the parish
was, as we have seen, not very uncommon. Earl Henry
did neither. He did not pull the collegiate church down,
neither did he give it to the parish. He kept it standing,
but disused. So unusual a course has been misunder-
stood, and people have fancied, though the existence of
the parish chancel in the south transept should have
taught them better, that the disused eastern limb was,
what architecturally it seemed to be, the chancel of the
parish church, and that the successive Earls of Arundel,
in keeping that part of the building in their own hands,
had been, for three hundred years and more, abusing
their rights as lay rectors. But the award, the surrender,
the grant, the transfer which actually took place, all hang
together. Taken together, they show that, within the
building which in common language would be called
'Arundel church,' the college possessed in absolute property the 'chorus,' the eastern limb, that they surrendered
it to the king, and that the king granted it to the earl.
And to those who have studied this class of buildings
there is nothing wonderful in the whole story. Or rather
the only wonderful thing is that Earl Henry did not pull

down the church which was granted to him. Had it been a church at the other end of England, which contained the tombs, not of his own forefathers, but of the forefathers of somebody else, he would most likely have dealt by it as John Dudley dealt by Fotheringhay.

The only point of doubt is whether Earl Henry took quite all that the grant gave him. Along with the church and churchyard, the college surrendered to the king, and the king granted to the earl, the tower or *campanile*. Now in the first trial one of the counsel for the vicar treated this as a *reductio ad absurdum*, as if it was impossible that the tower of the church could be the duke's property. It seems to me by no means impossible that it may be so; the words of the grant seem to imply it. In the various cases which I have gone through, the central tower has sometimes been destroyed with the choir, sometimes left standing. When it was destroyed, it must have been the property of the corporate body, which therefore passed to the grantee, and a grant of the tower is not uncommon in such grants. At Waltham the central tower was destroyed, and the parishioners built themselves a new tower at the west end. At Wymondham and Tewkesbury the parishioners bought the tower of the king. Here at Arundel, the college and the parish clearly had a joint right, if not a joint property, in the tower. But most likely the freehold was in the college; the words of the surrender and grant imply it. But, if so, the property of the college, and afterwards of the earl, in the tower was a property subject to the parishioners' right of joint use. The tower therefore could not have been pulled down by the earl or taken to his sole use. But I suspect that the freehold of it belongs to the Duke of Norfolk.[1]

[1] This view seems borne out by a curious passage in the award. 'Proviso quod omnes et singulæ reparationes dicti campanilis nunc necessariæ resarciantur et fiant citra festum Michaelis proximum futurum, ac quod dicti major, burgenses, et parochiani habeant pro interesse si velint unam

I have found it argued on the vicar's part that the example of Dunster does not apply, because the ground plans of Dunster and Arundel are not exactly the same, and because the division between the two parts of the church is not made in exactly the same way. I answer that, in the long list of examples which I have put together, we have many kinds of ground-plans, and many ways of making the division. Several of the churches of which I have spoken are not cruciform churches at all. Dorchester, Llantwit, Fotheringhay, Waybourne, have ground-plans which have no likeness to those of either Dunster or Arundel; but the division may be seen in all of them. At Dorchester and Fotheringhay it is a matter of distinct documentary evidence. The division was often made by a solid reredos; it was so at Wymondham, Binham, Ewenny, Waltham; but there is no reason to think that it was always so made. In some of the cases which I have gone through such a way of making the division is clearly impossible. It could hardly have been so at Dorchester or Fotheringhay; and the division is much less likely to be so made in a collegiate church than in a monastery. Even when the part which the canons occupied was their absolute property, they had not the same temptation which the monks had to fence themselves wholly off from the parishioners. An open screen would serve their purpose just as well as a solid reredos. To my mind therefore it proves nothing, that the two parts of Arundel church, or the two churches, whichever we choose to call them, were divided by a screen and not by a solid wall.

I have looked specially to this class of churches for five and twenty years and more; perhaps they have had a

clavem per quam possint reparationes dicti campanilis necessarias, si velint, supravidere, ita quod, si id non facient, imputetur eis.' This looks as if, though the parishioners had rights in the tower and bore a share of the cost of its repairs, yet the actual ownership of it was in the college. It was clearly not the parishioners who were actually doing the repairs.

special charm for me, because nobody seemed to understand them. And the result of this examination was, before I made any reference to documents, to make me say with perfect confidence that the claim now made by the Duke of Norfolk was in strict analogy with a great number of undoubted historical examples. The appearances of the building were consistent with the duke's argument, and they were not consistent with any other. But it is satisfactory to find how completely the documents support my view formed without them, and to find two successive courts decide in accordance with the plain facts of history. To me of course the question is simply one of historical fact, where the only object is to find out what the facts are. I certainly have no satisfaction in seeing a church, or part of a church, in private hands; but the plain facts of history cannot be got over. Two Acts of Parliament, of Henry the Eighth and Edward the Sixth, caused the property of the colleges and chantries, including in some cases the fabrics of churches, to pass into lay hands. Nothing but a repeal of those Acts of Parliament can take them away from their present owners.

I have two more remarks to make, one on each side. First, I can see no authority for the name 'Fitzalan chapel,' which has been given in modern times to the collegiate choir. I have shown that there is a good deal of laxity in the way of speaking of these buildings; but the name 'Fitzalan chapel' does not occur in the documents, and I can hardly conceive that such a name can ever have been in use. Secondly, I must protest against a late so-called 'restoration' at Arundel, which, as usual, destroys the history of the building. I was there in April 1880, and found that the parish altar, which in 1853 still stood in its ancient place in the south transept, had been moved under the central tower, to the confusion of the whole story.

[I might have spoken also of Crowland abbey, where the division is very plain, the parish reredos still standing across the western arch of the lantern. But at present the western limb is ruined, save only part of the north aisle which serves as the parish church. According to the Monasticon (ii. 205) this arrangement dates only from the seventeenth century; but I have a strong impression that I have seen a Crowland document of the fifteenth prescribing something of the same kind.]

WORKSOP AND BLYTH.

1875—1880.

THE county of Nottingham contains, at a short distance from each other, two churches of the class in which the monastic and the parochial church stood close together under one roof. These are the Benedictine priory of Saint Mary at Blyth, and the priory of Austin canons of Saint Cuthberht at Worksop. In each case the nave only, the parish church, is standing; of the monastic church there are no remains at Blyth, and only a ruined fragment at Worksop. The dates of the two foundations are not far apart. Both monasteries arose in the days of the Conqueror's sons. But the surviving part of Blyth still keeps the architecture of the date of its foundation, while at Worksop we find the Romanesque style, if Romanesque we can still call it, in its latest form. The effect of the two buildings as we draw near to them is widely different. Worksop, with its twin towers, proclaims at the first glimpse its character as a minster. Blyth, on the other hand, shows itself in the distance by a single tower, not without stateliness, but which would not suggest that it belonged to anything but an ordinary village church. Indeed, if a visitor could be set down immediately under the south wall of the church, he would not be the least inclined to suspect either the antiquity or the stateliness of the inside. Where the nave alone is left, where the cruciform shape of the building has therefore vanished, a slight change may easily destroy the external character of a church which within follows the full type of a minster of a high order.

The priory of Blyth was founded by Roger of Bully, famous in Domesday, but nowhere else, about 1090. The house was in a certain degree of dependence on the monastery of the Holy Trinity at Rouen. Yet the priory of Saint Mary at Blyth was an independent corporation. It was not counted as an alien priory at the dissolution of alien priories, though it was at least once taken into the King's hands during the war with France. All that now remains of the monastery and its belongings is the parochial part of the church, the constructive nave. Within we at once see that the main fabric cannot be much later than the time of the original foundation. The features of the nave, triforium, and clerestory are all of them early Norman. Some of the details are strikingly like those of the chapel of the White Tower. Any one would at first sight set down the nave of Blyth as being fully a generation earlier than the choir of Durham, which must have been going on at the same time. That is to say, Roger of Bully did not call to the work an architect of the same genius as Bishop William of Saint-Calais, or whoever it was that Bishop William employed. His work therefore lags a little behind. It is work which not only Roger of Salisbury but Randolf Flambard would certainly have looked on as old-fashioned. Every instance of this kind is instructive, as teaching the lesson to all who can take it in of the wide difference between questions of style and mere questions of date. The nave of Blyth can hardly have been finished before the early days of Henry the First, yet it has all the simplicity as well as the grandeur of the earliest Norman. Its vaulted roof was not contemplated by its original builders, but no one can regret its addition here any more than at Malmesbury. That the triforium on one side has given way to a range of very late windows we certainly regret, but we would not, in any repair of the building, wipe out the record of a change which is part of its history.

But more remarkable than these changes was a change in the general character of the building which makes the stateliness of the Romanesque interior come upon us as something of which the outside gave no sign. As not uncommonly happened in such cases, the parishioners seem to have striven at a somewhat later time to give their part of the church a distinctly parochial character. They built a new and wide south aisle, after the manner of Grantham, a change which was also made at Wymondham, and, on the greatest scale of all, at Leominster. As at Leominster, the new aisle, and not the Norman nave of the minster, became the main body of the parish church, and the parish high altar still stands at its east end, a position nearly but not quite the same as that at Arundel. Later again, as at Wymondham also, they built a western tower, in this case, as at Shrewsbury and Malmesbury, within the original nave, so that we have to add another to the long list of former examples of the now rare arrangement of a central and western tower grouped as at Wimborne. The transepts and the eastern limb, as forming part of the monastic church, have perished. But the eastern bay of the western limb is standing, but blocked off from the parish church. There is, in itself, nothing wonderful in this, as the Norman choirs often went far down into the western limb. But in Mr. John Raine's History of Blyth it is said that, though this bay was cut off from the church, the parish was held to be bound to repair its vaulted roof. This looks as if the grantee had taken a bay more than his share—perhaps a bay covered by the monastic roodloft. Altogether this, we fancy, very little known church of Blyth is a highly instructive building, both in the character of its original architecture and in the changes which it has since gone through.

The greater neighbour of Blyth, the Austin priory of Worksop or Radford, supplies in some points a contrast to its fellow. The beginnings of Worksop were rather later than those of Blyth, the foundation having been made in 1103 by William of Lovetoft. His name is not to be found in Domesday, which suggests the belief that he was one of the many new men who rose to importance under Henry the First. But if the foundation of Worksop is only a little later than that of Blyth, the style of the building is a good deal later. It is still Romanesque, so far as it keeps the round arch and something of Romanesque proportion, but the style is the very latest to which the name of Romanesque can be given. That is to say, the comparatively small church of Blyth was probably finished from east to west by its original founder, while the much larger pile of Worksop took a much longer time to build, and was not finished till quite the last years of the twelfth century. As at Durham, as in so many other cases, we can see that the eastern limb, and just so much of the western as was needed to form a support for the central tower, was built first, and that the western part was not carried on till after a longer or shorter interval. In the nave of Worksop the break is easily to be seen in the change of detail. All that is now left of the first work, that is, the eastern bay, is, as compared with Blyth, late and rich Romanesque, but the nine bays to the west of it are again much later and richer. We may be sure that their architect, had he been designing a perfectly new building, would have used the pointed arch. As at Peterborough and Ely, he used the round arch only because his own taste or the bidding of his employers told him to adapt the new work to the general proportions of the old. In fact, he did use the pointed arch where he could. He could not venture to alter the main lines of the pier-arch, triforium, and clerestory, but in the smaller and purely ornamental arches of the triforium range the pointed arch is actually used. This reverses the usual rule, according to which the pointed shape appears first in the constructive and afterwards in the merely decorated arches. Here again we see how far the ancient architects were from following any inflexible law, and how readily they adapted themselves to the requirements of any particular set of circumstances. The whole nave is a study, both for the grandeur of its general effect and for the richness and beauty of its detail; but we feel that that detail would have been more in place if it had been adapted to other constructive forms. The internal elevation of Worksop nave is a stately one, but there is a certain degree of trick in the treatment of the triforium and clerestory. Greater space is found for the triforium range by placing the clerestory windows over the piers, which take the form of columns alternately round and octagonal. Worksop had two western towers from the beginning, so that the change which was made in the general outline of the church at Blyth could not be made here. But an old drawing shows that a good deal had been done in the way of lowering roofs and putting in windows in the triforium range, just as at Blyth. These changes, which ought never to have been made, but which, when once made, form part of the history of the building, were, with questionable judgement, wiped out in a restoration made some years back. Of the monastic church the extent has been traced, an unusually long eastern limb ending in an apse. A chapel of the thirteenth century attached to the east of the south transept still remains, though ruined. Parts of the cloister and dormitory may be traced to the north of the nave, and the noble gateway of the priory remains at some distance to the south.

COWDRAY.

1875.

THE student of English antiquities has often to complain of the strange neglect which, amid a marked improvement with regard to our monuments of other kinds, is commonly the lot of our ancient domestic buildings. There is indeed a great difficulty of making the general public understand that there are any ancient domestic buildings at all—it is hard to persuade people that a mediæval building, when palpably not a castle, is not necessarily a church or a monastery. There is perhaps a certain class of houses to which this difficulty does not apply. These are the great houses of the reigns of the first two Tudor kings, the latest houses which can be in any sense called ancient, the earliest which can in any sense be called modern, as being the earliest which can be adapted to modern uses without spoiling them, the earliest which can suggest much practical teaching for buildings of our own time. It is instructive to be carried suddenly from the castles of Northumberland or South Wales to such a building as the ruined house of Cowdray in Sussex. Our feelings are exactly opposite in the two cases. When we see a castle in ruins, we feel that the castle is as it ought to be; when it is inhabited, we feel that it is as it ought not to be. At Alnwick and Bamburgh alike we grudge the presence of their several kinds of inhabitants. When we come to a ruined house as distinguished from a ruined castle, we mourn to see it in ruins; we regret its lack of inhabitants. At Alnwick we should feel annoyed at the presence even of a Vescy; at Cowdray, the dwelling-place of seven or eight successive Viscounts Montague, we are sorry that there is not a Viscount Montague dwelling there still. For the castle is a thing of the past, a thing of the past which is wholly gone; it is something which was called into being by circumstances which have long vanished. It is essentially an antiquity, a memorial of distant times, and, if it is made into a modern dwelling-place, it loses its character as an antiquity and a memorial. The habits of modern life, carried on in an ancient keep, are simply incongruous. Either the keep is utterly sacrificed, or else the habits of modern life are carried on with less convenience than they might be elsewhere. In a Tudor house on the contrary, great or small, the case is quite different. It is not a castle, a fortress—a dwelling-place certainly, but a dwelling-place of days when no dwelling was safe but a fortress; it is strictly a house, in which, if any signs of a fortress are shown, they are mere survivals, a house in which it is perfectly possible to live with comfort in our own times. The interest of a building is always greater when it has been uninterruptedly used for its proper purpose from its first days till now; and, on this ground, it is always sad to see an ancient house forsaken or ruined. Of this Cowdray is a special case. The house, one of the grandest structures of the early days of Henry the Eighth, lived on as the chief dwelling-place of its owners till near the end of the last century. Nearly at the same time—it is probably a case of modern legend when we are told that it was on the self-same day—Cowdray house was burned, and the last Lord Montague was drowned far away in the Rhine, as though fire and water had, as Æschylus says, conspired together against the family. At that time, to judge from what still remains and from old drawings, the house must have been absolutely perfect, and it would seem to have been hardly at all disfigured, at least on the outside, of which alone we are able to judge.

The house, built about 1520, belonged to that happy moment of our national art when purely domestic architecture was at its height. The notion of the great house, as something distinct from the castle, had now been brought to perfection. The turreted gate-house is doubtless continued by direct tradition from castle times; but it is merely continued, and its few really military features, as the holes for shooting out of, have become little more than survivals. On the other hand, the architecture is still purely English; it does not as yet Italianize. That is to say, the architecture proper does not; as the foreign influence may be found in tombs and other lesser features before it touches the main features of a church, so it may be found in inserted medallions and the like before it touches the main features of a house. There is nothing of this kind now visible at Cowdray, except one or two inserted coats-of-arms and the like, which must be a little later than the building itself, and some Jesuit-like work in the chapel, which must be later still. Otherwise, the house, with the quadrangular court—of which two sides have utterly vanished, and not one is absolutely perfect— the gate-house, the hexagonal kitchen-tower, the grand hall with its windows and buttresses and its vast oriel, generally the ranges of large windows throughout the house, are purely and perfectly English. Both the actual style and the arrangements of the building are exactly at the point which is best suited for domestic work. There was still the hall in all its stateliness, with its screens, its gallery, its oriel, its soaring timber roof, every feature of mediæval grandeur still untouched. But the master and his family were no longer cabined, cribbed, confined, as they were in the older houses. The solar keeps its old place in relation to the hall, but it has swelled into the great drawing-room, or rather series of drawing-rooms, whose large windows form a main feature of the quadrangle. But, while the modern architect makes a pretty drawing of a house and then gets his rooms into

B B

it how he can, here at Cowdray no one can mistake the
purpose of any part of the building. Each is marked by
its own proper character; the hall is clearly the hall, and
nothing else; the large rooms beyond it are no less clearly
what they are, and nothing else. The hall and the chapel
alone have pointed and traceried windows; the other
parts have the square window which best suits domestic
purposes. Buildings of this kind, in their grand simplicity, their perfect adaptation of everything to its proper
end, do indeed contrast with that endless striving after
something new, something queer, something unlike anything which has ever been done before, which seems the
main object of most designers of modern houses. There
are no breaks, no projections, no odd little bits put in,
not because they serve any practical end, but because the
architect was throughout haunted by the notion 'I must
make something picturesque.' At Cowdray, and in all
other buildings of the type of Cowdray, the whole house
and every part of it is meant to serve its own purpose.
Each part does serve its own purpose, and the reward of
building rationally and straightforwardly is the creation
of a magnificent and harmonious whole.

The history of Cowdray carries us into the thick
of the history of the sixteenth century. The house no
doubt marks the site of an earlier house or castle; but
the history of the present building begins with a daughter
of the famous Marquess of Montague who died at Barnet,
Lucy by name, whose marriages remind us of the real and
mythical countesses of that name at an earlier time. The
daughter of Montague and niece of Warwick married successively Sir Thomas Fitzwilliam and Sir Anthony Browne,
names which at once land us in the reigns of Henry the
Eighth and his children. Her son by her first husband
bought Cowdray in 1528 and built the house; her son by
her second husband inherited it. He was a friend of
Henry the Eighth, and an early possessor of Battle abbey,
though it may be well to bear in mind that the church

there was pulled down, not by him, but by an earlier possessor still. His son, another Sir Anthony, was raised to the peerage under Mary. Viscount Montague doubtless chose his title in memory of his mother's father, but he does not seem to have thought it needful to cast away a surname which was famous as early as the twelfth century. He stands out in our history as almost the only eminent layman who, having conformed to earlier changes and having played a leading part in the changes under Mary, refused to conform under Elizabeth. Lord Montague even argued stoutly in the House of Lords against the second abolition of the papal authority. In his peerage and his possession of Cowdray he was succeeded by several viscounts of the elder faith, though the family conformed to the established religion before it came to an end. This suggests a question—What, during this long time, was the use of the chapel? This is an apsidal building with a room, as in so many other cases, opening into it. It forms an important part of the building, and is the only part which now shows distinct signs of having been Italianized within. Did successive Viscounts Montague venture on anything so like to public celebration of forbidden rites as to have mass said in this chapel? The first lord moreover, quite at the end of his days, in 1591, received Queen Elizabeth at Cowdray as he had years before received Edward. Long before that time all the doubtings and haltings and compromises of the earlier part of her reign had come to an end, and men were, as they are now, either distinctly Protestant or distinctly Roman Catholic. Did Lord Montague go on with an illegal worship under her Majesty's very eyes, and was no worship of the kind prescribed by law provided for the royal visitor? Here is a question which at once strikes the stranger, and to which local research may perhaps find an answer.

It is, as we have said, not without a feeling of sadness

that we see a building in ruins which might still, but for
the accident of eighty years back, have been kept on in all
its splendour as one of the greatest houses of the best
house-building time. Its repair, which in more than half
of the vast pile would amount to rebuilding, is now hardly
to be thought of; but one thing at least might be done.
Never was a building so thoroughly disfigured, and indeed
endangered, by that baleful plant which is sometimes so
strangely thought to add fresh beauties to the buildings
which it defaces.. The whole is so utterly overgrown with
ivy that in many parts the proportions are utterly lost.
The outlines both of the great gateway and of the kitchen
tower can hardly be traced by reason of the presence of
the enemy in its full strength. The insidious weed has
so entwined itself into the great oriel of the hall that its
rear-arch seems ready to fall. Some hand should at least
be stretched forth to hinder this. We cannot afford to
lose one stone of such a house as Cowdray. It stands, like
others of its own class, as a memorial of what Englishmen
could do in the sixteenth century, of what they will not
do in the nineteenth. We can never look on a building
of this kind without once more asking the question, why,
while we have in our own land buildings like Cowdray
and Thornbury, buildings of the very stateliest architecture, an architecture which is the growth of our own soil,
whose associations are those of our own history, and
which is surely surpassed by the architecture of no other
nation in splendour, in consistency, in practical convenience—why, when we have such models as these at
home, we should ransack Venice and Verona and all the
cities of the earth, to bring back a scrap from this place
and a scrap from the other, whose sole merit is that,
whatever they are, they are not English. With such
buildings among us, it is indeed strange that our modern
architects and their employers will go everywhere for
models, rather than to the great works of our own land.
We can only say, for our own part, that if any Englishman

is thinking of building a house on any scale, from a palace to a cottage, he could not fail to learn something which might be useful in his work by a study, even in its ruin, of the house in which the first Viscount Montague entertained Edward and Elizabeth.

CHICHESTER.

1864-1875.

The city of Chichester has probably gained in general fame by the loss and recovery of its best known feature. Many people must have heard of the fall and the rebuilding of the spire whose notions of Chichester and its church were till then a little indistinct. The city, in short, is not one of our great cities, and its minster is not one of our great minsters. It lies off any great line of travel, and it is rather in a corner even of its own county. The county of Sussex, the county which contains the hill of Senlac and the hill of Lewes, has witnessed greater events than any other shire in England, but those events belong to districts at a considerable distance from Chichester. The city itself, though it plays a certain part in the civil wars of the seventeenth century, has never been the scene of anything very memorable. Its interest and history is mainly ecclesiastical, and, even among ecclesiastical towns, it can claim only a secondary place. But few memorable names figure among its bishops, or rather perhaps, the see being a poor one, those eminent men who have held it have commonly been translated elsewhere, so that we connect their names with their later bishoprics. The local saint, Saint Richard, and that most paradoxical of divines, Reginald Pecock, are the two most famous names which connect themselves more with Chichester than with any other place; and, after all, Saint Asaph may fairly dispute the possession of Pecock with Chichester. Altogether, the ecclesiastical capital of the South-

Saxons must be satisfied with quite a secondary rank among the episcopal cities of England.

Secondary towns and churches of this sort have however a kind of interest which does not always belong to places of greater importance. Local history derives a sort of special charm from being more purely local, and, in a place of this kind, the absence of greater memories leaves the mind more leisure to attend to the details of local customs, offices, and traditions. At Battle, at Evesham, at Waltham, a single illustrious remembrance well nigh excludes all others. At Chichester, as in many other of our cathedral and monastic towns, there is no memory of this kind; there is simply an old ecclesiastical foundation for the ecclesiastical antiquary to compare with other foundations of the same kind. Wherever there is a cathedral church, there is always something to study in the way of buildings; wherever there is an old-foundation church, there is always something to study in the way of peculiarities in its constitution and history.

The cathedral church of Chichester, like two or three others, fills a kind of debateable ground between minsters of the first and the second order. Chichester, Wells, and Hereford hardly aspire to rank in the same class with Canterbury and Ely, and yet it is hard to pull them down to the level of Ripon, Saint Davids, or Romsey. Of course we are here speaking merely of the scale, not at all of the architectural merit or historical interest, of the several churches. In these respects, a minster of the second rank may be fully equal to one of the first. There is no church in Christendom more worthy of a pilgrimage than the metropolitan church of Alby, yet in point of mere scale it is insignificant compared with many which seem commonplace beside it. Thus our present subject Chichester can hardly compare with the general effect of such a church as Southwell, which is distinctly its inferior in point of size. In fact, the value of Chichester rests rather in the deep interest of several particular portions than in any very great general grandeur of outline or splendour of detail. The outline is awkward. That the north-west tower has perished is not the fault of its original designer; but the west front can never have been satisfactory; it should either have had higher towers, or no towers at all. They seem to have been originally crowned with the characteristic wooden spires of the county; and this would doubtless have improved the general appearance, though there must always have been an awkwardness of effect about spires whose towers rise so little above the ridge of the roof. Even at Lichfield, this defect is felt in some degree. The central spire of Chichester was doubtless a noble object; still nothing but exaggerated local patriotism could ever have compared it with Salisbury, or even with Norwich. The true distinction of Chichester in the way of towers is to be found in an object which we suspect has been somewhat underrated. Chichester, alone among English cathedral churches, has had the great good luck to keep its detached bell-tower. This tower is plain and massive, very unlike the soaring lanterns of Bourdeaux and Boston, which it resembles in general design. As the single tower of the church, it would have been despised as paltry; as an adjunct, it is in every way admirable. Standing near the church, but not forming part of it, the shiftings of its apparent position produce never-ending varieties of grouping, and from every point of view they redeem the outline of the church from that character of commonplace which would otherwise have attached to it. Indeed it surpasses either of the Bourdeaux campaniles in the happiness of its position; both of them lose somewhat from standing so directly east and west of their respective churches. But the Chichester bell-tower is a gain from every point from which it can be seen. From one point it stands out in its own character, as the bold, massive, detached tower which relieves the north side of the minster, which otherwise lies too bare and open to the street; from another more distant point it supplies, and more than supplies, the loss of the missing tower of the west front. We do not know whether any barbarians ever threatened to pull down the Chichester tower, as some actually did pull down its fellow at Salisbury. But Salisbury could bear the loss better than Chichester. It may be doubted whether it is a merit in a building to be so complete in itself, so independent of grouping—so much, in short, like a model—as Salisbury is; but, such being the character of the building, it is clear that it could better afford to lose such an adjunct than a church like Chichester, which is neither such a perfect whole as Salisbury, nor yet a building in itself of any very varied or picturesque outline. The campanile is, in fact, not only the distinguishing characteristic, but the distinguishing merit, of the church of Chichester as seen from the outside.

It is within that we see far more of those peculiarities which make Chichester, inferior as its effect is to so many other churches, one of the most interesting studies of architectural history in England. The Norman of the nave must have been singular from the beginning. The vast rectangular piers, nearly as wide as the arches between them, are utterly unlike the common English form; and the singular process of casing after the fire late in the twelfth century makes them more remarkable still; there is a marked contrast between the plain and massive original work and the delicate coating which cleaves to it and follows its form. The double aisles again, or rather the chapels beyond the aisles, so common in foreign churches, are almost without a parallel in England; for the double aisles of some parish churches, as Coventry and Taunton, have quite another character. These chapels have the effect of making the nave, on a ground-plan, about the widest in England, while practically, as measured from pier to pier, it is one of the narrowest.

The new tower and spire were built closely after the pattern of those which they succeeded. The lower stages of the tower are therefore Norman. The new arches are close reproductions of the old ones, while care has been taken to make the foundations this time fully able to bear the weight which is to be laid upon them. Still we have a strong opinion as to the unreality of rebuilding a tower and spire in two or three styles, because its predecessor had been built at two or three distinct dates. We still hold that the right course would have been to rebuild the spire exactly as it was, but to adapt the internal supports, æsthetically as well as constructively, to the superstructure which they were to bear. Instead of passing off any part of it as a building of the twelfth century, we would have in this way distinctly marked it as a building of the nineteenth. And we may remark another point. We chanced to see the church at the moment when the tower was finished but when the spire was not begun. The proportion and the general effect was so admirable that we pleaded hard that it might stay as it was, finished only with some low capping. But it was ruled otherwise; the neighbourhood won back its great landmark, but the church was again, to our thinking, cumbered with a crown far too high for its size, and the loss of which was a real gain.

In the collegiate buildings attached to the minster there are several good points here and there, but, as a whole, they are not striking. The Bishop's chapel is by far the best thing, and the extraordinary shape and position of the cloister should be noted. It is even more distinctly unmonastic than that of Wells. It is simply a passage connecting two doors, one in the nave and the other in the presbytery: it thus takes in the south front of the transept. All peculiarities of this sort should be carefully attended to, as marking the difference between the arrangements of regular and secular foundations.

Two other buildings in the city, though of course on a much smaller scale, are in their way quite as well worth study as the minster itself. The old Guildhall is the choir of a friars' church of the usual type—the long simple choir, without aisles or surrounding chapels, forming a marked contrast to the complicated arrangements of cathedral and abbatial churches. The difference is less in size than in arrangement; the *Barfüsserkirche* at Basel is as big or bigger than the neighbouring minster, but it preserves the same simple ground-plan as its smaller fellows. This of Chichester, when the nave was standing, must have covered a great deal of ground from east to west. But the nave has unfortunately vanished. The arch between it and the choir is so wide that there can hardly have been a tower inserted between them, as has happened to so many churches of the type.

The other building is Saint Marys hospital, perhaps the best example in England of that kind of hospital which consists of a large hall divided into cells for the inmates, and opening at the east end into the chapel by an arch and screen. The object of course is to allow the inmates to attend divine service without going out of doors. The arrangement is in fact the same as that which was usual in monastic infirmaries, where the infirmary church is open to the domestic part of the building. It is the same as that which is found in many domestic chapels in castles and houses, where the chapel was often only large enough for the priest to say mass while the household 'assisted' in the hall, or in some other room from which they could look into the chapel. Among hospitals there are many such cases, sometimes with two stages, sometimes with one only. Of this latter class there is none which carries out the arrangement so thoroughly as this at Chichester. People who are not familiar with buildings of this kind are sure to mistake the hall for the nave of a church—the chapel, of course, being the chancel—and they are commonly scandalized at the sight of people living in it. But both wonder and scandal are thrown away: the arrangement is at once common, ancient, and convenient. It is merely part of the vulgar error of crying out 'church' at the

sight of any mediæval building, just as when an outcry
was raised against holding the Hampshire assizes in the
hall of the King's palace at Winchester, because people
fancied that a building with pillars and arches must
necessarily be a church.

In domestic antiquities Chichester is not rich, but the
city cross, of the same type as those at Cheddar and
Malmesbury, but infinitely grander, is perhaps the best of
its kind in England. It is a remarkable contrast to the
soaring form of the corresponding building at Winchester,
which almost rivals the outline of the Eleanor crosses.
In the neighbourhood of the city is the church of
Bosham, famous for its connexion with the history of
Godwine and Harold, and from its representation in the
Bayeux Tapestry. There can be no doubt that the tower
and part of the church are as old as Harold's time, yet
certainly they are not the least like the picture. Far less
interesting historically, but beyond all comparison superior
as a matter of art, is Boxgrove priory, one of the best
examples in England of a divided church, but rendered a
little perplexing, because, contrary to the usual fate of such
buildings, the parish church has been destroyed while the
monastic portion survives. The singular internal elevation
of the presbytery is known to most antiquaries, and should
be got up on the first opportunity by any to whom it is
still unknown. We need hardly say that the county of
Sussex in general is one of the richest for the ecclesiastical
inquirer. The village churches are small, but always
picturesque, and there are several larger parish churches of
much merit. But the strength of Sussex lies in its series
of second-class minsters, of which Boxgrove is only one
out of several. The architectural interest of Sussex is of
quite a different kind from that either of Northamptonshire or of Somerset, but it is equal in its own way to either
of them.

COLONIA CAMULODUNUM

COLONIA CAMULODUNUM.

1868-1876.

[Read at the opening of the Historical Section of the Archæological Institute at Colchester, August 1, 1876. The case of Lucas and Lisle has been fully gone into by Mr. Clements Markham in the 'Fortnightly Review' for September 1876.]

THE history of the town in which we are now met, as far as it concerns the general history of Britain, belongs mainly to three distinct periods; and, in two of these, Colchester, placed as it is in the extreme east end of the island, has a singular historical connexion with events which went on at the same time in its western parts. In strictly English history, the time when Colchester plays its most truly important part is in the tenth and eleventh centuries. But on the surface of history, as history is commonly written, the name of Colchester stands out in greater prominence at an earlier and at a later date, in the first century of our æra and in the seventeenth. To most minds Colchester will be the town which was overthrown by Boadicea and which was taken by Fairfax. The events of the intermediate age have had more direct bearings on the real destinies of the English kingdom and nation; but it is the earlier and later dates which have most firmly fixed themselves in popular memory. And, both at the earlier and at the later date, there is a singular historical connexion between Colchester and the land in which it stands and a widely distant part of Britain. It seems a wide step indeed from the land of the Silures to the land of the Trinobantes, from

Morganwg to Essex, from British Cardiff to Saxon Colchester. For myself the kindness of the Institute has bridged over the gap by calling on me to fill the same place at Colchester which five years ago I filled at Cardiff. And yet there are real, if accidental, points of connexion between the two lands and the two spots. Colchester has in its earlier days a privilege which is shared by no other city or borough of England. The first beginnings of its history are not to be found in British legend or in English annals; they are recorded by the pen of the greatest historian of Rome. It is in the pages of Tacitus himself that we read of the foundation of that Veteran Colony which, swept away in its first childhood by the revolted Briton, rose again to life, first to be emphatically the Colony of Rome, and to become in after days the fortress which the men of the East-Saxon land wrested by their own swords from the grasp of the invading Dane. But, in the very page in which he records the beginnings of the Trinobantine colony, he brings that colony into a strange, and at first sight puzzling, connexion with movements in the far Silurian land. Later on in his Annals, he has to record the overthrow of the new-born colony, the first of all the sieges of Colchester. The first clause of his narrative of that stage of British affairs brings in a name which, in legend at least if not in history, is held to be preserved in the name of the greatest fortress of Morganwg. Before Tacitus can tell us how much Suetonius did in the east of Britain, he has first to tell us how little Didius had done in the west. Now this same Didius is, at least by a legendary etymology, said to have given his name to *Caerdydd*, the fortress of Didius, as a more likely etymology sees, in the name of the town where we are met, the name of the fortress of the Colony. If then there be any truth in the popular etymology of Cardiff, the beginnings of Cardiff and of Colchester must be dated from nearly the same time. And, even without trusting too much to so doubtful a legend, we at least find the land of the Silures and the land of the Trinobantes brought close together in our earliest glimpse of both. The foundation of a Roman colony in the East is directly connected in the narrative of Tacitus with patriotic movements in the West. Alike in the days of Boadicea and in the days of Fairfax, warfare in the Silurian and in the Trinobantine land has to be recorded in the same page. In the royalist revolt of which the fall of Colchester was the last stage, no part of the island took a greater share than the land to check whose earliest revolt Colchester was first founded. When the royal standard was again unfurled at Colchester, it had but lately been hauled down at Chepstow; it was still floating over Pembroke. And one of the fortresses of the land of Morganwg, one of the lowlier castles which surround the proud mound and keep of Robert Fitzhamon, saw the last encounter in that last stage of the civil war which even local imagination can venture to dignify with the name of battle. The fight of Saint Fagans does not rank in English history along with the fights of Marston and Naseby; and the siege of Colchester, with all its deep interest, military, local, and personal, can hardly, in its real bearing on English history, be placed on a level with the siege of Bristol. Yet the siege of Colchester and the war in South Wales were parts of one last and hopeless struggle. The remembrance of its leaguers and skirmishes lives in local memory there as keenly as the last siege of Colchester lives in local memory here. And if the name of Fairfax may be bracketed in the East with the name of Suetonius Paullinus, in the West the name of Oliver Cromwell has left but small room for the memory of Aulus Didius.

Throughout the earliest stage of the history of the two districts their historical connexion is as clear as it is strange. I am not going to give a complete history of Colchester or of Essex, or to dispute at large on any minute points of controversy. I presume however that I may at least assume that Camulodunum is Colchester and not any other place, in the kingdom of the East-Saxons or out of it. I feel sure that, if I had any mind so to do, my East-Saxon hearers would not allow me to carry the Colony of the Veterans up to Malton in Yorkshire; and I certainly cannot find any safe or direct road to guide them thither. I trust too that there may be no civil war in the East Saxon-camp, that no one may seek to wile away the veteran band from the banks of Colne to the banks of Panta. Maldon has its own glories; its name lives for ever in the noblest of the battle-songs of England; but I at least can listen to no etymologies which strive to give a Roman origin to its purely English name. Let more minute philologers than I am explain the exact force of the first syllable either in Northumbrian Malton or in East-Saxon Maldon. Both cannot be contractions of Camulodunum; what one is the other must surely be; one is the town, the other the hill, of whatever the syllable common to both may be taken to be. I at least feel no doubt that it is the town in which we are now met which has the unique privilege of having its earliest days recorded by the hand of Tacitus.

But if it is Tacitus who records the foundation of the colony, it is not in what is left to us of his pages that we find our first mention of the name of Camulodunum. That unlucky gap in his writings which every scholar has to lament sends us for the first surviving appearance of the name to the later, but far from contemptible, narrative of Dio. Claudius crossed into Britain, and went as far as Camulodunum, the royal dwelling-place of Cynobellinus. That royal dwelling-place he took, and, on the strength of that and of the other events of his short campaign in the island which men looked on as another world, he enlarged the *pomœrium* of Rome and brought the Aventine within the sacred precinct. Whether the royal dwelling-place of Cynobellinus stood on the site which was so soon to become the Roman colony, I do not profess to determine. The Roman town often arose on a spot near to but not actually on the British site. Roman Dorchester—if any trace of it be left—looked up on the forsaken hill-fort of the Briton on Sinodun. Roman Lindum came nearer to the brink of its steep hill than the British settlement which it supplanted. I do not pretend to rule what may be the date or purpose of the earthworks at Lexden. It has been thought that they are part of a system which took in the site both of an older and a later Camulodunum, a system belonging to the time of British resistance to Teutonic invasions. If so, we have here at Lexden a defence raised against the East-Saxons, as at Wareham and Wallingford we have defences raised against the West-Saxons. But on this matter I could not decide. All I ask is that I may not be constrained to believe in King Coel's kitchen. But wherever the British settlement was, I cannot bring myself to believe that the site of the colony was other than the site of the present town. It was a site well suited for a military post, fixed on a height which, in this flatter eastern land, is not to be despised; it approaches in some faint measure to the peninsular position of Shrewsbury, Bern, and Besançon. On this site then the Colony of Veterans was founded while Claudius still reigned. When he had taken his place among the gods—Seneca to be sure had another name for the change in him—the temple of the deified conqueror arose within the site which the Roman occupied to hold down the conquered people. And now comes the difficulty, the strange relation in which two such distant parts of Britain as Camulodunum and the land of the Silures appear in the narrative of Tacitus. The Iceni are subdued; the Cangi have their lands harried; the Brigantes submit. But in the East and in the West, by the banks of the eastern and of the western Colne, another spirit reigns. The Silures, the people of Caradoc, still hold out. Neither gentleness nor sternness will move them; nothing short of regular warfare, regular establishment of legionary camps, can bow those stubborn necks to the yoke. With a view to this warfare in the West, the Colony of Veterans is planted in the East. Some have therefore carried Camulodunum elsewhere—though assuredly matters are not much mended by carrying it into Yorkshire; others, more daring still, have sought to depreciate the authority of Tacitus himself. But, as I read the passage, though the connexion is perhaps a little startling, though the wording is perhaps a little harsh, the general meaning seems plain. In order that the legions and their camps might be more easily established among the threatening Silures, a feebler defence was provided for the conquered Trinobantes. As I understand the terse phrases of the historian, the legions were removed from the east for the war with Caradoc, and a colony of veterans was thought enough to occupy a land where little danger was feared. How little danger was feared, how thoroughly the land was held to be subdued, appears from the defenceless state of the colony eleven years after. The colonists lived at their ease, as if in expectation of unbroken peace. The town was unwalled; the only citadel, the 'arx æternæ dominationis,' was the temple of the deified conqueror. The mission of the veterans was less to fight than to civilize their barbarian neighbours. They were sent there indeed as 'subsidium adversus rebelles;' but they were sent there also 'imbuendis sociis ad officia legum.' Sterner work than this had to be done among the hills where Caradoc was in arms; but those who founded the unwalled colony hardly dreamed that, before long, work no less stern was to be done there also. They little dreamed what feats of arms were to be wrought, upon the Roman as well as by him, in the land which they had deemed so thoroughly their own that its capital hardly needed warlike defences against an enemy.

For eleven years the colonists lived a merry life, the life of conquerors settled upon the lands of their victims. The dominion of law which the veterans set up at Camulodunum did not hinder the conquering race from seizing the lands and houses of the natives, and insulting them with the scornful names of slaves and captives. Such doings are not peculiar to the dominion of the Roman; but it does say something for the Roman, as distinguished from the oppressors of our own day, that it is from a Roman historian that we learn the evil deeds of his countrymen. Tacitus neither conceals nor palliates the wrongs which led to the revolt of eastern Britain, as wrongs of the same kind still lead to revolts before our own eyes, as they always will lead to revolts as long as such deeds continue to be done. Crime was avenged by crime, as crime ever will be avenged, till men unlearn that harsh rule which excuses the wanton oppression of the tyrant and bids men lift up their hands in holy horror when his deeds are returned on himself in kind. Fearful indeed was the vengeance of the revolted Briton; but when he used the cross, the stake, the flame, against his oppressors, he was but turning their own intruments of civilization against themselves.

The tale is one of the most familiar, one of the most stirring, in that history of the former possessors of our island which so often passes for the history of ourselves. We see the British heroine, as we might now see some matron of Bosnia or Bulgaria, calling on the men of her race to avenge her own stripes, her outraged daughters, the plundered homes of the chiefs of her people, the kinsfolk of their king dealt with as the bondmen of the stranger. But we are concerned with Boadicea, her wrongs and her vengeance, only as they concerned the Colony of Veterans at Camulodunum. The tale is told with an Homeric wealth of omen and of prodigy. The statue of Victory fell backwards; strange sounds were heard in the theatre and in the senate-house; frantic women sang aloud that the end was come. The men of the defenceless colony, and the small handful of helpers sent by Catus Decianus, guarded by no ditch or rampart, defended the temple of Claudius for two days till town

and temple sank before the assaults of the avengers. So
the first Camulodunum fell, in one mighty flame of sacrifice, along with the two other great settlements of the
Roman on British ground. London, not adorned like
Camulodunum with colonial rank, but already the city of
ships, the place where, as in after days, the merchants of
the earth were gathered, fell along with the Veteran
Colony. So too fell Verulam, doomed again to arise, again
to fall, and to supply out of its ruins the materials for the
vastest of surviving English minsters. All fell, as though
the power of Rome beyond the Ocean was for ever broken.
But their fall was but for a moment; the sword of Suetonius won back eastern Britain to the bondage and the
slumber of the Roman Peace. The towns that the Briton
had burned and harried arose again: a new colony of
Camulodunum, this time fenced in with all the skill of
Roman engineers, again grew up. It grew up to live on
through four unrecorded centuries, carefully marked in
maps and Itineraries, but waiting for a second place in
history till the days when Roman and Briton had passed
away, when the Saxon Shore had become a Saxon shore in
another sense from that in which it bears that name in the
Domesday of the tottering Empire.

 The Roman then passed away from the Colony of
Veterans, as he passed away from the rest of Britain.
But in the Colony of Veterans he left both his works and
his memory behind him. When I say that he left his
works, do not fancy that I mean that he left the temple of
Claudius behind him. On the grotesque delusion which
mistook a Norman castle for a Roman temple I might not
have thought it needful to waste a word. Only, when I
was last at Colchester, I saw, written up in the castle
itself, such names as 'Adytum,' 'Podium,' and the like,
implying that there was still somebody in Colchester who
believed the story. Perhaps there was also somebody who
believed that the earth was flat, and that the sun was only

a few miles from it. The scientific antiquary will give exactly as much attention to the one doctrine as the scientific astronomer will give to the other. Of the two stories I should be more inclined to believe in old King Coel, in his fiddlers, and even in his kitchen. Yet I have come too lately from the Illyrian land, my mind is too full both of its past and of its present history, to let me believe that Helen the mother of Constantine was the daughter of Coel of Colchester. The strange likeness between the names of the river and the settlement, between the *Colne* and the *Colony*, is, if not a puzzle, at least a coincidence. But King Coel will be at once sent by the comparative mythologist to the same quarters as Hellên and Romulus and Francus the son of Hector. Saint Helen, says Henry of Huntingdon, surrounded Colchester with walls. So she did many things at Trier which the last and most scientific historian of Trier is pulling to pieces in a way which must grievously shock some of his brethren. I trust then that I shall not shock anybody in Colchester by disbelieving in old King Coel. I do not think that I shocked anybody in Exeter by declining to believe that, when Vespasian marched off to besiege Jerusalem, it was because he was bent upon taking some city, and had found Exeter too strong for him.

But the walls are there, whoever built them, the walls which, at some date between the invasion of Boadicea and the invasion of the first East-Saxon settlers, were raised to shelter the Colony. And even the legend of Helen may be taken as pointing to the age of Constantius and Constantine as the most likely time for their building. Those walls are, as far as I have seen, unique among the inhabited towns of Britain. Neither York nor Lincoln nor Exeter, nor even Chester, can boast of being still girded by her Roman walls in anything like the same perfection in which Colchester is. Nowhere else in Britain, save in fallen Anderida and Calleva, have I ever seen the line of the old defences so thoroughly complete. But unluckily it is the line only. While the circuit of the walls is so much more perfect than at York and Lincoln, the fragments which still remain at York and Lincoln have kept much more of their ancient masonry than can be found at Colchester. Still Colchester can show far more than can be seen at Chester, where, though the Roman lines are all but as perfectly followed by the later defences, little is left of the actual Roman wall beyond its foundations. As the abiding wall of a still inhabited town, the Roman wall of Colchester is, I repeat, unique in Britain. And a Roman wall I do not scruple to call it. In so calling it I am far from meaning to rule that the whole circuit of the existing wall actually dates from the time of Roman occupation. I have no doubt that the lines are the Roman lines; I have no doubt that part of the wall is the actual Roman wall. But I have just as little doubt that it has been in many places patched and rebuilt over and over again; one great time above all of patching and rebuilding is recorded in the days of Eadward the Unconquered. But the wall has a higher historic interest, it becomes a more living witness of Roman influence, from the very fact that much of it is not actually of Roman date. It teaches us a lesson which is taught by several continental cities, but which Colchester brings out more strongly than any other place in England. This is the way in which certain forms of construction sometimes abide through all changes of architectural style and of everything else. In the walls of Colchester we indeed learn with how strong a life the arts and the memory of Rome lived on. Whatever be the date of any part of the walls, they are Roman; they are built *more Romano*. It is at Colchester as it is at Trier, as it is at Périgueux, as it is in a crowd of other places where the influence of Roman models had struck deep. In places of this kind the Roman construction lived on for ages. At Trier masonry of thoroughly Roman character is used at least up to the eleventh century; at Périgueux and in some other cities and districts of southern Gaul it cannot be said to have ever gone out of use at all. So here in Colchester we have to distinguish between three kinds and dates of construction. We have, in the walls at least, actual bricks of Roman date in the places where the Roman engineer laid them, bricks which formed part of the defences which withstood the first East-Saxon attack. We have bricks of Roman date used up again in the construction of later buildings, as at Saint Albans. And we have bricks, not of Roman date, but of thoroughly Roman character, made afresh at all times at least down to the fifteenth century. Here, where brick and timber were of necessity the chief materials for building, the Roman left his mark upon the bricks as in some other parts of Britain he left his mark upon the stones. Northern England reproduced the vast stones of the Roman wall in a crowd of buildings built *more Romano*, with masonry of massive stones. With such stones again, no less *more Romano*, did Æthelstan rebuild the walls of Exeter. Here at Colchester Roman models were no less faithfully followed; but here the *mos Romanus* naturally took the form of brick, and to build *more Romano* meant to build with brick and not with stone. It meant to build with bricks, either taken from some Roman building or cast in close imitation of those which the Roman buildings supplied. The brickwork of the best and most undoubted piece of the Roman wall is reproduced in a neighbouring church tower of the fifteenth century. Still differences may be seen among bricks which differ perhaps fourteen hundred years in age. The true Roman bricks can commonly be known by the distinctive mortar still cleaving to them, and in the later work many bricks are interspersed of a size and thickness which, so far from being Neronian, cannot even be Stilichonian. Still, in the sense of a fashion handed on by unbroken tradition, all the brick buildings of Colchester may be called Roman. In this sense the castle itself may be called a Roman building. So may the one tower of Primitive Romanesque to be found in Colchester, the tower of Trinity church, which, while other towers of its type are of stone, reproduces in material as well as in form the campaniles of Italy. Its western door has a triangular head; the arch from the nave into the tower is Saint Benet at Cambridge translated from stone into brick. But the midwall shafts, strange to say, are lacking; as if the mind of Colchester was so wholly set upon bricks that the art of turning a stone column was unknown there. Another far greater and more famous piece of brickwork is the ruined nave of Saint Botolfs priory. Here we have a building second only to Saint Albans as an instance of the use of Roman materials, not so much taught to assume new shapes, as brought back to what was their true Roman use before Italy began her imitation of the arts of Greece. But the walls are Roman in a yet stricter sense than any of the other buildings around them. As almost everywhere in Britain, the gates have perished. There is nothing to set even against the New Port of Lincoln; far less is there aught to set against the mighty gateways of Trier, Aosta, and even Nîmes. Can we deem that at Camulodunum, as at Rome itself, there were ever gateways of really good architectural design built of the favourite material? As it is, we must content ourselves with the walls. They are the old walls of the Colony, in many places patched; in some, we may believe, actually rebuilt. But they have undergone no change which at all destroys their personal identity. The wall is not an imitation, a reproduction, of a Roman wall; it it the Roman wall itself, with such repairs, however extensive, as the effects of time and of warfare have made needful. The walls of Colchester are Roman walls in the sense in which the walls of Rome are the walls of Aurelian. The circuit of the walls is very nearly perfect; in some places they stand free; everywhere they can be seen by going down courts and alleys. As so often happens in these Roman towns, the old line of defence no longer answers to the actually inhabited space. As at Chester, there are void spaces and gardens within the walls, while in other parts the town itself has spread far beyond them. Modern Colchester spreads itself away from its river over the ground to the south. This is doubtless partly owing to the foundation of the castle, the precinct of which takes up a large part of the northern side of the town. For at Colchester we must talk of sides; we cannot, as we commonly can in a Roman *chester*, talk of quarters. There is, now at least, no strongly marked cross at Colchester, such as there is at Gloucester, Chichester, and the city which is specially Chester. There too the foundation of the castle, and the large space taken up by its precinct, may well have disturbed the ancient arrangement. The successive enlargements of the ecclesiastical precinct have, in the same way, caused modern York to keep but little of the lines of the ancient Eboracum.

We come then to a time when the walls of the Colony were still standing, but when the legions of Rome were no longer marshalled to defend them. Was there ever a time when those walls stood, as the walls of Bath and Chester once stood, as the walls of Anderida and Calleva still stand, with no dwelling-place of men within them? That question I will not undertake to answer. I think I remember that, in one of his scattered papers and lectures, the great master of those times, the discoverer of early English history, told us that of all the towns of England there was none more likely than Colchester to have been continuously inhabited through British, Roman, British, and English days. If I am right in thinking that Dr. Guest said this, he doubtless had some weighty reason for saying it. I have not myself lighted on any direct evidence either for or against such a proposition. It is only in a very few cases that we have any direct evidence as to the fate of this or that particular town during the progress of the English Conquest. And of the circumstances under which the kingdom of the East-Saxons came into being, we know absolutely nothing. The

Chronicles are silent; no legend, no fragment of ancient song is preserved to us by Henry of Huntingdon. We have nothing but a dry list of princes. We hear of Æscwine as the first founder of the East-Saxon settlement; we find his remote descendant Sleda spoken of as the first East-Saxon king. In this there is no contradiction. The story of the growth of Essex is doubtless much the same as the story of the growth of East-Anglia and of the two Northumbrian kingdoms. Several scattered Teutonic settlements were gradually united under a more powerful chief; then, as the head of a nation and no longer the head of a mere tribe, that chief deemed himself great enough to take upon himself the kingly title. Such was Ida in Bernicia; such, we may believe, was Sleda in Essex. But we have no trustworthy details of the East-Saxons and their kings till their conversion to Christianity in the beginning of the seventh century. We have no trustworthy mention of the town of Colchester till the wars of Eadward the Unconquered in the tenth. All that we can say is that the Colony on the Colne, like the Colony on the Rhine, kept its name. One was Colonia Camulodunum; the other was Colonia Agrippina; but *Colonia* was name enough to distinguish either. Latin *Colonia* became British *Caer Collun*; and *Caer Collun* appears in every list as one of the great cities of Britain. British *Caer Collun* passed into English *Colneceaster*, with no change beyond that which the genius of the British and English languages demanded. In British and in English alike it remains the city of the colony. From this preservation of the name I argue, as I have argued in the case of the one English city whose name ends with the title with which the name of Colchester begins, the sister colony of Lindum, that, if Camulodunum ever was, like Deva, 'a waste *chester*,' it was only for a very short time. I inferred from the fact that Lindum Colonia kept its name in the form of English Lincoln, that, if Lindum Colonia ever lay in the state of a waste *chester*, it was but for a very short time. It was settled again and named again while the memory of its old name and its old rank were still fresh. And I make the same inference in the case of Colchester, though with one degree less of certainty, because I must stand ready to have it thrown in my teeth that the town is called, not from the Roman colony, but from the river Colne. Here is a point on which each man must judge for himself. If there were no colony, one could say for certain that the town was called from the river; if there were no river, one would say for certain that the town was called from the colony. As it is, I cannot get over the succession of *Colonia, Caer Collun, Colneceaster.* I feel that it is awkward to say that the likeness of the name of the colony and of the river is purely accidental: it would be more awkward still to hint that the river may have taken its name from the colony. But the colony is a fact; the keeping of its name is a fact; and, in the face of those facts, all that I can do is to leave the river to shift for itself.

It seems likely then that, whether Colchester was or was not continuously inhabited through all the revolutions of the fifth and sixth centuries, its time of desolation, if it had any, was but short. If it did not become the dwelling-place of Englishmen in the first moment of their conquest, it at least became the dwelling-place of Englishmen before its British and Roman memories were forgotten. But, as I just now said, of Colchester itself there is absolutely no mention in history between the days of Boadicea and the days of Eadward the Elder. All that I can find is a dark and mythical reference in the story of Havelock as told by Geoffrey Gaimar. But we must not forget, even within the walls of the colony, that Colchester is not the whole of the East-Saxon realm. It is not even its formal head. I must leave local inquirers to say whether there is any reason beyond the fact of the neighbourhood of Colchester to the East-Anglian march to account for that rank falling to the lot of a town of so much less fame as Chelmsford. Yet Colchester was once

somewhat of a capital. That one of the earliest seats of
Roman power in Britain should to modern ears be mainly
suggestive of oysters is really by no means inappropriate.
The shell-fish, as the unscientific call it, was so favourite an
article of Roman food that its remains are often set down
among the signs of Roman occupation. Not that Colchester,
inland as it stands, is in itself a seat of the oyster-fishery.
But, if not the seat, it was long the head; the town had
a jurisdiction over the neighbouring coasts, something
like that exercised over other waters by Bristol and by its
own successful rival London. Colchester is not a city in
the modern use of the word; it does not even bear the
name in Domesday. It has never been the seat of an
independent bishopric. That was because another of the
Roman towns which was overthrown by Boadicea, lowlier in rank in those early days, had, by the time that
the East-Saxons embraced Christianity, outstripped the
Veteran colony. London, already the home of commerce
before her first overthrow—again, under her new name of
Augusta, the home of commerce in the later days of
Roman power—was now, as an East-Saxon city, the head
of the East-Saxon realm, again the home of commerce,
the meeting-place of merchants and their ships. London,
not Colchester, became the seat of the bishopric of the
East-Saxons, and remained so till the strange arrangements of modern ecclesiastical geography gave Colchester
a shepherd, first in the realm of Hengest and then by the
ruins of Verulam. But the very greatness which made
London the head of the East-Saxon kingdom tended to
part London off from the East-Saxon kingdom. Among
the shiftings of the smaller English kingdoms, London
seems to have held her own as a distinct power, sometimes acknowledging the supremacy of Mercia, sometimes
the supremacy of Wessex, but always keeping somewhat
of an independent being. She parts off from the main
East-Saxon body; she carries off a fragment of it along
with her, to become what we may call a free Imperial

city, bearing rule, like other Imperial cities, over her subject district of the Middle-Saxons. London therefore soon falls out of our special survey of the East-Saxon land. But the East-Saxon land can number within its borders not a few historic sites besides the towns which Boadicea overthrew. There is the battle-field of Maldon and the battle-field of Assandún; there is the wooden church of Greenstead where Saint Eadmund rested; there is Earl Harold's Waltham and King Eadward's Havering; there is Barking, where the Conqueror waited while his first tower was rising over London, where Eadwine and Morkere, and perhaps Waltheof himself, became the men of the stranger, and where Englishmen first bought back their lands at a price as a grant from the foreign king. The East-Saxon land has thus its full share among the great events of our early history; but the history of the kingdom itself, as a kingdom, fills no great place in our annals. Essex supplied no Bretwalda to bring the signs of Imperial dignity to London or Colchester as Eadwine brought them to York. After some flittings to and fro, Essex passed, like the other English kingdoms, under the supremacy of Ecgberht, and by the division between Ælfred and Guthrum it passed under the rule of the Dane. It is in the great struggle of the next reign that Essex, and especially its two great historic sites of Colchester and Maldon, stand forth for a moment as the centre of English history, as the scene of some of the most gallant exploits in our early annals, exploits which seem to have had a lasting effect on the destinies of the English kingdom.

It was in the year 913, the thirteenth year of Eadward's reign, the year after he had taken possession of London and Oxford, that we hear for the first time of a solitary East-Saxon expedition. Eadward marched to Maldon; he stayed there till he had built a fortress at Witham, and had received the submission of many who had been under

Danish rule. This sounds like the emancipation of all Essex south of the Panta or Blackwater. Our next notice is nine years later, after Eadward and his sister, the Lady of the Mercians, had won back most of the central part of the island to English and Christian rule. We now again find Eadward carrying his war of deliverance into the East-Saxon land. He first fortified Maldon, the goal of his former march, the borough which seventy-three years later was to behold the valour and the death of Brihtnoth. But Colchester was still left in the hands of the enemy. The next year the Danes again broke the peace; and, during the whole former part of the year, fighting went on in central England between the Danes and the defenders of the various towns which King Eadward had already fortified. At Towcester, at Bedford, and elsewhere, the English defenders drove off the Danish invaders from King Eadward's new fortresses. Towcester was not yet surrounded by the stone wall which girded it before the year was out; but the valour of its defenders, fighting, we may suppose, behind a palisade or rampart of earth, was enough to bear up till help came and the enemy was driven away. During all this stage of the campaign, the warfare seems to be purely local. The Danes attack; the English defend; there is no mention of the King or of any royal army. Presently the tables are turned; the local force of various English districts begins to attack posts which the Danes still held among them. And now comes our first distinct mention of warfare on East-Saxon soil. Colchester is still held by the enemy; Maldon is held by King Eadward's garrison. The tale cannot be so well told as in the language of the chronicle:—'There gathered mickle-folk on harvest, either of Kent and of Surrey and of East-Saxons, and of each of the nighest boroughs, and fared to Colchester, and beset the borough all round'—*ymbsæton* is the emphatic word—'and there fought till they had won it and the folk all slew, and took all that there within was, but the men that there fled over the wall.' Colchester was thus again an English borough, won, as it would seem, by the force of a popular movement among the men of Essex and the neighbouring shires, without any help from the West-Saxon king. Then, in the same harvest, the Danes of East-Anglia, strengthened by wikings from beyond sea, set forth to attack the English garrison in Maldon. In the words of Chronicler, 'they beset the borough all round, and fought there till to the borough-folk there came more force from without to help them, and the host forsook the borough, and fared away from it; and then fared the men after out of the borough, and eke they that had come to them for out to help, and put the host to flight, and slew of them many hundred either the *ashmen*'—the men of the ashen ships—'and others.' Thus, of the two great points in the East-Saxon land, Colchester was won, Maldon was kept, and that without any help from the king. Local energy had done so much that, when shortly the Unconquered king came with his West-Saxon army, his march was little more than a triumphal progress. He came to Towcester; he girded the town with its stone wall, and received the submission of Northamptonshire. He marched to Huntingdon; he strengthened the fortress, and received the submission of the surrounding country. Then comes the fact which immediately concerns us here. That 'ilk year afore Martinmas fared Eadward king with West-Saxons' fyrd to Colneceaster, and repaired the borough and made it new there where it tobroken was.' Here then we have a distinct record of damage done and of damage repaired in the circuit of the walls of Colchester. Part of the wall was broken down in the siege, and the breach was repaired on the King's coming. It would be pleasant if we could tell, amongst the many bricks of various dates which are to be seen in the walls of Colchester, those bricks which were set in their place at the bidding of the founder of the English kingdom, and not by any earlier or later hand. If we can find the site of the breach which Englishmen made in winning Colchester from the Dane, Englishmen may look on that spot in the Roman wall with the same eyes with which all Europe looks on that spot in the wall of Aurelian where the newest bricks of all tell us where the army of united Italy entered her capital.

But the two great East-Saxon sieges of this memorable year have more than a local interest. They were the last warfare of the reign of the Unconquered king. After Colchester was won and Maldon saved, no sword was drawn against Eadward and his dominion. The rest of his reign is one record of submissions on the part of his enemies. At Colchester itself the men of East-Anglia and Essex, who had been under Danish rule, first bow to him; then comes the submission of the Danish host itself; then that of all Mercia; then that of all North Wales. The realm of the West-Saxon king now reaches to the Humber. Northumberland, Strathclyde, Scotland, are as yet untouched by his arms or his policy. But next comes the great day of all, the crowning-point of West-Saxon triumph, when the King of Scots and all the people of Scots, and Rægnold and Eadwulf's son, and all that were in Northumberland, Angles, Danes, Northmen, or any other, and eke the King of Strathclyde Welsh, and all Strathclyde Welsh, bowed to Eadward at Bakewell, and sought him to father and lord. The fights on East-Saxon ground, the storm of Colchester, the defence of Maldon, had taught the whole world of Britain that Eadward and his people were not to be withstood. The gallant gathering of the men of Essex, Kent, and Surrey, had led to the establishment of an English kingdom bounded only by the Humber, of an English Empire bounded only by the Northern sea.

Thus two East-Saxon sites, one of them our present place of meeting, have won for themselves a foremost place in that struggle with the Dane which welded England into a single kingdom. And one of those sites joins again with a third whose name we have not yet heard to form another pair no less memorable in the struggle which gave the united kingdom of England into the hands of a Danish king. If the days of Colchester and Maldon stand forth among the brightest days of English victory, so Maldon and Assandún stand out among the saddest yet noblest days of English overthrow. Our last East-Saxon memory showed us the invading Dane flying from before the walls of Maldon; our next East-Saxon memory shows us the Dane victorious in the hard hand-play, and the Ealdorman of the land dying in defence of the Saxon shore. The fight by the Panta, the fight where Brihtnoth fell, lives in that glorious battle-song which, were it written in any tongue but the native speech of Englishmen, would have won its place alongside of the battle-songs of ancient Hellas. The song is plainly local and contemporary; it comes straight from the soul of the East-Saxon gleeman of the tenth century. It is something to stand on the spot and to call up the picture of the valiant Ealdorman, lighting from his horse among his faithful hearth-band, marshalling his men in the thick array of the shield-wall, refusing to pay tribute to the wikings, and telling them that point and edge shall judge between them. Then we see the dauntless three who kept the bridge, Wulfstan, Ælfhere, and Maccus—Wulfstan the Horatius, his comrades the Lartius and Herminius, of the fight in which the legend of the Tiber was repeated in sober truth by East-Saxon Panta. Yet among the crowds to whom the legends of distant lands are as household words, how few have ever heard the names of the inborn heroes of our own soil. Then Brihtnoth, in his 'overmood,' in his excess of daring and lofty spirit, allows the enemy to pass the water : then comes the fight itself, the Homeric exploits on either side; the death-wound of Brihtnoth and his last prayer; the dastardly flight of Godric on the horse of his fallen lord, the fight over the body of the slain chief; the self-devotion of the true companions who in death are not divided, as they lie

'thegn-like' around their lord, their earl and ring-giver.
No tale is told with more spirit, no tale sets better before
us that great feature of old Teutonic, and indeed of old
Aryan, life, the personal and sacred tie which bound a
man to the lord of his own seeking. But the men who
fought on that day were Englishmen; the tongue in which
their deeds were sung was English; their deeds are therefore forgotten, and the song which tells of them sounds
in the ears of their children like the stammering speech
of an unknown tongue.

But if the banks of Panta saw the glorious death of
the local East-Saxon chief, the banks of another East-
Saxon estuary saw, not indeed the death but the last
struggle, of the champion, not only of Essex but of all
England. The fight of Maldon is handed down to us in
the glowing strains of native song; the song which told
of the fight of Assandún has perished: we have only feeble
echoes preserved to us in the Latin pages of the historian
who has kept so many such precious fragments, from the
song of Anderida to the song of Stamfordbridge. As to
the site of Assandún I will not enter on any discussion;
I think no one will doubt about it who has been there.
There is the hill on which Eadmund Ironside marshalled
his army for the last battle, the hill down whose slope he
rushed with his sword, as the faint echo of the ballad
tells us, like the lightning-flash, leaving in his charge the
royal post between the Standard and the West-Saxon
Dragon, and fighting hand to hand in the foremost rank
of his warriors. We hear from the other side how the
Raven of Denmark had already fluttered its wings for
victory; but it was only through Eadric's treason—treason
which no effort of ingenious advocacy can wipe out from
the pages which record it—that Eadmund, in the sixth
battle of that great year, found himself for the first time
defeated. The spot which saw Cnut's victory over all
England saw also a few years later his offering in his new
character of an English king. Then arose the joint work

of Cnut and Thurkill, the minster of stone and lime, whose material as much needed to be noted in the timber land of Essex as the material of the wooden basilica of Glastonbury needed to be noted among the rich stone-quarries of Somerset. Of that minster the first priest was Stigand, the man who won his first lowly promotion at the hands of the Dane, and who lived to be hurled from the metropolitan throne at the bidding of the Norman.

But the East-Saxon land contains a memorial of those times more precious even than the memories of Maldon and Assandún, a memorial too which forms a special tie between Eastern and Western England. It was on East-Saxon soil, just within the East-Saxon border, on the spot to which the willing oxen drew the Holy Cross of Leodgaresburh from the place of its first finding in the West, that Tofig first cleared the wild forest, that he first reared the minster of Waltham in its earlier and lowlier form, and gathered round it a band of pilgrims and devotees who changed the wilderness into a dwelling-place of man. It was on that spot that Earl Harold, patron of the secular clergy in the most monastic period of our history, patron of learning in a day when the light of English literature seemed almost to have died away, enlarged the church and the foundation of Tofig. It was for the good of this spot that he sought in lands beyond the sea, in the kindred land with which England had exchanged so many worthies—the land to which she had given Ealhwine and whence she had received Old-Saxon John —for men to help him in the work which he had planned for the weal of Waltham and of England. It was there that the doomed king, marching forth to the great strife for his land and people, went to make his last prayers and to offer his last gifts, and it was there that, as men of his own day believed, he received that awful warning which led his faithful bedesmen to his last field, standing afar that they might see the end. It was there, in his own minster, that his bones, translated from their earlier

South-Saxon resting-place, lay as the most precious among his gifts to the house which he had founded. And it was there, when his foundation had been changed to another form, when a choir in a new style of art had risen over his tomb, that the greatest of his successors, the first of a new line of English kings, lay for a moment by his side. The choir of Waltham has perished along with the choir of Battle; the place of Harold's tomb, like the place of Harold's standard, again lies open to the day; but if the East-Saxon land had nothing to boast of beside the unmarked spot where Harold and Edward met in death, that alone would place the shire where Waltham stands among the most historic shires of England.

Among his other possessions in all parts of England, Earl Harold held four houses in Colchester. This fact, I need not say, comes from the Domesday Survey, which tells us how those houses had passed away to the abbey of Westminster. The Domesday of Essex is very full; for Essex is one of those three eastern shires of which we have only the first and fuller account, while in most of the other shires we have only the shorter form which is found in the first volume of the Exchequer Domesday. Essex was one of those shires which came into the possession of the Conqueror, not, indeed, like Sussex and Kent, immediately after the great battle, but immediately after the submission at Berkhampstead. Like Kent and Sussex, its men had been in their place in the battle, and it became subject to a confiscation only less sweeping than that of Kent and Sussex. We do not find in Essex, as we do in many other shires, either one or two English landowners still keeping great estates, or a whole crowd of them keeping smaller estates. A few entries of English names towards the end of the record are all. We hear of no revolts in Essex after the coronation of William; the strength of the shire, like the strength of Kent and Sussex, must have been cut off on Senlac, and no foreign prince offered himself as deliverer to the men of Essex as Eustace of Boulogne offered himself to the men of Kent. Still there must have been some confiscations in Essex later than the time of the redemption of lands; for the penalty had fallen on one of the very commissioners by whom the redemption was carried out. Engelric, who must have played much the same part in Essex which Thurkill played in Warwickshire and Wiggod in Berkshire, as the Englishman who, by whatever means, rose high in William's favour, had fallen from his high estate before the Survey was made. Another man, English by birth though not by descent, Swegen the son of Robert, who took the name of the shire as a surname, he whose father had stood by the death-bed of Eadward and had counselled William on his landing to get him back to his own duchy, still kept great estates; but he had lost his office of Sheriff. Most of the familiar names of the Conquest appear in Essex as well as elsewhere; but the East-Saxon shire enjoys a singular privilege in not having had an acre of its soil handed over to the Conqueror's rapacious brother, Count Robert of Mortain. But Bishop Odo is there, and Count Alan, and the Count of Eu, and William of Warren and Hugh of Montfort, and many another name of those who found their reward in almost every shire of England. Among the names specially connected with the district stand out Geoffrey of Mandeville, father of a line of East-Saxon earls, Ralph Baynard whose name lives in London city, and the names specially belonging to Colchester, Hamo and Eudo. Of Colchester itself the record in the Survey is one of the fullest among the boroughs of England. It ought to be fully illustrated by some one who to minute local knowledge adds the power of comparing what the Survey tells us about Essex and Colchester with what it tells us about other shires and boroughs. A general historian from a distance cannot do this; a dull local antiquary cannot do it; it needs a man on the spot who knows the ins and outs of the land, but who also understands historical criticism, and who knows something of other parts of England as well as of his own.

Colchester does not appear, as one might have looked for, at the beginning of the East-Saxon record, but at the end. Nor can we find any such precious notices of the municipal constitution of Colchester as the other volume gives us of the municipal constitution of Lincoln, Cambridge, and Stamford. Colchester had been held by the Danes; but they had been driven out too soon and too thoroughly to allow of the formation of a patriciate of Danish *lawmen*. But we see the burgesses of Colchester already forming a recognized body, holding their folkland, their common lands, and claiming other common lands as having been unjustly taken from them. We specially see them holding the land for a certain distance round the walls. And it would seem that, not many years back, Colchester kept a precious record of its early municipal being, a treasure rare even in Italy and, one would think, almost unique in England, a town-hall or gild-hall of Romanesque style. Of this building the drawing of a single Romanesque doorway is the only monument. But while the walls are distinctly recorded in the Survey, there is no mention of the castle. There is therefore no entry of the destruction of houses to make room for the castle, such as we find in many other English towns. A long list is given of English burgesses who kept their houses, followed by a list of possessions within the borough which had passed into the hands of Norman owners. Among these of course appear the *Dapiferi*, Eudo and Hamo, and about the latter there is an entry of special interest. Whatever Hamo held had been held in the days of King Eadward by his English *antecessor* Thurbearn. First Thurbearn and then Hamo, besides a house, had a 'curia,' a rare word whose use I do not fully understand. And this 'curia' seems, I know not on what ground, to be identified with an existing house which keeps portions of Romanesque date. The first entry of all is also one of a good deal of interest, as marking the subdivision of property in Old-English times. The houses and other property of Godric—one of the many bearers of one of the commonest of English names—had been divided among his four sons. They had died on Senlac, or had otherwise brought themselves under the displeasure of the Conqueror. Of the four parts of Godric's property the king held two; Count Eustace had the third, and John the son of Waleran the fourth. The church of which Godric was patron had passed whole to Count Eustace; but his mill—a most important possession, and one always accurately noted in the Survey—was carefully divided.

Another point to be noticed in the Survey of Colchester is that the borough had clearly been, before the coming of William, allowed to make a money composition for military service in the *fyrd*. In many towns Domesday records the number of men which the town was to find when the King made an expedition by sea or land. Instead of this, we find at Colchester a payment of sixpence from each house for the keep of the King's *soldarii* or mercenaries, that is doubtless the housecarls. In another part of the kingdom Wareham and the southern Dorchester were subject to payments for the same object, while Wallingford had to find for the housecarls, not money but quarters. In the nature of the service due from Colchester to the king we may perhaps see the key to the fact that so many English burgesses of Colchester remained undisturbed by the Conqueror. The borough, as a community, had served King Harold, not with men but with money. Possibly it had not served King Harold at all, as the last yearly payment may have been made before the day on which King Eadward was alive and dead. In either case, it would have been hard, even for the astuteness of William's legal mind, to turn this payment of a customary royal due into an act of constructive treason against the Norman claimant of the crown. The community then, as a community, was guiltless, and fared accordingly. But volunteers from Colchester, as well as from other places, had doubtless flocked to the Standard of the Fighting Man; and they, whether dead or alive, paid the forfeit of their patriotism.

Here is a point which touches the general history of England. There are other curious entries with regard to the customs of Colchester which I leave to local inquirers to expound to us. I pass to the ecclesiastical history. The Survey mentions several churches; but there clearly was no great ecclesiastical foundation, either secular or religious, within the walls of Colchester. The two religious foundations which have given Colchester an ecclesiastical name arose after the taking of the Survey and beyond the ancient walls. They arose on the south side of the town, the side away from the river, a fact which accounts for the way in which the inhabited town of Colchester has spread itself. While on the northern side void spaces have arisen within the walls, houses have grown on the south side round the priory and the abbey, covering a large space which lies outside alike of Roman Camulodunum and of old English Colchester. The great abbey of Saint John, the foundation of Eudo, rose on a height opposite that on which the town itself stands; the priory of Saint Julian and Saint Botolf rose between the heights on the low ground just below the hill of Camulodunum. The history of Eudo's foundation is told in a document in the Monasticon which, in all points bearing on general history, is highly mythical. Eudo's father, Hubert of Rye, is a well-known man, he who sheltered William on his perilous ride from Valognes before the fight of Val-ès-dunes. But the embassies on which Hubert is sent between William and Eadward simply take their place among the Norman legends of the Conquest. There is also a very mythical air about the prominent part in securing the succession to William Rufus which the local story assigns to Eudo. We may however accept the purely local parts of the tale. Eudo's special position at Colchester, by whatever name we are to call it, appears in the story as the gift, not of William the Great but of William the Red. This at once falls in with the absence of all mention of the castle in Domesday. The castle was not one of the castles of the Conqueror; that vast pile, so widely differing in its outline from the towers of London and Rochester, was clearly a work of Eudo, a work dating from the reign of the second William and not of the first. It is a castle of the square Norman type, but covering a greater expanse of ground than Rochester, or even than London. It is therefore low in proportion to its height; no one would think of calling it a tower. Its vast rectangular mass is broken only by the apsidal projection for the chapel in the east wall, as in the later example at Kidwelly; in the Tower of London the apse is made in the thickness of the wall. The style is plain throughout; all the original windows are of the narrowest and simplest Norman type. The inside is divided into two courts, but it is a dead wall that divides them. There is nothing at Colchester like the arcades of William of Corboil, nothing even like those plainer arcades of Gundulf which so strangely reproduce in miniature the vast pile of Saint Sernin at Toulouse. Far vaster in mere bulk, the castle of Colchester has nothing to compare with the architectural detail of that of Rochester, any more than it can rival the general effect which the Kentish keep owes to its grand position. The Colne is not the Medway, and the castle of Colchester does not overhang even the Colne. It does not soar over the town, but simply stands within its walls. Low and spreading, standing on the same level as the rest of the town, it is simply the chief among the buildings of the town, while the tower of Rochester looks down, with a distinct personality of its own, on church and city alike.

The great Benedictine abbey began in the later days of Rufus; the priory of Austin canons began a little later in the early years of Henry the First. Both are among

the ties which connect the East of England and the
West. John Beche, last Abbot of Colchester, was one of
the three prelates who refused to betray their trust. He
was a sharer in the martyrdom of Richard Whiting on the
Tor of Glastonbury. The priory had ages before served,
as we have seen clearly, as a nursery for Llanthony. It
boasted the Lion of Justice himself among its benefactors,
as appears by his charter dated while Queen Matilda and
Bishop Robert Bloet of Lincoln were still living. The
abbey, like that of Shrewsbury, arose on a spot where had
stood the wooden church of the English priest Sigeric.
Of the material of the new building the local history does
not speak; the foundation stones whose laying it records
are quite consistent with a superstructure of brick, and
it appears in old drawings as a brick building. Saint
Botolfs, as we all know, is built *more Romano, more Camu-
lodunensi*, of bricks which are none the less Roman, even
if some of them may have passed through the kiln in the
twelfth century. So it is with the castle also, though
there brick is not so exclusively the material. A marked
difference may be seen in the bricks in the upper and the
lower part of its walls. The colony, like its metropolis,
remained in all ages and under all masters emphatically
a city of brick, and happily no one has been found to
change it into a city of marble.

I have now reached the point at which I commonly
find it expedient to bring discourses of this kind to an
end. But at Colchester I must follow another rule, as in
some degree I did at Exeter. The place of Exeter in
English history would be imperfectly dealt with, if we
did not bring the entry of William the Conqueror into
its obvious contrast with the entry of William the Deliverer. So at Colchester I cannot bring myself to stop at
the days of William the Red. I must leap over a few
centuries. To many the scene which the name of Colchester first calls up will be the scene which followed the

last siege, the day when Lucas and Lisle died on the green between the Norman castle and the Roman wall. I have already pointed out that there is, in some sort, an analogy between the beginning and the ending of Colchester history, between the warfare of Boadicea and the warfare of Fairfax. It is hardly allowed to me here to speak as freely of Fairfax as I can of Boadicea. Of Eudo the Dapifer I can perhaps speak more freely than of either. The strife of the seventeenth century is so closely connected with modern controversies and modern party-feelings that it cannot be made purely archæological ground like the strifes of the first century or of the eleventh. I perhaps need hardly tell you that my own personal feelings go with the side of Fairfax, though I trust I am fully able to understand and to honour all that was good and high-minded and self-sacrificing on the side of his enemies. But in summing up the last stage in the long life of this historic town, I must call attention to one or two obvious facts which are apt to be forgotten in forming an estimate of that great piece of local history. Remember then that the warfare of which the siege of Colchester forms the last and the most striking scene was a warfare wholly distinct from the earlier warfare of Edgehill and Naseby. Colchester was not, as seems to be the legendary belief, a fortress which had held out for the royal cause ever since the royal standard was first upreared at Nottingham. During the whole of the first war, Colchester and Essex were hardly touched. Even in Essex, a land so strong for the Parliamentary cause, the men of Colchester were noted for their special zeal, a zeal which they had shown, a little too fiercely, against their royalist neighbours at the abbey. The royalist movement of 1648, alike in Essex, in Kent, and in South Wales, was in the strictest sense a revolt, a rising against an existing state of things. Whether that revolt was to be praised or to be condemned, it is a simple fact that the enterprise of the Earl of Norwich and Lord Capel was not a continuation of the war which began at Nottingham, but a wholly new war of their own levying. Before Colchester was besieged by Fairfax, it had in truth to be besieged, though only for a moment, by those who presently became its defenders. Those defenders, who have been so strangely changed into local heroes, were in the days of their presence looked on simply as oppressors of whom the oppressed town was yearning to be rid. The day of deliverance came; two of the oppressors underwent a fate which has come, in local legend, to be looked on as martyrdom. Yet in the execution of Lisle and Lucas, Fairfax went on perfectly good technical grounds. They had been prisoners of war, and had given their word of honour never again to serve against the Parliament. I am far from insisting with any undue severity on the obligations of such promises as this. It is a question of casuistry whether such a purely military promise should or should not keep a man back from an enterprise to which he deems that loyalty or patriotism calls him. But, as a matter of military law, his life is fairly forfeit; the man who has been set free on certain conditions cannot complain if the sternest measure is meted out to him when he breaks those conditions. The military justice of Fairfax touched those only whose breach of military honour had fairly brought them within its reach. The escape of Norwich, the execution of Capel —Capel, a man worth Norwich, Lucas, and Lisle all put together—were the work of another power in which Fairfax had no share. Whatever may be thought of the political or personal conduct of either of the two lords, there was no stain on their military honour. The General therefore did not take on himself to judge men who, whatever they were in the eye of the law, were, on the field of battle, entitled to the treatment of honourable enemies. But, 'in satisfaction of military justice,' he let the laws of war take their course on men who, whatever may be pleaded in their behalf on other grounds, had, by the laws of war, lost all technical claim to honourable treatment.

One point more there is which brings the last siege of Colchester into direct connexion with earlier times. The site of Saint Johns abbey, the house of Lord Lucas within or close to its precinct, play an important part in the siege. The gateway, the only important part that now survives, occupied by the insurgents, was stormed by the Parliamentary forces, and doubtless what other remains of the abbey were left at the Dissolution now perished. Saint Botolfs too, standing immediately between the batteries of the besiegers and the walls of the town, was exposed to the fire on both sides. The eastern or monastic part, as commonly happened to the divided churches of the Austin canons, had already perished. The nave became in the siege the ruin which we now see it.

I have now brought my tale, and that by somewhat of a bound in its last stage, to its latest point. I have tried to sketch out the chief grounds on which the shire of Essex, and, above all, the town of Colchester, are entitled to a high place among the shires and towns of England. It is for others with more of local knowledge to fill up that sketch in detail. I have exhausted nothing; I stand in the way of no one who has specially mastered any portion of East-Saxon history. In the days of Boadicea and in the days of Fairfax I may even be deemed an intruder. But I am no less ready to invite every help, to welcome every light, on the times in which I may say that I myself have lived. That I have lived in those times makes me know perhaps better than other men how much there is still to be found out, how many things in them there are that to me at least are grievous puzzles. The greatest of English scholars, once a dweller in the East-Saxon shire, has made the history of the Holy Cross of Waltham plain to all men. But we still need a worthy commentator on the Song of Maldon. Even in those parts of the tale at which I have specially worked, I feel, better perhaps than others, how much I have left uncertain, how much there still is for others to fix by the light of sound and sober historic criticism. But, in any case, there is no part of the isle of Britain in which one who has lived in the tenth and eleventh centuries feels more at home than within the walls which felt the repairing hand of Eadward the Unconquered, in the land which beheld the exploits and the death of Brihtnoth, the land where Eadmund fought the last fight of the year of battles, the land where Harold knelt before the relic which was brought from the green hill of Montacute, the land to which he himself was borne from the craggy hill of Hastings. It is something that the hero of England should be in this way a common possession of the three branches of the great Saxon colony, that the Saxon of the West, the South, and the East, should be all bound together, as by a threefold tie, by the presence among them in life or death of the last king of the old stock, the king who died on Senlac and who no longer sleeps at Waltham.

[I have left what I wrote attributing the castle to Eudo. But last year there appeared an anonymous book, seemingly by a local writer, called the 'History and Antiquities of Colchester Castle,' which shows some research and criticism (though the form of the criticism is sometimes a little captious), but in which the author takes too much trouble over the nonsense of those who call the castle a Roman building. 'Solventur risu tabulæ' is the only treatment for them, as for Anglo-Israelites and such like. But the writer speaks of a charter of William Rufus, granting the castle to Eudo, which certainly looks as if the castle was not Eudo's building. This charter, he truly says, has escaped my notice. But he does not tell us whether the charter is printed anywhere, nor does he print it in full himself. He gives (p. 29) the words of the grant 'Sciatis me dedisse benigne et ad amorem concessisse Eudoni dapifero meo civitatem de Colecestria et turrim et castellum et omnes ejus civitatis firmitates cum omnibus quæ ad illam pertinent.' But he does not quote the opening words of the document, and the words which follow the grant are fatal to the notion of its being a genuine charter of William Rufus. The king grants the town and castle, 'sicut pater meus et frater et ego in ea quocumque habuimus.' A moment's thought will show that these words could not be used by the Red King, nor indeed by any sovereign after the Norman Conquest, except Henry the First, John, Mary the First, and William the Fourth. A date follows : ' hæc commissio facta fuit apud Westmonaster [sic] in primo natali post concordiam Roberti comitis fratris mei de me et de illo.' This has a suspicious ring about it ; but it would do just as well for Henry in 1101 as for William Rufus in 1091. And, if Eudo had anything to do with the treasons of that year, a fresh grant of the castle might well be needful, whether the castle was his own building or not. But it is passing strange that the writer does not give us the opening words.

It is perhaps safest to leave the matter open. The anonymous writer attributes the castle to the Conqueror. It is too great a work for Eudo. There is perhaps something in this. On the other hand there is the absence of any mention of the castle in Domesday. This again however is only a presumption, as the notices of castles in the Survey is a little capricious. But one would certainly have looked for some mention of it in so elaborate a description as that which Domesday gives of Colchester.]

CARLISLE

THE PLACE OF CARLISLE IN ENGLISH HISTORY.

In the course of the journeyings of our Institute through various parts of our island, in the course of the meetings which it holds year by year in our chief cities and boroughs, it often happens that the immediate scene of our researches specially calls back, as a matter either of likeness or of contrast, some other scene which we have examined in earlier years. Thus it was that, in the discharge of the office which the kindness of the Institute has so often laid upon me, I was once called on to flit over a large part of our island, from British Cardiff to East-Saxon Colchester. Strangely enough, I found that in two stirring periods of history, at some distance from one another, in the first century and in the seventeenth, the fates of the Silurian and the East-Saxon lands were twined together in a way which beforehand we should hardly have looked for. Here, on our second visit to this renowned border city, on my first visit to it in the character of an officer of the Archæological Institute, my thoughts have wandered to stages in our progress earlier than the meeting of the Institute at Cardiff. From the hill and the castle of Carlisle I would ask you to look south-eastward to the flats of Holderness, to the haven of Kingston-upon-Hull. I would ask you also to carry your eyes more directly southward, to that one among all the *chesters* that Rome has left us which has specially taken that once vague description as its own proper name, to the scene of the bloody victory of Æthelfrith and the peaceful triumph of Eadgar, to the City of the Legions by the Dee. Between Carlisle and Chester, between Carlisle and Kingston-on-Hull, I trust to show some instructive historic analogies and contrasts.

There are not many of the chief cities and boroughs of England which can point with undoubting certainty to a personal founder in strictly historic times. On founders who are purely mythical I need hardly dwell, and it would almost seem that they are passing out of date even in popular belief. I found at Colchester that, while yet wilder legends were still in vogue, old King Coel was well nigh forgotten in his own city, and that it needed rather hard work to get a copy of the music of his own song to sing on the battlements of what for the nonce we may call his own castle. Among more real personages, who do not claim to be looked on as grandfathers of the founder of the New Rome, it has happened in not a few cases that some well-ascertained man has founded a castle or a monastery, and that a town has grown up around his foundation. So it was, to take only two examples out of many, with the abbey of Saint Eadmund in one age and with the castle of Richmond in another. So in northern England Durham owes its being to the happy choice of Ealdhun, when he picked out the peninsula girded by the Wear as the fittest place to shelter Saint Cuthberht's body after its wanderings. So in southern England the younger Salisbury owes its being to the happy choice of Richard Poore, when he moved his church from the waterless hill of elder days to the merry field that looks up to it. But I speak rather of cities directly called into being as cities, as great military or commercial posts, by the policy of princes who strove to strengthen or to defend their kingdom. We believe that Edinburgh came into being at the bidding of Eadwine the Bretwalda as the outpost of Anglian Lothian against the Scot. We know that Taunton came into being at the bidding of Ine the King as the outpost of Saxon Somerset against the

Briton. But the foundations of Eadwine and Ine belong to a time so early that we can hardly look on them as cities or boroughs in the later sense. In the long list of English towns which first appear in history among the works of Eadward the Unconquered and Æthelflæd the Lady, it is hard to say on which spots they bade an uninhabited site to become for the first time a dwelling-place of man, and on which they simply strengthened sites which had, from the beginning of English settlement in Britain, been covered with English homes. But it is one of the works of Æthelflæd, and one of the works, if not of the elder Eadward, yet of the namesake of after-times who walked in his path and renewed his glories, which I would ask you to look to as fellows, in the way of likeness and of contrast, to the city in which we are now met. Chester, Carlisle, Kingston-upon-Hull, can all point without doubting to their personal founders. Let the eldest of the three, the work of the Mercian Lady, wait a while. I would first ask you, dwellers and sojourners within these ancient walls, at the foot of yonder historic castle, dwellers and sojourners on a spot which has played so great a part in English warfare, not to look with scorn on the lowlier, the more peaceful, the more recent, fame of the great haven by the mouth of Humber. I can hardly believe that the men of Hull would willingly exchange their founder for the founder of the Carlisle that now is. On the stairs of their town-house stands their founder's statue, a statue which fifteen years back I had often to pass, and which I could never bring myself to pass without showing some mark of worship to the greatest of England's later kings. Carlisle contains no such memorial of her founder, and, if she did, I am not sure that some years of very near acquaintance with him and his doings would lead me to pay him the like reverence. For while Hull may boast herself as the creation of Edward the First, the Carlisle that now is can claim no worthier founder than William the Red. I give the founder of

Hull his conventional number under protest. Lawyers
and courtiers have taught us to forget the worthies of
our own stock; but the men of the great Edward's own
day better knew his place in history; they reckoned him,
by a truer and worthier reckoning, as fourth of his name
among the Kings of the English, third among the Emperors of Britain. If we are to change the number of the
founder of Carlisle, we must change it the other way; for,
as we are standing here on soil which formed no part of the
realm of the Conqueror, he who was William the Second
for the kingdom of England might be deemed to be only
William the First within the earldom of Carlisle. Between
the founder of Hull and the founder of Carlisle, between
Edward the First and William the Red, the general
contrast is certainly as wide as any contrast that can be
found between any two of the princes and leading men of
our history. I need not now draw their portraits. The
portrait of the great Edward I have striven over and over
again to draw as occasion served. The portrait of William
Rufus I have so lately drawn in the fullest detail of which
I am capable that I am not as yet ready with a single
freshening touch. Between the father of his people and
their oppressor, between the foul blasphemer and the
devout crusader, between the man of the most debased life
and the mirror of every personal virtue, there is indeed
little likeness. And though the reign of Rufus does in
its way mark a stage in our national progress, it is hardly
in the same way as the reign of the king whom we may hail
as the founder of our later commerce and of our later law,
the king who made fast for ever the great political work
of the uncle whom he overthrew. And yet there are points
in which two men so unlike each other as the founder of
Hull and the founder of Carlisle may truly stand side by
side. Each gave a king to Scotland; each warred with the
Briton; and, if the Welsh warfare of Rufus brought him
but little of immediate gain or immediate glory, it did in
truth open the way for the victorious warfare of Edward.

But, before all things, each enlarged the borders of the kingdom of England in a way that was done by no king between them. That the ground on which I now stand is English ground is the work of William the Red. And that the city in which we are met has been for nearly eight hundred years a dwelling-place of man is his work also.

But it may be that some one stirred up by a praiseworthy local patriotism may arise and ask how the King's-Town-upon-Hull, whose plain English name bespeaks a comparatively modern origin, can be in any way set side by side with a city like this, whose British name points to an antiquity far older than the Conqueror's son. Hull, he may say, had undoubtedly no being before the days of Edward the First; do I mean to say, he may ask, that Carlisle had no being before the days of William the Red? And I must answer that, though each prince is, on his own ground, alike entitled to the honours of a founder, yet the work of Rufus by the Eden and the work of Edward by the Humber were not wholly of the same kind. They differed in this, that the one called into being a haven of peaceful trade, while the other called into being a border fortress for the defence of his kingdom. But they differed further in this. Edward was strictly a creator. If men already dwelled on the site of the King's-town-on-Hull, there was, till his keen eye marked the advantages of the site, nothing that could claim the name of town or borough. But William Rufus, in founding what has lasted from his day to ours, did but call into renewed being what had been in ages long before his. He called into being a city of men, and he girt it with walls and towers; but he called it into being on a site where men had dwelled in past times, and which had been defended by walls and towers of an older pattern than those with which the Red King fenced it in a second time.

As I have already hinted, if we had no record to tell us of the fact, the very name of *Carlisle* would be enough to teach us that the history of this city is essentially different from that of any other English city; and, above all, that its first being dates from a day long before the day of William Rufus. Alone among the cities of what we now deem the proper England, Carlisle bears an almost untouched British name, a name which was assuredly not given to it by a King of the English of Norman birth. This alone would show that, if Rufus was on this ground truly a founder, yet he was a founder only on ground where others had been founders long before him. Now here comes in the analogy between Carlisle and the other city with which I have already asked you to compare it. The part which was played at Carlisle by the son of the Conqueror was essentially the same as the part which had been played at Chester by the daughter of Ælfred. Rufus and Æthelflæd alike called into renewed being a city which had once been, but which was no longer. Deva, Caerlleon, the City of the Legions, had stood void of men for three hundred years, since Æthelfrith smote the Briton beneath its Roman walls. Under the Lady of the Mercians the 'waste chester' rose again, bearing an English version of its ancient name. But so renowned was the chester of the Legions, the chester of Æthelflæd, among the many chesters of the land, that it became emphatically the Chester, and has for ages been known by no other name.

Whether Roman Lugubalia, British Caerlluel, ever sank so low as Roman Deva, British Caerlleon, we have no means of judging. We know not whether it ever stood as a mere 'waste chester,' like Deva and Anderida. On the whole, the evidence looks as if Rufus had not found it utterly desolate. The story of its restoration looks that way; the history of the name looks that way. At Caerlleon-on-Dee, the British name was, according to the usual rule, turned round and translated. The Briton, according to the idiom of his tongue, had put his *caer* before the qualifying name; the Englishman, according to the idiom of his tongue, put his *ceaster* after it. *Caerlleon* became *Legeceaster*, as the southern *Caergwent* became *Wintanceaster*, *Winchester*. But on the spot where we now stand the British name has ever lived on. *Lugubalia* became *Caerlluel*, as *Venta* became *Caergwent*; but, while *Caergwent* has become *Winchester*, *Caerlluel* has not, in modern speech, become *Lulchester*, but, with the slightest change of sound, it remains *Caerlluel* to this day. As far as modern usage goes, it has not shared the fate of the Caerlleon by the Dee and the Caergwent by the Itchin; it has lived on, like the other Caerlleon by the Usk, the other Caergwent on the Silurian shore. And this fact, the fact that we speak of Winchester and not of Caergwent, while we speak of Carlisle and not of Lulchester, becomes the more remarkable when we light on another fact, namely that, for a season, on some mouths at least, Lulchester was the actual name of the city where we are met. There is just evidence enough, but only just enough, to show that the English form of the name was really known. In the ninth century we hear of Lulchester; in the eleventh we hear again of Caerlluel. This seems to prove almost more than if the name of Lulchester had never been heard at all. It does not absolutely prove continuous habitation; but, combined with other facts, it looks like it. And it does prove that, while there had once been an English day on the spot, it was followed by a renewed British day. In the case of the City of the Legions, some form of the name, British or Latin, must have lived on for Æthelflæd to translate into English. But it was she who translated it. In her father's day the spot had no English name; it was not the Chester of the Legions, it was simply a 'waste chester.' But William Rufus did not think it needful to translate the name of Caerlluel into either French or English. He did not think it needful to call again into being the English translation which had been once made, but which was by his time doubtless quite forgotten. Neither did he, like the founders of Richmond and Montgomery, give his creation a name in his own tongue, borrowed perhaps from some well-known spot in his own land. All this shows that, when Rufus came, the British name of the spot must have been in familiar use. It was perhaps more commonly *Luel* than *Caerlluel*; yet even the fuller name must have been far better known in his day than the name of Caerlleon could have been in the days of Æthelflæd. And this looks as if Caerlluel was not so utterly a waste chester in the days of Rufus as Caerlleon-on-Dee was in the days of Æthelflæd. But we must further remember that English Æthelflæd had every temptation to give her restored creation an English name. To the French-speaking Rufus—for he knew not our tongue like his greater brother—a British name would sound no more strange than an English one. If he found the name of Caerlluel as well established as the name of Eoforwic, he had no more temptation to change the name of Caerlluel than he had to change the name of Eoforwic.

But when we have fixed the name of the city, as far at least as writing it on paper is concerned, how are we to sound it? For the name seems to be sounded in one way within its own walls, in another way in other parts of the kingdom. Diligent students of Sir Walter Scott may have noticed that he gives the name of the city two distinct accents, according to the necessities of his metre. 'The sun shines fair on Cárlisle wall,' when the sovereignty of love is to be set forth; but, when an English raid is looked for beyond the Scottish border, the places whence it is most likely to come are marked as 'Naworth or Warkworth or merry Carlísle.' This last accentuation is that by which the city is best known to the rest of the world. The former is that which is used by its own inhabitants. But it is plain that in this case, as in some others, the stranger has preserved the true sound more accurately than the native. For it is the second syllable that qualifies the *caer* which answers to the English *chester*, and it is of course on the qualifying syllable that the accent should come. And it is whispered that, though the citizens themselves prefer the other sound, yet the neighbouring peasantry still keep the accent, according to etymology, on the second syllable. Exactly the same differences are to be marked in the sound of the Celtic name of a much smaller city, the episcopal see on the Taff. The Welsh *Llandáf* has, in the ordinary speech of other parts, become *Llandáff* or *Landáff*. In its own neighbourhood, the only known English form is *Lándaff*. This last sound is altogether unfamiliar out of the immediate neighbourhood. I well remember a witness being examined before a bench of magistrates in Somerset who mentioned something as having happened at *Lándaff*. Nearly every one who heard him understood him to speak of *Taunton*. The vowels were not quite the same; the consonants were quite different; but the trochaic run common to the two names did for one as well as for the other. I believe I may say, without boasting, that, if I had not happened to know a little of South-Welsh topography, no one would have found out what place the witness meant. I know not whether any such accidents have ever happened through the double accentuation of *Cárlisle* and *Carlísle*. If it ever should so happen, I trust that the foundation of William Rufus will not think it scorn to be mistaken for the foundation of Ine.

Such then are our analogies and contrasts. Between Carlisle and Kingston-on-Hull there is such fellowship as as may be deemed to arise between those two of the chief cities and boroughs of England which, alone or almost alone, can each claim as its personal founder a king of all England and a king who enlarged the bounds of England. Between Carlisle and Chester there is such fellowship as may be deemed to arise between cities which, after lying for a long time more or less thoroughly forsaken, were again called into being as cities of men, as border fortresses of the English realm. Other cities have in the like sort risen again: it may well be that most of the inhabited *chesters* throughout England did so. But in no other cases can we be so certain of the fact, so certain of the motive, as we can be of the work Æthelflæd in 907 and of the work of William Rufus in 1092.

But it rarely happens that any ancient and historic city, however close and instructive may be its points of likeness to its fellows, is left without some points in its history which are absolutely its own, and which might serve as its definition. I do not mean simply incidental definitions, based on some great fact in the history of the city. In this way we might define Chester as the city which beheld the last great victory of the heathen Englishman over the Christian Briton and which was the last of English cities to bow to the Norman conqueror. So we might define the elder Salisbury as the city which looks down alike on the field of battle which decreed that Britain should be English and on the field of council which decreed that England should be one. These are indeed events whose memory is now inseparably bound up with the historic spots where they took place; but the course of history might have taken such a turn as to cause them to take place elsewhere. York or Exeter, instead of Chester, might have been the last city to hold out against the Conqueror. Gloucester or Winchester, and not Salisbury, might have been the scene of his great act of legislative wisdom. To take the highest range of all, if York stands alone in Britain as the seat of Imperial rule, the peer of Trier and Milan and Ravenna, that post of supreme dignity might just as easily have fallen to the lot of London or Verulam or Camulodunum. If Lincoln stands out within our world as the head of aristocratic commonwealths, yet it might have been that the lawmen of Stamford or Cambridge should have held the place which was held by the lawmen of the Colony of Lindum.

I speak rather of definitions which enter as it were into the essential being of the cities themselves. It is after all an accident in the history of Exeter that she should have withstood William the Conqueror and welcomed William the Deliverer. It is an essential part of her personal being that she should have been the one city of Britain whose historic life is absolutely unbroken, the one city which passed from the Christian Briton to the Christian Englishman, it may even be without storm or battle, certainly without any period of abiding desolation. And Carlisle has her personal definition of the like kind. We can say of her that she is the one city which, having once become part of an English kingdom, again fell back under the rule of the Briton, the one city which became again part of the united English realm, and that by so strange a process as she beheld when the son of the Norman Conqueror drove out the one man of English blood who ruled as a prince in any corner of Britain.

It is a relief to one whose immediate business it is to speak specially of the city of Carlisle that he is not called upon to mix himself up with all the puzzles which surround the history and ethnology of Cumberland. He is not called upon to fix any limits to the extent of a name whose extent was ever changing. When Eadmund the Doer-of-great-deeds gave Cumberland, as perhaps the first of territorial fiefs, to his Scottish fellow-worker, when Æthelred, in one of his strange fits of energy, came to Cumberland on an errand of havoc, the site of Carlisle may perhaps have been in some way touched in either case. But the city of Carlisle was certainly untouched; for the city of Carlisle was a thing which had been and which was to be again, but which at that moment was not. Nor is he called upon to solve that most puzzling of problems, the history of Scandinavian settlement and influence in the land around us. That Scandinavians of some kind, Danes or Northmen, made their way into the land is plain alike from the record of history and from the traces which they have left to this day. On the eastern side of England, in Northumberland, in Lindesey, in East-Anglia, we know the time of their coming; we know the names of their kings and earls who reigned at York. Here we simply know that they did come, and, as a matter of actual record, we know that they did come by one fact only. But that is a fact which touches our immediate subject in the most direct way. The one thing that we know to have been done in this immediate region by Scandinavian hands is the thorough destruction which Scandinavian hands wrought in the city where we are come together, destruction so thorough that, for two hundred years, the city ceased to be a city. This fact concerns us most intimately; I do not know that we are at this moment called on to enter on the problem, how it was that Cumberland could be spoken of as specially Danish; how Henry of Huntingdon came to speak of it as the chief dwelling-place of the Danes, while the presence of Danes in it certainly did not hinder the succession of a line of Scottish princes. But I am not called on to speak of Cumberland. In the time that specially concerns me we have only to do with the name of Carlisle, not at all with the name of Cumberland. The land which the Red King added to the English kingdom was not the land of Cumberland, but the land of Carlisle. When, under King Henry, that land became an English earldom, it was an earldom of Carlisle, not an earldom of Cumberland. When, under the same king, the land became an English diocese, I need hardly say that its bishop was Bishop of Carlisle, not of Cumberland; by that time the territorial titles of bishops had altogether died out in England. The land which formed its diocese had no name; it had to be pointed at, as it is pointed at by Archdeacon Henry in his list of episcopal churches, as 'that land in which is the new bishopric of Carlisle.' The name of Cumberland, like the name of Westmoreland, as the name of a part of the immediate

English kingdom, dates only from the days of the Angevin. And, as for the problems of Cumbrian ethnology, let them be debated beyond the city walls. Of the city itself written history tells us only, what we have already heard, that the Dane overthrew the city and left it empty, and— a point on which I shall have to speak again—that, when the Norman came to restore and to repeople city and land, it was with a colony of Saxons that he repeopled them.

I have defined Carlisle as being that one among the cities of England which, having once become English, became British again. The unbroken English life of Carlisle begins with the coming of the Red King and the settlement of his southern colony. For two hundred years before he came, it had been British or nothing. For at least two hundred years before that it had been part of an English kingdom, that of the Angles of Northumberland. For at least two hundred years before that, it had shared the independence of those parts of Britain from which the Roman had gone, and into which the Angle or the Saxon had not yet come. Of the Roman and British life of the city we have little to tell, but that it had a long Roman and British life no man can doubt. Under various shapes and corruptions of its Roman and British name, we find it in every list of the cities of Britain. Luguballium, Lugubalia—I may be forgiven for cleaving to the shape which the name takes in the pages of English Bæda—occupies a site which seems marked out by Nature for a great fortress. It is a site which seems specially marked out as designed to guard a border, to defend a land against dangerous neighbours who may one day become wasting invaders. And this duty the hill of Lugubalia has had laid upon it throughout more than one long period, in the hands of more than one set of masters. I was once tempted to say that it is not without a certain fitness that the spot which was to be the bulwark of England against the Scot should of itself put on somewhat of a

Scottish character. I pointed out that the castle-hill of
Carlisle bore a strong likeness, though a likeness in miniature, to the castle-hills of Edinburgh and Stirling. In all
three the castle crowns a hill, steep at one end only. It
crowns it therefore in a different sense from those hill-
towns where the fortified akropolis forms the centre of the
city. At Edinburgh, at Stirling, at Carlisle, the castle
alike crowns and ends the city. It is at once an akropolis
and an advanced bulwark. All three strongholds are emphatically watch-towers, homes of sentinels, standing and
looking forth to guard the land of their friends and to
overlook the land of their enemies. But when I spoke of
Carlisle, the bulwark of England against the Scot, as
having itself a Scottish character, I was thinking of some
later ages of its history. In a wider view of the history
of our island, I might have expressed myself otherwise.
From one side we might look on all three as being for
several ages charged with what was essentially the same
historic mission. In a more general view than that
which concerns the fluctuating political boundary of
the English and Scottish kingdoms, each of these
fortresses, looking out as they all do, so significantly
and so threateningly to the north, might pass, from
the days of Eadwine, from the days of Rufus, as a
bulwark of Teutonic Britain against the Celtic lands
beyond it. That duty was at least as well discharged by
Stirling in the hands of an English-speaking King of
Scots as it was by Carlisle in the hands of a French-
speaking King of England. In a broad view of things,
the artificial boundary of the English and Scottish kingdoms, that is the boundary which parted off the Angle of
Northumberland from the Angle of Lothian, is of far less
moment than the boundary of Teutonic speech and civilization, whatever might be the name or the formal nationality
of its champions. But what distinguishes Carlisle from
its two northern fellows is that, while it has shared with
them the championship of Teutonic Britain against the

Celt, it, alone of the three, had already held an analogous place in days before any part of Britain was Teutonic.

It will be at once seen that, while Stirling and Edinburgh guard one natural line of defence, Carlisle guards another. Stirling and Edinburgh guard the northern line, the line of Antoninus and Valentinian, the line drawn across the isthmus between the firths, at the point where Britain becomes so narrow that some ancient writers looked on the land beyond this line as forming another island. It is strange how nearly Valentia, the recovered conquest of the elder Theodosius, answers to the Scotland of later history, the English kingdom ruled by kings bearing a Scottish title. Of that kingdom Stirling and Edinburgh were border fortresses against the true Scot, save so far as Teutonic speech and culture crept up the eastern coast to meet the kindred settlements which the Northman made in the lands which lay beyond the home of the Scot himself. Ages came when that was no mean function; but it was a function whose counterpart was called into only rare and fitful action in the days when the Cæsars ruled in Britain. To hold the land against the Celt was the calling alike of the Roman and the Teutonic lords of Britain. But the Roman could not be said to hold anything with a firm and lasting grasp beyond that great bulwark of which Lugubalia kept the western ending, as the Ælian bridge kept the eastern. Speaking without strict topographical accuracy, but with an approach to it near enough to convey the general idea, we commonly say that the Roman wall stretches from Carlisle to Newcastle. The Roman wall, the greater of the Roman walls, the only Roman wall in the sense which the word conveys in modern usage, the mighty bulwark of Hadrian, of Severus, and of Stilicho, may be fairly said to take Lugubalia as one of its starting-points. Not itself placed immediately on the line of the wall, the fortress looks out, as one of its chief points of view, on the station of Stanwix, the near neighbourhood of which may have caused Lugubalia itself to have been really of less military importance in the days of Roman occupation than in either earlier or later times. Yet the fortress itself does in some sort form part of the great bulwark, if it be true, as I have heard suggested, that the moat in advance of the wall to the south may be traced along the line dividing castle and city. On this point I venture no opinion; I leave it wholly to those of greater local knowledge to decide. Of one thing we may be sure, that the Roman was not the first to turn this natural fortress into a place of strength. He was possibly the first to fence in the headland with a wall of masonry—though indeed some have suggested that Lugubalia was defended only by a stockade; he was surely not the first to part it off by a ditch from the ground to the south of it. We may be sure that such a site was marked off as a place of defence even in the days when the art of defence was rudest. Here, as in so many other cases, the Roman did but seize on and improve on the works of the older inhabitants of the land. But we may be equally sure that it was at Roman bidding that the primitive stronghold became the akropolis of a city, a city where the arts and luxury of southern Europe were for the first time planted on this furthest border of Roman abiding power. From his own world the Roman had gone forth to bring the other world of Britain under his dominion. But, as he looked forth from the akropolis of this his most northern city, he must indeed have felt that there was yet another world beyond, a world within which the power of the Cæsars could spread itself only now and then, in moments of special, and at last of dying, energy.

Presently a time came when the Roman world, within and without Britain, was to be cut short, when the older barbarian world against whose outbreaks Lugubalia had been planted as a bulwark was again to be enlarged, again to take in lands and cities where the Roman had ruled and where he was still to leave his memory behind him.

We enter that unrecorded age whose silence is more eloquent than any record, that age of darkness whose gloom gives us a clearer teaching than we can often gain from the fullest light of contemporary history. The Roman has gone; the Teuton has not yet come. The second period of British independence and isolation has begun, the length of which was so widely different in different parts of Britain. In Kent many a man who had seen the eagles of Rome pass away from Britain must have lived to see the keels of Hengest draw near to the coasts of Thanet, and to take his part in the bloody fights when the Welsh fled from the English like fire. Nay, the life of man is now and then so long that some who were born under Roman law, subjects of the sons of Theodosius, may have stayed on to die as helpless elders when Ælle and Cissa left not a Bret alive within the walls of Anderida. Far otherwise was it here in Lugubalia. Two centuries at least of untouched Celtic independence must have passed before this corner of the island which the Roman had forsaken fell under the rule of any Teutonic conqueror. How are we to fill up that long gap through which even the most meagre records are speechless? It might indeed be easy to fill it up from the world of legend. We may at pleasure people merry Carlisle with the company which poets of earlier and later days have called into being to gather round the shadowy form of Arthur. The knights and ladies of Arthur's court, their loves and their exploits, I leave poets to deal with; I leave poets too to deal with the warfare of the British prince in lands far beyond the shores of Britain. But the question whether we are to look for a historic Arthur in so northern a part of our island is a fair question for critical discussion. If such an Arthur there was, we may fairly look on Caerlluel as in every way likely to have been his capital. But can any one here who bears in mind whence I have come reasonably ask me to become the prophet or champion of a northern Arthur? As a disciple of

Dr. Guest I must accept a personal Arthur; but both my local and my personal allegiance constrain me to place him and his exploits in a part of our island far away from this. I must accept an Arthur who was a thorn in the path of our fathers, a valiant enemy who did somewhat to delay the work which turned Britain into England. I must grant to him the glory of a victory of no small moment over the English arms; but I must place that victory far away from Lugubalia and the Roman wall, on the spot where he met Cerdic face to face beneath the rings of West-Saxon Badbury. Dwelling within sight of the Tor of Avalon, hard by a hill which bears Arthur's name and which looks out on the spot where men deemed that Arthur slept, I may join in honouring the memory of a gallant foe, the Hector, the Hannibal, the Hereward, of Britain; but I must be allowed to honour him on my own ground or on the ground of my immediate neighbours. If any man asks me to believe that the tyrant Arthur came with the men of Cornwall to win back his wife whom the King of the Summer-land had carried off to the sure shelter of the Glassy isle, I feel no special necessity laid on me to refuse so harmless a request. But I cannot let the hero of our *antecessores* in the south-western peninsula go further from us than to the lands which may be seen from his own southern hill. Two British names of which I have often had to speak have a tendency to get confounded both ways. We of the *Æstiva regio* where Arthur found his tomb may let him go so far from us as to keep his court at Caerlleon by the Usk; we cannot part with him on so long a journey as to let him go to keep it at Caerlluel by the Eden.

The fifth and the sixth century pass away; the seventh brings us face to face with deeds which are more certain, and with doers of those deeds of whom, if legend can tell us less, history can tell us more. At some time in that century, earlier or later, Lugubalia, beyond all doubt, passed under English rule. But was it earlier or later?

When Æthelfrith had done what Ceawlin had failed to do, when he had cloven asunder the solid British land which still stretched from the Clyde to the Severn sea, when he had smitten the monks of Bangor and left the City of the Legions a howling wilderness, are we to deem that the spot on which we stand was among the lands which the last heathen king of Northern England added to the Northumbrian realm? Or shall we deem it that Lugubalia bowed to Æthelfrith, but that what Æthelfrith won Cadwalla won back, when for the last time the Northern Briton went forth conquering and to conquer? Was the city and its fortress part of the immediate realm of the Bretwaldas Oswald and Oswiu? One thing is certain that, later in the century, Caerlluel formed part of the realm of Ecgfrith. It may have been part of his conquests from the Briton; it was at least not one of those among his conquests which were won only for a moment. For nearly two hundred years after Ecgfrith, the city remained part of the dominions of the Northumbrian kings, part of the spiritual fold of the bishops of Lindisfarn, and, by the grant of the conqueror to the holy Cuthberht, part of their temporal possessions also. In English mouths too at least, its name took an English shape, and British Caerlluel became, in the pages of Cuthberht's biographers, English *Luelceaster*. It had its abbots, its abbesses, one at least among them of royal birth, the sister of Ecgfrith, to whom and to others the holy Cuthberht foretold their king's coming end. Indeed, save his own holy island, few places stand out more conspicuously than Lugubalia in the history of the saint of Lindisfarn. We see him in the picture of Bæda himself, visiting the city with somewhat of the curiosity of an antiquary: we see him taken, as we have been this day, to look at its ancient walls, and to stand by the fountain which had been wrought in a wondrous sort in the days of Roman rule. Can we deem that, of the walls on which Cuthberht gazed we have this day gazed on any abiding fragments? Carlisle is not as dead Anderida, it is not as living Colchester, it is not even as Chester, which was dead and is alive again. Had Saint Cuthberht been taken to see the walls of any of those ancient cities, we could point with all assurance to the stones and bricks on which he looked, abiding in the place in which he saw them. In the walls of Carlisle I have believed myself to see Roman stones; I leave it to more minute local knowledge than my own to judge whether any of them still abide in the places in which Cuthberht can have looked on them. One would be glad indeed if we could thus directly connect the Carlisle of the present with the great Bernician saint; for it is simply through its connexion with him in life and death that we hear at all of the first English occupation of the city. The living Cuthberht prophesied within it; well nigh two hundred years later the dead Cuthberht appeared in a warning dream to its abbot Eadred, that Eadred who, from dwelling in the city of *Luel*, was known by the surname of *Lulisc*. Thus we learn that Lulchester was then still part of the Northumbrian realm. It was to be so no longer. The Dane was in the land, and Lulchester was to perish at his hands, though not to perish for ever. Its abbot had a share in placing a king on the throne of York, now that York was the seat of Danish kings, as it had once been the seat of Roman Cæsars. He had a share in guarding Saint Cuthberht's bones till they found that home at Cunegaceaster which sheltered them till Ealdhun found for them a nobler resting-place. But the city from which Eadred Lulisc took his surname ceased to be, and its site passed away from the rule of the foreign king of Deira for whom he found a kingdom, from the fellowship of the native saint of Bernicia for whom he found a tomb. Of the site where Lugubalia once stood we hear nothing; but it cannot fail to have shared the fate of that Cumbrian under-kingdom which afterwards came to form the appanage of the heirs of Scottish kingship, and over which the West-Saxon and

Danish lords of all Britain claimed at most the rights of an external over-lord.

Thus we learn from incidental notices, and from incidental notices only, that towards the end of the ninth century, the site, the walls, the ruined dwellings, of Luguballia, passed away from immediate English rule. They ceased to be part of any English kingdom. They had been part of the realm of the Northumbrian; they never became part of the realm of the West-Saxon. They formed part of a kingdom whose princes became the men—perhaps sometimes rather the men of the men—of Danish Cnut and of Norman William, but they were no part of the realm which owned the Danish and the Norman conqueror as its immediate sovereign. It is surely hardly needful for me to dwell on the exploded errors which were matters of more than local controversy, of controversy in the œcumenical columns of the Times no more than nine years back. There is surely no doubt now, there ought never to have been any since the day of our Institute's earlier meeting on this spot, why it is that Cumberland and Westmoreland do not appear by those names among the shires which are entered in the Norman Survey. Why Northumberland and Durham are not entered may still be a question, though to my mind it is not a very hard question; but the case of Northumberland and Durham and the case of Cumberland and Westmoreland have nothing in common. Northumberland and Durham might have been entered; we may therefore fairly ask the reason why they were not entered; but Cumberland and Westmoreland, by those names, were no more likely to be entered in Domesday than the earldom of Orkney or the county of Ponthieu. Domesday is a survey of lands which formed part of the dominions of the King of the English, not of lands which formed no part of his dominions. In the days of William the Great, nay, in the days of his sons and of his grandson, there were, as I have already said, no English shires bearing the names of Cumberland and Westmoreland. Of the lands which now bear those names, part already belonged to the English kingdom and formed part of an English shire. Those lands are duly entered in the Survey under the shire of which they then formed a part, the great shire of York, yet greater in those days than it is now. But the parts which immediately concern us, the site of Carlisle, the special land of Carlisle, are not entered in the Survey, for the simple reason that in the days of William the Great they formed no part of the English kingdom.

Again I repeat—it is no discovery of mine; it was announced in this city three and twenty years ago by a master of the history of Northern England, by Mr. Hodgson Hinde—it was not under the Conqueror himself, but under the son of the Conqueror, that the land of Carlisle was restored to the English realm, that the city rose again, strengthened by fresh bulwarks and colonized by new inhabitants. The tale which carries back Earl Randolf and his earldom into the Conqueror's day, which further turns him from an Earl of Carlisle into an Earl of Cumberland, has been copied over and over again; but no statement ever was more utterly lacking in authority. The reference commonly given is to a well-known passage in the printed text of the writer known as Matthew of Westminster. This would at most prove that a single inaccurate writer of somewhat doubtful personality had made a not very wonderful confusion; but the authority for the common tale is even less than this; it comes simply from a marginal note written by some unknown person in a copy of Matthew Paris. Genuine contemporary history knows nothing of the restored city of Carlisle till the days of William Rufus; it knows nothing of an earldom even of Carlisle till the days of Henry the Clerk. In the year 1092, so witnesses the Chronicle, 'the King William with mickle *fyrd* went north to Carlisle, and the borough set up again, and the castle reared, and Dolfin out drove that ere the land wielded, and the castle with his men set, and sith hither south went, and mickle many of churlish folk with wives and cattle thither sent to dwell in the land to till it.' There is the true tale. It is a curious instance of the way in which so much of our most trustworthy history has to be patched up from notices which are purely incidental, that it is from another record of this same event, from the entry in Floretus of Worcester, that we learn the destruction of the city by the Danes two hundred years earlier. That fact might otherwise have been passed by; but it was needful to put it on record to explain the state of things which the Red King found in Lugubalia and the coasts thereof.

No part of our fragmentary story is more thoroughly fragmentary than this, the central fact of the whole tale. The entry in the Chronicles stands by itself; we are left to connect it as we can with anything that went before, and with anything that came after. We are not told what led to this action of the Red King at this particular time. We find a certain Dolfin in possession of the land; but we are not told what he had done to lead to the attack which the King of the English made upon him; we are not even told who he was. But, from his name and from the whole circumstances of the story, we can hardly be wrong in setting him down as one of the house of the lords of Bamburgh and earls of Northumberland, as the son of that Gospatric who in his youth risked his life to save Earl Tostig, who afterwards himself ruled for a while as earl under the Conqueror, who had then for a while to find shelter with the Scottish king, but who appears in the end in Domesday as a considerable landowner in Yorkshire. And we can hardly be wrong in assuming that whatever Dolfin held he held as the man of Malcolm. Here then was a corner of Britain still ruled by a man of the loftiest English birth, a man sprung by the female line of the stock of West-Saxon kingship, but held under the supremacy of the King of Scots. The land now becomes in one sense more English, in another less. Up to 1092 there was still an English ruler in Britain; there was still a man of English blood holding an earldom, a lordship, or whatever it is to be called, which so far formed a distinct state as to be no part of the immediate dominions either of the Norman or of the Scot. Here was still a ruler who, sprung from Northumbrian earls on the one side, from West-Saxon kings on the other, might, with the minutest accuracy, be set down as an 'Anglo-Saxon.' As long as such a ruler still reigned, there was still something like an English power in Britain twenty-six years after the Norman landed at Pevensey. But its existence as an English power implied separation from the now united English kingdom; it implied dependence on the Scottish crown. After the change which the Red King wrought at Carlisle, no man of purely English descent ever again ruled in Britain; but this sentimental loss might be looked on as counterbalanced by the reunion of the severed land with a kingdom of England which was soon again to become an English kingdom. The French-speaking founder of Carlisle made way for a king who was English by birth and speech, if not by blood, and who handed on his crown to descendants who came of the old kingly stock by the same tie of female descent as Dolfin and Gospatric themselves.

We are not told what it was that led the Red King to march with a great fyrd to Carlisle and to drive out Dolfin. Save for this expedition, the year 1092 was a year of peace. The events recorded under it are mainly ecclesiastical. Just before his march into Carlisle, the King would seem to have been at Lincoln, ready for the hallowing of Remigius' minster, a hallowing which did not come just yet. The year before had been a busy one indeed. King William had made peace with his brother Duke Robert, and the two had dispossessed their younger brother Henry, Ætheling, Count, and Clerk.

Malcolm of Scotland had meanwhile harried Northumberland as far as Chester-le-Street, and had been driven back by the Normans and English of the land. The three sons of the Conqueror, all now reconciled, had come to England together; they had all gone northwards; they had entered Malcolm's dominions; but, instead of a battle, the mediation of Robert and Eadgar had led to a treaty and to an act of homage done by Malcolm to the King of the English. Then the brothers had quarrelled again, and Robert and Eadgar had gone away to Normandy. So much for 1091. In 1093 a Scottish embassy comes to William Rufus during his momentary fit of reformation at Gloucester. Then Malcolm is summoned to the court of his over-lord; Eadgar is sent to bring him honourably; he comes, but the capricious Rufus refuses to see him; Malcolm goes home in wrath; he invades England for the last time, and dies at Alnwick.

Here there are two years, 1091 and 1093, both full of warlike dealings between England and Scotland, parted by a year of peace as far as the two kingdoms are concerned, but in which we find these remarkable doings on the borders of the two, the driving out of Dolfin and the establishment of the English power at Carlisle. We may be sure that these events had some reference either to what went before or to what came after. One might suppose that Malcolm, like some other kings, betrayed his ally and vassal Dolfin, and that the surrender of Carlisle to William was one of the articles of the treaty agreed upon between him and the King of Scots. But if this were so, William would surely have taken possession of his new dominion on his way southwards, and would not have waited till seemingly the latter part of the next year. It is far more likely that the occupation of Carlisle was a piece of capricious aggression on the part of Rufus, an act which, whether it was or was not a breach of the letter of the treaty, was sure to kindle the wrath of Malcolm to the uttermost. A King of Scots might reasonably be wrathful at the wrong done to a vassal of Scotland, and still more at the standing menace which was now set up against the Scottish kingdom itself. We cannot be certain, because it is not recorded; but we may be strongly tempted to believe that the occupation of Carlisle held a foremost place among the complaints which Malcolm and his embassy had to make to Rufus, and to which Rufus, when he had risen from his bed of sickness and penitence, characteristically refused to hearken.

The whole later history of Carlisle—one might say, the whole later history of England—witnesses to the importance of the step which was now taken by the Red King. The whole later relations between England and Scotland, from that day till the union of the crowns, were influenced by the presence of a great and strong English city so close to the Scottish border. The step, whatever may have been its moral aspect towards Malcolm, towards Dolfin, or towards Dolfin's subjects, was, as an act done by a king of England, for the strengthening of his kingdom, the act of a keen-sighted general and a far-sighted statesman. And William the Red, though he did not always choose to be either, could be both whenever he did choose. What became of Dolfin we know not; as concerns Dolfin's subjects, the story suggests that they could not have lost much, and that there were not very many of them to lose anything. The words of one of our best authorities, literally taken, would imply that the city was a mere uninhabited ruin. But it is always dangerous to press descriptions of this kind too far. Some dwelling-places of man may likely enough have still gathered round the ancient walls, more likely within than, as at Anderida, without. It is enough that Lugubalia had ceased to be a city and a fortress, and that, at the bidding of William the Red, it again became both. How much, in wall and castle, may be his work, how much may be the work of his brother, I must leave local knowledge to settle. What William wrought, Henry, as Simeon of Durham witnesses with some pomp of words, undoubtedly strengthened. Of the work of one or other of them a good deal is left, though it may be hard to say how much is the work of the elder and how much of the younger brother. The keep is there, though sadly disfigured; and it is needless to say that other parts of the castle keep work of later times, that they suggest memories of stirring scenes in later history, memories of Richard of Gloucester and of Mary of Scotland. But those to whom the city and castle themselves have a distinct being will perhaps be inclined to dwell less on those later memories; they will rather strive to trace out every scrap that carries them back to the days of the sons of the Conqueror, seeing that to the days of the Conqueror himself there is nothing to lead us.

As for the land, as distinguished from the city, at the time when the Red King came, our story certainly implies that it was, to say the least, not very thickly inhabited. No part of Britain was thickly inhabited then according to modern standards; but the land of Carlisle must have seemed empty of men even according to the standard of the eleventh century. To drive out those whom he found in the land, and to plant in it a colony of his own subjects, might be an act of wise policy on the Red King's part. It might even be a wise way of disposing of men who might be dangerous in other parts of the kingdom. Dissatisfied Normans, oppressed Englishmen, would be turned into loyal subjects, when they were set to guard the border city of England against the Scot. But this is not the kind of migration of which the Chronicler speaks; at least he speaks of another kind of migration as well. The land must really have lacked inhabitants of any kind, when William found it a wise step to bring churlish folk from southern England to dwell in the land and to till it. I need not dwell on the guess, in any case a mere guess, and to my mind not a likely guess, which connects this settlement with the dispossession of English—sometimes

of Norman—owners to make way for the New Forest.
The important point is that the colony planted by William
Rufus in the land of Carlisle was strictly a Saxon colony.
It was a Saxon colony in a land for which Briton, Angle,
Scot, and Dane, had often striven, but where the Saxon was
altogether a new comer. Now in all discussions on the
ethnology of Cumberland this Saxon colony seems to be
wholly forgotten. Yet its coming is an undoubted fact, and
perchance the fact of the eleventh century may have left
some signs even in the nineteenth. I merely throw this
out as a subject for local inquiry. Are there any distinctively Saxon elements to be traced within the land colonized by Rufus, that is, I would again remind every one,
not all modern Cumberland and Westmoreland, but the
special land of Carlisle, the old earldom, the old diocese?
In the neighbouring land of Bernicia I have sometimes
seemed to notice points in language and nomenclature
that were distinctively Saxon. The *chesters* of that land,
as opposed to the *casters* of Deira, are, if not distinctively
Saxon, at least English as opposed to Danish. And I
began to doubt whether it might not be owing to the
coming of Octa and Ebussa, when I heard, along the
Roman wall, such names as Bellingham and Ovingham
sounded with a soft *g*. Surely, I said in my heart, here
are folk who are *Westsaxonibus ipsis Westsaxoniores*.

One thing we must not forget, namely, that the ecclesiastical side of Carlisle is not the work of William Rufus
—we could hardly expect it to be so—but the work of
Henry the First. Early in the reign of the Lion of
Justice, the fallen abbey of Eadred rose again in the shape
of a new priory of Austin canons, of which the King himself, if not the founder, was at least a benefactor. Here,
as in many other places, from Wells to Manchester, from
the tenth century to the nineteenth, the chapter or other
ecclesiastical body is older than the bishopric. Nearly
thirty years after the foundation of the priory, King Henry

planted his English confessor Æthelwulf in the new episcopal chair of Carlisle. It was not till the next century that the unbroken succession of the Carlisle bishops begins; still Henry is none the less the founder of the see, although for many years his foundation remained vacant. Henry the First was the last king till Henry the Eighth who could write himself a founder of English bishoprics, and in the case of Carlisle the material church dates from his time as well as the succession of its pastors. To the priory of Austin canons the bishop became at least a nominal abbot, and, as at Bath, as at Durham, the name of *abbey* clave to the episcopal church or its precinct. According to the common use of the Austin canons, the building was divided between the monks and the parishioners, one of the few instances of that arrangement in strictly English cathedral churches. As all on the spot know, the parishioners kept till quite lately the small fragment of the western limb which survived the civil wars. The division would seem to have had the most important effects on the building. In the western church the grand simple Norman of Æthelwulf's day is left untouched. The church of the canons was rebuilt in the thirteenth and fourteenth centuries, and was crowned with the noblest window of its class that England, and therefore that the world, can supply. But surely never was building built with less regard to its neighbour than the builders of the eastern limb of Carlisle abbey showed to the western. Did they simply cast the despised parish church out of all reckoning? Or did they dream of building it afresh some day or other in the same style and on the same plan as its greater neighbour? As it is, between rebuilding and destroying, the church is left a shapeless fragment, magnificent in parts, but without connexion or outline as a whole. Still I at least rejoice that something of the nave of Henry and Æthelwulf is left to us.

Again, in a land which is emphatically the earldom of

Carlisle, we must remember that, as Henry was the first to give bishops to Carlisle, Henry was also the first to give her earls. And they were bishops of Carlisle, earls of Carlisle. The limits of the land added to England by Rufus were the limits of their diocese and their earldom. If Henry founded bishops and earls, it was in a city founded by Rufus that he founded them. Yes, I would again say to the citizens of Carlisle, the Red King is your founder, and you cannot escape him. You might better have liked the Conqueror, to whom an old-standing blunder assigned you. You might better have liked Ecgfrith or Æthelfrith, Cadwalla or Arthur. You might better have liked one whom the monk of Saint Evroul gives you, even Divus Julius himself. The future Dictator is, I suppose, carried thus far northward by the same kind of process which has carried Hengest, out of the narrow Kentish range which history gives him, to Stonehenge and Sprotburgh and I know not where else besides. But the journey which Cæsar never took was taken by the king into whose body some thought that the soul of Cæsar had passed. The Roman must be satisfied with having called Corinth and Carthage into a restored being; it was his Norman *avatar* that did the same good turn by Carlisle. You must be content that the work of calling your fallen city into a new being was the work of him who every morning got up a worse man than he lay down, and who every evening lay down a worse man than he got up.

I am near the end of my discourse, but some might think that I am still near the beginning of my subject. Yet I have really reached its goal. I have carried the history of Carlisle through those stages of its history which give the city its distinctive historical character, those which work out what I would call its personal definition. We have seen, at Lugubalia, as in other parts of the land, the Roman city left as a city of the forsaken and independent Briton, to pass under the rule of an English kingdom. In this Lugubalia has simply fared as other cities, except so far as it would seem to have been one of those more favoured places which passed from British to English rule without any intermediate period of desolation. The thing which forms the distinctive character of Carlisle is that its time of desolation came later, that the coming of the Danes wrought, not only the overthrow of the city, but its separation from English rule. The forsaken site became part of a British kingdom, which presently bowed to an external English supremacy, but which, instead of passing under immediate English rule, became an appanage of the Scot. Then at last the land returns, if not to English rule, at least under the rule of England, and the Norman builds up again what the Dane had overthrown. But I should hardly have said 'at last;' Carlisle was yet again to pass under the rule of a king of Scots, and to be again restored to the realm of England. When all the sons of the Conqueror had passed away, when the nineteen years of anarchy had come with his grandson, King David, in all zeal for his Imperial niece, cut short the kingdom of his other niece's husband, and added Carlisle, with other lands and fortresses of Northern England, to the Scottish dominions. Just then subtle questions of homage were not likely to be argued, and the King of Scots doubtless held Carlisle by whatever right he held, if not Dunfermline, at least Lothian. But what one Henry had strengthened, the next won back, and, while Dunfermline and Lothian passed under the mere outward supremacy of the Angevin king, Carlisle again became part of his immediate kingdom. In this way the distinctive feature of the history of Carlisle, its falling away from England and its recovery by England, was really acted twice over. But the second loss, the second recovery, were but a feeble after-shadow of the first; they did not involve the destruction of the city and its calling again to a renewed life. For the moment indeed the question might have been asked, whether the rule of David was not more English than the rule of Stephen, if in courtesy we look on Stephen as exercising any rule at all. Practically, Carlisle, with the other parts of England which were ceded to David, obtained a happy exemption from the horrors which laid waste the rest of the kingdom, and, as soon as the kingdom had again a settled government, they again became members of the English body.

The place of Carlisle in English history is thus fully ascertained. The city has run a course of its own in the earlier times of our history; it now finally takes its place as an English city in order to discharge one special function among English cities. Carlisle has now to be, before all other spots, the bulwark of England against the Scot. So I must speak in obedience to the received rules of language; but we should ever bear in mind that warfare with the Scot hardly ever meant warfare with the true bearers of that name, allies as they so often were of the English overlord; the truer name of the warfare of which Carlisle was for many ages the centre would be warfare, as in the old days before England had a single king, between the northern and the southern English kingdoms. One king marched from Westminster, another from Dunfermline, each at the head of armies of the English speech, strengthened, it may be, or weakened, by wilder allies from the Celtic background which overshadowed both English realms alike. In this warfare the border city was ever the main object of attack and defence. The time would fail to tell how many times Carlisle was besieged by the Scottish invaders, how many times it was the trysting-place of the hosts of England. The annals of Carlisle at this stage are written in the Chronicles of the kindred Austin priory of Lanercost. It has a strange sound when we read how, in the year of the Great Charter, the Scottish Alexander took the city, as David had

taken it before him, and how he presently did homage—
for Carlisle, for Scotland, or for what?—to the French
prince whom the Norman barons of England had chosen
to take the place of the rebel tyrant from Anjou. But
the Scottish occupation under Alexander was yet shorter
than the Scottish occupation under David; two years
later the Scottish king, ere he could be absolved from
ecclesiastical censures,. had to give up Carlisle, not to the
Lord Lewis to whom he had so lately done homage, but to
the Lord Henry, chosen and hallowed King of England.
Through the wars of the Edwards, the name of Carlisle
meets us at almost every page; it stands out specially as
a spot bound by another tie to one of the other spots with
which at starting I compared and contrasted it. The
needs of warfare and of policy caused the city of William
Rufus to be many times honoured with the presence of the
founder of Hull. Edward, father of parliaments, held
three famous parliaments within your walls, and, as the late
Mr. Hartshorne told you three and twenty years ago, the
good estate of the river Thames and its traffic was discussed
in this distant corner of the English kingdom. From
Carlisle the Hammer of the Scots set forth on his last enterprise, when the enfeebled frame of the mighty warrior and
lawgiver sank beneath the weight of cares and labours
beside the sands of Solway. A generation later the
presence at Carlisle of Edward King of Scots may be a
momentary puzzle; but the personage so described was
no Scottish conqueror like David or Alexander; Edward
Balliol, faithful vassal of his Southern overlord, found it
convenient to make use of Carlisle as something between
a court and a place of shelter. In the sixteenth century
Carlisle again received a Scottish sovereign; but that
sovereign was a deposed queen flying from her own people.
In the seventeenth and in the eighteenth century, the city
was again occupied by Scottish armies; in the earlier case
it was by a Scottish army in league with the English

Parliament, in the latter by a Scottish army marching in the cause of a pretender to the English crown whose claims were at least Scottish rather than English. And in this last occupation we are after so many ages brought back to a race which has been for a long while out of our sight. If most so-called Scottish armies were more truly to be called armies of Englishmen of Lothian or of converted Britons of Strathclyde, we cannot say this of the Highland host of Charles Edward. Then the true Scot—or, for aught I know, the true Pict—showed himself on English ground in his true garb—his true garb, I say, for the devices of the famous army-tailor to whom the present so-called Highland dress is said to be owing, must have come at a later date. Let some student of the antiquities of dress tell us the exact distinction between the two. If that distinction should prove to be very wide, it might save King George the Fourth, who doubtless clad himself in the more modern fashion, from Lord Macaulay's gibe that he 'thought that he could not give a more striking proof of his respect for the usages which had prevailed in Scotland before the Union, than by disguising himself in what, before the Union, was considered by nine Scotchmen out of ten as the dress of a thief.'

I have rushed with somewhat headlong speed through several stirring ages. But to tell what Carlisle, after the city had put on its characteristic character, did and suffered, is rather the business of other members of the section, and not of its president. For detailed notices of such points we look to local zeal and local research; my business is rather to point out what Carlisle is, to fix its place among the cities of England, to trace out what is special and distinctive in the history of the one English city which still keeps its almost unaltered British name, the city where a foreign king, the most deeply hated of his line, showed himself as the enlarger of the English kingdom, the man who, if he drove out the last separate ruler of the old English stock, drove him out only to become himself the founder of a Saxon colony, and to give England her abiding bulwark against her northern neighbour, so often her northern enemy.

THE END.

LONDON: PRINTED BY
SPOTTISWOODE AND CO., NEW-STREET SQUARE
AND PARLIAMENT STREET

BY THE SAME AUTHOR.

COMPANION VOLUMES TO THIS WORK.

HISTORICAL and ARCHITECTURAL SKETCHES;
chiefly Italian. Illustrated by the Author. Crown 8vo. 10s. 6d.

'For these essays we have only words of unqualified praise. They are full of valuable information, and are delightfully interesting.'—WESTMINSTER REVIEW.

'Full of valuable teachings and suggestions to all who are ready to profit by them.'
THE ACADEMY.

'There is not perhaps among us any man more thoroughly versed in history than he, and the moment he puts himself into a place which history has consecrated, all its associations seem to come crowding upon him in pictures which he knows how to present to sympathetic readers in a sentence, or even in mere allusion.'—THE STANDARD.

SUBJECT and NEIGHBOUR LANDS of VENICE.
Being a Companion Volume to 'Historical and Architectural Sketches.' With Illustrations. Crown 8vo. 10s. 6d.

'This is a delightful book to read...... Mr. Freeman is not merely accurate, he crams so much knowledge into a small space, that abridgment can no farther go. Each sketch is a bird's-eye view...... It is rare indeed that a traveller combines so many qualifications as Mr. Freeman for describing what he has seen...... His various sketches are thus invaluable guides for those who travel not only just for the sake of recreation, but with eyes and ears open to take in all that can be gleaned from the records of the past...... Mr. Freeman's charming volume...... Its merits cannot be so easily enumerated...... We trust that we have said enough to induce our readers to consult Mr. Freeman's book for themselves.'
THE SPECTATOR.

'To the architect, the archæologist, the entire scheme will be replete with interest; to the rare traveller in these seldom-visited lands it will be a guide-book little less than indispensable.'—BRITISH QUARTERLY REVIEW.

'A book that will surround the localities which he describes with more living interest than almost any work that could be named.'—DAILY NEWS.

HISTORICAL ESSAYS. FIRST SERIES. Third Edition. 8vo. 10s. 6d.
CONTENTS:—The Mythical and Romantic Elements in Early English History—The Continuity of English History—The Relations between the Crown of England and Scotland—St. Thomas of Canterbury and his Biographers, &c.

HISTORICAL ESSAYS. SECOND SERIES. Second Edition, with additional Essays. 8vo. 10s. 6d.
CONTENTS:—Ancient Greece and Mediæval Italy — Mr. Gladstone's Homer and the Homeric Ages—The Historians of Athens —The Athenian Democracy—Alexander the Great—Greece during the Macedonian Period — Mommsen's History of Rome — Lucius Cornelius Sulla—The Flavian Cæsars, &c. &c.

HISTORICAL ESSAYS. THIRD SERIES. 8vo. 12s.
CONTENTS:—First Impressions of Rome— The Illyrian Emperors and their Land— Augusta Treverorum—The Goths at Ravenna —Race and Language—The ByzantineEmpire —First Impressions of Athens — Mediæval and Modern Greece—The Southern Slaves— Sicilian Cycles—The Normans at Palermo.

HISTORY of the CATHEDRAL CHURCH of WELLS. As Illustrating the History of the Cathedral Churches of the Old Foundation. Crown 8vo. 3s. 6d.

OLD ENGLISH HISTORY.
With Five Coloured Maps. New Edition, revised. Extra fcp. 8vo. 6s.

COMPARATIVE POLITICS.
Lectures at the Royal Institution. To which is added 'The Unity of History.' 8vo. 14s.

The GROWTH of the ENGLISH CONSTITUTION from the EARLIEST TIMES. Third Edition. Crown 8vo. 5s.

GENERAL SKETCH of EUROPEAN HISTORY. New Edition. Enlarged, with Maps, &c. 18mo. 3s. 6d. (Vol. I. of Historical Course for Schools.)

EUROPE. 18mo. 1s.
[*Literature Primers.*

The HISTORY and CONQUESTS of the SARACENS. Six Lectures. Third Edition, with New Preface. Crown 8vo. 3s. 6d.

MACMILLAN & CO., London, W.C.

www.ingramcontent.com/pod-product-compliance
Lightning Source LLC
Chambersburg PA
CBHW021415300426
44114CB00010B/499